STATS™ 2000 DIAMOND CHRONICLES

Don Zminda, Editor

Jim Callis, Thom Henninger, Chuck Miller

and Tony Nistler, Assistant Editors

STATS
PUBLISHING

Published by STATS Publishing

A division of Sports Team Analysis & Tracking Systems, Inc.

Cover by Marc Elman, Ben Frobig and Chuck Miller

Cover photo by the Associated Press

STATS is a registered trademark of Sports Team Analysis and Tracking Systems, Inc.

First Edition: March, 2000

ISBN 1-884064-78-7

Acknowledgments

STATS Diamond Chronicles is packed with opinions and analysis that we hope you'll find fascinating. Numerous people contributed to this book, and we'd like to thank them all:

STATS CEO John Dewan and President Alan Leib are leading us into the new millennium. Helping them stay on course is Jennifer Manicki, who provides invaluable assistance to both of them. Two vice presidents, Sue Dewan and Bob Meyerhoff, play critical roles in our company's future, directing our Research & Development/Special Projects teams. Sue works with Jim Osborne and Andy Tumpowsky. Bob teams with Athan Arvanitis and Joe Sclafani.

The members of the Publishing Products Department handled a majority of the writing and editing responsibilities, under the direction of vice president, Don Zminda. He, Thom Henninger and Tony Nistler oversaw the editing of this book, while Jim Henzler, Don and baseball expert and former STATS employee Mat Olkin, provided the best of their America Online columns for this book. Chuck Miller was responsible for design and layout. Thanks also to Taylor Bechtold, Jim Callis and Marc Carl, who proofread parts of this manuscript.

Getting the word out about the *Diamond Chronicles* and all other STATS Publishing ventures depends on Marc Elman and his promotions group. Marc works with Ben Frobig, Mike Janosi, Antoinette Kelly and Mike Sarkis. Ben, our graphics man, designed this book's cover.

The wonderful statistics that hold this book together were gathered by our Data Collection Department. Allan Spear heads the group, which includes Jeremy Alpert, Scott Berg, Michelle Blanco, Jon Caplin, Jeff Chernow, Mike Hammer, Derek Kenar, Tony Largo, Jon Passman, Jeff Schinski, Matt Senter, Bill Stephens and Joe Stillwell. With a vast reporter network making statistical collection possible, Jeff Chernow oversaw the compilation of MLB data during the 1999 season.

The Commercial, Fantasy and Interactive Products and Sales departments are key components of the STATS family. Vince Smith heads our Commercial Products staff, which includes Ethan D. Cooperson, Dan Matern and David Pinto. Steve Byrd oversees the Fantasy Department, which consists of Bill Burke, Sean Bush, Jim Corelis, Mike Dreckman, Dan Ford, Brian Hogan, Stefan Kretschmann, Walter Lis, Marc Moeller, Mike Mooney, Oscar Palacios, Jim Pollard, Corey Roberts, Eric Robin, Jeff Smith, Yingmin Wang and Rick Wilton. Michael Canter leads an active Interactive group that includes Tracy Altman, Dave Carlson, Jake Costello, Joe Lindholm, Will McCleskey, Dean Peterson, Pat Quinn, John Sasman, Meghan Sheehan, Morris Srinivasan, Nick Stamm and David Thiel. Jim Capuano directs a Sales team comprised of Greg Kirkorsky and Jake Stein.

Our Financial/Administrative/Human Resources/Legal Department keeps the office running smoothly and efficiently at our Morton Grove, Ill., home. Howard Lanin oversees the financial and administrative concerns of the company with assistance from Kim Bartlett, Mary Ellen Gomez and Betty Moy. Susan Zamechek assists in finance and keeps the office functional on a day-to-day basis. Tracy Lickton is in charge of human resources while Carol Savier aids with legal matters. Art Ashley provides programming support throughout the building.

—Chuck Miller

To the Ford clan:
Mom, sisters Pua and Lani, and brother Tim.
And especially to baby sister Momi,
who traded all her Dan Ford baseball cards to me,
little brother Chris, who helped perfect the art of one-on-one whiffle ball,
and my late Dad, who took me to my first game at Wrigley Field
and imparted his love for the Game.

—Dan Ford

Table of Contents

Introduction

Thank goodness for the busy offseason of trading, because otherwise the baseball world has been consumed by the two R's—Rose and Rocker. The Jim Gray interview of Pete Rose during the World Series generated a hailstorm of debate, and it was no different in our office.

Has the commissioner's office given Rose a fair shake in his legal battle for reinstatement? Should Rose be allowed to join his peers as a Hall of Fame candidate? It's possible no other topic flooded the internal e-mail system at STATS with more commentary than Charlie Hustle's interrogation by Gray.

Join the debate as it unfolds in this fourth edition of *STATS Diamond Chronicles*. The heated exchanges about Rose epitomize our passion for the game of baseball and the people who play it. But beware.

There's a lot more in these pages than Rose and Rocker. The book is loaded with analysis of trades, the Hall of Fame selections, the annual baseball awards and more. You'll find that the people who make up STATS aren't always on the same page when it comes to whether the Blue Jays were ripped off in the Roger Clemens-David Wells deal, or whether Ivan Rodriguez or Pedro Martinez should have won the Most Valuable Player Award in the American League.

Sometimes analysis wins out over argument. Kerry Wood's elbow surgery last April generated plenty of interesting talk and numerical study of pitch counts. This book is filled with numbers, which often are used to *support* an argument.

Do the Yankees win out as the best franchise in all of sports during the last century? Should Frank Thomas start targeting the first pitch to break out of his two-year skid? Was an umpire's use of video replay to determine if a ball was fair in an early-season game a legitimate act? Was the Tony Batista-Dan Plesac trade the worst of 1999? Is Homer Bush the best player named Homer to ever play the game?

These are just some of the topics you'll encounter in the Y2K edition of *Diamond Chronicles*. They're mixed in with tons of trivia and tidbits, wisdom and wisecracks. We hope you'll enjoy reading these exchanges as much as we enjoyed the heat of the debate.

When the free-for-all is over, you'll get more-indepth analysis of numerous baseball issues from our America Online columnists. *Diamond Chronicles* houses a year's supply of the written word from Don Zminda (Zee-Man Reports), Jim Henzler (STATS Focus) and Mat Olkin (Fantasy Baseball Advisor). If you missed them during the season, you'll find them here. Some of their work is timely, some of it is timeless, but all of it is engaging and entertaining.

—Thom Henninger

Dramatis Personae

(in alphabetical order)

The following people contributed their opinions and insights throughout this book:

Jeremy Alpert	Matt Greenberger	Dave Mundo	John Sasman
Jim Callis	Thom Henninger	Rob Neyer	Jeff Schinski
Jim Capuano	Jim Henzler	Mat Olkin	Matt Senter
Dave Carlson	Bill James	Jim Osborne	John Sickels
Jeff Chernow	Greg Kirkorsky	Brent Osland	Todd Skelton
Ethan D. Cooperson	Stefan Kretschmann	Oscar Palacios	Allan Spear
Brian Cousins	Dan Matern	Jon Passman	Bill Stephens
John Dewan	Bob Meyerhoff	David Pinto	Joe Stillwell
Ryan Ellis	Chuck Miller	Pat Quinn	Tom Tippett
Marc Elman	Mike Mittleman	Corey Roberts	Don Zminda
Dan Ford			

In addition, Jim Henzler, Mat Olkin and Don Zminda wrote several columns, all of which can be found in the STATS Baseball area on America Online (keyword: STATS). Look for their perspectives throughout the 2000 season on AOL.

Voices From the Network

February 9, 1999—The Death of Early Wynn

JAMES: According to *The Sporting News* of July 27, 1963, Early Wynn "may be the last pitcher ever to hurl 300 victories."

ZMINDA: Wynn used to talk about that himself when people asked him if he was upset that Spahn beat him to 300. He'd say, "No, because I might just be the *last* guy to win 300." As I recall, Jack Brickhouse always agreed with him.

February 16—Yeah, But He Dissed Me

OLKIN: Brien Taylor's stats since injuring his shoulder in a fight:

W	L	G	GS	IP	H	ER	BB	SO	ERA
3	15	41	28	108.2	107	131	175	86	10.85

February 18—The Roger Clemens Trade

OSBORNE: Roger Clemens has been traded to the Yankees for David Wells, Homer Bush and Graeme Lloyd.

SICKELS: What the hell were the Blue Jays thinking? David Wells and Roger Clemens are roughly the same age, and you can pluck guys as good as Lloyd and Bush out of the minors for nothing. Plus the Yankees are in the same division. A totally stupid trade.

COOPERSON: How soon before Mittleman writes that this is bigger than Babe Ruth?

ZMINDA: As Jim Callis put it, Gord Ash must have been thinking like a guy in a Strat-o league: "Yeah, I lost Clemens, but I got a guy who went 18-4 *and* a pitcher with a 1.67 ERA *and* a .380 hitter!" If they could play this season using the '98 cards, Toronto would be a good bet for a wild card. But they're not. It's a stupid trade.

PINTO: But they did get the first Homer to homer in a good long time.

DEWAN: For baseball purists (I count myself as one), this trade makes no sense. John Sickels hits that one right on the head. But as much as we all hate to consider the dollars involved, I would assume that Toronto is saving a heck of a lot of money with this deal. Does anyone know how much?

PINTO: I have to agree with John and Mike on this. Trades are seldom made for talent anymore, they are made for money. In a way, Toronto got a lot more for Clemens than the Mariners did for Randy Johnson.

Toronto wasn't going to win the pennant anyway. And now we can see if Clemens can win 30 games with this team. Anyway, the Yankees should win 100 games again this year.

MITTLEMAN: Before everyone gets on the bandwagon to dump Toronto for this deal, you have to realize all that was involved.

1) Did the Jays want the circus of a disgruntled Clemens reporting to Dunedin?

2) How many teams could they interest in taking Clemens without renegotiating his contract?

3) How could the Jays pluck enough major league-caliber players to fill not only the rotation void, but the holes in the bullpen, due to Quantrill's absence, and at second base? Seems to me, they did all this in one fell swoop.

They avoided the problem at spring training of having a clubhouse disturbance. They have replaced 36-year-old Clemens with 35-year-old Wells, albeit not as good but a Cy contender in any case. They shore up the bullpen with Lloyd, who can fill in for Quantrill until he's back later in the year, and they add a young second baseman with potential who is better than Grebeck and Cora right now. Most important, the Yanks were the only team with enough financial resources to trade for a Clemens ($16 million over the next two years) and give up three players (roughly $7 million-plus Wells is a free agent after next year) without agreeing to a contract extension for Clemens in advance.

ZMINDA: I'm not faulting Toronto for unloading Clemens, but unless they think they're going to contend this year, what do these three guys do for them? Wells has some trade value, but the other two guys aren't going to get them anywhere. If they'd gotten a mid-level prospect or two, I'd like this a lot better. Their problem is that they were holding out for young players they were never going to get, like Scott Elarton.

ROBERTS: A radio station in Toronto, FAN 590, reports the following trade rumor—the Blue Jays would trade David Wells to the Angels for Jim Edmonds. There is also a report that GM Gord Ash has vehemently denied this rumor.

GREENBERGER: Just read in *Baseball Weekly*, not 10 minutes ago, that the Angels would be trading an outfielder for a starter. *Baseball Weekly* wouldn't lie.

February 23—The Gant-La Russa Feud

PASSMAN: Excerpts from an AP story on Ron Gant's continuing feud with Tony La Russa:

On Tuesday, Gant even accused La Russa of racism.

"Rickey Henderson didn't like him, Royce Clayton didn't like him," Gant told reporters in Clearwater, Fla. "He treated Ozzie Smith like dirt. Brian Jordan didn't like him. I don't know too many people who did like him."

All of those players are black. "You do the math," Gant said. "Something's not right there."

La Russa did a slow burn when the comments were relayed to him.

"That's called unforgivable," La Russa said. "That's lower than cheap. But I'm not going to sue him. I'll turn the page."

Gant also said McGwire batting third and the pitcher eighth hurt everyone else in the lineup.

"The Cardinals were the laughingstock of the league for that lineup," Gant said. "Guys on every team were coming up to me and saying 'What's this about?' All I could say is 'Nobody knows what he's thinking about.'"

PALACIOS: By the way, it was La Russa who started the volley of bad comments between Gant and him. The comment in the AP story makes La Russa sound like a civilized person, but he isn't.

"That's called unforgivable," La Russa said. "That's lower than cheap. But I'm not going to sue him. I'll turn the page."

Yet again, he isn't the only manager without manners.

Why don't we read other La Russa quotes about Gant from the previous two months:

"I really hope he goes to Philly and whiffs for them like he whiffed for us. And we'll see what excuses he makes."

La Russa also made incredibly insensitive comments about Jeff Brantley. So he's probably not a racist. But he definitely doesn't have the people skills required in the real world.

February 25—Is He Crazy?

OLKIN: Wohlers Comeback:

Chipper Jones stood with the bat on his shoulder, frozen by a Wohlers fastball.

What the hell is Chipper Jones doing standing in against this man? And is it any surprise that he was "frozen"?

February 25—The Strike Zone

OSBORNE: Anybody hear about the memo from Bud Selig saying that the umpires will strictly enforce the strike zone as it is described in baseball's rule book this year? Anybody think this will actually happen?

SCHINSKI: I read about that in the paper. That is what's going to be attempted this year. We'll see how many umpires follow it. I would think that the umpires would be against it. With it in place, it would be good time to argue that balls/strikes calls should be able to be appealed.

ZMINDA: Sandy Alderson of the Commissioner's Office announced this last week. Richie Phillips immediately told Alderson to butt out and that the umps already *were* enforcing the strike zone. Of course, that's "my strike zone," open to individual interpretation by each of Richie's boys.

I don't recall who said this, but the current situation in baseball is like getting ticketed by a cop for going 52 in a 55-MPH zone; when you complain, the cop says, "Well, that's *my* speed limit. It's fair because I call it the same for all drivers."

March 2—Hall of Fame Veterans Selections

PINTO: Today the Hall added Frank Selee, Smokey Joe Williams, Orlando Cepeda and Nestor Shylock. I just pulled out Bill's manager book and read the page that compares Ned Hanlon and Selee. In it he says that Selee won't be elected to the Hall of Fame. Bill, I wonder how much your article on the two brought Selee back to the attention of the Hall's committee.

JAMES: Anything's possible. I've been claiming credit for George Davis; heck, I might as well claim Selee, too.

Seems like a reasonable group, doesn't it? Cepeda's all right. Selee was a great manager, although he was a great manager so long ago that I'm not sure there is any point in honoring him. Nestor Chylak is as good or as bad as any other umpire, as far as I'm concerned. . . at least I remember him. Smokey Joe's probably a good pick. There's no Vic Willis here that I see.

March 4—Tom Hall and Herb Score

PINTO: Does anyone know why they lost their effectiveness early in their careers?

ZMINDA: Score had problems with his control after coming back from the eye injury. He said there was no connection with the injury, but not too many people believed him. Al Lopez got him for the White Sox and tried all kinds of things to improve his control, like having him pitch in front of a mirror. It didn't help. They say he never lost his velocity, he just couldn't get the ball over the plate.

March 5—Show Kerry the Money?

PALACIOS: The Cubs gave Kerry Wood $700,000 for one year when they could have automatically renewed him for $200,000. I guess you could say that a half a million raise is nice but the Cubs could have paid him much more. Wood may remember this five years from now, and he may sign with another team. If Wood is the future, they should treat him as such. The Cubs were not "team players" with this deal.

And Wood may not be a "team player" with the Cubs either from now on. His agent is probably telling him to take a day off whenever he feels anything in his arm. With this type of contract, Wood should not take any chances, even if it means not making the World Series.

Wood's goal from now on should be to stay healthy until arbitration. The playoffs and World Series are distant second and third goals.

The Cubs paid more than $5 million for Mark Clark! Couldn't they pay Wood more now? I hope Wood gets them for $7 million in his first arbitration hearing.

COUSINS: I'm not arguing that the Cubs aren't tight with their money, but I think you're being a bit too critical. This is by far the largest contract for a player with less than one year of major league service.

PALACIOS: Todd Helton, a one-year-player, just received a multi-year contract worth 15 times Wood's contract. If the Cubs want to set the right precedent, this is what they should do:

1. Stop giving huge contracts to players like Mark Clark or Mel Rojas.

2. Except for the Dominican Republic, the Cubs should have part-time scout operations elsewhere. They should actually go full-time in Mexico, Venezuela, the Caribbean and Central America. This way, instead of giving large contracts to players like Mark Clark, they can sign players like Francisco Cordova or Ricardo Rincon (who served no time in the minors and went directly from the Mexican League to the major leagues).

3. Stop trying to build your minors using the draft alone and scout everywhere. Then bring up youngsters to fill your holes instead of relying on expensive veterans.

4. Assign a "shadow" agent to their players. Someone who will watch out for the player's *and* team's interest. When Greg Maddux was struggling with the Cubs, it was Scott Boras, not the Cubs, who recommended Maddux to see a sports psychologist. Had the Cubs cared about Maddux like Boras did, perhaps he would have been more loyal to the Cubs.

March 16—What Wood Have Been

OLKIN: According to ESPN Radio, the early word from Cubs management is that Kerry Wood has suffered significant damage to his ulnar collateral ligament. Speculation is that he will need Tommy John surgery.

COOPERSON: I seem to recall a Bill James e-mail that Wood's big strikeout game last year virtually guaranteed that he'd have a great career.

ZMINDA: Actually, this is what Bill wrote about Wood after the 20-strikeout game:

"But I think it is also very well documented that early success with an immature arm almost always leads to arm injuries by mid-career. It's such an extreme case that it's hard to know how to balance them. But if I was a betting man, I'd bet that he doesn't win 100 games in the majors."

DEWAN: Don, don't let facts cloud the issue!

JAMES: I know you're apologizing in your heart, there.

SICKELS: I've been warning people about Kerry's elbow since he was drafted. His high school pitching coach made him throw both ends of a doubleheader once.

CALLIS: I'm not going to say that throwing both ends of a doubleheader is good for anyone, but I think it's a little simplistic to blame the arm injury on that. The guy blew major league hitters away for five months last year, then got hurt. I can't imagine he was pitching hurt the whole time.

Everyone has theories about how much a young pitcher can take. There's no set answer. Virtually every pitcher has a serious injury at some point in his career, often early in his career. That's just a fact of life.

OLKIN: This just in: an MRI has confirmed that Wood has suffered a complete tear of his ulnar collateral ligament.

CARLSON: Let's just say for sake of this argument that Kerry Wood can't play again because doctors can't fix his injury correctly for whatever reason. Would his be the greatest one-season career in baseball? If not, who would it be?

JAMES: Henry Schmidt pitched for Brooklyn in 1903, going 21-13 in 301 innings. Schmidt was a Texan who absolutely hated living in Brooklyn, refused to report the next spring, and never again pitched in the major leagues. He was probably the best one-season pitcher of the 20th century, at least before Kerry.

HENZLER: Although we don't have pitch counts before the 1980s, it would seem possible to generate a reasonable estimate based on a number of peripheral pitching stats. I suppose there are ways to fine-tune the calculation, but I determined the average number of pitches required to record the following three events since 1987: Strikeout, 4.795; Walk, 5.125; Hit, 3.259.

Using the pitch totals for these three events, I then computed the average number of pitches for all other non-strikeout outs as 3.143.

Using these parameters, Kerry Wood is thus estimated to have thrown 2,773 pitches last year. He actually threw 2,838, a difference of 2.3 percent.

Anyway, I ran a program to spit out all the pitchers who threw an estimated 2,500 pitches at age 21 or before, at least since 1969. Draw your own conclusions.

Pitchers Throwing at Least 2,500 Estimated Pitches at Age 21 or Earlier—1969-99

Pitcher	Year	Age	IP	EstPit	W-L	ERA	Career W-L	Career ERA
Javier Vazquez	1998	21	172.1	2,842	5-15	6.06	5-15	6.06
Kerry Wood	1998	21	166.2	2,773	13-6	3.40	13-6	3.40
Ismael Valdes	1995	21	197.2	2,920	13-11	3.05	52-40	3.23
Steve Avery	1991	21	210.1	3,159	18-8	3.38	88-76	4.10
Alex Fernandez	1991	21	191.2	3,104	9-13	4.51	96-75	3.76

Pitcher	Year	Age	IP	EstPit	W-L	ERA	Career W-L	ERA
Tom Gordon	1989	21	163.0	2,628	17-9	3.64	104-94	4.14
Jim Abbott	1989	21	181.1	2,898	12-12	3.92	85-100	4.12
Greg Maddux	1987	21	155.2	2,604	6-14	5.61	202-117	2.75
Jose Rijo	1986	21	193.2	3,231	9-11	4.65	111-87	3.16
Dwight Gooden	1986	21	250.0	3,740	17-6	2.84	185-103	3.33
Edwin Correa	1986	20	202.1	3,410	12-14	4.23	16-19	5.16
Juan Nieves	1986	21	184.2	3,057	11-12	4.92	32-25	4.71
Bret Saberhagen	1985	21	235.1	3,362	20-6	2.87	156-109	3.35
Dwight Gooden	1985	20	276.2	4,050	24-4	1.53	185-103	3.33
Mark Gubicza	1984	21	189.0	2,910	10-14	4.05	132-136	3.96
Dwight Gooden	1984	19	218.0	3,410	17-9	2.60	185-103	3.33
Storm Davis	1983	21	200.1	3,010	13-7	3.59	113-96	4.02
Fernando Valenzuela	1982	21	285.0	4,246	19-13	2.87	173-153	3.54
Mike Witt	1982	21	179.2	2652	8-6	3.51	117-116	3.83
Fernando Valenzuela	1981	20	192.1	2,880	13-7	2.48	173-153	3.54
Britt Burns	1980	21	238.0	3,481	15-13	2.84	70-60	3.66
Rich Dotson	1980	21	198.0	3,096	12-10	4.27	111-113	4.23
Dan Petry	1980	21	164.2	2,632	10-9	3.94	125-104	3.94
Phil Huffman	1979	21	173.0	2,789	6-18	5.77	6-18	6.03
Don Robinson	1978	21	228.1	3,330	14-6	3.47	109-106	3.79
Roger Erickson	1978	21	265.2	3,983	14-13	3.96	35-53	4.13
John Henry Johnson	1978	21	186.0	2,859	11-10	3.39	26-33	3.90
Dave Rozema	1978	21	209.1	2,946	9-12	3.14	60-53	3.47
Gary Serum	1978	21	184.1	2,708	9-9	4.10	10-12	4.72
Jerry Garvin	1977	21	244.2	3,757	10-18	4.19	20-41	4.43
Moose Haas	1977	21	197.2	3,116	10-12	4.33	100-83	4.01
Dave Rozema	1977	20	218.1	3,108	15-7	3.09	60-53	3.47
Mark Lemongello	1977	21	214.2	3,200	9-14	3.48	22-38	4.06
Dennis Eckersley	1976	21	199.1	3,115	13-12	3.43	197-171	3.50
Mark Fidrych	1976	21	250.1	3,499	19-9	2.34	29-19	3.10
Pete Falcone	1975	21	190.0	3,134	12-11	4.17	70-90	4.07
Dennis Blair	1975	21	163.1	2,708	8-15	3.80	19-25	3.69
Dennis Eckersley	1975	20	186.2	2,952	13-7	2.60	197-171	3.50
Frank Tanana	1975	21	257.1	3,933	16-9	2.62	240-236	3.66
Tom Underwood	1975	21	219.1	3,422	14-13	4.14	86-87	3.89
Kevin Kobel	1974	20	169.1	2,537	6-14	3.99	18-34	3.88
Frank Tanana	1974	20	268.2	4,079	14-19	3.12	240-236	3.66
Terry Forster	1973	21	172.2	2,793	6-11	3.23	54-65	3.23
Bert Blyleven	1972	21	287.1	4,245	17-17	2.73	287-250	3.31

Pitcher	Year	Age	IP	EstPit	W-L	ERA	Career W-L	ERA
Vida Blue	1971	21	312.0	4,571	24-8	1.82	209-161	3.26
Bert Blyleven	1971	20	278.1	4,167	16-15	2.81	287-250	3.31
Don Gullett	1971	20	217.2	3,196	16-6	2.65	109-50	3.11
Bart Johnson	1971	21	178.0	2,982	12-10	2.93	43-51	3.94
Wayne Simpson	1970	21	176.0	2,679	14-3	3.02	36-31	4.37
Tom Griffin	1969	21	188.1	3,091	11-10	3.54	77-94	4.07
Mike Nagy	1969	21	196.2	3,133	12-2	3.11	20-13	4.15
Clay Kirby	1969	21	215.2	3,398	7-20	3.80	75-104	3.84
Al Santorini	1969	21	184.2	2,931	8-14	3.95	17-38	4.29
Bob Moose	1969	21	170.0	2,679	14-3	2.91	76-71	3.50

JAMES: I think the work Henzler is doing on pitch counts is fascinating, and I would hope we could find somewhere to publish some of this kind of information. . . estimated pitch counts for various pitchers. You may remember (some of you) that about 1991 or 1992, ESPN asked us if we could figure out how many pitches Nolan Ryan had thrown in his career. I suggested a method much like what Jim is doing now, a little more focused on Ryan but fundamentally the same, and we got an answer for them, which they used on the air. We had the advantage of the fact that nobody really *knew* what the answer was.

On the more general issue of the relationship between pitches and injuries. . . that is an extremely tangled vine, and I'm not sure how much one can say with confidence. Craig Wright believes that throwing a large number of pitches with an immature arm is damaging or even destructive, and has written extensively about this. While I believe that Craig is Wright, pun intended, I cannot prove it, nor, I believe, could he prove it to the satisfaction of a skeptic. The reason for that is that it is just an immensely complicated issue. For example:

1. Throwing 3,000 pitches in a season is vastly different if that's 40 games of 75 pitches, rather than 25 games of 120 pitches.

2. Throwing a 120-pitch complete game is quite different if it's a two-hour game rather than a three-hour, 30-minute game. One of the biggest reasons that complete games have disappeared is just the length of the games, the length of time. As Jim Kaat once said, when asked why he worked so fast, "Because if the game goes over two hours, my fastball turns into a pumpkin." There's a lot more strain on the arm working an extra hour, even if the pitches are the same, and this makes 1995 very different from 1965.

3. Mechanics. Some pitchers just have lousy mechanics, and they're going to destroy their arms quickly anyway.

4. Averaging 28.00 batters per game is vastly different if you do it for 10 games rather than 25.

Because of these factors and others, developing a single number which represents the strain on a pitcher's arm is a challenge which has been impossible for me so far. I've made several efforts to do so, but I've really gotten nowhere.

Complicating this further, the "trend line" analysis of future ERAs is suspect, because there is a "self-sorting" mechanism that works against you. I'm not sure that makes sense. . . let's say that you try to compare pitchers who have thrown 3,000 pitches in a season to those who have thrown 2,000 pitches in a season, and you compare their future-season performance. Well, there is a problem with that, which is that *the guys who throw 3,000 pitches in a season are just a lot better than the guys who throw 2,000 pitches.* That's why their managers work them so hard: because they're better. So if you compare how they do in future seasons. . . well, of course there is a *relative* advantage of the 2,000-pitch guys against the 3,000-pitch guys. To make it work, you absolutely have to from quality groups, so that you're comparing 3,000-pitch guys to 2,000-pitch guys *of equal quality.*

You could solve that problem, if you weren't dealing with 20 other things at the same time. Another big problem is that this is most interesting when you're studying young pitchers. But when you're studying 21- and 20-year-old pitchers, you're talking about guys who were in college last year and in high school three years ago, and you just don't have any real record about their work history. You can assemble some of it if you really work at it, but it's tough, and there's a tremendous risk of missing something. I have a friend who managed Darren Dreifort on an amateur team when Dreifort was 18; he got him late in the year, after Dreifort's previous team folded, and, according to my friend, Dreifort had thrown about 300 innings. Try finding records of *that* league. . . hell, Kent Earl doesn't have any records, and he was coaching in the league.

What I'm saying is, I think Henzler's stuff is fascinating, and I think it opens a window on the issue, but I wouldn't get wildly optimistic about what we're going to be able to see working through that window. The issue is just so complicated that, in my experience, it defies systematic analysis.

OLKIN: In doing some hit-and-miss research, the highest single-season average pitch count I've found (using Henzler's method) is Nolan Ryan, 1977—137. Bobo Newsom, 1938, is the only one I've found that's even close, except for Ryan's other big seasons in the 1970s. I've been surprised at how few pitchers ever have averaged 130 pitches per start in a season. If Henzler's method is reasonably accurate, the old-time pitchers didn't throw significantly more pitches per start than today's starters—although they probably did make many more starts on short rest.

P.S. Wilbur Wood threw 376 innings in 1972—and averaged only around 109 pitches per start. ·

JAMES: Couple of things I forgot to mention.

1. Pitch Selection. There are different stress levels associated with different pitches. Knuckleballs are zero-stress, of course, and this makes knuckleball pitchers an exception to all the

other rules about what a pitcher can do, but also, a lot of baseball people believe that throwing the slider is hard on the arm. I don't know, and I'm suspicious of the theory, but what do I know? I don't know how to prove that it is or isn't a high-stress delivery. There are people who argue that throwing the screwball is hard on the arm; there are people who argue that it isn't. Roger Kahn argues in *The Boys of Summer* that Branch Rickey taught his pitchers an overhand curveball that, as I recall his phrase, "places a line of strain on the pitcher running from his shoulder through his fingertips," which caused his pitchers to burn out early. Who knows?

2. Weather. I remember that John McNamara had Greg Swindell throw something like 140 pitches on a cold late-April day about 1990; I always though Swindell was never the same after that game. But throwing the same number of pitches on a hot August afternoon in a quick game. . . well, maybe it wouldn't mean anything.

And all of this has to be sorted out in an environment in which large numbers of pitchers just suddenly lose effectiveness without any injury being announced or revealed. I don't know how you can sort it out. I've never figured out any way to handle the complexities of the issue.

OLKIN: Using Henzler's estimated pitch-count formula for the 26-inning game of May 1, 1920: Cadore, 333 pitches; Oeschger, 308 pitches.

HENZLER: The danger of shrinking the general to the specific. . .

Largest Errors, Estimated vs. Actual Pitches—1988-99

Pitcher	Date	Est	Actual	Pct Diff
Chris Bosio	06/21/88	128	88	45.5
Jeff Fassero	08/19/93	135	94	43.6
Greg Maddux	07/22/97	112	78	43.6
Jaime Navarro	08/11/92	125	88	42.0
Bob Wolcott	07/15/96	112	79	41.8
Ed Whitson	05/06/90	113	80	41.3
Ed Whitson	04/20/90	120	85	41.2
Andy Benes	04/19/92	125	89	40.4
Andy Ashby	07/05/98	105	75	40.0

(starts only, minimum 9 IP)

OLKIN: I understand the danger, but the estimate is still useful in that it sets a range. Even if the error with Cadore was as large as it was with Bosio, we'd still have Cadore throwing 228 pitches.

JAMES: It would seem apparent from this list that pitchers who have very good control are inclined to use fewer pitches to record an "undescribed out" than pitchers with poorer control. If you had a week to work on it, you could use this knowledge to refine Henzler's system into even more accurate estimated pitch counts.

March 19—Read My Numbers

OLKIN: New Toronto manager Jim Fregosi's explanation for moving Jose Cruz Jr. out of the No. 2 hole in favor of Homer Bush:

"For me, in order for someone to hit second, you must be able to handle the bat and take pitches."

In 675 professional games, Bush has drawn 110 walks. Cruz has accumulated nearly that many (98) during his 209-game major league career.

JAMES: We would have in our system the "percentage of pitches" taken for each hitter, right? It's a good guess that the percentage is higher for Cruz than for Bush. If you had specific numbers addressing the issue that Fregosi raised, I think you could send them to a Toronto writer and probably get them in the paper.

DEWAN: We can actually also provide data for "handling the bat"—namely how often he puts the bat on the ball—that would probably put part of Fregosi's comment in a favorable light.

From *Player Profiles*: Homer Bush—3.38 career pitches per plate appearance. Cruz—3.82.

JAMES: But that's *pitches*; what I was specifically interested in is pitches *taken*, which would respond directly to Fregosi's comment.

March 22—Red-Faced Workload?

HENZLER: Couple of things I noticed when working with Giants spring training leader boards this morning.

Which one doesn't belong?

Spring Training HR Leaders—NL

Player	HR
Mark McGwire	8
Sammy Sosa	8
Tripp Cromer	5

Jack McKeon clearly believes in working his starters during spring training:

Spring Training IP Leaders—NL

	Player	IP
1.	Pete Harnisch	18.2
2t.	Steve Avery	16.2
2t.	Jason Bere	16.2
6t.	Brett Tomko	16.0

Last year, Dave Burba (when he was with the Reds) led NL hurlers with 38.0 spring training innings. Harnisch and Mike Remlinger tied for second with 33.0 apiece. And Steve Cooke tied for seventh with 29.0.

March 25—Triples-Challenged

MILLER: Prior to the 1997 season Jim Henzler wrote:

Most At-Bats With No Career Triples

Player	AB
Craig Worthington	1,234
Mark Parent	1,077
Gaylord Perry	1,076

Parent now has 1,303 at-bats without a triple. He's atop the world now! (Unless someone else has skyrocketed past Mr. Parent during the 1997 and 1998 seasons.)

HENNINGER: While Mark McGwire *has* tripled during his career (five times), he hasn't executed a three-bagger since 1988. He's gone nearly 4000 at-bats since his last triple, and he's homered nearly 400 times during that span. If only they would move the fences back about 40 feet at Busch Stadium.

March 25—Small-Market Blues

ROBERTS: The Royals will try anything.

From the Fox Sports website:

Failed experiment: Canadian national softball pitcher Mike Piechnik, who was impressive in a Royals tryout camp, won't be signing with the team. He sent video of his underhanded delivery with stops and strange movement, so the Royals could look it over. They determined it would be an illegal pitch in the majors.

JAMES: I *wish* the Royals would try anything. Unfortunately, if there's a choice between losing and doing something original, they're pretty much committed to the former.

PASSMAN: From today's *Washington Post*:

"Baseball has simply become too greedy for a city like Montreal," explained Roger Landry, publisher of the city's largest newspaper, La Presse, *and a former Expos vice president.*

Actually, I think it's become too greedy for a lot of cities.

Good article, though. Another interesting quote from the article: "If Montreal is married to hockey, baseball has been a favorite mistress."

It basically says that there is no government money available to help the franchise, and they've all but given up the team to Washington D.C.

CARLSON: I don't think this saddens the league in a way. Canadian franchises in a sports league add zero value to what the league can get from the TV contracts (and in some ways it can hurt since the networks have to figure in the chance of a Canadian market getting into playoff games and hurting ratings by not having two U.S. markets have a significant interest spike).

PINTO: I saw this on the wires today:

The Minnesota Twins are offering $99 full-season packages that include an autographed Kirby Puckett bat for every pair of seats. About 500 of the $99 season tickets have been sold since they went on sale two weeks ago, and the Twins expect another 200-300 to go before the April 6 home opener against Toronto. "Not only is it a heck of a deal with the bat, but more importantly it crosses all financial guidelines in terms of people's ability to become a full-time season-ticket holder for this baseball team," team spokesman Dave St. Peter said. The tickets are for upper deck general admission seats that regularly sell for $4 per game. The cost of a seat with the season-ticket deal is $1.22 per game. It is the cheapest 81-game season ticket in the majors.

I may buy a pair just for the bat!

March 28—Catchers Leading Off

PINTO: A wire story I saw today from the AP's Alan Robinson:

Jason Kendall is on the brink of possible Major League Baseball history, and he didn't even know it. Catchers are asked to call pitches, settle down pitchers, direct the defense, but one thing they do not do is lead off. Jason Kendall does.

Kendall will begin the season as the Pittsburgh Pirates' leadoff hitter and, about mid-May, likely will become the first catcher to lead off more than 32 times in a season.

Since 1970, Jeff Newman (32) and Butch Wynegar (31) are the only catchers to lead off more than 30 times in a season. Before that, catchers led off about as often as they steal bases.

Oops. Jason Kendall does that, too, setting an NL record for a catcher with 26 steals last season

He also led the majors by being hit by pitches 31 times last season. And his .327 average was the highest by any Pirates player in a non-strike season since Dave Parker hit .334 in 1978. Kendall wasn't aware until Friday that so few catchers have led off. He suggests it is a reflection of the changing times of a sport in which catchers long ago shed their images as roly-poly heavyweights who love to hit and love to eat.

I think this last paragraph is a lot of hooey. I don't remember many catchers from *any* era who were roly-poly and good (I'm not sure if Ernie Lombardi was fat or just a huge, muscular man). There have been a lot of slow catchers, but not because they were fat, but because catching wears on your legs. The fact is catchers have led off, it's just that when it becomes obvious a catcher is a good leadoff man, he stops catching. Brian Downing and Craig Biggio come to mind, but I bet someone can think of others.

The problem has always been that managers have set ideas of what a leadoff man should be, and it's often based on position. Seventy-two percent of games last year were led off by a center fielder or second baseman. (There was not one game led off by a catcher last year). Ralph Houk always led off with his second baseman (I went through my formative baseball years watching Horace Clarke, career .308 OBP, lead off for the Yankees). The second thing they seem to look for is speed. Of course, the first and foremost thing they should look for is the ability to get on base. But managers stereotype; first basemen and catchers are slow, right fielders hit for power, shortstops are there for their defense.

When I have some time, I'm going to try to look for catchers who should have been leading off. Mike Scioscia and Jim Sundberg come to mind immediately. Scioscia should have been leading off for the Dodgers in the mid-1980s, but Sundberg actually had a better, but still untraditional leadoff man on his team, Mike Hargrove.

What it really comes down to is the speed vs. OBP argument. If I said to someone last year, "The Mets should lead off Olerud," they would reply that he's too slow and would clog the bases. It's the Wade Boggs vs. Vince Coleman argument. I remember one year in looking at these two, they scored about the same number of runs; Boggs had a much higher OBP, but Coleman's speed brought him around to score more often per time reached. So they seem to be even right? Wrong. Because the effect of OBP is spread throughout the lineup.

Let's look at 1987:

Wade Boggs vs. Vince Coleman—1987

Category	Boggs	Coleman
AB	551	623
H	200	180
AB - H (outs)	351	443
Runs	108	121
OBP	.461	.363

Coleman scored more runs, but made almost 100 more outs doing so. That's three games worth of outs. If a team scores five runs a game, that's 15 more runs for the team if you put Boggs at the top instead of Coleman. It may not seem like much, but 15 runs were probably the difference between the Mets being the wild-card and being a game out last year.

It's interesting that the Pirates have come full circle here. They had a fast second baseman who couldn't get on base, and now they are going to their only good on-base average player. It's a bold move.

Back to the article:

"Nowadays, you've got to be in shape with all the weightlifting, the nutritional supplements, everybody in the game is stronger and faster," he said Friday. "It's no different for a catcher. They're taking the labels off catchers that were on them for a long time."

Last season, Kendall batted second or third, so moving up to first doesn't seem like all that big a deal. He may be called on to steal bases more than before, but he already stole much more than the average catcher.

"I honestly think he doesn't care where he bats," manager Gene Lamont said.

Kendall's answer: "I honestly don't. I'm still going to hit the same way I did before. If I get a 2-0 or 3-1 fastball, I'm swinging. I'm not taking the pitch. I'm not changing my approach."

Something is working this spring. His on-base percentage is nearly .500, far better than the .319 of Tony Womack, the Pirates' leadoff hitter last season.

PASSMAN: It's a stereotype, but not an altogether incorrect one. Think about it, from the high school and little league level, where does the biggest kid invariably end up? Behind the plate. Just look at the Bad News Bears.

JAMES: Random reactions to Pinto on Kendall:

1. Ernie Lombardi was fat. There were a number of good catchers in that generation who were quite obese, including Lombardi, Shanty Hogan and Spud Davis.

2. There is also a "selection mechanism" that contributes to catchers being slow, probably contributes as much or more than the wear-and-tear effect. If a player can't run, they'll *make* him a catcher. Mike Macfarlane is a good example. When he came up he was very slim—he's still slender—and if you watch him run, you don't realize that he's slow. But he's *really* slow; even running hard, he just doesn't move. That's why they made him a catcher. He was too slow to play the infield.

3. One catcher who could have led off was Johnny Bassler, 1920s Detroit Tiger who hung around in the PCL until the late-1930s. He had a .441 on-base percentage in 1924, over .400 some other seasons, no power. But they hit him eighth anyway.

4. I think Bob Stinson led off some. I agree that Scioscia should have led off. The Dodgers had seasons when they just had nobody to lead off, but they wouldn't let Scioscia do it.

Looking for catchers who were fat or could bat leadoff. . . don't see a lot in either category. I don't find many *good* catchers who were fat. Smokey Burgess, of course, Wilbert Robinson, Frankie Hayes. Terry Kennedy was kind of pudgy, but not good for very long, and Mike LaValliere pretty much ate himself out of the league, but had outstanding defensive skills.

Muddy Ruel could have been a leadoff man, but wasn't. Roger Bresnahan, Rick Ferrell, Wally Schang. Most of the *catchers* who had high OBPs also had enough power to bat somewhere else, like Tenace, Daulton and Tettleton. I would be tempted to lead off Tenace, but I don't think he did much.

HENNINGER: One of my boyhood favorites, Earl Battey, fit the roly-poly mold and was a decent defensive catcher for some solid Twins teams in the early '60s. He didn't hit for as much power as you might have expected, though.

COOPERSON: Didn't Bresnahan lead off?

JAMES: Bresnahan did lead off in mid-career; that's right.

Another catcher who *got* fat was Joe Torre. Part of the deal with Lombardi was that he sort of had permission to *get* fat and fatter because he couldn't move anyway, so he kind of read it as it doesn't matter. I think that's Earl Battey, too. Battey was very solidly built, and he got fat toward the end of his career, but I don't think he was fat when he was 26-30 and hitting 15-26 homers a year.

Torre, in the years that he was catching (up to 1970) was getting fatter and fatter. He went on a serious weight program the winter of 1970-71, moved to third base, and has never put the weight back on.

March 30—Baltimore vs. Cuba

PALACIOS: Forget about trying to sign players defecting from Cuba, we should go raid their umpires! Boy, except for three pitches that left me scratching my head, the strike zone that they were calling was beautiful.

I think even Scott Erickson found the strike zone refreshing. He threw a big breaking ball, a breaking ball perhaps not seen in the majors in years. The pitch started at the hitter's head and it ended right below the hitter's knee. The pitch probably crossed the plate at the hitter's belly—and it was called a strike.

He threw the pitch at 62 MPH. And it was unhittable. He threw it only once, as if he has been practicing that pitch as joke in the bullpen and he finally got a chance to use it.

It is really sad not to see these big breaking balls in the majors. I love breaking balls because they are not just about talent, but about work ethic and intelligence. And of course, with our ridiculous strike zone, those curveballs are dead.

Next time our umps go on strike, let's ask Fidel for a humanitarian donation of umpires. The umps would qualify as a humanitarian donation because they would aid the mental health of American baseball fans.

March 30—The 1999 Mets

JAMES: Hey, what do you guys think of the Mets? ESPN did a show on them. . . you have to like a team with Piazza and Henderson, and actually they have a lot of guys I have always liked. That's the problem: they have a lot of guys I would have loved to have 10 years ago.

Hershiser, Bonilla, Henderson, Leiter, Ventura. . . what is this, 1988? They've got Brian McRae and Mariano Duncan, who weren't actually all that good when they were good, and they got Edgardo Alfonzo now playing second base. I just wonder if they might not lose 90 games, but I don't really know how to figure out teams in the free-agent era. Be interested to know what you all think.

CAPUANO: They'd go to the World Series if they had Jose Offerman.

PINTO: They released Duncan yesterday.

I think Henderson is going to be a big improvement at the top of the order. If they have Henderson last year they win the wild card.

Pretty much every move they have made this winter offensively has improved their OBP, so they should score more runs. I have to like an offense with Henderson, Olerud and Piazza at the top.

Leiter's arm is probably five years younger than he is due to his years of not pitching much. I worked with him during the playoffs last year and he struck me as someone who knows his business.

Met fans think that getting rid of Mel Rojas is a big plus.

I think the Mets will challenge the Braves this year for the East title. I think the Braves' lack of offense is going to catch up with them, and for the first time in nine years they are going into a season without four proven starters.

CALLIS: I think the Mets are a bit overrated, but I do see them as a legit wild-card contender and can't envision them losing 90 games. Their rotation and bullpen are both fairly deep. Alfonzo came through the minors as a shortstop, and I don't see how he'll have much of a problem playing second. He's played there before for the Mets, and his bat is all the better there than at third.

OLKIN: I'm continually amazed by the complete transformation Bobby Valentine's shown. Back in Texas, he'd assemble a staff full of hard-throwing wild men and pitch them to death. They'd lead the league in walks every year, and eventually all of them got injured.

Then he went to Japan and came back a completely different manager. Now he's all about pitch-count limits and putting the ball in play. Many of the moves the Mets have made (the signing of Olerud and Ventura, the replacement of Baerga with Alfonzo, the decision to leave Ordonez at short and put up with his hitting) have significantly strengthened their infield defense. This goes hand-in-hand with his newfound fondness for control pitchers who put the ball in play.

Look what he's done with Rick Reed. He had them bring in Masato Yoshii, Armando Reynoso. . . Al Leiter, a strikeout-flyball pitcher, came over in a trade, and suddenly cut his walks and began throwing grounders.

What's more, he's become a born-again pitch-count watcher. Perhaps he's had no choice, coming in after the downfall of Bill Pulsipher and Jason Isringhausen. But based on what he did to Texas' staff, you'd never think he'd be one to keep his starters on a short leash.

PASSMAN: Without any statistical, analytical, or otherwise intelligent reasoning, I also think this year's Mets are overrated. It seems like they have a lot of the pieces to the jigsaw puzzle, but none of them seem to fit right. Maybe I keep flashing back to past Mets teams, maybe I keep thinking about how last year's Orioles had all this talent, but didn't come close to putting it together. Maybe I've just been sniffing too much marker fumes.

April 1—Wohlers Continues to Struggle

COUSINS: So much for him gaining his control back!

In today's game against the Astros, Wohlers pitched two-thirds of an inning, walking five, giving up two earned runs and throwing a wild pitch. I think the closer's job might be Rocker's after all.

April 5—Fast Start

SPEAR: Darryl Kile is leading the majors in hitting!

NL Batting Average Leaders—1999

Player, Team	Avg
Kile, Col	1.000 (2/2)
Vander Wal, SD	1.000 (2/2)
Bichette, Col	.800 (4/5)
Castilla, Col	.800 (4/5)
Manwaring, Col	.500 (2/4)
Joyner, SD	.500 (1/2)
Lansing, Col	.400 (2/5)
Hamilton, Col	.400 (2/5)
Rivera, SD	.250 (1/4)
Gwynn, SD	.250 (1/4)

Kile once hit .094 (5-for-53) for an entire season!

April 5—More Wohlers

JAMES: Mark Wohlers:

1. Just noticed that Wohlers last year had a 10.18 ERA, but was 8-for-8 in save opportunities. That's gotta be a record, doesn't it?

2. He's in the game today, has thrown strikes. Not very many, but he has mixed in a strike now and then among all the bad pitches.

3. The announcers just said that he is pitching better today because he is "missing close." Swear to God they said that, while he was in the middle of walking a guy on four straight. Don Sutton said that. The other announcer said "We're not going to know the end of the Mark Wohlers story for a long time yet." Are you serious? I thought they were going to release him *tonight*. You mean there's more of this yet to come?

ZMINDA: They can't release him. Turner Productions has been planning to make "The Mark Wohlers Story." I think Steve Blass has the title role.

CARLSON: And Rip Torn will play the evil Rupert Murdoch, who offers another crappy pitcher too much money, forcing Turner to pay Wohlers even more money.

NEYER: Bill, to reinforce your message from yesterday, I ran across the following in the AP's game story of the Phils-Braves:

The Phillies added two runs in the ninth against Mark Wohlers, the former Braves closer trying to make a comeback from a disastrous season. He was closer to the plate than a year ago but still walked four and surrendered a run-scoring double to Anderson off the center-field wall.

"Closer to the plate, but still walked four". . . it's like even the writer feels sorry for Wohlers.

I hope Montgomery pitches well this week, so the Royals can get something good for him.

PINTO: Happy Opening Day!

April 6—Let's Eat!

OLKIN: From today's *Boston Globe*:

O'Leary reported to camp having lost about a dozen pounds. He said at the time that if he didn't feel right, he'd start eating again. That's a philosophy you'd expect from a guy known in the clubhouse as Yummy because of his passion for all things delicious.

April 7—Move Over, Minnie Minoso

MUNDO: Don't know if you all saw this, but the Schaumburg Flyers (the new Chicago-area Northern League team) are inviting Ted "Double Duty" Radcliffe to *pitch* a game for them on June 19!

April 7—Magic Numbers in April

PINTO: On the front page of the sports section of my local paper was a box with "Red Sox Magic Number" and in large face print, "161." My first reaction was, "that's silly," but then, why not? What makes a magic number so much more magical in September than in April?

Magic numbers would be great things to watch through the year; they start at 163, and always go down; it's easy to tell when a team has been eliminated (magic number exceeds games remaining + opponent games remaining); and, well, they are just magical. You could get Sigfried and Roy or Penn and Teller to sponsor their display on sports news shows. When a team reaches 81, they sawed their magic number in half. When they are eliminated, they've done a disappearing act. The possibilities are endless.

Abracadabra.

COOPERSON: Amazingly, many people who follow the game don't understand how to figure out a magic number!

PINTO: I always had a complicated way of doing this. Someone showed me a simpler way to do it last year (it turned out, it was the same way, I had just never done the algebra to reduce the terms).

Take two teams, A and B. The magic number for A to eliminate B is the combined number of wins by A and losses by B that will result in A guaranteed to finish ahead of B. In a 162 game season, it's 163 - (A wins + B losses). Example; if A is 80-60, and B is 70-70, 163 - (80 + 70) is 13. If A wins 13 games, they would have 93 wins. Since B has only 22 games left, the most they can win is 92 games! Notice that you can turn this around and get a legitimate answer. B's magic number to eliminate A is 163 - (70 + 60) or 33. Since B has only 22 games left, it would need at least 11 losses by A to have a chance at winning. If the magic number goes negative, then the team is eliminated.

April 9—Error Prone

PASSMAN: Mike Sirotka committed three errors in the top of the fifth today against Kansas City. This has to be some kind of record (excluding any recreational league softball games I may have pitched in).

SPEAR: I'm pretty sure Tommy John committed three in an inning once.

ELLIS: Pokey Reese made four errors playing shortstop last year on Opening Day.

JAMES: Didn't Willie Davis commit three errors in one inning in the 1965 or 1966 World Series? Would it be the second game of the 1966 Series that Davis committed three errors in the game? My memory is that all were in one inning, two on one play and another later in the inning.

Also, I think Brooks Robinson once made three errors in an inning.

PASSMAN: I figured it would be rare for a player to commit three errors in an inning, but nearly impossible for a pitcher.

JAMES: I think Mark Wohlers is capable of making any number of errors in an inning, if you push him. Also, not having checked, I suspect that the ratio of errors to innings for pitchers is probably as high or higher than for the other infielders. I suspect we'll find it's got precedent.

April 11—Grimsleygate

SKELTON: Bat Thief Reveals Himself!

From the Associated Press:

Jason Grimsley has finally come clean.

The pitcher was the one who crawled through the bowels of Comiskey Park five years ago to replace the corked bat of teammate Albert Belle that was being held in the umpires' room.

The confession by Grimsley, then with the Cleveland Indians and now with the New York Yankees, was reported Sunday in The New York Times, *clearing up one of baseball's ongoing mysteries.*

"That was one of the biggest adrenaline rushes I've ever experienced," Grimsley told the newspaper.

In the first inning of a Cleveland-Chicago game on July 15, 1994, White Sox manager Gene Lamont was tipped off that Belle, then with the Indians, had a corked bat.

Lamont challenged the use of the bat and umpire Dave Phillips took it and put it in his locker. The Indians panicked, knowing the bat was indeed corked.

Grimsley, 6-foot-3 and a slim 180 pounds, volunteered for the mission to get it back.

The Times reported that he took a cork-free bat belonging to Paul Sorrento—all of Belle's bats were corked. Grimsley said he knew there was an escape hatch in the ceiling in the clubhouse and figured there was one as well in the umpires' dressing room.

With the help of an unidentified Indians' employee, he navigated his way to the spot. Crawling on his belly, a flashlight in his mouth, he finally found it, dropped down on a refrigerator and swiped the bat from Phillips' locker.

"My heart was going 1,000 miles a second," Grimsley told the Times.

PASSMAN: Well, at least if I ever get locked out of my apartment, or need to break into the Democratic National Headquarters, I'll know who to call.

COOPERSON: Almost as impressive a theft as the Phils trading Grimsley for Curt Schilling!

April 13—Jose Offerman

JAMES: Jose Offerman has had at least two hits in every game this season. He had four hits on Opening Day, two hits a game since then—14 hits in six games.

HENZLER: Did you know his anagram is "Major Offense"? He just hit his third triple of the season, driving in two runs. He's batting .484.

April 13—Flush the Nickname Down the Jake

OLKIN: From today's *Akron Beacon Journal*:

The Indians reportedly have asked broadcasters from channels 19 and 43 to refrain from calling Jacobs Field "The Jake," which happens to be slang for toilet. Though nobody knows for sure, there is speculation that the request came indirectly from Tribe owner Dick Jacobs.

April 13—White Sox Lament

PALACIOS: Sure, now they decide to hit.

Robin Ventura—1999

Year	Team	G	AB	R	H	2B	3B	HR	RBI	BB	SO	Avg	OBP	Slg
1999	NYM	8	32	3	12	3	0	1	9	4	6	.375	.432	.563

Albert Belle—1999

Year	Team	G	AB	R	H	2B	3B	HR	RBI	BB	SO	Avg	OBP	Slg
1999	Bal	6	22	4	9	2	0	1	5	5	1	.409	.519	.636

Last year Thomas after nine games: .273. Last year Ventura after nine games: .344. Last year Belle after nine games: .133.

JAMES: I always said Frank would be great; all he needed was to have some great hitter like Darrin Jackson hitting behind him.

April 13—More Small-Market Blues

JAMES: Mike Benjamin is now the Pirates' starting shortstop? Man, that's sad.

HENZLER: Bill, you must not be getting your weekly dose of Peter Gammons. Here's what he said this past Sunday:

"It is an offensive game, as we saw 11 runs scored in an Opening Day matchup of Tom Glavine vs. Curt Schilling, 14 in Kevin Brown vs. Randy Johnson, 19 in Mussina-Wilson Alvarez. Still, we have seen Kevin Mitchell 'play' right field, and Sadler wins more games. So does Mike Benjamin (emphasis added)."

Will we ever see Mike Benjamin playing right field? Now that would really be sad.

OLKIN: Diamondback fans got to see Tony Womack play right field last night.

April 16—Same Old Cubbies

ZMINDA: Benito Santiago just grounded into a triple play.

HENZLER: I wonder what Fernando Vina's triple-play pivot percentage is.

ELMAN: I happened to be in the Ops room and they had Santiago at first by two-and-a-half steps. Ouch!

April 16—The Struggles of Rojas and Navarro

ZMINDA: The Dodgers have traded Mel Rojas and Dave Mlicki to the Tigers for minor leaguers Robinson Checo, Rick Roberts and Apostol Garcia. What's next for Mel. . . even up for Jaime Navarro, maybe?

STEPHENS: As desperate as the White Sox are to dump Navarro and his enormous salary, I don't think they'd pull the trigger on that one.

PINTO: The funny thing is, the Tigers probably have improved themselves.

HENNINGER: Maybe the Tigers will be fortunate enough to get a better year out of Mlicki than they are likely to get out of Willie Blair.

MITTLEMAN: Rojas makes $4.85 million and Mlicki gets $2.25. That's better than $7 million saved by trading two guys the Dodgers didn't need. Rojas is a free agent after this year while Mlicki goes into his fifth-year arbitration (the most expensive one).

PASSMAN: Is it just me, or is the thought of Mel Rojas in Tiger Stadium frightening? Mel throwing in that bandbox. If you've never caught a home run, maybe a road trip to the Motor City is in order.

I also thought I heard that Wohlers and $5 million went to Cincy for John Hudek. I hope for the Reds fans that the money goes towards player salaries and nowhere near Marge or Schottzie 2.

DEWAN: I would trade Jaime Navarro straight up for any other player on the 40-man roster of any team in baseball. I probably would trade Navarro for any player in Double-A or Triple-A baseball.

JAMES: How about an empty roster spot? Wouldn't you have to think a 24-man team would be better than adding Jaime as the 25th?

HENNINGER: I think the ChiSox were crazy not to pick up a couple of innings-eaters last year, instead of running Fordham, Eyre and Parque out there before they were ready. No matter how he pitches, at least Navarro is eating innings some young kid is not ready for. I hope they don't trade him.

JAMES: Is there a Rick Reed type in the minors now? There must be somebody. . . you know what I mean. Reed was a damn good pitcher for at least six years in the minors before he could overcome the fascination with radar guns. There must be somebody out there like that?

MITTLEMAN: John's comments shouldn't be construed as sarcastic re: Navarro since the White Sox would gladly get rid of him for a dog and a beer to save the $5 million they owe him this year. No one will take him at that price and when you consider how much starters are revered today on the market, it's really sad.

April 20—The Early Surprises of 1999

PALACIOS: Maybe St. Louis will have the magic this year. I'm speechless:

Kent Bottenfield—1999

W-L	IP	H	R	ER	BB	K	#Pit	ERA
1-0	7	3	0	0	3	4	95	0.98

Once a starter prospect, Bottenfield became a journeyman reliever. La Russa used him as a starter again out of desperation last year, and since his move, Bottenfield has turned into a $100 million pitcher while making barely over the minimum. We should make sure Bottenfield is still pitching as a righthander.

As if this wasn't enough, second baseman Joe McEwing has been another Cardinal miracle. Another early surprise has been Einar Diaz with Cleveland. He became a different player last year in the minors (just like McEwing had an unexpected great year in Triple-A last year). After having unexpected great seasons in Triple-A, can Diaz and McEwing shock baseball by continuing their hot play in the majors this year?

JAMES: This would qualify Tony La Russa for the Johnny Oates award. Oates does this every year. In 1998 he got 39 wins out of Aaron Sele and Rick Helling. This year Oates has gotten a 3-0 start out of Mike Morgan. *Mike Morgan.* I'll bet you he gets Morgan to the wire like 15-9 or something.

April 21—Dubious Debut

ALPERT: Brett Hinchliffe of the Seattle Mariners made his first major league start this past Sunday. He was thrown out in the fourth or fifth inning for throwing at and hitting a batter. My question is: Does anyone happen to know if a pitcher who is pitching in his first major league start has ever been thrown out of that game?

FORD: I don't know about pitchers, but Bill Sharman of the Brooklyn Dodgers was tossed out of a game—and he *never* played a single inning in the majors. I'm thinking it was during the 1951 race, but I know it was in the '50s. He was a bench player called up from the minors, and got ejected when the umpire was getting razzed from the Dodger dugout.

I'm not sure, but I think he may be the same Bill Sharman who starred for the Boston Celtics in the NBA.

ZMINDA: Yes, it was the NBA Bill Sharman who got tossed out. He was quite a good minor league baseball player.

April 21—St. Louis Lineup Changes

HENZLER: Have you seen the lineup Tony La Russa has concocted for the Cardinals today? Mark McGwire and Eric Davis were both banged up last night, so they aren't starting today. But neither are J.D. Drew and Edgar Renteria. Here are the top three hitters in the order, with their career OBPs entering 1999:

1.	David Howard	.292
2.	Placido Polanco	.292
3.	Shawon Dunston	.296

But wait, Eli Marrero, he of the .392 career slugging percentage, is "replacing" McGwire at first base and batting cleanup. Alberto Castillo, with a .204 career average, is catching.

Joe McEwing, the hottest Cardinal hitter with an average of .442, is nevertheless batting eighth. Oh well. At least he isn't batting behind the pitcher.

PINTO: Gee, Andruw Jones could actually lead off for that team.

HENZLER: Boy, I sure wish the Cardinals could somehow get him. Perhaps he could guide J.D. Drew through the same growing pains he seems to be experiencing. Of course, since Drew is nearly a year-and-a-half older than Jones, perhaps it's Drew who should be doing the mentoring.

If you're just trying to be pejorative, I'm sure you're aware that Jones has walked 11 times in 45 official at-bats this year, a rate more in line with his performance in 1996 and the minor leagues.

April 29—Not Speechless in Seattle

OLKIN: In today's *Detroit News*, ex-Tiger Brian Hunter admits that if he were a manager, he wouldn't want Brian Hunter, either:

"Buddy [Bell] was one of my biggest fans. And that's nothing against Larry Parrish, but he made it very clear he wants his outfielders to hit 20-plus home runs. If I was a manager, I'd want that, too. Unfortunately I don't fall into that category."

April 29—The Bleeding Continues

PALACIOS: Mel Rojas does deserve some sort of credit for this line:

Detroit	IP	H	R	ER	BB	K	#Pit	ERA
Mlicki	4.1	4	6	4	5	1	84	2.35
Nitkowski (L, 0-1)	0	0	1	1	1	0	5	7.71
Rojas	1.2	8	11	11	1	1	43	17.47

I mean, it's hard to give up 11 earned runs on 43 pitches.

PASSMAN: I agree. I mean, I have not followed baseball to the depth and for the length of some here, but this has to be among the worst outings ever. He also hit two batters in the game.

I do find it humorous that the player who struck out is considered one of the top hitters in the game (Edgar Martinez). You'd think it would have been someone else, like Rafael Bournigal.

April 30—In Relief of Mel Rojas. . .

OLKIN: Carlos Perez' opponent OPS:

Carlos Perez, Opponent OPS by Pitch Count—1999	
Pitch	**Opp OPS**
1-15	.258
16-30	.500
31-45	.616
46-60	.823
61-75	1.758
76+	2.153

	AB	H	Avg	OBP	Slg
pitch 1-60	64	12	.188	.246	.344
pitch 60+	23	15	.652	.680	1.217

Now *that's* what you call hitting the wall.

DEWAN: Looks like a relief pitcher to me!

April 30—Small-Market Blues Revisited

ROBERTS: What is everyone's opinion on the planned "walkout" tonight when the Royals host the Yankees in Kansas City? Do people really think that this is going to change the way the wealth is spread in the major leagues?

Being a Royals fan, I have to agree with the reasoning behind the walkout. However, if I was at the game, I don't think that I would walk out with five innings left in the game, just to prove a point that will probably not result in anything anyway. Any thoughts?

PALACIOS: Not to be harsh, but perhaps Royals fans should go to more ballgames. The Royals are a young team this year and they can create excitement on the field. I doubt that the T-shirt demonstration will make Steinbrenner "see the light."

Anyway, Steinbrenner is not one of the wealthiest owners in the majors. The Minnesota Twins are currently owned by a billionaire. Why should Steinbrenner, who made his money making ships in Cleveland (not even in the ocean) have to give money to a billionaire.

The Minnesota Twins owner lost $10 million last year. That's less than one percent of what he's worth. I spend more than one percent of my net worth on baseball every year, and I don't get box seats.

If you're going to lose money in baseball, don't get in the business. I am against revenue sharing, but not against other means of spreading the talent (not dollars).

CALLIS: I'm tired of all the whining about large-revenue/small-revenue teams. A lot of the teams decide what category they want to fall into, or flip back and forth. The Angels are one example.

Here's my solution. Move the Royals if they're having such a tough time. I'm sure D.C. would welcome them. Their problems are caused just as much, if not more, by inept management than by the size of their market.

May 3—Pitchers' Hitting

SPEAR: You know, these aren't bad numbers at all from the Marlins pitching staff.

Highest Batting Average, Team Pitchers—1999

	Avg	AB	R	H	2B	3B	HR	RBI	SB	CS	TBB	SO	OBP	Slg
Marlins	.286	42	5	12	4	0	1	7	0	0	2	14	.311	.452
Expos	.216	37	4	8	0	0	0	2	0	0	4	18	.293	.216
Phillies	.213	47	4	10	1	1	0	4	0	0	4	20	.275	.277
Mets	.200	50	1	10	1	0	1	2	0	1	2	16	.231	.280
Braves	.183	60	6	11	2	1	1	6	0	0	2	23	.210	.300
NL Avg.	.149	47	3	7	1	0	0	3	0	0	3	17	.200	.170

May 3—All the Poop That's Fit to Print

OLKIN: Actual Headline from the *Detroit Free Press*:

Higginson on target in toilet and at plate

May 4—More Mel

STEPHENS: Mel Rojas' line from May 3 against Tampa:

Detroit	IP	H	R	ER	BB	K	#Pit	ERA
Blair (L, 0-4)	2.1	6	8	7	4	1	75	7.76
Rojas	0.2	3	5	5	2	1	31	22.74

Hmmm. . . I'm starting to like Jaime Navarro more and more these days.

May 4—Longball Shortage in Denver

COOPERSON: Does Jim Leyland have them bunting? The Rockies rank 13th in the NL with only 21 homers so far—that's exactly half as many as Arizona has hit.

DEWAN: The Rockies have only played five of 22 games at home. That's pretty much the whole story.

May 4—But How Many Fans Can the Pathfinder Seat?

PALACIOS: Signs our society's values are changing:

In the 1960s, we were spending billions of dollars on our space programs, while we were spending under $100 million in each of our new multi-purpose parks.

These days the tables have turned. It cost us $266 million to put the Pathfinder on Mars, but Safeco Field will cost $415 million ($340 million from public funds).

In both cases, we're spending the money on things that improve our morale as a society, but baseball does more for our morale than knowing the mass of carbon dioxide on Mars. However, I am tired of the old arguments of ballparks helping the local economies.

After all, a modern good-size mall employs more people than a major league team. When Bloomington lost the Vikings and the Twins, they cried for the 400 jobs those two teams supported. The Mall of America was built on the exact same size, and it provides over 10,000 jobs.

I agree that ballparks help local economies. However, the same way that having street sweepers helps our local economies. We spend a lot of money to have clean streets, and clean streets don't help our local economies directly either.

But clean streets, new ballparks, and even the Mars Pathfinder help our morale. Maybe some day, some young college talent will tell his or her sweetheart that s/he has to go home because there's no better city than Milwaukee. "I love Milwaukee. It has Miller Park!"

PASSMAN: I think it actually depends on the market. Bill could probably agree or disagree with me on this, but in the pre-Rockies days, the Royals used to draw a lot of fans from neighboring states like Colorado, Nebraska and Oklahoma, who would take a long weekend or even a week to go to KC for a few games. So, not only were these people paying money for games, but for motels, restaurants and other activities.

I know Milwaukee is the same. They draw a good number of their fans on trips from places like Madison, Green Bay, Eau Claire, etc. These people invariably spend money at places to stay, eat, etc.

Chicago doesn't necessarily draw the same way. The Cubs always will do well at Wrigley, because well, they're the Cubs and because it's Wrigley. The White Sox, well, people aren't gonna come up from Peoria to see the Sox when they can see the Cubs. I think we lose perspective in this market that it's a different situation elsewhere.

Plus, it's difficult to put a price on being called "major league." Though they do not have an MLB team (yet), how much conscious thought did you ever give a city like Charlotte 15 years ago when the only major sport there was NASCAR? Now, they have the NFL and the NBA, and Charlotte is thought of as a "major league" city. Did the population increase exponentially in the that time? Sure, it grew because it's a growth market, but I don't think it was a tremendous increase. No, Charlotte is thought of far more often because they plunked down the coin for a stadium and an arena to become a player.

And they've been rewarded with a greater chunk of the American geographical psyche. Nashville is heading that way as well.

May 5—Cubs Pitching as a Cure for One's Ills

DEWAN: The Rockies have scored in each of the first seven innings against the Cubs today and lead 9-5 in the seventh. As I recall, scoring in every inning is extremely rare—more rare than a perfect game if I'm recalling correctly. Can anyone verify this?

CARLSON: I was very interested, so I wrote up something very quickly. Most innings scored in during a nine-inning game:

Most Innings Scored, 9-Inning Game—1987-99				
#Inn	Team	Date	H/A	Score
8	Milwaukee	8/28/92	A	22-2
8	Montreal	4/11/93	A	19-9
8	Cleveland	6/15/96	A	10-3
8	Oakland	6/27/96	A	18-2
8	Colorado	6/30/96	H	16-15
8	Baltimore	9/5/97	A	13-9
8	Kansas City	9/14/98	H	16-6

They could be the only team (at least since 1987) to do all nine. Obviously, those two victorious home teams did it in as many innings as they could, since they didn't bat in the ninth.

ZMINDA: There have been only two games since 1900 in which a team has scored in all nine innings: Giants vs. Phillies (6/1/23); Cardinals vs. Cubs (9/13/64).

No AL team has ever done this, although a number of home teams have scored in all eight innings without a chance to bat in the ninth.

CARLSON: So, what's more incredible? That the Rockies may score in all nine innings today, or that Gary Gaetti just hit his second homer in two days?

ZMINDA: The Rockies scored two in the ninth to tie the record. Now maybe they'll even win the game!

COUSINS: What's the record for most innings scored in a row? The Rockies have scored in 13 straight going back to yesterday.

ZMINDA: The Red Sox have the record, scoring in 17 straight innings in September of 1903. The Rockies are one inning away from tying the NL record of 14 held by the 1894 Pirates and 1949 Giants.

OLKIN: The Rockies have scored in each of their last 13 innings against the Cubs. That can't be lucky.

May 6—Olerud Streak

SPEAR: John Olerud has reached base via hit or walk in each of his last 45 games, going back to last season. Over that span he's got a .391 batting average and .530 OBP.

PINTO: The lower limit of this record is 74. In 1941, Joe DiMaggio had a 56-game hit streak. He walked in the game before the streak began, walked in the game the streak ended, then had a 16 game hit streak on top of that.

May 11—A Pitcher Should Never Beat Himself

MUNDO: Today's Mets/Rockies game features Bobby Jones vs. Bobby Jones.

May 11—Baseball and the 2000 Olympics

PALACIOS: As you know, professional baseball players will be allowed to participate in the 2000 Olympics. But the Olympic games are from September 15 to October 1, meaning most Major League Baseball players won't be able to attend.

However, this may be a moot point for the United States. Only two teams from the Americas will qualify for the Olympic games out of 10 teams. There are only two weaklings from this group: Guatemala and Brazil. Panama and Nicaragua have had their moments in international baseball. One good starter on each of those teams could create havoc. The other six teams will create a qualifying tournament that will probably be more exciting than the Olympic games themselves: United States, Cuba, Dominican Republic, Puerto Rico, Canada and Mexico.

There are many sad things about baseball in the 2000 Olympics: no MLB players, games featuring Italy vs. the Netherlands and Egypt vs. Cuba. It's too bad so many strong teams will stay home, while so many bad ones will make the game look bad to the soccer-loving world. Does anyone know if Japanese major leaguers will play?

CARLSON: Does NBC have the World Series in 2000? I think they may have it this year so FOX would in 2000. Otherwise, I'd think if NBC had the Olympics, MLB playoffs and World Series right next to each other, they'd somehow try to convince baseball to end the regular season two weeks early, let the MLB players play in the Olympics, and then come back for the playoffs. I'm sure the teams and managers would be against that for injury and continuity reasons, but I'm sure that kind of setup would give NBC both higher Olympic baseball ratings and probably a slightly higher playoff ratings also. But I think it's moot if Fox has the 2000 World Series.

PALACIOS: The 2000 Olympics will be a moot point because the United States may not qualify. We're going to have a squad featuring guys like Brooks Kieschnick. Maybe Steve Balboni will go.

I know Dave Nilsson will ditch his team to play for Australia. Many old Hispanic ex-major leaguers stay in shape in other leagues. Who knows? Fernando may pitch for Mexico, and he may have one last good day in him to eliminate a U.S. team made of Class-A and Double-A players.

If the Japanese League takes a break, teams from the Americas could be reinforced, including, possibly, the United States.

Is MLB not going to have September callups? If they do, and those players cannot go to Australia, even if the U.S. makes the Olympics, it will be a disaster.

This is my prediction:

1. Japan (if their league pauses and MLB doesn't)

2. Cuba

3. U.S./Puerto Rico/Dominican Republic (basically the other Americas qualifier).

FORD: The Japanese major leagues do take a break. From the end of the season until their World Series, they take about a month off because of the monsoon season. And it just may coincide with the schedule for Olympic play. If it's off a bit, I foresee the Japanese making adjustments so their best players could represent them in the Olympics.

ELMAN: Didn't we learn anything from the NHL? I don't think there was much if any extra excitement added to the NHL by letting its players compete in the Olympics. Plus, the supposed match-ups never came around because the teams had no time to play together and gel. Why the obsession of having to kick butt in *every* international competition, regardless of scheduling conflicts? What is wrong with losing because the "best players in the world" are in the middle of their season and could not compete? It's the Olympics, not the World Championships of baseball. If you want to find the best baseball team, schedule a tournament when *everyone* is available. Of course, that won't happen because of the dollars involved with players and sports in general.

If you ask me, it was a lot more fun watching the Olympic basketball tourney in the pre-Dream Team days. College kids busting their asses for the team, often in fairly close games, is more fun than wondering if the Dream Team will win by 40 or 50.

May 19—Unlucky 13

PASSMAN: It's hard to be a White Sox fan, but at least there's some solace in giving up 13 runs on three straight nights. Ron LeFlore will be signing autographs in Skokie on Saturday. I have a reason to go on as a South Sider.

HENNINGER: Dan Ford and I talked about Cleveland's back-to-back 13-run performances on the way home yesterday. Now Cleveland does it again.

People in 13-run pools have to be wondering if they are witnesses to an omen from the Higher Powers that be. I wonder if any team has recorded 13 runs in three consecutive games before Cleveland did last night. In the dead-ball era, I wonder if there's any chance that 13 runs in a game might not happen much more in a season than it did this week in Chicago.

ZMINDA: Our day-by-days go back to 1951, and I had Henzler run a program to see if any teams had scored exactly 13 runs in three straight games. The Tribe was the first. A bunch of teams had done it twice in a row.

HENZLER: I ran it for scores between one and 10. There were four six-game streaks of certain scores:

Consecutive Games Scoring Certain Number of Runs—1951-199				
Runs	**Team**	**G**	**First Game**	**Last Game**
2	Twins	6	7/30/80	8/5/80
3	Astros	6	7/12/84	7/17/84
3	Indians	6	6/19/93	6/24/93
7	Brewers	6	9/6/89	9/12/89
(includes tie games)				

CARLSON: Only three more 13-run games to go to tie the record.

May 19—Where's Mel Rojas When You Need Him?

OLKIN: The 20th-century record for the most runs in a game is 49. The Reds currently lead the Rockies 24-12 with one out in the top of the seventh inning. Thirteen runs to go!

ZMINDA: Welcome to Coors:

Jeffrey Hammonds Through Yesterday

AB	R	H	2B	3B	HR	RBI
38	3	5	1	0	0	3

Jeffrey Hammonds Today

AB	R	H	2B	3B	HR	RBI
6	5	4	1	0	3	5

He's raised his average from .132 to .205, and the game ain't over yet!

May 20—The Day After

MITTLEMAN: How about this? Ron Villone notches his first save of the season for the Reds yesterday and gets it by pitching three innings while his club enjoyed a 12-run lead in yesterday's embarrassing debacle at Coors Field.

COOPERSON: Probably was a tougher assignment than protecting a three-run lead in most ninth innings!

SPEAR: This is a pretty good pitching line, especially considering the game!

Cincinnati	IP	H	R	ER	BB	K	#Pit	ERA
Neagle	1.2	7	6	6	1	1	41	8.17
Parris (W, 2-0)	3.1	3	3	3	2	1	50	4.80
White	1	3	3	3	1	2	27	6.52
Villone (S, 1)	3	2	0	0	2	2	47	0.00

ZMINDA: I'd say Villone ought to get some Cy Young votes out of this.

May 20—Beware of Conspiracy

ZMINDA: Was There a Second Batsman Hiding in the Bushes?

From today's *USA Today*:

OF Paul Sorrento hit a 491-foot home run over the grassy knoll in center field, the longest in the history of The Ballpark in Arlington.

Despite evidence from eyewitnesses, the Devil Rays are insisting that Sorrento acted alone.

MILLER: I saw the highlight, and a kid made a great dive to beat out another kid for the ball!

ZMINDA: That kid was working for the CIA. He grabbed the ball so no one else could get their hands on the evidence!

OLKIN: According to the CIA, there was no "ball."

CARLSON: According to some theorists though, there were actually three different balls that couldn't have come from the same bat.

May 23—A Record Not Likely to be Broken

OLKIN: Texas starter Mike Morgan just hit Baltimore's Brady Anderson for the second time. . . this *inning*.

COOPERSON: Mike Morgan would have done this earlier in his career, but he usually gets traded during the inning.

May 23—Paying Homage to Homer

PINTO: Some of you may remember this e-mail from last year:

Homer Bush has never hit a homer. Of the 10 men named Homer who have played Major League Baseball, only three have hit homers at all. Homer Summa holds the Homer homer record with 18. Also, Homer Bush is the first Homer to try to homer since Homer Spragins in 1947.

Of course, Bush did homer, and for me at least it was one of the high points of 1998.

I was at the Red Sox game today with my college roommate Jim. Bush was getting ready to lead off the third inning against Pedro Martinez, and we were discussing the fact that he had been the first Homer to homer since 1947. So Pedro gets ahead of him 1-2, and then Homer gets a hold of one. It's hit hard, but at first I thought it was going to be caught. Then I see O'Leary turn around toward the wall to watch it, and I start thinking "I'm going to see Homer Bush homer!" Well, I guess the crowd was shocked that Bush could get a hold of a Pedro pitch, because there's dead silence, except for me screaming "Go!" at the ball. Anyway, it hit about half way up the wall for a double. I was disappointed, but I turned to Jim and said, "My life would be complete if I saw Homer homer." I cheered for him the rest of the game, but that was his only hit.

He only needs 17 more to catch Homer Summa.

ZMINDA: I saw Ken Singleton single once. It did not change my life.

PINTO: Actually, I think he was married at the time.

May 25—Who You Gonna Call?

SPEAR: Active Leaders in Save Percentage:

Pitcher	Saves	SvOp	Pct
Troy Percival	119	136	.875
Trevor Hoffman	196	225	.871
Robb Nen	162	189	.857
Jose Mesa	112	131	.855
Randy Myers	347	407	.853
Rod Beck	257	303	.848
John Wetteland	266	314	.847
Mark Wohlers	112	133	.842
Mariano Rivera	95	114	.833
Billy Taylor	84	101	.832
Ricky Bottalico	78	94	.830
Ugueth Urbina	68	82	.829
Billy Wagner	74	90	.822
John Franco	410	499	.822
Rick Aguilera	281	346	.812
Jeff Montgomery	296	365	.811
Gregg Olson	208	258	.806
Todd Jones	105	131	.802
Doug Jones	293	366	.801
Roberto Hernandez	206	258	.798

(minimum 50 saves)

DEWAN: It's incredible that Jose Mess-Up is actually fourth on this list!

May 26—Two Martinez Lunch

PINTO: In case you were wondering, this is the first time two Martinezes have hit grand slams on the same day. Certainly 1995 was good to them, as they combined for four slams that year (Dave, Edgar and two by Tino). In fact, Edgar's slam today was the first non-Tino slam by a Martinez since June 7, 1995, when Edgar hit his last one. Coming into today, Tino had had the last five Martinez slams, and his seven over his career are the Martinez record.

Jose Martinez of the 1969 Pirates hit the first Martinez slam on September 8, 1969. It was the only home run he ever hit in the majors. It would be nearly 14 years until another Martinez hit a slam, when on June 5, 1983, Buck Martinez of the Blue Jays lifted one. Of course, no Martinez grand slam history would be complete without a mention of Carmelo Martinez. On April 27, 1990, I was sitting in the ESPN studio with John Saunders and Jerry Matalon when Carmelo hit a grand slam. In trying to come up with an interesting fact, I noticed that

Carmelo's previous grand slam had come exactly one year before, on April 27, 1989, making him the only Martinez to slam exactly one year apart.

By the way, we are approaching the 66th anniversary of the last grand slam homer by a Homer: June 8, 1933, by Homer Peel.

SPEAR: Today is the first time in major league history that two players with the same last name hit grand slams on the same day! Carlos Lee (May 17) and Travis Lee (May 18) just missed earlier this season.

May 26—Could He Be Traded for Jaime Navarro?

OLKIN: LaTroy Hawkins allowed eight earned runs in 4.1 innings today. If he gets the loss (which seems likely, as the Twins trail 11-3), his record over his last 21 starts will be:

W-L	IP	H	ERA
1-12	118.1	167	7.07

HENNINGER: Amazing. There was a stretch late in the first half of last season where I thought LaTroy was going to take the next step. But I guess he fell down the stairs.

ZMINDA: I have no doubt that in some alternative universe somewhere in space, LaTroy Hawkins is a perennial Cy Young candidate, and Dave McCarty is challenging for the Triple Crown. "Universe MLE," I think it is.

HENNINGER: These guys were viewed as studs a few years ago. They talked about McCarty like they talk about J.D. Drew now. He was widely considered the most polished college hitter in his draft. Now he's gone the way of Brooks Kieschnick.

CALLIS: Have to correct this. . . McCarty was highly regarded, but not nearly as much as Drew. McCarty was a line drive-hitting first baseman, while Drew was a center fielder with more power in addition to more speed and the ability to play a premium position. McCarty went with the No. 3 pick, but he closed with a late rush to do so. Talking to scouts at both times, they thought McCarty could be a very good player, while Drew had Hall of Fame talent.

May 28—Roger Clemens' Winning Streak

COOPERSON: Roger was better in the year prior to the streak than he has been during it.

Roger Clemens, Year Prior to Win Streak vs. Win Streak		
	6/1/97-5/31/98	6/1/98-present
W-L	16-13	19-0
ERA	2.51	2.64
Complete Games	7	5
HR Allowed per 9 IP	0.29	0.57
Run Support per 9 IP	4.24	5.36

ZMINDA: Yes, but that was before he "learned how to win."

DEWAN: Ethan, that's a great item!

May 31— The *Other* Homer

PINTO: Besides being the all-time Homer homer leader, Homer Summa did something else of note on today's date:

1927—Detroit first baseman Johnny Neun made an unassisted triple play against Cleveland. He caught Homer Summa's liner, tagged Charlie Jamieson between first and second and then touched second base before Glenn Myatt could return. The Tigers beat the Indians 1-0.

June 3—A Byrd in the Bush. . .

COOPERSON: Last summer the Braves released pitcher Paul Byrd, largely because the team had a surplus of pitching and Byrd wasn't considered a great prospect. So far in 1999:

Greg Maddux:	4-3, 4.54
Tom Glavine:	3-6, 4.99
Paul Byrd (Phi):	7-3, 3.45

So there.

June 3—Going Nine

PINTO: Complete-game streaks:

Pitcher	Streak	Ended
Bobby Witt	9	8/30/88
Orel Hershiser	8	9/28/88
Mike Moore	6	8/30/87
Dave Stewart	6	8/14/88

In the 1990s:

Pitcher	Streak	Ended
Tommy Greene	5	6/10/93
Pat Hentgen	5	9/3/96
Curt Schilling	5	Current

Ended is that date they didn't get a complete game. I based this on all appearances, not just starts.

June 3—There's No Instant Replay in Baseball!

SCHINSKI: I was surprised no one made mention of the use of replay in the game a few nights ago. What do you think? Is it good for the game? Should the Marlins' protest be upheld? Personally, I think replay should be used. The technology is there; why not use it.

CARLSON: I think it was wrong for Pulli to use it in the game, not because I disagree with why he used it (it did inevitably make the right call), but because MLB doesn't have instant replay, so he should have just made the call and lived with it. The thing I have a problem with is that the umps second guess themselves too much, and let managers convince them to overturn their own calls. This situation (where he initially called it a double, then called it a homer after the manager complained, and then called it a double again after looking at the replay) reminds me of a Cubs game in 1990 when Ryne Sandberg hit a home run, which they called a homer, and then the San Francisco manager came out and argued that it was foul. Somehow he must have offered a steak dinner or something and the ump changed the call to foul (even though the replay showed it was five or six feet fair of the pole). Of course, if the ump had looked in the camera that day, Ryno would have had a homer.

In my opinion, judging homers fair or foul, or the Florida homer situation, are the only good uses of instant replay in baseball. Any other use (tags or whether a guy beat the throw at first) would slow down the game way too much. Plus, all of those calls are right in front of the umpires when they make it, so usually they are right. A home-run call is made usually at least 200-plus feet away from where the call needs to be made (except in the playoffs when they put more umps down near the poles), so I can see where a replay would be helpful there.

SCHINSKI: There is no mentioning in the rulebook about replay. The way I understand it, anything not mentioned in the rulebook is left to the discretion of the umpires. Based on that, Pulli was within his rights. He thought it would be best to use replay and it turned out he was right. I don't see any problem with that.

OSBORNE: Pulli claimed that somehow he needed the replay because he was confused about the ground rules. I don't know how the replay helps in this situation, but I guess it's OK in that case.

But, if it's being used to aid in a judgment call—fair/foul, ball/strike, safe/out, homer/off-the-top-of-the-wall—I think it is a horrible precedent to set. Every close call going to replay would be a real hassle.

Once Pulli decided to let replay affect that call, he justifies every other close call to be challenged by the managers. They can argue, "That pitch caught the corner. Check it out on replay." Now, if he doesn't use the replay, it's not fair. You need to consistently use it, or else consistently not use it. I think a replay rule in baseball would be a disaster.

FORD: I think we should drop the Bomb on Serbia. The technology is there; why not use it?

June 3—Underrated Power

COOPERSON: Most Home Runs, 1999, by Players not on All-Star Ballot:

Player, Team	HR
David Bell, Sea	13
Preston Wilson, Fla	12
Luis Gonzalez, Ari	11
Todd Greene, Ana	10

June 9—Nouveau Winners

COOPERSON: A look at the National League leaders in pitching victories in 1999 reveals some surprising names. Among the league's top four, we find three hurlers who had fewer than 30 career wins entering '99; two of the four had losing records, and only Curt Schilling was an established major league starter.

Most Wins, NL—1999

Pitcher, Team	1999		Career Prior to '99	
	W-L	ERA	W-L	ERA
Jose Lima, Hou	10-2	2.72	25-30	4.80
Kent Bottenfield, StL	9-2	3.97	18-27	4.27
Curt Schilling, Phi	8-3	3.12	84-77	3.36
Paul Byrd, Phi	8-3	3.33	12-8	3.78

June 9—Slammin' Shortstops

HENZLER: I'm guessing you may have noticed the staggering numbers Alex Rodriguez has compiled since returning from the disabled list. He's hit .393 with 10 homers and 19 walks in the 23 games since coming back.

For the season, Rodriguez is generating 15 runs per 27 outs, the best among players with at least 100 plate appearances. He may not be able to sustain that torrid pace, but he still figures to have a fighting chance at becoming only the third shortstop since Honus Wagner (Vaughn—1935 and Yount—1982) to lead the majors in RC/27.

And if Rodriguez doesn't, maybe Derek Jeter will. They currently rank 1-2 in RC/27. Nothing close to this has ever happened before. In fact, only once have two shortstops finished the year in the top 10. That was 1949, when Eddie Joost and Vern Stephens ranked seventh and eighth, respectively.

Most Runs Created Per 27 Outs—1999

Player, Team	RC	RC/27
Alex Rodriguez, Sea	36	15.02
Derek Jeter, NYY	70	13.13
Rafael Palmeiro, Tex	61	12.48
Jeff Bagwell, Hou	65	11.96
Sean Casey, Cin	59	11.91

(minimum 100 PA)

June 10—Scoring's Up

COOPERSON: These games are nearly 10 times more frequent in Major League Baseball as they were 10 years ago.

Frequency of Games in Which Both Teams Score 10+ Runs

Year	Frequency
1987	Once every 175.4 games
1988	Once every 350.0 games
1989	Once every 526.5 games
1990	Once every 191.4 games
1991	Once every 191.3 games
1992	Once every 175.5 games
1993	Once every 98.7 games
1994	Once every 114.3 games
1995	Once every 96.0 games
1996	Once every 68.7 games
1997	Once every 119.3 games
1998	Once every 93.5 games
1999	Once every 57.9 games

June 10—Three-Homer Games

COOPERSON: This wasn't a story for Mac last year, but everyone wants this list today.

Players With Two Three-Homer Games in Same Season

Player	Team	Year—Games
Johnny Mize	St. Louis	1938—July 13 vs Bos Braves, July 20 vs NY Giants
Johnny Mize	St. Louis	1940—May 13 @ Cincinnati, Sept 8 vs Pittsburgh
Ralph Kiner	Pittsburgh	1947—Aug 16 vs St. Louis, Sept 11 vs Bos Braves
Ted Williams	Boston	1957—May 8 @ Chi White Sox, June 13 @ Cleveland
Willie Mays	San Francisco	1961—Apr 30 @ Mil Braves (4 HR), June 29 @ Philadelphia
Willie Stargell	Pittsburgh	1971—Apr 10 @ Atlanta, Apr 21 vs Atlanta
Dave Kingman	Chi Cubs	1979—May 17 vs Philadelphia, July 28 @ NY Mets
Doug DeCinces	California	1982—Aug 3 vs Minnesota, Aug 8 @ Seattle
Joe Carter	Cleveland	1989—June 24 @ Texas, July 19 @ Minnesota
Cecil Fielder	Detroit	1990—May 6 @ Toronto, June 6 @ Cleveland
Geronimo Berroa	Oakland	1996—May 22 @ NY Yankees, Aug 12 vs Minnesota
Steve Finley	San Diego	1997—May 19 @ Cincinnati, June 23 @ San Francisco
Mark McGwire	St. Louis	1998—Apr 14 vs Arizona, May 19 @ Philadelphia
Jeff Bagwell	Houston	1999—Apr 21 @ Chi Cubs, June 9 @ Chi White Sox

June 15—Pedro the Magnificent

COOPERSON: Is Pedro headed for a pitching triple crown as the league leader in wins, ERA and strikeouts?

Pedro Martinez, AL Ranks—1999

Category	No. (Rank)
Wins	11 (1)
ERA	2.16 (1)
Innings Pitched	95.2 (2)
Strikeouts	143 (1)
Strikeout-Walk Ratio	7.15 (1)
Hits-Innings Pitched	0.79 (3)
Pitches per Start	117.8 (1)

June 15—Fargo or Bust

PALACIOS: Montreal's attendance has dipped to 8,986 per game, which pretty much guarantees that Montreal will no longer be a major league city. Here are other attendance numbers for comparison:

Average Attendance—1999

Team	League	Avg Att.
Buffalo	International (AAA)	8,610
Indianapolis	International (AAA)	7,401
Pawtucket	International (AAA)	6,861
New Orleans	Pacific (AAA)	6,710
Columbus	International (AAA)	6,646
Akron	Eastern (AA)	6,627
Salt Lake	Pacific (AAA)	6,513
Lansing	Midwest (A)	6,164
Grand Rapids	Midwest (A)	5,758

Montreal drew more than 40,000 on Opening Day, and has failed to draw more than 20,000 since.

Minnesota, another team hurting in attendance, applied to play a series in Fargo, ND, but they were turned down. Perhaps it would have been in the best interest of baseball to have allowed that three-game series in Fargo.

COOPERSON: The Expos actually had a very good team with decent attendance back in 1993 and 1994. Had they pushed for the stadium *then*, and had the strike not come when it did, the history of baseball in Montreal might have been very different. Timing was everything.

June 23— Magglio Ordonez

DEWAN: Can you spot the trend?

Magglio Ordonez' monthly batting averages as of today:

April:	.280
May:	.330
June:	.380

June 25—SABR's Top 100 Players of All Time

PINTO: To any of you who are members of SABR, I apologize.

That has to be the worst survey I have ever seen. Who's doing the voting? Old men, 12-year-olds and people from Ohio? There's so many things wrong with it, but I'll just take one that really made me mad.

First of all, how could any survey rank Pete Rose 48th all time? Never mind the gambling, the guy wasn't that good. He was at best the fifth-best player on the Reds! As if that wasn't bad enough, they rank Rickey Henderson 60th!

They are both leadoff men, and last I looked leadoff men were supposed to get on base and score runs:

Rose vs. Henderson, Career

Category	Rose	Henderson
Games	3,562	2,655
Avg	.303	.283
OBP	.375	.405
Slg	.409	.427
Runs	2,165	2,039
Runs/Game	0.61	0.77

Henderson has played 900 fewer games, but has scored only 100 fewer runs. And this doesn't even take into account Henderson's ability to steal bases or his power. (Rickey is currently tied for 100th on the all-time homer list with Eric Davis and Steve Garvey with 272 home runs). Are there any sabermetricians in SABR?

When I recover from this, I'll list the 20 active players who are better than Roberto Clemente.

MILLER: David, what do you have against people from Ohio?

OSBORNE: In the 1998 *Diamond Chronicles*, STATS had Pete Rose as better than that: 46th overall.

HENZLER: David, I agree. It's easy to isolate on specific injustices, but the one I really can't fathom is the ranking of Barry Bonds. A very good argument could be made that he should rate no lower than the third greatest left fielder of all time, and possibly even second. And yet he ranks 65th overall. That's at least 40 pegs too low, in my estimation.

PINTO: It's a good thing I didn't read that part of the book.

DEWAN: The *Diamond Chronicles* list is very good. For example, Bonds is in the top 20. Henderson in the 30s. Rose at 46 doesn't bother me.

PINTO: You could make an argument that Barry might be the best ballplayer of all time. If you believe he's the best ballplayer of this generation, and if you believe that ballplayers are getting stronger, faster and more athletic as training, medicine and nutrition improve, then he could easily be the best. I have no doubt if you could pluck Babe Ruth out of 1921 and put him in a home-run contest against Bonds, Bonds would wipe him out.

OSBORNE: I'd have a much bigger problem if Bonds finished ahead of Babe than with Henderson getting nosed out by Rose.

PINTO: It's certainly better than SABR's if Henderson and Bonds are ahead of Rose.

HENZLER: Another way to decry the ranking of Bonds is to see that he rates only eight spots ahead of Lou Brock (73). It may be sacreligious as a St. Louisan to say this, but Brock probably shouldn't rank in the top 200.

The fact that Rickey is only 13 spots ahead of Brock only adds to the fatuity. Henderson and Brock have played roughly the same number of games (2,655 Rickey, 2,616 Brock). Considering Henderson has the far superior on-base percentage (.405-.343), has hit nearly twice as many homers (272-149), has scored over 400 more runs (2,039-1,610) and stolen roughly 40 percent more bases (1,312-938), Brock's proximity to Henderson is almost an insult.

GREENBERGER: If you look at the comments in *Baseball Weekly* as a window into the mind of the average SABR voter (that elusive beast), it's clear that statistics aren't all that important:

6. Joe DiMaggio: "Baseball's most enduring example of how the game should be played." Yeah, keep making lefts until you get back to home plate.

8. Willie Mays: "Fans knew he loved the game and was out there having fun." He looked like he could barely keep a straight face with the Mets.

29. George Brett: "Batting crown in three decades." Yeah, but did he get at-bats in as many decades as Minnie Minoso?

51. Rod Carew: "Best AL singles hitter of his era." How about the fact that he's by far the greatest stealer of home who ever converted to Judaism?

Does Brett really belong that high? Isn't Morgan way too low? Is Tony Gwynn that much better than Reggie Jackson? Who do you pick first when you're making your team?

I won't argue with the Ruth pick.

PALACIOS: SABR members have also been scratching their heads. This message is part of the SABR discussions on why the rankings turned out as they did:

From John Stuart:

What I found disturbing in the article was that of 865 ballots counted, four—count 'em, four—members of the Society of American Baseball Research did not vote for Babe Ruth nor Lou Gehrig. I can see one vehement "Yankee Hater" leaving these two out for grudge reasons. But for an organization that prides itself on the detailed historical and statistical study of the National Pastime, how can four card-carrying members of SABR leave out two players that even my wife (a non-baseball fan) would intuitively pick? Unless these four have some compelling quantitative evidence that Ruth and Gehrig are not Top-100 players, then their ballots should have been tossed out in the ash-can.

This is the main problem with the rankings. Four people didn't include Ruth or Gehrig. Seven didn't include Ted Williams or Hank Aaron. Eight not for Musial. Ten not for DiMaggio. Eleven not for Cobb. Thirteen not for Mays. Fourteen not for Hornsby. Fifteen not for Wagner.

The top 100 is created by people leaving great players off the ballot. So, we're not really saying that Gehrig is greater than Cobb. . . it's just a handful of people (seven) who for whatever reason didn't include Cobb that puts Gehrig ahead of Cobb.

I'd like to see the votes for the elite points, as I've read them called. That would give a much better top 10 or so of the all-time greats as opposed to allowing the list be made by a few people who didn't make a check by these players.

Once the list gets down to about 50 or so, the list is probably more representative of who we actually think since the players near here are more arguable as being in or out of the Top 100.

The way the ballot was constructed, it probably would have been better just to list the 100 names as being the greatest players, i.e. not in order. And then, show the list of the top five or 10 or 20 or so based on the "elite" points.

June 28—Pudge and the Stolen Base

SASMAN: Though he's cooled off as of late, Ivan Rodriguez has allowed just 10 stolen bases this season. (He's nailed 20 runners, giving opponents a 33 percent success rate.) That's not the best part, however. He's also stolen 15 bases in 18 attempts. If he keeps it up, he would be the first catcher in the history of baseball to steal more bases than he allows.

Best Stolen Base vs. Stolen Bases Allowed Differential—1987-99

Player	Year	SB	Allowed	Net
Ivan Rodriguez	1998	9	38	-29
Ivan Rodriguez	1997	7	37	-30
Ivan Rodriguez	1994	6	37	-31
Brad Ausmus	1994	14	47	-33
Benito Santiago	1989	11	46	-35
B.J. Surhoff	1988	21	57	-36
Brad Ausmus	1995	16	54	-38
Ivan Rodriguez	1996	5	46	-41

(miminum 80 G at catcher; five SB)

The worst mark since 1987 belongs to Jason Kendall, who had a -131 in 1996 with five steals and 136 allowed.

June 29—Homer Myth Exploded!

ZMINDA: At the SABR convention, Neil Munro pointed out that Homer Summa was *not* the last Homer to homer. Homer (Dixie) Howell, a catcher for three NL teams in the '40s and '50s, hit 12 homers, the last coming in 1952. And that ain't just whistlin' "Dixie."

PINTO: If they called him Dixie, he wasn't a homer!

June 30—Halfway Home?

COOPERSON: I haven't heard anyone mention this, but Griffey's next home run will be career No. 378, which is half of 756.

June 30—AL vs. NL

OSBORNE: I found these numbers to be interesting. Which league has the better hitters?

Stats represent average team in league (c-rf means stats as one of the eight fielding positions—not as pitcher, DH, or PH).

National League—1999

	Avg	AB	R	H	2B	3B	HR	RBI	SB	CS	TBB	SO	Slg
Total	.270	2,588	380	700	138	16	83	362	59	24	277	495	.432
As c-rf	.278	2,324	348	648	127	13	78	331	54	22	253	407	.445

American League—1999

	Avg	AB	R	H	2B	3B	HR	RBI	SB	CS	TBB	SO	Slg
Total	.274	2,621	395	718	138	13	88	373	52	24	276	453	.437
As c-rf	.273	2,301	342	629	120	9	72	315	45	19	234	386	.427

At first, I was surprised to see the NL with better power numbers among position players. I figured a heavy-hitting fielder would be more likely to be in the traditional hitters' league. But maybe because of the DH, the AL teams are able to fill their power needs in that way, while the NL has to get any power it can find in the field.

July 1—If Only He Was Striking Out Two Guys Per Inning

MILLER: Randy Johnson's last two starts:

ERA	G	W	L	GS	CG	ShO	IP	H	R	ER	HR	TBB	SO
1.59	2	0	2	2	2	0	17.0	12	3	3	1	2	31

Randy Johnson's opponents last two starts:

ERA	G	W	L	GS	CG	ShO	IP	H	R	ER	HR	TBB	SO
0.00	2	2	0	2	1	2	18.0	1	0	0	0	4	16

Johnson nearly had back-to-back no-hitters thrown against him!

HENZLER: Johnson's Game Scores were 85 and 77 his last two starts. His total of 162 has been the highest recorded since 1987 by any pitcher who suffered losses in both games.

Highest Game Score Total Over Two-Game Span, Both Losses—1987-99				
Pitcher	Tot	Avg	1st Game	Last Game
Randy Johnson	162	81.0	6/25/99	6/30/99
Andy Hawkins	155	77.5	7/1/90	7/6/90
Jimmy Key	152	76.0	6/15/87	6/20/87
Francisco Cordova	150	75.0	8/28/98	9/3/98
Jose Rijo	148	74.0	8/6/94	8/11/94

(starts only)

July 1—Now Warming Up in the Bullpen. . .

ZMINDA: Andy MacPhail unveils another veteran ex-Twin righthander.

Holy Doug Dascenzo! Gary Gaetti (career ERA 0.00 for two appearances) was warming up in the Cub pen in the ninth inning of today's 19-12 loss to the Brewers. The crowd booed Riggleman when he went to the mound in the ninth but decided to leave in Scott Sanders.

HENNINGER: I was listening to the Cubs game in my car when Gaetti was warming up. You could clearly hear the crowd chanting, "GA-RY, GA-RY, GA-RY, GA-RY. . ."

COOPERSON: I was recently told I look like Gary Gaetti. Maybe I could pitch in his uniform.

July 1—Hitting in Safeco Field

HENZLER: Have you seen Michael Knisley's column in this week's *Sporting News*? In it, he talks about the effect Safeco Field will have on Ken Griffey's home runs. And he asserts, "Safeco, the way it's currently configured, could cost Griffey 10 home runs a season. . . The 379 homers he needs to push Aaron are out of the question."

Well, I guess we'll have to wait for the ballpark to actually open before we know for sure, but 10 home runs a year seems like an awful lot to me.

For the sake of simplicity, let's assume Griffey averages 300 at-bats per season at home and on the road. During his career, he's averaged 22 homers at home and 19 homers on the road per 300 at-bats. Since 1996, when he's gone on a 188-homer rampage, those rates are 28 home, 26 road.

So Griffey, if Knisley is right, might dip to 18 homers a year at Safeco. And if that's the case, that would mean the new ballpark would have a home-run index of 64, assuming Griffey's rates are truly indicative.

For perspective, the *worst* home-run index for the years between 1996-98 was at the Astrodome, where it was 84. In other words, Safeco would be an extraordinarily poor home-run park. The anti-Coors, if you will.

CALLIS: This is just another example of a reporter writing something without taking five minutes to check out that 10 homers a season is an enormous amount. Likewise, I wish I had a dollar for every reporter who thought Albert Belle was a lock to break Maris' AL home-run record after signing with the Orioles. His home-road home-run breakdown in Chicago was 43-36, and the three-year park factors for righty home runs are 94 in Chicago and 107 in Baltimore. So if you ignore the fact that Albert wasn't hurt by Comiskey and focus solely on the park factors, he would have been expected to improve his home-run production by 13 percent at home, which would mean about 3-4 homers.

July 2—More Pedro Facts

COOPERSON: By my count, there have been only six seasons this century where a pitcher threw at least 100 innings and had a strikeout-walk ratio of 7.00 or better. Pedro Martinez is currently at 7.50. That would rank him fourth-best this century among pitchers with at least 100 innings pitched, third-best among guys with at least 200 innings. Only Maddux ('95 and '97) threw 200 innings with a strikeout-walk ratio better than 7.50.

HENZLER: I'll go even further. Martinez has struck out 165 batters while allowing just 90 hits and 22 walks this season. His strikeout-hit-plus-walk ratio is the best in history among pitchers with at least 100 innings.

In fact, Pedro currently holds the previous record in this category, at least among non-re-lievers.

Best Strikeout-Hit-Plus-Walk Ratios—1876-1999

Pitcher	Year	IP	K	H	BB	K/(H+BB)
Pedro Martinez	1999	116.2	165	90	22	1.47
Bruce Sutter	1977	107.1	129	69	23	1.40
Pedro Martinez	1997	241.1	305	158	67	1.36
Sandy Koufax	1965	335.2	382	216	71	1.33
Randy Johnson	1995	214.1	294	159	65	1.31
Randy Johnson	1997	213.0	291	147	77	1.30
Randy Johnson	1999	137.2	188	109	36	1.30
Mariano Rivera	1996	107.2	130	73	34	1.21
Mike Scott	1986	275.1	306	182	72	1.20
Curt Schilling	1997	254.1	319	208	58	1.20

(minimum 100 IP)

QUINN: It seems odd that the statistics go back to 1876, but the top 10 only goes back to 1965.

HENZLER: Well, it really should make perfect sense. Take a look at this chart. It shows the strikeout-hit-plus-walk ratios by decade. As you can see, the ratios have been steadily rising since the '20s:

Strikeout-Hit-Plus-Walk Ratios by Decade—1876-1999

Decade	K	H	BB	K/(H+BB)
1870-79	4,239	18,753	1,553	.2088
1880-89	64,851	155,661	37,818	.3352
1890-99	50,160	182,417	62,617	.2047
1900-09	79,410	191,011	55,707	.3219
1910-19	98,899	224,281	78,193	.3270
1920-29	69,328	241,928	74,464	.2191
1930-39	81,667	240,046	79,886	.2553
1940-49	87,842	220,418	87,854	.2849
1950-59	108,862	218,774	88,241	.3546
1960-69	182,438	268,647	100,046	.4948
1970-79	203,741	344,432	130,770	.4287
1980-89	218,147	358,866	131,164	.4452
1990-99	234,420	346,005	130,206	.4923

As you can see, there was a spike in the 1960s. If we look only at the years before 1965, there aren't many hurlers with ratios above 0.90:

Best Strikeout-to-Hit-Plus-Walk Ratios—1876-1964

Pitcher	Year	IP	K	H	BB	K/(H+BB)
Sandy Koufax	1962	184.1	216	134	57	1.13
Sandy Koufax	1963	311.0	306	214	58	1.13
Dick Radatz	1964	157.0	181	103	58	1.12
Dick Radatz	1963	132.1	162	94	51	1.12
Sandy Koufax	1964	223.0	223	154	53	1.08
Dick Radatz	1962	124.2	144	95	40	1.07
Jim Maloney	1963	250.1	265	183	88	0.98
Sammy Ellis	1964	122.1	125	101	28	0.97
Lindy McDaniel	1960	116.1	105	85	24	0.96
One Arm Daily	1884	500.2	483	446	72	0.93
Walter Johnson	1910	370.0	313	262	76	0.93
Sandy Koufax	1957	104.1	122	83	51	0.91
Walter Johnson	1912	369.0	303	259	76	0.90
Herb Score	1956	249.1	263	162	129	0.90
Jim Whitney	1884	336.0	270	272	27	0.90
Walter Johnson	1913	346.0	243	232	38	0.90

(minimum 100 IP)

July 6—Road, Sweet Road

COOPERSON: What's going on here? Can't the Brewers simply wait for their new park?

Brewers Home & Away—1999

	Home	Away
W-L	11-23	29-18
Pct	.324	.617
Runs/Gm	4.65	6.19
HR	35	68
Slg	.432	.485
ERA	5.41	4.92
Nilsson Slg	.538	.688

July 6—Hard Luck Unit

CARLSON: Randy Johnson is just about the unluckiest pitcher in baseball in the last 12 years:

0-3 Over Three Straight Starts, ERA Under 2.00—1987-99

Pitcher	ERA	IP	ER	Span
Carlos Perez	0.63	14.1	1	9/14-9/24/97
Randy Johnson	1.44	25.0	4	6/25-7/5/99
Doug Drabek	1.59	22.2	4	4/21-5/1/89
Greg Maddux	1.64	22.0	4	5/16-5/27/92
Orel Hershiser	1.80	20.0	4	8/28-9/8/89
Chuck Finley	1.96	23.0	5	9/18-9/28/90
Jack Morris	1.99	22.2	5	4/21-5/1/89

HENZLER: Just to amplify Dave Carlson's note, the Big Unit has compiled an average game score of 80.0 during his last three starts. No other pitcher since 1987 has averaged better than a 67.7 (Greg Maddux, May 16-27, 1992) over three consecutive losses.

Furthermore, Johnson's three-game average is the second highest generated by any pitcher this season. He himself holds the top mark, with a rate of 80.3 in a completely separate streak. But none of the other pitchers in the top 10 have even lost a game:

Highest Game Score Total Over Three-Game Span—1999

Pitcher	Tot	Avg	W-L	1st Game	Last Game
Randy Johnson	241	80.3	3-0	5/25	6/4
Randy Johnson	240	80.0	0-3	6/25	7/5
Pedro Martinez	238	79.3	3-0	5/1	5/12
Pedro Martinez	232	77.3	3-0	4/25	5/7
Mike Hampton	230	76.7	3-0	4/29	5/10
David Cone	227	75.7	2-0	4/20	5/1
Pedro Martinez	227	75.7	3-0	4/20	5/1
Andy Ashby	223	74.3	3-0	4/10	4/21
John Smoltz	222	74.0	3-0	4/19	4/30
Pedro Martinez	221	73.7	3-0	5/7	5/18

(starts only)

July 9—Strikeouts-R-Us

HENZLER: Don't know if anyone's discussed this. I don't see too much baseball in my cableless house.

But could this be the year another single-season record gets toppled?

Pedro Martinez currently leads the American League with 184 strikeouts. If he continues that pace (based on team games), he'll wind up with 351. That's well short of Nolan Ryan's record 383, but still more than anyone else has managed in over two decades.

But Randy Johnson has 200 now and will make one more start before the All-Star break. He's on pace (team games) for 377, and he's turned it up a notch in recent outings. Of course, he's also on pace for 274 innings, and no one has thrown that many in over a decade.

JAMES: Strikeout rates reached a historic peak in 1967-1968, then went downward until 1981. From 1982 to the present they have been going back up again. They passed the 1967-68 high water mark about 1994, maybe 1993, and have pushed on to levels about 10 percent higher. We have the odd phenomenon in the late 1990s of historically very high batting averages—the highest in 50 years—with record levels of strikeouts.

July 12—More Hard Luck

CARLSON: Poor Randy:

Lowest ERAs Over an 0-4 Starting Span—1987-99

Pitcher	ERA	IP	ER	Span
Randy Johnson	1.41	32.0	5	6/25-7/10/99
Tom Candiotti	2.22	28.1	7	6/7-6/23/91
Orel Hershiser	2.25	28.0	7	8/28-9/13/90
Nolan Ryan	2.29	19.2	5	7/7-7/29/87
Mike Morgan	2.43	29.2	8	6/17-7/3/89

July 12—Back When Ronald Reagan Was President. . .

COOPERSON: Since his last major league triple, Mark McGwire has had 4,561 at-bats, with 193 doubles, 421 home runs, 1,037 RBI and 1,021 walks. He even has two sacrifices since then!

July 14—You Just Can't Replace Carlos Baerga

PALACIOS: Puerto Rico pulls out from the Olympic baseball qualification tournament:

Puerto Rico pulled out of the PanAm games, citing that Major League Baseball did not free up the players needed to participate in the tournament. "It strikes me as a little strange that nine countries didn't have a problem and one did," said Mike Moore, Pan Am Games vice president.

Puerto Rico suffered a blow when Carlos Baerga became tied up by the San Diego Padres. Puerto Rico pulled out Tuesday, making it impossible to find another country to replace it.

Team Canada also suffered from players rejecting invitations.

After the Women's World Cup stole the spotlight from Major League Baseball, MLB didn't learn from the power of an international event. Women's soccer showed the world what their sport is all about. Meanwhile, MLB will be responsible for mediocre baseball being shown worldwide.

Mariano Duncan will come out of retirement to play for the Dominican team. Dennis Martinez will also start for Nicaragua.

Team Canada announced its roster, which included four Triple-A players, 10 Double-A players, 14 Class-A players and two independents. The four Triple-A players are: Alex Andreopoulos, Stubby Clapp, Aaron Guiel and Ryan Radmanovich. Rob Butler, currently in Double-A, is on the team as well.

The United States will play its first game on July 26 vs. Canada:

July 26	USA vs Canada
July 27	USA vs Mexico
July 28	USA vs Cuba

The games will be held at the brand new CanWest Global Park (capacity: 6,200).

CALLIS: I don't want to sound like an MLB apologist, because they screw up left and right, but Oscar, what are you talking about? How is this MLB's fault?

Carlos Baerga's departure makes Puerto Rico unable to compete? I don't buy it. My guess, from covering international baseball, is that Puerto Rico didn't think it had a chance to win and decided to save money by not participating. Puerto Rico, Mexico and the Dominican Republic all declined to attempt to qualify for the 1996 Olympics, and that was all about politics and trying to save money. And they probably wouldn't have qualified anyway.

None of the teams from the Americas is going to have major leaguers. And there aren't going to be any on the teams that go to the Olympics next year. MLB has made players not on the 40-man rosters available to *all* nations. The United States has been stung because the Yankees (Nick Johnson) and Giants (Jason Grilli) wouldn't let top prospects participate. The U.S. roster, while it does include some nice prospects, also features the likes of Shawn Gilbert and Jeff Manto.

Are you advocating that MLB shut down for 2-3 weeks for an Olympic qualifying tournament that will send two teams to Sydney? That makes little sense to me.

PALACIOS: It is in the best interest of the game that the best baseball is shown to the world. MLB does share the responsibility that the world will once again see mediocre baseball.

The real reason why baseball is so popular outside of the United States is the amateur world series. However, the amateur sports world has really been hurting over the past decade. Amateur championships are hurting because pros have been allowed to participate. If the pros don't pick up the baton from the amateur sports, then there will no longer be ambassadors of the game to the rest of the world.

Professional baseball needs a World Cup, like soccer does. It is no coincidence that soccer is the most popular sport in the world, and the World Cup deserves much of the credit.

The Olympics could have served as this World Cup for baseball. But MLB and the Olympics did not want to accommodate their schedules. MLB wouldn't have had to shut down for two to three weeks. All the games are going to be played in eight straight days if the U.S. makes it to the finals.

By MLB not releasing the best players, it didn't hurt the U.S. only. It hurt half of the baseball world.

Yes, the Dominican team always fields a weak national team, but that's because anyone with talent is signed at the age of 15. What are the Dominicans, Puerto Rico and Venezuela supposed to play with when their best talent is off limits?

How come there's outrage when an 18-year-old basketball player leaves high school for the NBA, but there isn't such an outrage when a 15-year-old leaves everything behind to play baseball?

Finally, there were a lot of people jumping on Juan Gonzalez for not participating in the All-Star Game. A lot of these people had official ties with MLB.

This criticism is two-faced considering that MLB shares responsibility for undermining a worldwide All-Star event.

CALLIS: I still think you're way off base on this.

Even if MLB just shut down for the eight days of games, that would be a fiasco. And they would have to shut down more, once travel and practice time are factored in. Again, why would they shut down for an Olympic qualifier that sends two teams to Australia?

And how is MLB the villain? They made the vast majority of players in every organization available to the various nations. That seems pretty nice to me. Adam Kennedy is better than anyone the Cardinals have playing second base right now, but he'll be in Winnipeg. Peter Bergeron and Lance Berkman could start in the outfield for Montreal and Houston, respectively, but they'll be gone, too.

The concept of a World Cup is nothing new. And contrary to what you're saying, both MLB and the MLBPA are working toward creating one. The Olympics won't work because they interfere with pennant races (not to mention other foreign leagues). But there have been plenty of stories and columnists predicting a World Cup in the next five years.

Sadly, Carlos Baerga probably won't be able to participate.

As for 18-year-olds leaving college to play basketball, that's fine with me. Same with 15-year-olds signing as foreign free agents. If they want to sign, go ahead.

July 23—Jose Guillen

ZMINDA: The Pirates traded Jose Guillen and minor leaguer Jeff Sparks to Tampa Bay for Joe Oliver and minor leaguer Humberto Cota. Guillen goes from being the "the next

Clemente" to a guy who got traded for Joe Oliver (although Cota's a pretty good prospect, I guess).

HENZLER: But hey, at least Guillen has proved he's a .267 hitter:

Jose Guillen—1997-99

Year	Tm	G	AB	R	H	2B	3B	HR	RBI	BB	SO	Avg	OBP	Slg
1997	Pit	143	498	58	133	20	5	14	70	17	88	.267	.300	.412
1998	Pit	153	573	60	153	38	2	14	84	21	100	.267	.298	.414
1999	Pit	40	120	18	32	6	0	1	18	10	21	.267	.321	.342
Totals		336	1,191	136	318	64	7	29	172	48	209	.267	.301	.406

HENNINGER: But the Bucs wouldn't let him prove he could hit 14 homers again.

July 26—Canada Dims U.S. Olympic Hopes

PALACIOS: Canadian baseball team beats U.S., 7-6.

As I have been saying, it would not be surprising if the U.S. baseball team does not qualify for the Olympics. Actually, it's expected that the U.S. won't. The tournament favorites are Cuba and the Dominican Republic.

The first sign of what may be bad things to come was Monday night's loss to Canada in 11 innings by the score of 7-6. Of course, the U.S. may not have made the Olympic Games in baseball even if major leaguers had been allowed to play because it takes one Eiji Sawamura-like performance to shock the baseball world.

In a single-elimination tournament you could have seen Pedro Martinez facing Randy Johnson. Or Greg Maddux facing the awesome Puerto Rican firepower of Roberto Alomar, Juan Gonzalez, Ivan Rodriguez, Bernie Williams and Carlos Delgado.

It would have been great. Instead of a great baseball tournament, it's football season in all but 11 cities.

COOPERSON: Is it bad if the U.S. loses?

CALLIS: If the U.S. loses, in all likelihood baseball will be dropped by the Olympics after 2000. Even if it remains, it likely will be superceded by a MLB/MLBPA-sponsored World Cup in the near future.

August 10—Greg Vaughn

ZMINDA: Interesting fact I discovered while looking up something about Greg Vaughn: there have been 14 home runs hit on 3-0 pitches in the National League this year, and Vaughn has three of them.

August 10—Tripp Cromer

PINTO: Now that Homer Bush homers have become rather commonplace, it comes to my attention that Tripp Cromer has never tripled!

August 12—Worst Trade of the Year?

SASMAN: I know I wasn't the only one who was amazed when the Diamondbacks traded a 25-year-old power-hitting shortstop (Tony Batista) for a 37-year-old lefty specialist (Dan Plesac).

Since then, Batista has hit 17 homers and slugged .588 in 52 games for the Blue Jays. He now has 22 homers on the year, which are more than every other shortstop aside from A-Rod (sorry Derek and Nomar).

In return, the Diamondbacks have used Plesac a total of 11 innings, during which he's allowed 14 hits and eight walks and has a 5.73 ERA. Oh yeah, and the Diamondbacks threw in John Frascatore in the deal. Somehow, he's managed to go 7-0 for the Blue Jays in just 20 innings.

Nice move, Showalter.

PINTO: Yet, for all that, it hasn't hurt the Diamondbacks. They have the biggest lead of any NL division leader, and the best ERA in the NL.

STEPHENS: I still think any deal involving the "Great" Mel Rojas deserves consideration for Worst Trade of the Year.

August 13—Do You See Rojas in the Box Score?

SASMAN: It's now 12-11 after six innings in today's Montreal-Colorado game. In the last four half-innings, the teams have scored 5, 5, 6 and 5 runs. Today is the only instance since 1987 of four consecutive half-innings of at least five runs.

PINTO: It's also only the third time since 1987 that there have been four innings of five-plus runs in a game.

August 13—Home-Run Mark Falls

PINTO: Marvin Benard just hit the 54th homer of the day, tying a record that has stood since 1962.

PINTO: Carl Everett has hit No. 55 on the day to set a new record. The record set on June 10, 1962, was on a day with 20 games. Seventeen games were played today.

August 17—Ouch!

ROBERTS: An interesting piece of baseball trivia on this day 42 years ago:

1957—Richie Ashburn, known for his ability to foul pitches off, hits spectator Alice Roth twice in the same at-bat. The first one breaks her nose, and the second one hits her while she is being removed from her seat on a stretcher. Ironically, she is the wife of Earl Roth, the sports editor of the *Philadelphia Bulletin*. The Phils won 3-1 over New York.

August 19—Olerud Sets Mets Walk Record

SPEAR: In case you missed it last night, John Olerud set a Mets record for most walks in a season. With his three last night, Olerud now has 100 walks this year.

Mets Single-Season Walk Leaders—All Time

Player	Year	BB
John Olerud	1999	100
Keith Hernandez	1984	97
Darryl Strawberry	1987	97
John Olerud	1998	96
Bud Harrelson	1970	95
Keith Hernandez	1986	94
Lee Mazzilli	1979	93
Wayne Garrett	1974	89
Howard Johnson	1988	86
Darryl Strawberry	1988	85
John Olerud	1997	85

August 24—But Did He Mention Homer Bush?

QUINN: Peter Gammons mentions David Pinto:

At the end of last night's "Baseball Tonight," I heard Peter Gammons mention David Pinto right before giving a Mark McGwire statistic. I'm sure I got this wrong, but it was something like: "Another David Pinto special statistic shows McGwire has seven two-homer games this year and only four two-single games."

August 24—Run on Runs

CARLSON: With the Yankees' recent 21-run game. . .

Number of Games in Which a
Team Scored 20-Plus Runs

Year	G
1999	8
1998	1
1997	0
1996	7
1995	2
1994	3
1993	2
1992	1
1991	1
1990	2
1989	0
1988	1
1987	4

August 25—Is That All There Is?

COOPERSON: Career numbers for Kent Mercker:

Through and including his no-hitter: 16-13, 3.04, 210 H in 269.1 IP.

Since his no-hitter: 44-45, 4.66, 772 H in 726.0 IP.

August 25—Where Are the Tablesetters?

COOPERSON: Why don't the Cardinals win more?

You'd think this team with McGwire would score lots of runs and win lots of games. Well, since the day the Cards got him (July 31, 1997), they're only fifth in the NL in runs per game (and they're much closer to ninth than they are to first):

Most Runs Per Game, NL Since July 31, 1997

Team	R/G
Rockies	5.32
Giants	5.28
Astros	5.22
Braves	5.05
Cardinals	4.90
Cubs	4.88
Phillies	4.81
Mets	4.80
Reds	4.77

August 25—Sammy vs. the Cubs

PALACIOS: Forget about the Sosa-Big Mac Race! Sosa has as many homers (52) as the Cubs have wins. Never has a player finished with more homers than his team has wins.

These are the closest:

Number of Individual HR Hit Closest to Number of Team Wins

Year	Team	W	Player	HR
1884	Wilmington Quicksteps	2	Charlie Bastian	2
1934	Boston Braves	38	Wally Berger	34
1952	Pittsburgh	42	Ralph Kiner	37
1950	Pittsburgh	57	Ralph Kiner	47

My projection is that the Cubs will go 13-25 the rest of the season, finishing with 65 wins. STATS is projecting Sammy Sosa to finish with 65 homers. So Sammy could make history.

August 26—Swing Away, Big Hurt

PALACIOS: Guess first-pitch fastball, Frank!

Frank Thomas, First-Pitch Avg vs. Overall—1991-99

Year	0-0 Avg	Overall Avg	Diff
1991	.490	.318	+.172
1992	.373	.323	+.050
1993	.420	.317	+.103
1994	.375	.353	+.022
1995	.296	.308	-.012
1996	.339	.349	-.010
1997	.339	.347	-.008
1998	.266	.265	+.001
1999	.296	.311	-.015

American League, First-Pitch Avg vs. Overall—1991-99

Year	0-0 Avg	Overall Avg	Diff
1991	.314	.260	+.054
1992	.305	.259	+.046
1993	.323	.266	+.057
1994	.331	.272	+.059
1995	.332	.270	+.062
1996	.347	.277	+.070
1997	.338	.271	+.067
1998	.337	.271	+.066
1999	.341	.276	+.065

When Frank Thomas was an MVP player, he used to kill the first pitch. These days, despite being an above-average hitter overall, he's below average with a 0-0 count. It's almost like he's letting pitchers have the first strike for free.

Frank's got to be more aggressive with an 0-0 count. Yes, working the count is good, but you have to keep pitchers honest. Frank's head is just messed up.

Frank, just guess first-pitch fastball. Who cares if it is a breaking ball? So you guess wrong and you miss the pitch. Who cares? You're a .315 hitter after an 0-1 count.

Frank's talent has not diminished. He just can't hit the first pitch. Could it be from being cold on the bench? Don't DH, Frank!

DEWAN: Oscar, I don't see anything in the information you provided that might not suggest the exact opposite of what you are saying. In essence, maybe Thomas is now going after the first pitch much more often than he used to. In fact, it may be the case that he should lay off the first pitch. Until recently, Thomas' walk rate has been way down this year. If I recall correctly, his walk rate last year was also slightly below his own historic rate.

Take a look at how often he is going after the first pitch compared to the past, not only the result.

I completely concur with your last comment. ("Don't DH, Frank!")

August 27—Benny and the Mets

SASMAN: Would the real Benny Agbayani please stand up?

	AB	H	HR	Avg	OBP	Slg
Through 6/25	96	33	11	.344	.427	.760
After 6/25	137	32	0	.234	.305	.328

Benny Agbayani—1999

Are we really that surprised?

ZMINDA: Yeah, I loved it when Jayson Stark wrote a column unfavorably comparing J.D. Drew's production with Benny's.

August 27—Sosa Surge

ZMINDA: With yesterday's homer he needs 17 in 36 games to tie McGwire's record, 18 to beat him. I'm really starting to think that he can do it. He's hit 10 homers in his last 12 games, and over a much longer period, 49 home runs in his last 103 games. One homer every two games is a very reasonable pace for him. Unless he goes into a slump (possible) or the pressure starts to get to him (I doubt it), this could go down to the wire.

HENNINGER: The tag on Sosa is that he hits a lot of meaningless home runs. Well, we know one thing: the Cubs will play a lot of meaningless games the rest of the way.

PALACIOS: It's not Sammy's fault that Steve Trachsel, Rod Beck, Dan Serafini and Company suck. If he's hitting in meaningless games, it is because the pitchers are making the games meaningless.

Opponents' batting average against the Cubs in the first inning this year is over .300. Opponents are hitting .291 with runners in scoring position against the Cubs.

Sammy's hit .290 with six homers when it's close and late this year. What's amazing is that Sammy will get to 60-plus homers this year without facing Cubs pitching.

ZMINDA: Maris was hitting "meaningless" homers in September of '61 also, after the Yankees broke the race open. Ditto Ruth in the late stages of '27. I don't see how it cheapens the achievement.

August 29—Jim Leyland and Pitch Counts

PALACIOS: Jim Leyland certainly knows how to (over)work his starters:

Pedro Astacio—1999		Livan Hernandez—1998	
Date	Pitches	Date	Pitches
7/16	116	7/14	107
7/21	121	7/20	126
7/25	131	7/25	113
7/30	116	7/30	128
8/5	122	8/4	124
8/10	119	8/10	138
8/15	131	8/15	137
8/20	115	8/21	148

On August 27, 1998, Hernandez goes just three innings and gets bombed. On August 26, 1999, Astacio goes just two innings and gets bombed.

After August 27, 1998, Hernandez had a 6.44 ERA.

August 30—Phillie Frustration at Coors Field

COOPERSON: How could the Phillies, within the period of a week, have a two-game span where they score 33 runs, then get shut out in Coors Field?

August 30—Millwood Fires Zeroes

COOPERSON: Saturday afternoon in St. Louis, the Atlanta Braves' Kevin Millwood went where no major league starting pitcher has gone in 1999: he pitched into the 10th inning.

Millwood allowed no runs and only two hits against the Cardinals, becoming only the sixth hurler in the last nine seasons to work 10 innings without allowing a run; no one in that span has pitched more than 10 innings in a game. The list of 10-inning shutout performances since 1991:

10 Shutout Innings, Single Game—1991-99

Pitcher	Team-Opp	Date	H	Pitches	W-L	Team Result
Mark Portugal	Hou vs Phi	6/11/91	6	122	ND	Won, 1-0 (11)
Kevin Appier	KC @ Cle	7/23/92	2	95	ND	Lost, 0-1 (14)
Bobby Jones	NYM vs StL	9/29/93	4	139	ND	Won, 1-0 (16)
Bret Saberhagen	NYM vs SD	7/15/94	5	131	ND	Lost, 2-1 (14)
Darryl Kile	Col @ SD	9/20/98	3	103	W	Won, 1-0 (11)
Kevin Millwood	Atl @ StL	8/28/99	2	119	ND	Won, 3-0 (13)

September 1—Bonds Still Hurting

SASMAN: Barry Bonds the first six weeks after he came off the DL compared to the rest of the season:

Barry Bonds—1999

	G	AB	R	H	2B	3B	HR	RBI	BB	SB-CS	Avg	OBP	Slg
6/9-7/25	34	111	27	22	1	1	7	24	23	7-1	.198	.371	.414
Rest of Yr	44	160	48	54	13	1	23	53	31	7-1	.337	.443	.862

September 3—Home-Run Marks

ZMINDA: Sosa just hit No. 57. Mark McGwire, your record is doomed!

PINTO: With his fifth homer of the season, Homer Bush sets the single-season Homer home-run record!

September 10—Where's Dave Kingman?

COOPERSON: We all know the Reds' Greg Vaughn is on a torrid home-run pace, with seven dingers in his last seven games, and five in his last three contests. Vaughn has had a very strange season for Cincinnati, with 36 homers despite a meager .234 batting average. He's on pace for the lowest batting average ever by a player with 40-plus home runs:

Lowest Batting Average by Player With 40-Plus Home Runs

Player, Team	Year	HR	Avg
Jose Canseco, TB	1998	46	.237
Harmon Killebrew, Wsh	1959	42	.242
Jay Buhner, Sea	1997	40	.243
Harmon Killebrew, Min	1962	48	.243
Gorman Thomas, Mil	1979	45	.243

September 14—So, Why Isn't He Batting Eighth?

PINTO: With two RBI tonight, Shane Reynolds now has 14 on the year, the most by any pitcher this year, and the most by a pitcher since Tim Lollar drove in 15 for the Padres in 1984.

September 15—Nothing a Trade to Colorado Can't Cure

ZMINDA: Scott Karl, Mr. Consistency:

Scott Karl—1997-99

Year	Team	W-L	Pct	G	IP	H	R	ER	HR	TBB	SO	ERA
1997	Mil	10-13	.435	32	193.1	212	103	96	23	67	119	4.47
1998	Mil	10-11	.476	33	192.1	219	104	94	21	66	102	4.40
1999	Mil	10-11	.476	30	180.2	224	112	96	18	65	70	4.78

The pressure's really going to be on him now to work 12 scoreless innings (hopefully fanning the side in each inning) without inadvertently picking up a win.

September 16—Rickey Henderson

HENZLER: You gotta love Rickey Henderson. Right now, entering Wednesday's game, Rickey is generating 8.89 runs per 27 outs. According to my calculations, the only left fielder in baseball generating more is Barry Bonds (10.04).

The National League's RC/27 average is simply runs scored per game, which is an even 5.00 (actually 5.0017).

Among players who've accumulated at least 200 plate appearances, and whose primary position is left field, the MLB average is 6.27. Obviously, left field is an offensive position, so you'd expect a higher rate. But Henderson is clearly a cut above average, even as he approaches his 41st birthday.

NEYER: The point of this little exercise, in case you didn't already know, is to find out if Rickey's having the best season ever by a 40-year-old player. I don't think that he is, because of his relatively limited playing time. But in terms of RC/27 compared to league, he's right up there, at least among the candidates I've come across.

Highest RC/27 Index at Age 40

Player	Year	RC/27	Lg RC/27	Index
Willie Mays	1971	7.97	3.91	2.04
Rickey Henderson	1999	8.89	5.00	1.78
Ty Cobb	1927	7.75	4.92	1.58
Dave Winfield	1992	6.77	4.32	1.57
Sam Rice	1930	7.26	5.41	1.34

I'm sure I'm missing somebody, but it's obvious that Rickey's having an amazing season, even if he'll only end up playing in the neighborhood of 115 games.

September 16—Manipulating the Numbers

ZMINDA: I ran into Jerome Holtzman at Comiskey last night, and he told me that MLB is going to make *Total Baseball* count the 1887 walks as hits (that was a one-year rule that was immediately dumped) to get Cap Anson's career hit total over 3,000. Maybe this will encourage more people to buy the *All-Time Handbook*.

September 30—Big Unit is Big in September

JAMES: On September 22, 1992, Randy Johnson gave up six hits and struck out 12 Kansas City Royals, but was outdueled by the great Chris Haney, who pitched a two-hit shutout to beat the Mariners, 3-0.

The significance? That was the last time that Randy Johnson lost a game in September. September 22, 1992.

COOPERSON: More important, that was two days after Mickey Morandini's unassisted triple play for the Phillies at Pittsburgh.

September 30—Left of Center

FORD: The *Chicago Sun-Times* has been running daily articles reviewing events of the 20th century on a year-by-year basis. Today's issue featured 1908, which of course is the last year the Cubs won the World Series. The article offered this tidbit:

The Cubs win second World Series in a row playing at a West Side field (West Side Grounds) near where Cook County Hospital now stands. Near the left-field line was a mental hospital where patients used to hang out the windows to watch the games, giving birth to the expression, "You're out in left field."

October 2—1990s Hitting Explosion

JAMES: I was looking at the *Sourcebook* last night, and noticed that in 1992—just seven years ago—the National League All-Star outfield included Ray Lankford, who hit .293 with 86 RBI, and Andy Van Slyke, who hit .324 but with only 14 homers, 89 RBI. Doesn't it seem unbelievable that just seven years ago, a player could be a National League All-Star with those kind of numbers? I'd have to think that kind of performance now would just about be the National League average for an outfielder.

October 4—Stereotypes Die Hard

PALACIOS: Is the stereotype going to fade now?

Latin American players have been labeled as not being able to draw walks. Of course in the past most Latin American players were middle infielders, and middle infielders as a whole don't walk at the same rates as other players.

In 1999, we had six Latin American players in the top 12 in walks in the AL. Is this stereotype going to fade now? Or must we wait for a new crop of baseball announcers before it does?

Most Walks—1999

Player, Team	BB
Jim Thome, Cle	127
Jason Giambi, Oak	105
Albert Belle, Bal	101
John Jaha, Oak	101
* Bernie Williams, NY	100
* Roberto Alomar, Cle	99
* Edgar Martinez, Sea	97
* Rafael Palmeiro, Tex	97
Brady Anderson, Bal	96
Rusty Greer, Tex	96
* Jose Offerman, Bos	96
* Manny Ramirez, Cle	96

(* Latino)

October 4—Who Were the Best of 1999?

JAMES: Hey, guys, let's take our own MVP/Cy Young/Rookie of the Year polls. Same system as the pros use. . . 10 names on the MVP ballot, three on the Cy Young, three on the Rookie of the Year. Send ballots to me. I'll total them up if I get a decent number.

October 4—So Long to Candlestick Park

COOPERSON: The Phillies lost 67 of their last 87 games at Candlestick/3Com Park.

October 8—One Triple Away

PINTO: If Rickey has a triple this postseason he will tie George Brett for most postseason triples.

Most Triples, Postseason

Player	3B	AB
George Brett	5	166
Rickey Henderson	4	176
Mariano Duncan	4	152
Tris Speaker	4	72
Devon White	4	189

Despite his speed and power, Henderson never has been a great triples hitter. He has 60 for his career, compared to Brett who had 137. (Kaufmann Stadium with Astroturf was a great triples park.)

Rickey has a total of 19 extra-base hits in the playoffs, tying him for fifth among active players (10 doubles and five homers to go with the four triples).

October 11—And the Winner Is. . .

JAMES: OK, I've calculated the results of my poll and am ready to report. Twenty-eight people participated in my poll, about the same number as participate in the *real* votes, which works out well. The 28 people who participated were Jeremy Alpert, Matt Armbrister, Jack Cavin, Mike Corner, Brian Cousins, Bill Deane, John Dewan, Bruce Dickson, Ryan Ellis, Dan Ford, Bill James, Barry Koron, Rob Neyer, Oscar Palacios, Pete Palmer, Dave Pinto, Mat Olkin, Lee Panas, Pat Quinn, John Sasman, Jeff Schinski, Alan Schwarz, Jeff Smith, Allan Spear, Bill Stephens, Mike Webber, Rick Wilton and Don Zminda. I think everyone took the time and made the effort to vote carefully, and I appreciate all of your time and effort.

To cut to the chase, five of the six awards appear to be clear-cut, and I would predict that in all five of these cases, our award winner will also win the BBWAA voting. Those five were:

NATIONAL LEAGUE MVP

Not only was Chipper Jones an overwhelming choice for the National League MVP, but Jeff Bagwell was equally obvious as the No. 2 man, and Mark McGwire was way ahead of anyone else for third place. Jones got 22 of 28 first-place votes, while Bagwell got four firsts and 18 second-place votes, and Mark McGwire was listed third on one-half the ballots, 14 of 28.

After the top three, almost everybody in the league got a vote or two. I exaggerate, but 29 players figured in the National League MVP voting:

1.	Chipper Jones (22)	355
2.	Jeff Bagwell (4)	259
3.	Mark McGwire	160
4.	Mike Piazza	102
5.	Matt Williams	89
6.	Edgardo Alfonzo	83
7.	Sammy Sosa	80
8.	Robin Ventura	69
9.	Randy Johnson (1)	63
10.	Craig Biggio	58
11.	Larry Walker (1)	57
12.	Jay Bell	43.5
13.	Vladimir Guerrero	38.5

14. Sean Casey	37	
15. Luis Gonzalez	35	
16. Bob Abreu	34	
17. Brian Giles	24	
18. Carl Everett	12	
19. Greg Vaughn	11	
20. Mike Hampton	9	
21. Barry Bonds	8	
22. Scott Williamson	7	
23. Kevin Millwood	5	
24. Todd Helton	4	
25. Fernando Tatis	3	
26. Scott Rolen	2	
27. Billy Wagner	2	
28. Barry Larkin	2	
29. Andruw Jones	1	

AMERICAN LEAGUE CY YOUNG

The American League Cy Young voting was even more obvious, with Pedro Martinez being a unanimous selection, and Mike Mussina an overwhelming choice as the No. 2 pitcher. The voting for the No. 3 spot was fairly close:

1. Pedro Martinez (28)	140
2. Mike Mussina	64
3. Mariano Rivera	21
4. Bartolo Colon	14.33
5. David Cone	7.33
6. Aaron Sele	2.33
7t. Tim Hudson	1
7t. Troy Percival	1
7t. Jeff Zimmerman	1

NATIONAL LEAGUE CY YOUNG

To my great surprise, Randy Johnson was the favorite of 75 percent of our electors. I didn't expect this. I went into this thinking, based on my conversations with friends, that Billy Wagner of Houston would be the winner. He didn't draw a single first-place vote:

1. Randy Johnson (21)	123
2. Mike Hampton (5)	57
3. Kevin Millwood (1)	47.5
4. Billy Wagner	10.5

5. Jose Lima (1)	8
6. Kevin Brown	4
7. Greg Maddux	1
8. Scott Williamson	1

This could be the one of these five obvious votes which *could*, perhaps, turn around in the BBWAA poll. Obviously, if a man wins 21 of 28 votes in one poll, you would have to bet on him to win 51 percent in a second poll. However, while Johnson has the best ERA and the historic strikeout total, Mike Hampton's won-lost record is a full five games better. There have not been a lot of Cy Young votes which were won by a player with a won-lost record five full games worse than another pitcher. If the BBWAA voters are more impressed with won-lost records than ERA, they could vote the other way.

And they might not necessarily be wrong. Most of you who have thought about it at all are probably assuming that Bank One Ballpark, where Johnson compiled his numbers, is a hitters' park, thus his numbers are really even more impressive than they look. This is not necessarily true. While Bank One Ballpark *was* thought to be a hitters' park, and while Johnson himself posted an ERA almost a run higher there than he did on the road (2.06 on the road, 2.96 in Arizona), the season's data, as a whole, show BOB to be a *pitchers'* park—thus, Johnson's ERA may be *less* impressive than it looks. One reason for this unexpected result is Brian Anderson, who didn't pitch a lot of innings, but posted a 2.97 ERA (7-0 record) in Arizona, but a 7.93 ERA (1-2 record) on the road.

AMERICAN LEAGUE ROOKIE OF THE YEAR

Two national publications have stated that Carlos Beltran would *not* be the American League Rookie of the Year, while a third has published an article (written by a participant in our poll) saying that he should not be. Regardless of who should win, it is very clear that, in fact, Beltran is going to win the award.

Beltran is not an overwhelming favorite of our voters, being listed first by 16 of 27 voters (one person did not submit a rookie of the year ballot). Sixteen of 27 in our poll could turn out to be 11 of 28 in the BBWAA poll, but that won't matter, because the other candidates will split the vote so much that no one else has any real chance to win. Beltran may not be the best candidate, but he is the one *obvious* candidate; even the people who think that Zimmerman or Garcia or Hudson or Daubach should win the award still tend to vote for Beltran second or third. He is going to win the award:

1. Carlos Beltran (16)	98
2. Jeff Zimmerman (6)	44
3. Freddy Garcia (2)	42
4. Tim Hudson (3)	26
5. Brian Daubach	12
6. Chris Singleton	9

7t.	Billy Koch	4
7t.	Carlos Febles	4
9.	Carlos Lee	3
10.	John Halama	1

NATIONAL LEAGUE ROOKIE OF THE YEAR

Again, this one was a complete surprise to me. I went into this thinking that there were many fair Rookie of the Year candidates, but no one who was heads above the others. In fact, reliever Scott Williamson of Cincinnati was even more dominant than Beltran in the voting:

1.	Scott Williamson (16)	101
2.	Warren Morris (5)	61
3.	Preston Wilson (4)	42
4.	Ronnie Belliard (1)	18
5.	Kris Benson (1)	8
6.	Michael Barrett	5
7t.	Matt Mantei	3
7t.	Alex Gonzalez	3
9t.	Scott Elarton	1
9t.	Erubiel Durazo	1

Two players were mentioned in the NL Rookie of the Year voting (Scott Elarton and Matt Mantei) who were not actually rookies. Obviously, I would rather not have had that happen, but the same thing *has* happened, historically, in the BBWAA vote; several players have drawn Rookie of the Year votes, over the years, who were not eligible.

AMERICAN LEAGUE MVP

OK, I've stalled long enough. The one award which was *not* clear-cut in our voting was the American League Most Valuable Player vote, which was split seven ways. Derek Jeter of the Yankees, although named first on only seven of 28 ballots, had enough votes to win our poll. Another interesting note here. Whereas the National League vote was split wildly after the top three players, in the American League the same nine names appeared on almost every ballot, even in the seven through 10 spots, where Jason Giambi and Bernie Williams were mixed up with A-Rod and Griffey and a few odd votes for Jim Thome, Omar Vizquel and others. But whereas in the National League the No. 15 finisher had 40 percent as many points (35) as the No. 5 finisher (89), in the American League the No. 5 finisher had 193 points, and the No. 15 finisher had five—a 38-to-1 ratio:

1.	Derek Jeter (7)	247
2.	Manny Ramirez (4)	223
3.	Pedro Martinez (7)	211
4.	Ivan Rodriguez (4)	205
5.	Nomar Garciaparra (3)	193

6. Roberto Alomar (2)	174
7. Rafael Palmeiro (1)	130
8. Shawn Green	70
9. Bernie Williams	64
10. Jason Giambi	41
11. Alex Rodriguez	33
12. Ken Griffey Jr.	30
13. Jim Thome	10
14. Omar Vizquel	6
15. Mariano Rivera	5
16. Carlos Delgado	4
17. Juan Gonzalez	3
18t. Mike Mussina	1
18t. Albert Belle	1
18t. Magglio Ordonez	1

I will offer the prediction, based on this vote, that Derek Jeter will be the American League MVP. Obviously, given the nature of the vote, we can't have *too* much confidence that the BBWAA vote will follow the same lines as our own. For the last 40 years, New York players have generally not done well in MVP voting, perhaps because there is an overcompensation for a perceived bias in their favor. This could cost Jeter a couple of votes, and a couple of votes in a close race could well be enough.

But if Jeter loses votes to that, Pedro Martinez *certainly* will lose votes because some writers won't vote for a pitcher, making it difficult for Pedro to win. Manny Ramirez may split his vote with teammate Roberto Alomar; Ivan Rodriguez competes with Rafael Palmeiro, and Nomar Garciaparra with Pedro. The top seven MVP candidates are two from Texas, two from Boston, two from Cleveland—and one from New York.

In addition to this, Jeter is legitimately the best player, in my humble opinion. I think he is going to win.

One other prediction: the 1999 vote could erupt into a historic controversy, not unlike the 1947 American League vote or the 1971 National League Cy Young Award. The vote may be close enough that one voter who has an off-the-wall opinion—let's say, one guy who leaves Jeter or Ivan Rodriguez completely off the ballot—could swing the vote. If a few reporters pick up on that quickly, it could be one that people will talk about.

Thanks again for participating. I learned a lot from doing this.

October 12—The Division Series: Boston vs. Cleveland

JAMES: Watching a mediocre broadcast of a great baseball game. . . how would you guys evaluate the decision to walk Nomar twice with a righthander on the mound and a lefty with

103 RBI up next. McCarver assured us that you "couldn't really question the decision," which it seems to me you probably can if you want to. Garciaparra is certainly a greater hitter than O'Leary, but if you walk Nomar, then a double or triple by O'Leary is as damaging as a home run by Garciaparra, and a home run by O'Leary is more damaging than *any* outcome of an at-bat by Garciaparra. Is the difference between Garciaparra and O'Leary really great enough to justify that risk?

Also, was it just me, or did McCarver have an absolutely awful night? I've never been a McCarver fan, but I've always respected his knowledge of the game. It seemed to me he was just off all night. He never took a real look at the game's key decision (to pitch to O'Leary rather than Garciaparra, no matter what.) He didn't seem to know that Jose Offerman was a great hit-and-run man, when that was relevant, or that Offerman rarely grounds into double plays. He insisted for three innings that Martinez didn't look exactly right, when he really couldn't have looked much better.

In the ninth inning, he second-guessed the decision to let Dave Roberts (a lefty) hit, saying that the Indians could "at least use Richie Sexson," who had 116 RBI. Richie Sexson, excuse me? You've got a 6-foot-7 righthanded hitter with a .305 on-base percentage and a 117-34 strikeout-walk ratio facing Pedro Martinez. What would you have, about a 75 percent chance of a strikeout? And four runs down with the bases empty, what in the hell do you care how many RBI he had? It just seemed like a really inane comment. . . but then, maybe it was just me.

COOPERSON: Always good to hear about our friend Jose. For what it's worth, Dave Campbell (ESPN radio) also said that Pedro wasn't throwing his hardest.

PINTO: There's been a lot of talk among the pundits lately about not letting particular hitters beat you. I think a lot of it comes from the Mets pitching to Chipper Jones and getting beat by him, especially in the 2-1 game. But nobody ever blames the Mets offense for not scoring three runs.

Nomar's a good hitter, but he doesn't take a walk. If you throw him nothing but pitches outside the strike zone, he's more likely to make an out than get a walk, and if he does get a hit, it probably won't be a home run. But if he gets a hit, the manager gets second-guessed, and if you walk him and the next guy hits a homer, that's OK. Bobby Valentine gets vilified for pitching to Jones in a 2-1 loss, but his team was in the game. If he pitches around Jones and Jordan or Klesko homers, it's a 4-1 game and the Mets offense is in a bigger hole. I tend to agree with Valentine and disagree with Hargrove.

A little off the subject, but has anyone noticed how often in these series batters are striking out on pitches in the dirt (or at least very low in the strike zone). There are a lot of hitters out there who don't have the discipline with two strikes to take that pitch, and not many teams that can exploit that. I thought the Yankees and Mets staffs did a good job of exploiting this weakness of both the Rangers and Diamondbacks.

HENNINGER: One commentator last night—was it McCarver or Dave Campbell?—noted that a Cleveland writer had written a piece about how Garciaparra has killed the Indians and should be pitched around in this series. The commentator suggested that Hargrove took that advice to heart.

As for the difference between Garciaparra and O'Leary, the 1999 numbers suggest the difference was minimal. That commentator pointed out that Garciaparra had batted .451 with 17 RBI against Cleveland in 1999, which is true. He had four doubles and five homers as well in 51 at-bats. O'Leary also posted 51 at-bats against Cleveland, and recorded four doubles, three homers, a .351 average and 13 RBI in 1999.

October 12—Tracking the MVP Vote for Bias

JAMES: The following e-mail from Barry Koron has provoked me to develop a new method, which I think is potentially of great interest:

Albert Belle has never won it, but Albert Belle has never been the best player in the American League in any season. Didn't mean to imply that he ever was, just that his MVP vote totals are lower than they should be for a guy with his numbers. I've read that his teammates love the guy, think he plays very hard, and feel he deserves more credit in this area. —BK

This caused me to wonder whether Albert Belle's performance in MVP voting has in fact been worse than it should have been, over the years. Thinking about this, I realized that one could evaluate the question objectively by tracking the player's league rank in MVP voting against his league ranking in Win Shares. In 1991, for example, Frank Thomas was the second-best player in the American League, according to the Win Shares method. That's nine points, since the player who is listed second on an MVP ballot receives nine points. However, Thomas finished third in the MVP voting, which is eight points. Thus, in 1991, Thomas' performance on the field was one point better than his performance in MVP voting, nine to eight. In 1992, Thomas was again the second-best player in the American League (nine points again), but finished eighth in the MVP voting (three points). In 1993, however, Thomas was once again the second-best player in the league (nine points), but this time *won* the MVP Award. This left him, through 1993, only two points behind where he should have been:

	Frank Thomas—1991-93	
Year	Performance	Voting
1991	9	8
1992	9	3
1993	9	14
Total	27	25

In 1994 Thomas won the MVP Award and deserved it; in 1997 he again deserved the award, but finished third in the voting. Summarizing the decade as a whole:

Frank Thomas—1991-98		
Year	Performance	Voting
1991	9	8
1992	9	3
1993	9	14
1994	14	14
1995	6	3
1996	2	3
1997	14	8
1998	0	0
Total	63	53

For his career, Thomas is 10 points "behind" in MVP voting. This is historically normal, since MVP voters are reluctant to give the same player the MVP Award every year. I haven't run Barry Bonds or any historic players, but I wouldn't be surprised if Mickey Mantle in his career was "short" by 100 points or so, and players like Stan Musial, Ted Williams, Barry Bonds and Willie Mays would all be "behind" in career MVP voting by very substantial margins, just because the voters don't want to give them the MVP Award every year.

Albert Belle in 1998 was probably the best player in the league (14 points), but finished eighth in the voting (three points); thus Belle *was* ignored in the voting in 1998. Previous to 1998, however, Belle had actually done *better* in MVP voting than is quite justified by his performance. In 1993, when Belle was about the 10th-best player in the league (according to Win Shares), he finished seventh in the MVP voting. From 1994 through 1996, when Belle was the second- or third-best player in the league each season, he finished second or third in the MVP voting each year. For the decade as a whole, Belle is light by seven points—39 points performance, 32 points voting. These are the top 10 players in the American League through the 1990s in combined performance and MVP voting points:

Player	Performance	Voting
Frank Thomas	63	53
Ken Griffey	31	45
Albert Belle	39	32
Juan Gonzalez	8	37
Roberto Alomar	29	15
Mo Vaughn	6	27
Kirby Puckett	15	17
Alex Rodriguez	20	11
Cecil Fielder	8	20
Rickey Henderson	14	14
Cal Ripken	14	14

Rickey Henderson deserved the American League MVP Award in 1990, and won it, and Cal Ripken the same in 1991—but neither player has been in the top 10 in the AL MVP voting in any other year in the 1990s, or has deserved to be.

The most "fortunate" player in MVP voting—the most overrated player—as you can see, has been Juan Gonzalez, who has won two MVP Awards, but was not considered by the Win Shares method to be one of the 10 most valuable players in the American League either season. There are six players in the American League who have been +10 or more in the 1990s: Juan Gone (+29), Mo Vaughn (+19), Dennis Eckersley (19 and 0, +19), Joe Carter (15 and 0, +15), Griffey (+14) and Fatso Fielder (+12).

As a whole, the scales balance—59 points in each league each season, 59 points in performance, 59 in voting—so if there are players who are "lucky" in the voting, there must be players who are "unlucky." There are five American League players in the 1990s who have been "slighted" by 10 points or more. Those are Paul O'Neill (6 to 16, -10), Frank Thomas (53 to 63, -10), Edgar Martinez (8 to 19, -11), Roberto Alomar (15 to 29, -14), and Chuck Knoblauch (0 to 21, -21).

Just my opinion, but I think it would be difficult to read these results as supporting the theory that voters vote for players they like or against players they don't like. Has Juan Gonzalez "charmed" his way into two MVP Awards? Do reporters dislike Paul O'Neill? Do reporters despise Chuck Knoblauch? Of course not.

A more fair interpretation, I think, is that there are simply some modest differences between the way the Win Shares system sees value, and the way that reporters see value. Reporters put a lot of stock in RBI. RBI men like Gonzalez, Vaughn, Joe Carter and Cecil Fielder do better in MVP voting than there is any real reason they should. This has always been true. For some reason, reporters are convinced that driving in runs is more important than scoring them. There are some other differences—Knoblauch was ignored because the Twins were stringing together bad seasons one after another, etc.

Thanks, Barry, for suggesting the line of research. Once again, I must reflect on how lucky I am to be able to make a living doing crap like this.

October 16—Postseason Odds for Slow Starters

PINTO: Since this is bound to come up:

There have been 53 postseason series of seven games that have started 2-0. The 2-0 team won 41 of those. (8-2 in LCS play, 33-10 in World Series play)

There have been 23 postseason series of seven games that have started 3-0. Nineteen were sweeps, three went five games, and one went six games. None have gone seven, and no team has come back from 3-0 in a seven-game series.

October 18—Ventura's Game-Winning Homer

PINTO: I've been looking at the rule book, trying to decide in my own mind what the score of last night's Mets game should have been. There are decent arguments for scores of 4-3, 5-3 and 7-3. While I think 4-3 is probably the correct score, I think the official scorer could have given Ventura a grand slam even though he didn't complete his home-run trot.

The pertinent rules are 10.07(f), 10.07(g) and the exception to 4.09(b).

10.07(f) talks about the number of bases to award a batter on a game-ending hit, and basically it says that you can't get a double if all you need is a single to end the game. But 10.07(g) states:

"When the batter ends a game with a home run hit out of the playing field, he and any runners on base are entitled to score."

"Entitled" is the key word here. The ball was hit out of the park, making the runners entitled to score. I think this argues that the runner on second who crossed the plate should count. But the official scorer called it a single (Ventura never reached second). If Ventura had reached second, I wonder if the second run would have counted.

In fact, the official scorer had a rule he could have applied to give Ventura a home run, a rule that everyone covering the playoffs missed last night in relation to Chris Chambliss' 1976 LCS-winning home run. The exception to rule 4.09(b), which says that the winning run has to physically cross the plate and the batter has to reach base on an automatic run (bases-loaded walk or HBP):

"An exception will be if fans rush onto the field and physically prevent the runner from touching home plate or the batter from touching first base. In such cases, the umpires shall award the runner the base because of the obstruction by the fans."

Although the rule does not mention home runs, in 1976 it was applied to Chambliss, who I believe never touched all four bases on his homer. If I had been the official scorer last night, I think I would have invoked this rule, claiming that the Met players were acting as fans obstructing batters and runners. Since they all were entitled to score, I would have given Ventura a grand slam.

October 19—The Atlanta Braves

HENZLER: The Braves went 34-12 during the regular season versus teams with .575 winning percentages or better (9-3 NYM, 6-1 Hou, 8-1 Cin, 5-4 Ari, 2-1 NYY, 4-2 Bos). Since 1951, no other team has won so many games against such a high caliber of competition:

Highest Winning Pct. vs. Teams With .575-Plus Records, Single Season—1951-99

Year	Team	Record	Pct
1999	**Braves**	**34-12**	**.739**
1994	Yankees	11-4	.733
1997	Orioles	11-4	.733
1976	Orioles	13-5	.722
1990	Expos	13-5	.722
1997	Marlins	13-5	.722
1994	Royals	15-6	.714
1951	Yankees	15-7	.682
1959	White Sox	15-7	.682
1974	Dodgers	12-6	.667

(regular season only; minimum 15 decisions)

It's interesting to note that only the '97 Marlins and '51 Yankees actually went on to win the World Series.

If we reduce the standard to records versus .550 teams, the Braves don't pick up any more decisions. But their winning percentage shines a bit better. Here again though, only two teams—the '55 and '63 Dodgers—went on to capture the ultimate prize:

Highest Winning Pct. vs. Teams With .550-Plus Records, Single Season—1951-99

Year	Team	Record	Pct
1999	**Braves**	**34-12**	**.739**
1955	Dodgers	15-7	.682
1959	White Sox	15-7	.682
1983	Giants	20-10	.667
1963	Dodgers	12-6	.667
1974	Dodgers	12-6	.667
1957	Yankees	14-8	.636
1958	Dodgers	14-8	.636
1978	Royals	26-15	.634
1969	Orioles	19-11	.633
1976	Orioles	19-11	.633
1983	Padres	19-11	.633

(regular season only; minimum 15 decisions)

October 20—Tight NLCS Ties Mark

COOPERSON: In their just-concluded thriller of a National League Championship Series, the victorious Atlanta Braves and the New York Mets did something that had been done only once before in the history of postseason baseball: they played five straight one-run games in the same series. In 177 previous postseason series, only the 1972 World Series—in which six of seven games were decided by a single tally—had seen five consecutive one-run games.

Most Consecutive One-Run Games in a Postseason Series

No.	Series	One-Run Wins	Series Winner
5	1972 WS	A's 3, Reds 2	A's (4-3)
5	1999 NLCS	Braves 3, Mets 2	Braves (4-2)
4	1915 WS	Red Sox 4, Phillies 0	Red Sox (4-1)

PINTO: They also played the only postseason game ever to end on a bases-loaded walk.

October 20—Bullpen

PINTO: Can anyone tell me how the bullpen got its name?

ZMINDA: There's several theories. The most common story is that most old ballparks had advertising signs for Bull Durham tobacco on the outfield walls near where the relief pitchers warmed up. Dickson's *Baseball Dictionary*, however, says that the term was used as early as the 1870s. It was common then for overflow crowds to stand in roped-off areas by the foul lines, and that's where the pitchers warmed up. The term bullpen, he says, was used as early as the Civil War to denote holding areas for cattle or prisoners, and it was used in baseball literature as early as 1877. I would give the Dickson story more credibility.

October 23—Mitch Williams Memorial Moment

COOPERSON: Six years ago today the Phillies led Toronto, 6-5, after 8 1/2 innings.

October 27—Is the Longball the Key?

JAMES: Reporting research/offering for comment. First entry is from a man who I think is named Jeff Silmaneser, although I'm not sure that's right.

I have always suspected that the most efficient base deployment/timing in baseball is the home run. Those bases always coordinate to change the scoreboard. The 1999 Oakland A's had an .801 OPS, and the 1999 Boston Red Sox had a .798 OPS. The A's got theirs via lots more walks and homers, and the Red Sox got theirs via many more singles, doubles, and triples.

The A's, with identical OBP and SLG to the Red Sox, used their scoreboard-efficient BB and HR to score 893 runs; the Red Sox used their inefficient base hits to score only 836. Will bet you my eyeteeth that a systematic study would show that for the same OBP and SLG, that teams score more runs when their offense is disproportionately homer-weighted. Chess players know that it ain't how many pieces are attacking; it's how well they're coordinated. Whether they're accomplishing the same thing at the same time. Homers would seem to "bunch" offensive output; base hits would seem to "scatter" offensive output. Have any studies been done on this? —Jeff

I had never done anything precisely relating to this, and I thought it was an interesting idea, so I decided to follow up on it. I have a spreadsheet which has in it the complete batting records of all major league teams 1980-1990 except 1981, for obvious reasons. I loaded that spreadsheet, and sorted the teams by their on-base-plus-slugging—a statistic, by the way, which I hardly ever use, and don't really believe in. Anyway, with the teams so arranged, I then created five columns to measure the extent to which each team was similar to the adjacent teams in on-base percentage, the extent to which they were similar in slugging percentage, the extent to which they were similar in the total of the two, the extent to which the teams were different in terms of home runs hit, and the total of these four things. By this method, I identified 17 "matched sets" of teams that were similar in on-base percentage and slugging percentage, but approaching that in different ways.

For the record, the 17 sets of teams, with the home-run hitting team listed first, were:

The 1984 Detroit Tigers and the 1982 Kansas City Royals
The 1985 Baltimore Orioles and the 1988 Boston Red Sox
The 1986 Detroit Tigers and the 1984 Toronto Blue Jays
The 1987 New York Yankees and the 1983 Milwaukee Brewers
The 1987 Baltimore Orioles and the 1983 Boston Red Sox
The 1984 Oakland A's and the 1980 St. Louis Cardinals
The 1987 California Angels and the 1990 Cincinnati Reds
The 1986 Seattle Mariners and the 1984 Kansas City Royals
The 1984 Baltimore Orioles and the 1990 Cleveland Indians
The 1983 California Angels and the 1983 St. Louis Cardinals
The 1984 Chicago White Sox and the 1990 Minnesota Twins
The 1986 Oakland A's and the 1980 Pittsburgh Pirates
The 1984 California Angels and the 1990 Chicago White Sox
The 1983 Los Angeles Dodgers and the 1983 Houston Astros
The 1990 Baltimore Orioles and the 1984 Milwaukee Brewers
The 1986 Los Angeles Dodgers and the 1989 Cardinals
The 1982 Oakland A's and the 1984 Pittsburgh Pirates

In the first match, for example, the 1984 Tigers hit .271 as a team with 187 homers but 602 walks, giving them a .305 on-base percentage and a .432 slugging percentage, combined .736. The 1982 Kansas City Royals hit .285 as a team but with only 132 home runs and 442 walks, giving them a .308 on-base percentage, .428 slugging percentage, combined .736—the same as the Tigers, and with similar on-base and slugging percentages.

In the aggregate, the 17 "Type A" or "Type Oakland" teams hit .254 as a whole, with a .290 on-base percentage and a .398 slugging percentage, combined .687. Here, why don't I chart that:

Team or Group	Avg	HR	OBP	Slg	OPS
1984 Det	.271	187	.305	.432	.736
1982 KC	.285	132	.308	.428	.736

Team or Group	Avg	HR	OBP	Slg	OPS
Group A Avg	.254	168	.290	.398	.687
Group B Avg	.268	111	.294	.394	.688

To cut to the chase, it's a small study, but this study strongly suggests that your hypothesis is absolutely correct—and, indeed, that the effects are significant. Group A above, the teams that hit .254 with 168 homers, scored an average of 726 runs. Group B, the teams that hit .268 with 111 homers and essentially the same OBP and slugging, scored an average of only 700 runs—26 fewer. The Type A offense outscored its Type B partner in 15 of the 17 matches, and by an average of 26 runs.

Well, thanks for suggesting this. . . always nice to learn some little thing.

October 27—Chad Curtis

COOPERSON: The Yankees' Chad Curtis joined an elite group of players when he ended last night's World Series Game 3 with a 10th-inning homer. Only 10 other players have ended a World Series game with a home run, and only Eddie Mathews, Carlton Fisk and Kirby Puckett had done so in extra innings:

Game-Ending Home Runs in World Series

Player, Team	Opp	Game	Year	Inn
Tommy Henrich, NYY	Bkn	Gm 1	1949	9
Dusty Rhodes, NYG	Cle	Gm 1	1954	9
Eddie Mathews, Mil	NYY	Gm 4	1957	10
Bill Mazeroski, Pit	NYY	Gm 7	1960	* 9
Mickey Mantle, NYY	StL	Gm 3	1964	9
Carlton Fisk, Bos	Cin	Gm 6	1975	12
Kirk Gibson, LA	Oak	Gm 1	1988	9
Mark McGwire, Oak	LA	Gm 3	1988	9
Kirby Puckett, Min	Atl	Gm 6	1991	11
Joe Carter, Tor	Phi	Gm 6	1993	* 9
Chad Curtis, NYY	Atl	Gm 3	1999	10

(*series-ending home run)

October 27—Pete Rose and Jim Gray

SCHINSKI: A few things:

1. I liked seeing Rose at the ceremony on Sunday. It was great that the fans gave him such a big hand. I thought he absolutely belonged there and I am glad Bud Selig allowed him to be there. I thought the ceremony in general was great as well.

2. I thought Jim Gray was very unprofessional in the interview he had with Rose after the ceremony. This isn't the first time Gray has done this but frankly I think NBC should be embarrassed for what Gray did to Rose.

3. I give Chad Curtis a lot of credit in the interview with Gray for telling him off for the way Gray treated Rose. I was very surprised he did it considering he had just hit the homer to win Game 3 and I thought he would be caught up in the emotion of the moment. It shows me Curtis has a lot of class.

4. I hope Bug Selig sees the support Rose is getting from the fans and players and lifts the ban on Rose.

DEWAN: I wholeheartedly agree with your first three points. However, I don't believe that Jim Gray should be the reason Pete Rose gets into the Hall.

OSBORNE: I can agree with Jeff's first two points, but I don't think what Chad Curtis did should be considered classy. I understand why he acted that way and why a lot of people enjoyed seeing Jim Gray get publicly embarrassed on live TV, just as he had done to Rose, but I still found Curtis' actions to be simply rude, distasteful and classless.

PINTO: It's too bad Game 2 of the World Series wasn't at Shea Stadium. Pete Rose would have been booed mercilessly.

The Atlanta fans don't know anything about baseball. They weren't cheering much for their team. Turner Field is more like a place to be seen than a place to watch a ballgame. The fact that they cheered more loudly for Rose than they did for Williams or Aaron tells you something.

A couple of years ago I was listening to Ray Knight tell Pete Rose stories. He was saying how Rose helped him out when Ray came up from the minors, buying him meals, giving him a place to stay, etc. I couldn't help thinking as I listened to Knight talk of Bill James' essay on Hal Chase.

I never liked Rose as a player, and I like him even less as a human being. Every once in a while you have to punish a bastard like that for his excesses, least others begin to think that sort of behavior is okay. Let him rot.

OSLAND: Whew, thanks. I thought I was still the only person who couldn't stand Rose. He's a complete jerk who gambled on baseball while he was a part of it. His skills and achievements on the baseball field are enough to get him into the Hall, but his own arrogance and stupidity are keeping him out. The only thing that I'm sorry about is that somehow Jim Gray was able to make one of the biggest losers in the game seem like a sympathetic person.

HENNINGER: It's hard to say if the outcry against Jim Gray means a majority of baseball fans have forgiven Rose and want the ban dropped, but if that's the case, I'm a bit surprised. Fans can be very unforgiving of players after an extended holdout or a drug arrest, but then Rose is easily forgivable, even if he has been in complete denial about his gambling and hasn't expressed any remorse about betting on baseball. I don't see his gambling as being any less serious than most of the crimes players "get away with," and holding out isn't even a crime. I suppose many fans have doubts whether Rose even bet on baseball, but my gut says the MLB line that the evidence was not refutable is true. Two other things work in Rose's favor with the public. Ten years have passed, and Rose probably is viewed as more likable than most of today's athletes, even though I don't find Rose at all likable. A lot of people didn't like all of Ronald Reagan's policies, but they often supported him because they liked him.

MITTLEMAN: This was my column from yesterday:

Is Pete Rose His Own Worst Enemy?

To hear NBC's bulldog sports reporter Jim Gray tell it, Pete Rose is his own worst enemy and if he has any interest in setting things right he should apologize or admit what he did was wrong. It's not too hard to guess that Gray also believes that Rose should make his peace in front of 100 million viewers during one of Gray's bombastic interviews.

Game Two of the 1999 World Series was prefaced by baseball's latest promotion—The All-Century Team. It was a pageant-like atmosphere reminiscent of the kind of schmaltz we witnessed during the All-Star Game in Fenway Park this past summer. The only problem was that baseball's Darth Vader managed to get himself elected to the team and was present on the field for the ceremonies. Not only that, but the loudest, warmest and longest ovation was given to Rose by the throng at Turner Field in Atlanta. Commissioner Bud Selig looked as though he needed a laxative to relieve the discomfort he obviously felt from the message the fans were sending.

Selig, in his infinite wisdom, got boxed in royally this time. He now finds himself in the awkward position of upholding the ban on Rose from baseball which disqualifies him from the Hall of Fame, but also orchestrating a celebration of the greatest players in history and including Peck's Bad Boy in the process.

Selig never imagined that fans would be so dumb as to elect Rose ahead of Stan Musial or Frank Robinson, but that's precisely what happened. It took a special committee of overseers to rectify the injustice perpetrated on Stan the Man. That begs the question as to why allow the fans a part in this at all if Selig knew ahead of time they couldn't be trusted to get it right To be honest, it looks good on Selig because the punishment handed out to Rose is full of the same hypocrisy as the procedure to elect an All-Century Team.

Did Pete Rose gamble with bookies while he was managing a big league team? Sure he did. Did he bet on baseball? Probably, but we'll never know for sure because Rose insists that he didn't in the face of the Dowd Report, which supposedly has betting slips that the FBI claims is in Rose's handwriting. The problem is that Rose cut a deal before the public was shown the evidence and could judge for itself. Should Rose be reinstated? It's been 10 years and Rose certainly has paid his debt to baseball and society, but baseball remains paranoid about gambling issues ever since Shoeless Joe and the Black Sox scandal of 1919. Reinstatement should be addressed and Selig avoids it like the plague, even though Rose filed nearly two years ago and has yet to be given a response.

But, to those who suggest that Rose should remain out of baseball because he does not show enough contrition—get a life. Isn't that the same baloney fed to us by those who claimed to want to forgive President Clinton in the Lewinsky Affair? Reality suggests they were only interested in his entrapment, not an apology.

Some people are never happy until they can kick a man in the stomach repeatedly when he is down. Apparently, NBC's Jim Gray is such an insect. Gray is a parasitical embarrassment to his profession who made a name for himself for being tenacious with boxer Mike Tyson after he bit the ear off Evander Holyfield that fateful night in Las Vegas. There is a big difference between trying to get a rational explanation out of a deranged fighter moments after being disqualified from a bout as opposed to using the same interrogation method against the all-time hits leader, who has lived in disgrace the past 10 years, on a World Series night supposedly honoring the best and the brightest.

Everyone has their own opinion of the Rose matter. For the record, mine is simple. Rose did not violate these ethical codes while he played the game. His Hall of Fame-caliber accomplishments listed in the record books are attributable to him as a player. His gambling sickness was exposed while he was a manager and no longer playing the game and there should be a distinction. Not that it mitigates his error or transgression in any way, but in so far as Hall of Fame balloting is concerned and what it is supposed to represent, he should be allowed in.

Notwithstanding the mortal sin gambling represents to those inside the sport, if we are going to evaluate accomplishments and morality on a post-playing days basis, then there are a lot of cases to be made for several Hall of Famers to be expelled. Is gambling worse than assault, wife-beating, fraud and other offenses attributable to a few members of the Hall of the Fame whose names will not be revealed here and now? That question deserves an answer from the Commissioner's office.

Despite Bud Selig's opinion to the contrary, maybe the fans do get it right. Their election of Rose to the All-Century Team dovetails nicely with recent polls which suggest that nearly 75 percent of the fans believe the Hit King should be reinstated to baseball and his entry to the Hall of Fame should be reviewed. A player with 4,256 hits, more than any of the greatest legends of the game, who was nicknamed Charlie Hustle for his trademark 100 percent effort given all the time, certainly has endeared himself to the public, if not the lawyers who run baseball.

Whether Rose eventually gets reinstated or not will not keep this writer awake at night. You won't see petition drives, telethons or conscience-raising columns about Pete Rose again. But any time a character like Jim Gray invades my household through my big screen television with his pitiful attempt to beat up and sensationalize a sad character like Pete Rose, using an ill-mannered, bloodsucking mentality during a majestic World Series game—I will scream.

PALACIOS: Jim Gray did the interview like Rose played baseball.

Had Gray gotten Rose to apologize on TV, Gray would have gone down in baseball history. His interview would be played as much as the TV clip of Rose's 4,191st hit.

Gray's interview was selfish. As selfish as dislocating a catcher's shoulder in an All-Star game. Gray could have walked through hell in a gasoline suit to get Rose to apologize on TV.

Pete Rose and Jim Gray deserve each other.

SPEAR: Last year during the Braves-Cubs Division Series, I was working for the Cubs' PR staff and was assigned to work with Jim Gray, basically to help him get around Wrigley Field and to keep an eye on him to make sure he didn't go where he wasn't supposed to go.

In my four hours with him, I came to the conclusion that he is nothing more than an egotistical weasel. He almost got into a fight with a Wrigley Field security guy because he wouldn't let Gray into Scottie Pippen's skybox, and he was incredulous that the Cubs wouldn't let him into their clubhouse right before game time to get a picture of something posted on the clubhouse bulletin board.

I think his egotistical weaselness is what makes him a good reporter. He will stop at nothing, including breaking rules, to get what he thinks is the story, and because of it he does seem to get some pretty good scoops.

But he's still a weasel and Chad Curtis is now one of my all-time favorite players.

STEPHENS: I'll admit, Pete Rose wasn't my favorite baseball player. But based on what he did on the field, he should be in the Hall of Fame. What Jim Gray did was inexcusable in my mind. The greatest players of all time were honored that evening, but Gray had to ruin it by badgering Rose into answering the questions about his alleged gambling. There is a time and place for those questions, and Sunday night was not that time.

Allan, I must agree with you. Chad Curtis is now one of my favorite players of all time for what he did last night.

JAMES: Pete Rose:

1. The agreement that Pete Rose signed with baseball specifically says that there is *no* finding—*no* finding—that Pete Rose bet on baseball. The ban is *not* a lifetime; it is an indefinite ban, with the clause about no finding that Pete Rose bet on baseball clearly intended to lead Rose and his attorneys to believe that he would be reinstated after a couple of years. The question we should be asking is not whether Pete Rose will admit to something that Major League Baseball has acknowledged it cannot prove, but when Major League Baseball will decide to live up to the agreement that it made.

2. I wish that one-tenth of the people who believe that the Dowd report has irrefutable proof that Rose bet on baseball would actually read the damn thing, and tell me what this proof is.

DEWAN: Very interesting, Bill. Nevertheless, I still find it very believable, and even probable, that Pete Rose bet on baseball. It's almost a natural extension of his being. He's a compulsive gambler. He believes in his team. He bets on his team. And he rationalizes that, since he's betting on himself, he's not doing anything detrimental to baseball.

In essence, you're saying, and he's saying, there's no proof. OK, I accept that. But do you believe he bet? I believe he did. For that reason, I'm OK with him being banned from the Hall. I am OK with Rose being set out as an example of, if you gamble, you lose. Or, we know you gambled but we can't prove it, you lose.

But I'm also OK with it if he's admitted. But he shouldn't be admitted because everyone now feels sorry for him because of Jim Gray's idiocy. As to your other point, that MLB misled him: they shouldn't have done that, and they should own up to it by, at a minimum, responding to his reinstatement request.

JAMES: What I am in favor of is people negotiating in good faith and living up to the agreements that they enter into. Suppose, John, that you had an employee who:

a) was having serious personal problems, impacting heavily on his job performance, and

b) you also suspected was stealing from the company.

Suppose, however, that this employee had a guaranteed contract, so that you couldn't simply fire him. Suppose that the employee firmly and vigorously denied that he had ever stolen from the company.

Suppose, then, that you negotiated an exit agreement from the contract, *in which you specifically acknowledged that his exit was not based on the charges of dishonesty.*

Five years pass. The employee cleans up his personal problems. He applies to come back to the company, or perhaps someone calls from another company, asking about employing him.

Would it be ethical, then, for you to say to the other managers "No, we can't hire him back, we fired him because he was stealing from the company?" Would it be ethical for you to suggest to the other company that you thought that the man was a thief, having explicitly agreed that he wasn't?

John, you and I. . . well, I guess no one else reading this would know this, but you and I have operated for many years with no contract between us, and I have no problem with that because I have absolute confidence in your integrity. You guys publish books with my name on them, use my game designs, etc, and I do things for you, and it's all just based on handshake agreements. We trust each other, and we can trust each other, because when I enter into an agreement, I damn well mean it, and so do you. But what Major League Baseball is saying to Pete Rose is, "That agreement you forced us into. . . that isn't worth the paper it's written on. That's just what we had to agree to get rid of you." And that's not right.

STILLWELL: I think the majority of fans seem to think that admittance to the Hall is a right to all who played the game extremely well. Most players seem to think that as well, judging by comments made by players like Phil Niekro or Orlando Cepeda when they were passed over on several ballots. I believe HOF selection is strictly an honor and a privilege. The Hall is not obligated to take anyone. Pete Rose was compensated very generously in salary for his exploits on the field, and nothing in his contract ever said he had to make the Hall.

I sometimes wonder if Bud Selig makes decisions based on whatever will be least popular with fans. Even if he does, this is one rare instance where he, and baseball, have not sold out the game. The Hall of Fame's selectivity, I believe, is what makes it so special for all of us. I always thought it was sick that fans suddenly believed a man who helped fix a World Series (Joe Jackson) should suddenly be let into the Hall because Hollywood made a couple of sympathetic movies about him. Jackson was declared innocent, too.

MEYERHOFF: Frank Deford proposed this morning that MLB cut the baby in half.

One half: Admit Rose to the Hall based on what he did as a player.

Other half: Ban him from other aspects of the game based on what he did when he was not a player.

OSBORNE: It appears baseball is more content to give him the other half of the baby, letting him participate at the World Series celebration.

NEYER: I don't know that such a thing as "irrefutable proof" could exist in this case. However, the betting slips, in his handwriting and containing his fingerprints, seem like enough proof to me. As I'm sure you've been told at some point, the dates do indeed match up with real games.

JAMES: *If*, in fact, they *are* betting slips; *if*, in fact, it *is* his handwriting; *if*, in fact, these "slips" became the basis of actual bets; and *if*, in fact, it was his money, rather than a matter of Paul Janszen asking him what he thought about some games. . . No one actually knows any of these things.

Rose's fingerprints and (perhaps) Rose's handwriting are on a document which is, on the surface of it, totally non-incriminating. It's just a sheet of paper such as I might write or you might write or anyone else might write. The only thing that makes it even remotely incriminating is that Paul Janszen, who hated Rose and was intent upon destroying him, *claimed* that this was a betting slip.

People say "betting slips" as if this was a technical term; when you place a bet with a respectable bookie, he hands you a betting slip as a receipt. People talk as if Rose had written "These are my bets for 4-9-86" across the top of a sheet of paper. It isn't anything like that. It's just one sheet of paper on which some notes are scribbled, "Phi at Chi, w." The entire basis of the alleged betting slips is something less than 40 words on essentially one piece of paper. It isn't enough material for anyone to determine definitively whether it is or isn't Rose's handwriting.

NEYER: I agree with you, Bill, that MLB did not deal fairly with Pete Rose.

But the more I think about this, the more I wonder. . . if Pete Rose really is innocent of the betting charges, why hasn't he sued Major League Baseball? It's now been 10 years. Back in the early 1990s, people would ask Rose why he didn't do something drastic, and he would say, "It's only been a few years. When the time is right, something will happen."

JAMES: As to why somebody hasn't done something, there could be a million reasons. To cite two of the most obvious:

1. Rose or his lawyers perhaps screwed up the negotiations with the Commissioner's office, getting vague language when they needed something specific. Perhaps Rose hasn't broken with his old lawyers, who don't want to re-hash their own poor performance.

2. Rose may view it as an either/or thing. *Either* Rose sues, or he tries to pursue forgiveness, not both. He has simply chosen to pursue forgiveness.

But really, we can't know why Rose doesn't do something, and that simply isn't evidence.

My point is to focus on what is the actual evidence. I really have only two points in this immensely complicated discussion:

1. Regardless of whether Rose is innocent or guilty, Major League Baseball should act ethically and honorably toward him.

2. The actual evidence that Rose bet on baseball, when you sort through all the BS, is very, very slight, and miles short of the overwhelming evidence that Major League Baseball *claims* that it has.

This, from my standpoint, is just more BS. It's not evidence that he bet on baseball. It's just something that people use to buttress their position, rather than actually look at the evidence.

GREENBERGER: I never liked Rose—his talent always was obscured by his ego. So it's easy for me to admit that I'm predisposed to assume his guilt. However, if he isn't guilty, why can't he clear his name? Who can possibly gain from dirtying his name? Wouldn't MLB want to have him as part of the family if there was any way to do so without really crossing a line? I mean, MLB isn't exactly impressing me as a bastion of solid values in its general operations. I have to believe the evidence is pretty solid because MLB certainly would benefit from having Rose as part of the machine.

JAMES: Everybody has their own reason why we should believe that Pete Rose is guilty, even though the evidence against him is completely unconvincing. John Dewan has his argument about why Rose must be guilty, Neyer has his argument, you have yours. . . everybody has one. This is unworthy of you. Rose is innocent unless there is convincing evidence that he is guilty. There isn't. Major League Baseball has signed an agreement stating that there isn't. Major League Baseball should honor that agreement, and all of us should call upon them to do so.

If there is convincing evidence that Pete Rose bet on baseball, what is it? The Dowd Report says that there is convincing evidence that Pete Rose bet on baseball. It also says that "each of Pete Rose's accusers has stood before the bar of justice and engaged in the most painful act of integrity," by which it means that they had all pled guilty to felonies. What is this evidence?

October 27—Millennium Hype

MITTLEMAN: Our local sports-talk radio show is going nuts here in Toronto, trying to expand this team-of-the-whatever hype. It seems that people here have a hard time distinguishing the best franchise of the last 100 years. They are hung up between the Yankees, Habs, Packers and Celtics. What do you think and why? Try and keep an open mind and not be biased by your love of a particular sport.

ZMINDA: I think the most reasonable criteria are consistent dominance over time, and total number of titles won. Championships by decade:

	Championships by Decade			
Decade	Yankees	Canadiens	Celtics	Packers
1900-09	0	0	—	—
1910-19	0	1	—	—
1920-29	3	1	—	1
1930-39	5	2	—	4
1940-49	4	2	0	1
1950-59	6	5	2	5
1960-69	2	5	9	0
1970-79	2	6	2	0
1980-89	0	1	3	0
1990-99	3	1	0	1
Total	**25**	**24**	**16**	**12**

The NFL, NHL and NBA teams are at a bit of a disadvantage since the NBA didn't start until 1946, the NHL until 1917 and the NFL until 1920. Even so, you can quickly eliminate the Packers, who have only 12 titles overall and only one since the '60s. No other NFL team has won more than nine championships.

The Celtics, with 16 titles since the NBA began in 1946, are impressive, but the Yankees have won 15 championships since that time, and the Canadiens have won 19. And most of the Celtics' titles came in a 13-year period with Bill Russell, when they won 11 championships. That eliminates Boston in my estimation.

That leaves the Yankees and Canadiens. The Yankees have won one more title, but the Canadiens started later, and they've won at least one title in every decade of their existence. That's impressive, but the NHL had far fewer teams than MLB up until the 1970s, including the six-team setup that existed from 1942-43 to 1966-67. And when the Canadiens won their first title in 1919, the NHL had exactly *three* teams. I'd say the Yankees were the team of the century for that reason, but a strong argument could be made for Montreal.

October 28—Joe Torre and Yankee Dominance

COOPERSON: The Yankees dropped just three of 25 postseason games in cruising to the last two World Series titles, and have pushed their manager, Joe Torre, to the head of the class in terms of postseason success. Torre has far and away the best career postseason winning percentage among managers with at least 15 games under their belt:

Best Postseason Winning Percentage, Managers

Manager	W-L	Pct	WS Titles
Joe Torre	35-14	.714	3
Joe McCarthy	30-13	.698	7
Sparky Anderson	34-21	.618	3
Tom Kelly	16-8	.667	2
Bob Lemon	15-9	.625	1

(minimum 15 postseason G)

October 31—Dante Bichette to Cincy

PINTO: I saw a wire story today that the Reds had acquired Dante Bichette to take the place of Greg Vaughn. Obviously, the Reds don't believe in the Coors Effect:

Dante Bichette, Home vs. Road—1993-99

Category	Home	Road
Avg	.360	.268
OBP	.397	.303
Slg	.642	.431
AB	2,094	1,956
H	754	524
HR	136	65
RBI	537	289

Note that playing in two tough hitters' parks (Anaheim and Milwaukee) his home-road split was:

Dante Bichette, Home vs. Road—1988-92

Category	Home	Road
Avg	.244	.263
OBP	.280	.291
Slg	.395	.399

Anyway, I think by the end of next year we'll be doing big falloff graphics for Bichette. He's about to turn 36; it would not surprise me if he were out of baseball by the end of next year.

JAMES: As we all said about Andres Galarraga.

PINTO: Yes, we did say that about Galarraga. Obviously, we missed something, and that something might be the effect of Coors on overall strength. You would think if you spent years in a rarified air environment, when you came down to sea level you'd be stronger and have more endurance than your stuck-at-sea-level buddies. We'll see.

November 4—The Juan Gonzalez Trade

PINTO: I'm not a big Juan Gonzalez fan, but he turned out to be a much better player than I thought he would be. When he was young, he was a slugger who didn't walk. I remember having a discussion with Scott Ackerson, a "Baseball Tonight" producer at the time as to who would hit more home runs for their career, Griffey or Gonzalez. He liked Gonzalez because he was bigger and stronger. I argued that Gonzalez had a hole in his swing that Griffey didn't, and that Griffey's home-run swing was more natural. So far I've been right, but not by much. Gonzalez' hole has closed somewhat; now he's a slugger who walks some but hits for a good average. Now, if you are the Red Sox, whose missing piece was a slugging outfielder, it might be a good move. But the Tigers had a lot of holes this year, and Gonzalez is going to do nothing to improve the pitching staff, and losing Justin Thompson is going to do nothing to improve the pitching staff. I don't know what the demographics of Detroit are; Gonzalez may bring the Latin fans to the ballpark. But I don't see this as a move to improve Detroit, I see it as a move to bring fans to a new park by having a superstar in the lineup.

For Texas, it really depends on how the youngsters develop. The Randy Johnson deal turned out to be pretty good for Seattle when Garcia and Halama both had good years. Also, Texas' offense was good enough that if the pitching staff does indeed improve, it can handle the loss of offense without a loss of wins.

Finally, it also comes down to who do you keep for you future. If the choice is Gonzalez or Ivan Rodriguez, I think it's a no-brainer to keep Rodriguez. Ivan's combination of skills is much harder to come by. Griffey vs. A-Rod is a tougher call. My preference would be to keep A-Rod. His upside at this point is much higher than Griffey's. Like Ivan, his combination of skills is much harder to come by (although there seems to be a lot of hard hitting shortstops out there now). He's also still in his growth phase, while Griffey is likely starting to decline. However, Harold Reynolds made a good point to me this year; Griffey is the draw. His feeling is that more fans are going to come see Junior than A-Rod, so Seattle should keep him; that if Griffey is going to break Aaron's home-run record, that's a draw you want to have on your team. Griffey seems to have made the choice for Seattle, however.

While we're on the subject of slugging shortstops, Peter Gammons asked me which of the big three would be considered the best 15 years from now—Jeter, Garciaparra or Rodriguez. My answer was that Rodriguez would be the best hitter, Garciappara the best fielder, but Jeter would combine the two better and be considered the best of the three. Having a chance to really watch Jeter during the playoffs, I'm not sure he's not the best now. He's so smooth in the field. He gets on base more than the other two, but he lacks their home-run power. I'm sticking with Jeter, but I'd be curious as to what all of you think.

COOPERSON: Is anything sacred in baseball anymore? Is there any player who is truly untouchable? With Juan Gonzalez being dealt by the Rangers to Detroit, four of the top five RBI men of the last four years have changed teams since 1996. And the one who hasn't changed teams, a guy named Junior, appears headed out of Seattle any day now. The leaders in RBI since 1996:

Most RBI—1996-99

Player, Team(s)	RBI
Ken Griffey Jr., Sea	567
Juan Gonzalez, Tex	560
Albert Belle, Cle-CWS-Bal	533
Mark McGwire, Oak-StL	530
Rafael Palmeiro, Bal-Tex	521

HENZLER: Should Griffey find another home next year, it would mark the first time, at least since 1900, that each of the top five RBI guys in any four-year span played for more than one team between Year 1 and Year 5 (the year after, such as Gonzalez next season).

November 8—The Shawn Green Trade

ZMINDA: Gammons is reporting that the Dodgers have traded Raul Mondesi and Pedro Borbon for Shawn Green, then signed Green to a six-year, $84 million contract. I like Shawn Green, but he's had one good year ('98) and one great one ('99). How much does this make Griffey or Rodriguez worth?

November 9—Who's On First?

KIRKORSKY: How does Palmeiro win the Gold Glove after playing 28 games at first? Who votes on this stuff?

COUSINS: Isn't it the players and coaches that vote on Gold Gloves?

JAMES: Yeah, but in defense of the voters, did you look at the American League first basemen? I don't know who I would vote for. . . Doug Mientkewicz.

Should do a list of the worst Gold Glove selections ever. . . this would have to be on the list, since Palmeiro wasn't really a first baseman. One year Joe Rudi won the Gold Glove as an outfielder when he had been playing first base almost all year. Another time Jim Kaat won the Gold Glove at pitcher when he had missed two-thirds of the year with an injury; another year he won the Gold Glove after he had made *eight* errors, giving him an .826 fielding percentage for the season.

The fact that the players vote doesn't mean that the voting structure works. A badly designed voting structure will sometimes produce irrational results, no matter who votes.

SKELTON: Sounds like the American presidential-electoral system. I wonder if half of the electorate voting for Gold Glove at first base decided to stay home because they felt their vote wouldn't matter.

MITTLEMAN: Players do not vote for Gold Gloves. Managers and coaches decide Gold Gloves.

PINTO: In a recent Rob Neyer column on ESPN.com, Rob wrote:

The point is, the managers and coaches had eight or 10 choices. . . and instead, they went off the board, and rewarded a guy who deserves a Gold Glove about as much as Brooke Shields deserves her own TV show.

I will not see Brooke disparaged, despite the fact that she went to Princeton. Certainly, she's no Calista Flockhart (outweighing her by at least 80 pounds), but she's a much better actress than your Neve Campbells, Heather Locklears and Jennifer Love Hewitts (I believe there actually are two Heather Locklears, since I don't think it would be possible for one person to do Dynasty and T.J. Hooker at the same time). Let's see more Brooke Shields! Maybe she just needs the right vehicle; a nutty teacher in an all-boys high school? An undercover cop in Harlem? Maybe a revival of the "Donna Reed Show" (can't you just see her vacuuming while wearing pearls)? The possibilities are endless.

Come on, Rob, use your fame and access for good! Get Brooke a better TV show!

November 11—Those Lovable Losers

HENZLER: The logical successor to Ernie Banks?

No offensive player started and lost more games during the 1990s than Mark Grace:

Most Losses, Non-Pitching Starts—1990-99

Player	Losses
Mark Grace	758
Jay Bell	721
Todd Zeile	714

At least the Cubs won at a .477 clip in Grace' starts. That was better than Gregg Jefferies (543-633), whose teams played .462 ball in his starts. That percentage was the worst for any player with at least 1,000 starts during the 1990s. Among guys with 500 starts, Marty Cordova's Twins (257-349, .424) played the worst.

November 15—Big Unit Wins NL Cy Young Award

SCHINSKI: For those who don't know, Randy Johnson won in a close race with Mike Hampton.

PINTO: Well that's great! It's nice to see the voters put his won-lost record in the proper perspective.

From June 25 through July 15 he started five games and was 0-4, while posting a 1.13 ERA. In 40 innings he allowed 25 hits, 5 ER, 12 BB and 62 K. Make that the 4-0 or 5-0 it should have been and no one gives anyone else a first-place vote.

November 16—Pedro in a Landslide

SCHINSKI: Pedro Martinez won the AL CY Young in a landslide. He received all the first-place votes.

COOPERSON: Terrible choice. How could baseball writers possibly have chosen Boston's Pedro Martinez as the '99 AL Cy Young winner? Well, all Martinez did was lead the American League pitchers in just about every significant pitching category, winning the pitching Triple Crown by topping the league in wins, ERA and strikeouts. Here are *some* of the categories in which Pedro topped the AL last year:

Pedro Martinez—1999

Category	No.
Wins	23
ERA	2.07
Strikeouts	313
Winning Pct	.852
Strikeout-Walk Ratio	8.46
Opponent Avg	.205
Opponent On-Base Pct	.248
Baserunners/9 IP	8.69
Hits/9 IP	6.75
Strikeouts/9 IP	13.20

November 18—Pudge Over Pedro

STEPHENS: In a stunner. . .

Pudge Rodriguez was named MVP of the American League, edging Pedro Martinez by 13 points.

PINTO: I just want to say right off that when STATS had its own MVP vote at the end of the season, my 1-2-3 picks were Pudge, Jeter and Martinez, so I'm not bothered in the least that Pudge won this thing. What is bothering me is the coverage. The stories I've seen so far have focused on Martinez not winning the award, rather than Pudge earning it.

Catchers, shortstops and second basemen are defensive players first. When you get good offense out of them, that's a plus. When you get great offense out of them, it's an MVP season. Remember Cal Ripken in 1991? Well, Ivan had a great offensive season at the toughest defensive position. Like it or not, Pedro shines in one dimension, defense. An everyday player like Pudge or Jeter, who shines both offensively and defensively deserves the award more. Now if it's just Martinez vs. Ramirez or Palmeiro, Martinez wins hands down because the other two are as one-dimensional offensively as Martinez is defensively.

I'm glad Pudge won it, I think he deserves it, but I'm not glad he won because Pedro was left off ballots. That's idiotic. I can't see Pedro lower than fourth on anyone's ballot. The other person who was totally overlooked by the voters was Jeter. The man was on base in almost every game, hit for power, and played stellar defense, and his team had the best record in the league. Finishing behind Palmeiro is an embarrassment.

GREENBERGER: David, what are you saying? Palmiero won a Gold Glove!

SCHINSKI: I agree with what you said, David. It makes me wonder if the two who left Martinez off believe the MVP should be reserved for non-pitchers since pitchers already have their own award (the Cy Young).

QUINN: "SportsCenter" tried to interview the two voters who left Martinez off their ballot. One of the two was on vacation. The other answered ESPN's questions. He said since starters only pitch every fourth or fifth of their teams' games, he believes they are less valuable.

SENTER: He also said that he did believe that pitchers do have their own MVP award, the Cy Young, and that the MVP Award should go to a batter.

HENNINGER: I saw the *Minneapolis Star-Tribune* writer—a guy with the surname Neal—defend his position, saying pitchers play in a small percentage of games. Still, Martinez had a direct hand in nearly two dozen wins. I wonder how many games some of the other candidates can say they played such an obvious role in winning. I find it hard to believe that doesn't justify putting him on your ballot somewhere.

PINTO: A friend of a friend sent me this in response to my MVP e-mail:

Martinez' "defensive" value far outstrips the value provided by any position player on offense. Even the most prolific offensive player only has a minimal impact on a game, given the fact that a player bats only four or five times a game.

My response is:

A catcher, is extremely involved in the home game, since he is involved in every pitch with the pitcher. He's setting targets, blocking bad pitches, throwing out runners, trying to pick up on batter adjustments; the catcher's involvement is more subtle than a pitcher's, but it's there more than any other non-pitcher.

A pitcher exerts so much control over the outcome of a game that it is quite possible for a pitcher, as was the case with Martinez this year, to appear every five days and still be more valuable to his team than an everyday player.

Well, this is another bone I have to pick with Martinez getting the MVP. He didn't appear every five days. He started every 5.6 games. (If you count the time he was late and came in in relief, 5.4 games). Secondly, he only pitched 213.1 innings. Among starters who have won the Cy Young Award, it's the fifth-lowest number of innings, and the four with fewer all occurred in strike-shortened years. The Red Sox babied him all year. If they had a day off where they could start him with 4 days rest and give their fifth pitcher a day off, they didn't do it. Now, where you only have to win the wild card, that's a good strategy. But if they had to win the division, those three or four extra starts that they couldn't get out of him might have made a big difference. It's like Tony Gwynn winning the batting title a few years ago without enough PA to qualify. It's nice, but he would have been more helpful to his team if he were there for 150 games.

Bottom line: the Red Sox won 83.9 percent of the games in which Martinez appeared, and 51.9 percent of those in which he did not. What could possibly speak better of his "value"?

Well, half the game is offense, and the Red Sox did step up in the games Pedro started, scoring 5.9 runs in those games, vs. an overall runs per game of 5.2. It wasn't like Pedro was squeaking out a lot of 1-0, 2-1 victories. He did win a 1-0 game vs. the Tigers, but he also had plenty of games with enough runs for a competent pitcher to win. He wasn't like Randy Johnson putting up a run and a half ERA over five games and going 0-4.

No position player, no matter how dominant on offense and defense (Rodriguez is the best example in the AL and Edgardo Alfonzo comes to mind in the NL) could have that kind of an impact (with the possible exception of Babe Ruth in the dead-ball era). In a typical year, there is no pitcher who so affects his team's fortunes, but in 1999, Martinez clearly was the difference between the Red Sox failing to make the playoffs and their successful run at the wild-card berth.

And as I stated earlier, his inability to pitch a lot might have been the difference between winning and losing the division.

JAMES: You may remember that I predicted a month ago that the AL MVP might erupt into exactly this controversy, for exactly this reason—that some people might leave Pedro off their ballots.

My two cents worth, if anybody wants it, is that some people *do* underrate the contribution of a pitcher relative to a position, but some people also overrate it. I haven't run all the math for this year's contest, but I'm skeptical that any modern pitcher, pitching 220 innings or whatever Martinez pitched—less than one-sixth of his team's innings—can have as much impact as the best position players.

The "degree of outcome control" for a pitcher is less than it is for a hitter; always has been, and is in every category of batting/pitching performance. The most strikeout-prone hitters strike out more often, per plate appearance, than Martinez or any other pitcher generates strikeouts—badly phrased, but true the last time I looked, at least. Some hitters hit home runs more often than any pitcher allows home runs; some hitter hit home runs *less* often than any pitcher allows home runs. Some hitters walk more often than any pitcher walks batters, and some batters walk less often than any pitcher walks hitters.

What offset that, for the first 100 years of baseball history, was that pitchers pitched so many innings that the gross impact was equal; whereas the busiest hitter might face 750 pitchers in a season, the busiest pitchers would face 1200 batters in a season. But that's not true anymore. Martinez faced 835 batters, only about 10 percent more than the top hitters. And without that advantage, it is difficult for a pitcher to have as much impact as a top position player.

Tom Tippett's analysis of the race is largely parallel to the analysis that I myself would have done a few years ago. My ways of thinking about this issue have changed somewhat since then, maybe for the better or maybe not, but anyway I see things a little differently, so let me explain how I see it.

Tom: Pedro Martinez pitched 213.1 innings and allowed 56 runs, so he allowed 70 fewer runs than the average pitcher over that span. This was by far the leading performance by an AL pitcher this season.

Bill: Yes, but the flaw in this logic is that value does not consist in being better than average, since a team does not start out the season with 81 wins. Value consists of being better than the replacement level.

Suppose that you have a player who has an effective winning percentage of .505, and another who has an effective winning percentage of .510. Is the second player twice as valuable as the first? Of course not; he's more like one or two percent more valuable, given equal playing time.

How many runs would a replacement-level pitcher for the Red Sox have allowed? My best guess, based on logic that I'm not going to retrace right here, is that a replacement-level pitcher with the Red Sox in 1998 would allow about 6.83 runs per nine innings.

Martinez allowed 56 runs, but seven of those were unearned. I hold a pitcher one-half responsible for unearned runs, one-half free of responsibility—that pegs Martinez at 52.5 runs allowed.

A replacement-level pitcher allowing 6.83 runs per game would allow 161.9 runs in 213.1 innings. Martinez is thus about 109 runs better than the replacement-level pitcher.

Tom: AL teams scored an average of 837.5 runs this year, or 93 for each of the nine batting order positions. According to the *STATS Major League Handbook*, Ivan Rodriguez created 100 runs in 141 starts, which are 19 more runs than the league average hitter created in that number of starts. Rodriguez wasn't close to making the top 10 in runs created in the league, but he did show well in the Triple Crown stats.

Bill: Tom doesn't even mention that the Ballpark in Arlington, which according to the 2000 *Handbook*, was the best hitters' park in the American League in 1999. If he had factored this in, that would have wiped out a substantial portion of Rodriguez' narrow edge.

Rodriguez created 5.95 runs per 27 outs. A marginal hitter, playing in the same park, would probably have created about 2.67 runs per 27 outs. Rodriguez, then, is about 55 runs better than a marginal American League hitter, given the same number of outs in the same ballpark. (I used the three-year ballpark figure to estimate these, not the 1999 figure. He'd lost a run or two if I had used the 1999 figure, but I think it is more likely that the multi-year figure is a more accurate gauge of the actual park effects.)

Thus, I agree that it is unlikely that Rodriguez' was actually more valuable than Martinez.

Tom: On the other hand, Rodriguez plays one of the toughest defensive positions on the field, a position where superior offense is all the more valuable. Using the most basic runs-created formula (the one that leaves out SB/CS), AL teams got an average of 76 runs created out of the catcher position. Pro-rate that to 141 starts and you get an average output of 66 runs created, a figure that Pudge exceeded by 34.

I have Martinez at 109 runs, Rodriguez at 55 runs plus defense. Even allowing that Rodriguez plays the most demanding defensive position, which he does, and that he plays it better than anyone has played it in 30 years, which he does, that's still a truck load of defense. I might be able to get him to 30 runs credit for his defense, maybe even 35. I don't see any way to get him to 54.

Tom: The runs-created leader, Manny Ramirez, created 150 runs, or 57 more than a league-average hitter.

Bill: Well, let's consider the case for Derek Jeter, since Jeter created 146 runs and has to be at least four runs better than Ramirez in the field.

Jeter created 146 runs, and did this in what was, again according to the clever folks at STATS, Inc., the worst hitters' park in the American League in 1999. Again going to the multiyear chart, I use a park factor of .96, and estimate that a replacement-level hitter in Yankee Stadium would have created about 2.54 runs per 27 outs.

Given Jeter's outs and some other trivial adjustments, that's 42 runs. Jeter has an advantage of 104 runs—only five runs less than Martinez.

But Jeter also plays a part in the prevention of runs. How large a part? He's a shortstop, and a good one. I would value his defense at probably 20 to 25 runs.

In addition to that, since Jeter plays in a more run-scarce environment than Martinez, it is likely that one hundred runs saved or created by Jeter have more impact in the won-lost record than 100 runs saved by Martinez.

Tom: I guess the bottom line for me is that I think Pedro had one of those rare outstanding seasons where a starting pitcher is indeed more valuable than any everyday player. It's telling, I think, that both of the Texas-based voters had Palmeiro and a few others ahead of Rodriguez.

Bill: I agree that Martinez had as good a season as any pitcher has had in several years. I still doubt that he had as much impact on the won-lost record of his team as Jeter or probably a couple of other guys.

I'll stand by what I wrote before: some people undervalue pitchers, but some people overvalue them.

The Rangers have now won three MVP awards in four years, and probably did not deserve any of them. This illustrates again one of the central lessons of sabermetrics: that the misperception of statistics is a larger cause of players being overrated or underrated than playing in New York, playing for a championship team, or being nice to the press.

Tom: I concur with Bill's comment that replacement value is a better way to evaluate players than comparing them to league averages, and I knew that someone would take issue with my use of averages. My question is how much of a difference that makes in this type of analysis.

Seems to me that when you're evaluating the best players in the game, all of whom are well above average and replacement value, it would make a difference only if the gap between average and replacement value differs from position to position.

Bill: Well, it makes a difference for many reasons, two of which are relevant here. One is proportionality. Suppose that you have two pitchers in a league with an ERA of 4.00, one who pitches 100 innings with an ERA of 3.95, which we will assume translates to an effective winning percentage of .505, and the other who pitches 200 innings with an ERA of 3.99, which we will assume translates to an effective winning percentage of .501. According to your theory, the difference between "average" and "replacement level" is not relevant, because they are both above average and better than replacement level.

But it *is* relevant. If you compare them to the league average, the pitcher pitching 100 innings with an ERA of 3.95 is far better, since he saved .56 runs (.05 x 100 / 9), whereas the pitcher pitching 200 innings with an ERA of 3.99 has saved only .22 runs (.01 x 200 / 9).

But if you compare them to replacement level, which would be an ERA of about 5.5, then the pitcher who pitched 200 innings would be far better, saving 33.56 runs (1.51 x 200 / 9), whereas the other pitcher would have saved only 17.22 runs (1.55 x 100 / 9). And, of course, this is obviously the more correct answer, since everybody desperately needs average pitchers, and a pitcher pitching 200 innings is more valuable than a pitcher pitching 100 innings at a level a tiny bit better.

This, however, is not the real reason it makes a big difference in this case. The problem with the analytical model that you're using—a problem that I myself didn't see for 20 years—is

"What do you do with the defense?" I think we would agree that run creation and run prevention can be sorted into four groups: Batting, Baserunning, Pitching and Fielding.

Baserunning is fairly trivial, and can be combined with Batting. The real challenge is accommodating Fielding, which has statistical markers similar to and overlapping with pitching, but which must be credited to position players.

The real problem with the analytical model that you're using is that it has no place to put fielding. If you evaluate a pitcher by comparing him to the average, what do you do with two pitchers on the same team, one of whom is above average, and the other of whom is below average? Let's say Pedro Martinez and Mark Portugal. You wind up saying, measuring from the average, that the Boston fielders made a *positive* contribution to Pedro Martinez, but a *negative* contribution to Mark Portugal. This makes no sense.

But using the theory of marginal runs, the position of the fielders is easy to see: the fielders move the margin. If you compare a pitcher on a good defensive team (Minnesota) and a pitcher on a poor defensive team (the White Sox), the margin is different, but the margin is the same for every pitcher on any one team.

Tom: Of course you're right that replacement value is the correct way to look at this issue. I managed to convince myself that value-above-replacement and value-above-average would be arithmetically equivalent for players in the MVP race. As you point out, playing time is one of the key differences between using averages and replacement value. My mistake was in implicitly assuming that all of the leading MVP candidates were everyday players with comparable playing time.

I started out making the case for Pedro over Rodriguez, and I would still vote for Pedro given a choice between these two. But I agree that Jeter was more valuable than Rodriguez, and I've come around to the view that Jeter should have been MVP.

In a column last week, Rob Neyer estimated replacement value as one run created per game below average, and if that's the way we estimate replacement value, it shouldn't matter which measure we use. After reading Rob's column, I took a quick look through some of the *Abstracts* to see if I could find any other method for estimating RV. I couldn't find anything, so I'm wondering if any of you can share with me the latest thinking on estimating RV for a particular position?

Bill: It's an element of the Win Shares system.

Tom: I agree with Bill that Rodriguez was not the best position player candidate and that Jeter was a better candidate than Ramirez because of the positions they each play. If the decision is between Jeter and Martinez, I go with Jeter, because their runs created/prevented were similar, and I'd go with the position player unless the pitcher has a clear edge, if only because Pedro has already been honored with the Cy Young.

Bill, you gave Jeter credit for saving 20-25 runs with his defense. That seems like a lot to me. I'd be interested in hearing how you arrived at this estimate.

Bill: Well, it's a hell of a lot if you measure from the average. It's not much if you measure against the marginal shortstop.

November 20—Bradley Passes Go, Collects $200

PINTO: The Montreal Expos purchased the contract of outfielder Milton Bradley. I understand he's a real gamer, although you might get board watching him. The Expos hope to have a Monopoly on such players, but the game of life lately has given the team more chutes than ladders. The whole operation appears to be run by Uncle Wiggley, but they feel they are just Uno player away from success.

December 2—Mark Loretta

JAMES: A couple of notes from spending too much time with *Player Profiles*:

1. Mark Loretta this year split time between first base (66 games, 493 innings) and shortstop (74 games, 592 innings). In all my years as a baseball fan, I can never remember having seen a shortstop-slash-first baseman. I can't recall that I have ever heard of such a thing. I remember Ruben Amaro used to play late-inning defense, sometimes at shortstop and sometimes at first base, but he was a backup; Loretta was a regular. Who was the last player to play 50 games in a season at first base, and 50 games in the same season at shortstop? Honus Wagner? Has this ever happened before?

2. Over the last five years, Ramon Martinez has a better winning percentage than his brother Pedro. Pedro over the five years is 86-39, a cool .688 winning percentage. But Ramon over the same five is 51-22, a .699 percentage—11 points better than his little brother.

KRETSCHMANN: Here's the list (and Amaro appears to be the only one who got there with a bunch of late-inning replacements):

50 Games at 1B and 50 Games at SS, Season

Player	Year	1B-G	SS-G
Dave Altizer	1907	50	78
Dots Miller	1914	91	60
Ruben Amaro	1964	58	79
Ruben Amaro	1965	60	60
Mark Loretta	1998	70	56
Mark Loretta	1999	66	74

December 15— Pro Player Stadium, We Hardly Knew Ye

PASSMAN: The Florida Marlins have selected Bicentennial Park, a currently unused park (in the traditional sense) in downtown Miami as the new future home for the Marlins. Adjacent to public transportation, highways, and with 15,000 parking spaces within a 10-15 minute walk to the park, the Marlins hope to move in April, 2003. HOK will do the designing.

December 22—John Rocker Speaks

OSBORNE: These comments from Rocker are incredible!

Does anybody know what action, if any, baseball *could* take against Rocker for these kinds of statements? Any predictions on what, if anything, *will* happen to him? Marge Schott and Al Campanis essentially got the death penalty for far less than this. Granted, that was baseball punishing ownership and this involves a player.

I'm interested in the thoughts of people on this list. Chalk it up to freedom of speech and do nothing? Punitive action from the league? From the Braves? What do you think should happen?

It'll be interesting to see how the Braves and Rocker respond to the public reaction to the article.

COOPERSON: Baseball didn't do anything to Campanis. The Dodgers fired him, and no team would hire him.

HENNINGER: Trade him to the Mets and make him ride the No. 7 train to work.

PASSMAN: There's no point in punishing him. The punishment he deserves he'll get from his teammates when they segregate themselves away from him (particularly the Latin Americans); the fans in Atlanta, New York and everywhere else who will boo him unmercifully; and the media, who will continue to rip him daily. He'll essentially have to wear the Scarlet Letter, at least until some other bonehead athlete does something even dumber.

HENNINGER: He'll have some angry African-American teammates as well. One report on the *SI* article I saw says Rocker called an unidentified black teammate "a fat monkey."

JAMES: I think Passman's got it. It is totally wrong for authorities to punish people for expressing opinions that they don't like. It was wrong to do it to Schott, but they could get by with it because she wasn't protected by a union. They can't do anything to Rocker, because the union would sue, and would win.

GREENBERGER: Will his teammates and the fans punish him? Sure they'll boo him in Shea, but they were doing that already. Yes, it's two days before Christmas, but I can't feel all that confident that come May, anyone will remember what a mass of hateful hot air Rocker released. I hope I'm wrong.

JAMES: The essential question posed by Rocker's outburst is: "Does it help reduce hatred to punish people who express hateful thoughts?" I would argue that it does not, that intolerance of intolerance is simply another form of intolerance. If you allow people to express their anger and bitterness, you can help those people come to terms with the things that bother them. If you muzzle them, they become more bitter and more alienated.

SKELTON: I don't think there can be an effective punishment for Rocker. As Bill said, if the league hopes to do anything, the union would protect him.

Meanwhile, the fans can't do much to affect Rocker, either. Rocker is a jerk. No matter what the fans or the media say, he will not be fazed. Fans and media have been ripping Albert Belle for years and I doubt he goes home at night and cries, wondering why more people don't like him. Rocker has already expressed that fans (especially New Yorkers) have merely reinforced his belief: they are crude, uneducated and hostile. Rocker, like Belle, is a talented ballplayer who will likely have a productive career, all the while being booed mercilessly. If fans try to force him out of the league (i.e. by throwing stuff at him, etc.), the fans will cause harm to their own team (forfeits). It appears as though Rocker's freedom of speech will indeed protect him.

God bless America (sic)

GREENBERGER: Punishment may not work, but to call speaking out against hate speech or hateful actions equally intolerant as the hate itself gets you nowhere. Good men must take a stand and send a message that intolerance and prejudice will not be accepted without protest and the presentation of a message of that combats hate—justice, mercy, tolerance and acceptance. Are we so unsure of our values that we're afraid that condemning Rocker's words is somehow not the right thing to do?

Rocker's probably not a bad guy, but if your kid came home talking about the lousy foreigners, you would have a talk with him. Rocker needs the same message.

JAMES: I encourage everyone to speak out against hate speech. I discourage punishing anyone for what they say.

December 23—The Mike Hampton Trade

ZMINDA: The Astros, if you haven't heard, traded Mike Hampton and Derek Bell to the Mets for Roger Cedeno, Octavio Dotel and minor leaguer Kyle Kessel.

If you're going to dump salaries, this is not a bad deal at all. The Astros must be doing handsprings about getting rid of Derek Bell; Cedeno's probably not as good as he played in '99, but then neither is Hampton. In a couple of years Dotel could be a much better pitcher than Hampton, and almost anyone would rather have Cedeno than Bell.

I still wonder about a first-place team about to move into a new stadium deciding it has to cut salaries. It might be a good deal long-term, but the Mets should have the better of it next year. This is what baseball's come to: teams like the Rangers and Astros, in new parks and successful, deciding they can't afford to keep some of their best players.

JAMES: Well, not just being the devil's advocate, it sure seems to me that the Astros have probably gotten all the best of this trade (note to self: insert sarcastic crack about Don Zminda's ability to analyze a trade. . . locate past failures in this regard, etc., to destroy credibility of opponent. Subsequent note: Hey, it's *Don*, you idiot, and Christmas is two days away.) Anyway, Hampton is, I would assume, a free agent at the end of the 2000 season. I think if you analyze these "under the gun" trades where a team has to trade a player or lose him to free agency, you will find that the team being "forced" into the trade, on balance, wins big. If you could sub-divide from those "forced" trades those on which the team being forced to make a trade was pro-active, rather than just scrambling around to make some kind of a deal, I would bet you would find that the team being forced to make the trade often comes out way, way way ahead in the long run, and the run being not necessarily so long. The best example, of course, is the Randy Johnson deals in Seattle. Seattle was afraid of losing Mark Langston to free agency, so they were forced into making a deal with Montreal—a deal which brought them not only Randy Johnson, but also three other pitchers, one of whom was pretty decent for a couple of years. After they got about 10 good years out of Randy Johnson, they were "forced" to trade him—for Freddy Garcia and John Halama. I think, if you study trades, you'll find a lot of those kind of deals. One year, when the Astros were a month away from losing Larry Andersen to free agency, they traded him to the Red Sox for a minor league third baseman: Jeff Bagwell.

If they keep Mike Hampton, all they've got is one year of one pitcher. If they did anything at all in this trade, that's nothing. Getting rid of Derek Bell—that just sweetens the pot. Getting Cedeno. . . hey, he doesn't *have* to be as good as he was last year.

There are two points at which the Astros, if they can't sign Hampton, can trade him—now, and next year, at the start of the pennant race. Well, if you assume that the Astros are going to be in the pennant race next year, can they trade Hampton at that point? Obviously not. This is it. If they're going to get something out of Hampton, they have to do it now. I think the Astros, really, have taken advantage of a bad situation to improve their team.

January 11, 2000—Hall of Fame Vote

ZMINDA: Carlton Fisk and Tony Perez have been elected to the Hall of Fame. Highest vote-getters (375 needed to be elected): Fisk 397, Perez 385, Rice 257, Carter 248, Sutter 192, Gossage 166, Garvey 160.

I'm not surprised Fisk and Perez got in; however, I was a little surprised that Gossage didn't do better the first time around. Jeff Reardon, very high on the all-time saves list, got only 24 votes and is off the ballot forever after one year. I don't think he belongs, but that surprised me. Also, I'd like to know which guys cast ballots for Charlie Hough, Bruce Hurst, Lonnie Smith, etc. Hubie Brooks ("He can flat hit," Tim McCarver used to say) was the only guy who didn't receive a vote. Why are people like that even on the ballot, not that the Hall of Fame is supposed to make sense.

DEWAN: Gossage being so low on the list doesn't make sense. He should be a first-time ballot Hall of Famer. Is he the second-best relief pitcher of all time (to Hoyt Wilhelm)?

ZMINDA: I definitely think Gossage deserves it, and Bruce Sutter also. I'm not sure I'd rate Gossage as the second-best reliever of all time, but he'd certainly rank very high.

January 11—In the News

PINTO: I'm back at work today, and a couple of things caught my eye in the wires today:

OWNERS GIVE SELIG SWEEPING POWERS

(AP) - Owners gave commissioner Bud Selig sweeping new powers Wednesday, allowing him to block trades and redistribute the wealth in order to restore competitive balance in baseball. To enforce his authority under baseball's "best interests" clause, the 30 owners also unanimously adopted a new constitution that grants him the ability to fine teams up to $2 million—the previous limit was $250,000. He can fine club employees $500,000, up from $25,000. Since the end of the 1994-95 strike, just one team not among the top half by payroll has advanced to the postseason—the 1997 Houston Astros—and the eight playoff teams were among the 10 top spenders last year. The bar for player salaries is about to be raised again, with the New York Yankees close to a $118.5 million, seven-year contract with shortstop Derek Jeter.

Why when I read this do I get the image of a communist dicator consolidating power and announcing a new five-year plan? Didn't Bowie Kuhn use this sort of power as a personal vendetta vs. Charlie Finley? Since Selig is owner of a small-market team, isn't this a tremendous conflict of interest? And the question I've been wondering about for years, what makes a used-car salesman so qualified to be commissioner of baseball? While some has argued to me that Selig's moves of expanded playoffs and interleague play have improved baseball, they have done so at making baseball less unique among the major sports. And through it all, Selig has not addressed the one issue that really matters, bridging the gap of mistrust between the player's union and owners.

BUSH GETS $7.3 MILLION FROM BLUE JAYS

(AP) - Homer Bush, who hit .320 in his first full season as a starter, agreed Wednesday with the Toronto Blue Jays on a three-year contract worth $7,375,000. Bush, a 27-year-old second baseman, was acquired by Toronto last February from the New York Yankees along with pitchers David Wells and Graeme Lloyd in the Roger Clemens trade. Given a chance to play every day, Bush had 32 steals, five homers and 55 RBI. After making $227,000 last year, Bush gets a $150,000 signing bonus and annual salaries of $1.4 million, $2.5 million and $3,325,000. Toronto will defer $400,000 this year, $1 million next year and $1.6 million in 2002 at 1 percent below the prime rate. Bush was Toronto's last player in salary arbitration.

When I first read the headline, I couldn't figure out why the Toronto Blue Jays would be contributing to an American presidential candidate. (A few years ago, on the front page of *USA Today* there was a picture of a baseball stadium, and above it was the headline, "Cardinals oppose abortion." I actually wondered for a minute why the St. Louis team would have a consensus on the subject.) Anyway, the Blue Jays obviously recognize the value of having the future Homer homer king on their team. It's the next best thing to Mark McGwire.

January 28—Strikeouts and Young Pitchers

JAMES: I have done a small study here which I have nothing to do with except share with my friends. I will pass it along here in the perhaps vainglorious hope that Don Z. can include it in a book somewhere, and it might thus at least be published in some form.

It is a well-known fact that a pitcher's strikeout rate indicates his potential for development. If you take two pitchers of the same age and the same level of performance, the one who has a higher strikeout rate will very probably out-perform the other in the following season and in the rest of his career. But if this is true for individual pitchers, I wondered, could it also be true for teams?

I have a vague recollection of having studied this issue before, but I couldn't tell you for sure whether I have or haven't. It is the sort of issue that I find very intriguing, because:

a) All statistics which give any indication of future performance are therefore interesting, and

b) One can see an obvious reason why this *might* be true—what is true of the individual obviously might be true of the team—but also very obvious reasons why it might *not* be true. Thus, it's a clean puzzle; you can't go into the study with any strong sense of what you're going to find.

For my first effort to study this issue, I took all teams from 1980 through 1990, except 1981, and figured to reach team the ratio between their wins and their strikeouts. The highest win-strikeout ratio in the era, for example, was by the 1985 Pittsburgh Pirates, a team which had only 57 wins, but 962 strikeouts, a ratio of 16.9-1. The lowest win-strikeout ratio was for the 1980 Kansas City Royals, a team which won 97 games, but had only 614 strikeouts.

For each of the ten seasons in the study, I identified four groups of teams, with only two teams in each group:

Group 1A was the two teams with the highest win-strikeout ratios in that season.

Group 1B was two teams with similar won-lost records, but with fewer strikeouts.

Group 2A was the two teams with the lowest win-strikeout ratios in that season.

Group 2B was two teams with similar won-lost records, but with more strikeouts.

For the ten-year study, there were 20 teams in each group. For each team in each group, I then looked up their won-lost record in the following season, the second following season, and the third following season. My intention, of course, was to see whether teams with high ratios of strikeouts to wins would improve more rapidly than teams with lower ratios of strikeouts to wins.

This study showed, first of all, that bad teams with high strikeout totals improved no more rapidly, as teams, than bad teams with lower strikeout rates. Contrasting Group 1A to Group

1B, the average performance was as follows:

	Group 1A		Group 1B	
Base Year W-L Record	68-94	.419	68-93	.422
Base Year Strikeouts	978		841	
Next Year W-L Record	73-83	.467	73-83	.470
2nd Following Year	78-83	.484	77-84	.478
3rd Following Year	81-81	.500	79-83	.486

No real difference. Bad teams improved toward the average at (essentially) the same rate of progress, whether they did or did not have strikeout staffs.

However, at least within this very small and very imperfect study, the same was not true on the opposite end of the spectrum: good teams with low strikeout rates did in fact crash to earth more rapidly than good teams with higher strikeout rates. Here we contrast group 2A (very low ratio of strikeouts to wins) with group 2B (comparable teams with more strikeouts):

	Group 2A		Group 2B	
Base Year W-L Record	91-71	.563	91-71	.562
Base Year Strikeouts	759		929	
Next Year W-L Record	80-77	.509	83-73	.530
2nd Following year	84-78	.517	85-76	.528
3rd Following Year	82-80	.507	86-76	.532

Well, that's intriguing, but certainly not convincing enough evidence to argue *anything*. I decided to more or less repeat the study, with minor variations, using a different group of teams.

For the second study, I used all teams from 1946 to 1960. From these, first I sorted out the top 20 percent and the bottom 20 percent in team wins; this turned out to mean 91 wins or more or 91 losses or more. Then I sorted those groups of teams by their strikeouts relative to the league, and took out the top 15 and the bottom 15 teams in each group. This left us, again, with a group 1A which was bad teams with relatively high strikeouts, a group 1B which was bad teams with relatively low strikeouts, a group 2A which was good teams with relatively few strikeouts, and a group 2B which was good teams with more strikeouts. The process of arriving at the groups of teams was a little different, but the composition of the groups is essentially the same.

The data from this study is not *exactly* the same as the data from the 1980s study, but it is consistent with that data. As was true in the other study, I found that a high strikeout rate was no indicator whatsoever of a bad team's development:

	Group 1A		Group 1B	
Base Year W-L Record	58-96	.378	55-98	.361
Base Year Strikeouts	641		522	
Base Year K relative to Lg	+13		-106	
Next Year W-L Record	64-90	.416	64-90	.414
2nd Following Year W-L	69-85	.445	69-85	.449
3rd Following Year W-L	71-84	.458	70-84	.456

The data on the other end, however, once again showed that good teams with more strikeouts had a stronger tendency to remain good teams than did good teams with fewer strikeouts:

	Group 2A		Group 2B	
Base Year W-L Record	94-60	.611	96-58	.623
Base year Strikeouts	660		736	
Base Year K relative to Lg	-24		+132	
Next Year W-L Record	88-66	.570	94-60	.613
2nd Following Year W-L	87-68	.561	92-61	.601
3rd Following Season	83-73	.533	92-62	.599

The 1946-60 era was dominated by a relatively few teams that tended to remain strong throughout the era. This probably explains the higher winning percentages in this study for good teams in follow-up seasons.

If I could speculate briefly on what this all means. . . a high strikeout rate on a bad teams probably is not telling, in general, because few of the pitchers on a bad team will actually stay with the team as the team develops. Using the 1985 Pirates as an example, how many pitchers who were on that team were still with the team two years later? Basically, one—Bob Walk. Otherwise, the entire staff turned over. The strikeout rate of a bad team is not an indicator of growth potential because it isn't really even an indicator of who will be with the team in future seasons.

A good team, however, counts on the pitchers they have. If those pitchers decline, the team may decline. Thus, the strikeout rate of a pitching staff may be an indicator of the team's ability to withstand baseball's competitive gravity, which tends to push all teams in the direction of .500.

PINTO: Since among individuals you compare pitchers by age, does that matter for the overall staff, also? Is a young strikeout staff more likely to develop than a young staff that doesn't strike out a lot of batters?

JAMES: In truth, David, it is almost impossible to show that the age of a pitcher has any significance at all in projecting his future. This is counter-intuitive, I know, but true nonetheless; John Dewan, who has studied pitcher projections as much as I have, can confirm this based on his independent research.

If you take a 25-year-old pitcher and a 35-year-old pitcher of the same ability and the same strikeout level, it is almost impossible to demonstrate that there is any difference in their future performance. In practice, we do pay some modest heed to a pitcher's age in making projections, but this is more a concession to expectations, expediency and common sense than it is supportable by research. Certainly if you take a 35-year-old pitcher who strikes out 7.00 men per game and a 25-year-old pitcher who strikes out 6.00 men per game but is equally effective, you'd have to bet on the 35-year-old pitcher to have a better future career.

February 1—Rocker and Free Speech

PINTO: A couple of weeks ago I sent out a letter comparing Bud Selig's consolidation of power to a communist dictator. Now he's taken the next step, and has gotten into mind control.

His reason for suspending and fining Rocker:

"Major League Baseball takes seriously its role as an American institution and the important social responsibility that goes with it," Selig said. "We will not dodge our responsibility."

I guess one of those responsibilities isn't defending free speech.

When Marge Schott was driven out of baseball, Bill James complained about this very thing. To my shame, I did not agree with him at the time. My reasons then were:

1. MLB owners are an exclusive club, and owners serve with the blessings of other owners. If they don't like someone, they don't have to let them in, and if someone offends them, they can throw them out.

2. Free speech is a political right. While the government can't prosecute people for their beliefs, it's perfectly all right for individuals or corporations to publicly disassociate themselves from such people. I should have known better. The lesson of history is that if you appease, you lose.

Rocker said something stupid. No one has defended him. He's going to lose money because of this, if not in salary then in endorsements (if you remember, Wade Boggs lost all his endorsements after his affair became public). He's going to have to put up with extremely hostile fans on the road, and possibly in Atlanta. He's been contrite about what happened. The situation up to this point had been handled correctly. But Bud the dictator needs to bend all to his will.

Bud Selig is a dangerous man on a power trip. He needs to be stopped before he invades Poland. Go MLBPA!

ZMINDA: I'm with you all the way on this one, David.

This is how twisted all this is. In the "tease" in the upper left-hand corner of page 1 of today's *USA Today*, the big Late Sports headline is "BASEBALL SUSPENDS ROCKER" with a color picture of him hanging his head and a sub-headline "Racist remarks will cost him spring training, $20,000." Obviously this is *the* important story in sports this morning, the one of most vital importance to all of us, at least according to the editors at *USA Today*.

Underneath it, in smaller letters, depicting a (obviously) less important story, is another headline: "RAVENS STAR CHARGED WITH MURDER"

I guess there's a lesson in this, but I'm not sure what it is.

PALACIOS: Cut them a little slack here. The murder story didn't come across the wire until 12:33 a.m. Eastern Time. The front page of the sports section was finished at that point. They probably had 1.5 hours before press time.

On the other point, I agree that Rocker shouldn't be punished.

I have spoken in Spanish while walking in Manhattan, so I guess I'm one of those people that Rocker offended. It's no shock that people say what he said. I heard those things in 8th grade. And I watched some of those people change.

Basically, hate the sin, but not the sinner.

What's really irritating me is people jumping on the bandwagon against him. Rocker at least was interesting when he was insulting. The other people make we want to puke.

As for Bud Selig, what makes him think that America wants moral guidance from a car salesman? Meanwhile, Bobby Chouinard gets nothing for pistol-whipping his wife? Come on Bud, stop playing the press.

ZMINDA: There's no reason to cut *USA Today* any slack. They had the murder story, not in great detail but all the essentials including the circumstances, who was murdered, who was charged, etc. There's a fairly substantial one-column story on it in the front page of the sports section of the same paper I described. That's more than enough to highlight it as the lead story. Instead, they not only bury it underneath the Rocker story, they don't even refer to Lewis by name in the headline. It was their judgment that more people are worked up over some things John Rocker said to a reporter than over something an athlete has been accused of actually *doing*, up to and including murder. And they're probably right. Compare the coverage given to the Rocker story with the coverage of Bobby Chouinard being accused of choking his wife, then aiming a pointed gun at her head and saying "Is this what you want?" I'll bet that three-fourths of the people in America have never heard about the Chouinard case, while basically everybody knows about Rocker and has an opinion on it.

I find that very bizarre.

PINTO: Yes, Selig should be happy he doesn't have any murders in the majors. He might have to suspend them for a year.

I had not heard about Chouinard until now.

ZMINDA: My point exactly.

JAMES: I hadn't heard of the Chouinard case, either, but entangling the discussion of the action against Rocker with Chouinard, Lewis, Carruth, O.J., Ty Cobb or Pacer Smith isn't helpful in my opinion. The action against Rocker is not wrong because there are murderers in sports. The action against Rocker is wrong because it is wrong.

We should be grateful to Bud Selig, I suppose, in the same way that one might be grateful to an armed rapist who shoots himself in the groin. Selig has almost certainly overstepped the boundaries of his power, with the predictable result that an arbitrator will now tell him that he cannot do what he should never have been trying to do. This will clarify the legal situation, I would suppose, by clearly stating that baseball players cannot be punished for what they say.

We live in a country which is hyper-sensitive about censorship, but apparently quite willing to accept censorship so long as it is directed at people we don't like who express opinions that we don't like. If a mayor suggests that his city's art museum ought not to exhibit a work in which elephant dung is splattered on an image of the Virgin Mary, the mayor is accused of censorship, although:

a) no one has even suggested that the artist should be punished for his expression, and

b) no one is telling the artist that he should or must refrain from similar work in the future.

But in this case, we have censorship of the most vulgar and direct form. Rocker is subjected first to compulsory counseling under the threat of punishment, and then:

a) is actually punished, and

b) is explicitly told that he must refrain, apparently, from any future expression which anyone might find to be offensive.

Throughout most of our history, we have lived with many forms of government and private censorship, and the constitution has not been interpreted to prohibit this. In this last 50 years, the tide against censorship has rolled in so strongly that actions which can be characterized as "censorship" only by extension and inference will still draw howls of protest from the left.

But when the censorship is directed at someone who is. . . well, not like us, the artists who screech like scalded banshees at the merest shadow of censorship directed at *them* become suddenly mute, if not openly supportive. This is not right. I am opposed to censorship, but I am opposed to it everywhere. I am opposed to the censorship of those that I despise as strongly as I would object to the censorship of those that I admire.

SKELTON: I'm sorry, but I have to disagree with all of the harassment Mr. Selig is getting in this current Rocker affair. Don't get me wrong, I dislike Mr. Selig as much as the next guy, but as Bill said, we sometimes have to defend that which (or whom) we don't like.

Bud Selig reserves the right to punish John Rocker as he, the commissioner, chooses. As much as we like to think of baseball as our game, it is private a industry (with an antitrust exemption, no less). With as much noise as it makes, and power it exudes, the MLBPA should not be able to appeal and overturn Selig's ruling.

I believe we can, in good conscience, reasonably assume that when John Rocker is being interviewed by *Sports Illustrated* he is a representative of the Atlanta Braves and Major League Baseball. Thus, he is subject to the restrictions of his employment.

The fact that the appeal must be heard by an outside arbitrator is indicative that the buck stops with Bud. You can't go over his head. This is what happens when you make someone the overlord of baseball.

It would be interesting to see if Selig will appeal the arbitrator's decision if the suspension is revoked and/or the fine waived. Bud could appeal the case to a court of law and win.

The First Amendment of our beloved Constitution says that "Congress shall make no law [which] inhibits. . . the freedom of speech."

Congress can't, but the almighty Bud can. You may not like it, but you must defend it if you claim to defend what is right.

JAMES: The constitutional right to punish employees who say things you don't like? I don't think I've ever heard that theory before.

COOPERSON: In many cities in this country, public, taxpayers money has been used to finance baseball (and other sports') stadiums. That means the tax money paid by homosexuals, foreigners (all of them, and they are s-o-o-o-o many of them) and other minority groups. When some idiot who does nothing but benefit by the paying of those tax dollars into baseball coffers rips on those taxpayers, baseball has every right to punish him, severely. I don't think the management of STATS would be too happy if a STATS employee publicly and unjustly ripped a client of ours.

JAMES: Just trying to understand your logic here. Suppose that the Chicago White Sox were a client of ours, which I think they are, and suppose that you, Ethan, were to unjustly rip a White Sox player in a forum which became public. By your logic, then, as I understand it, STATS would be justified in fining you and suspending you? If not, why not?

PINTO: I agree with you here to a point, Ethan. I think that the Braves could justify firing Rocker if it could be shown that what he said had a negative impact on the team, either financially or in the win column. For example, if people started boycotting Braves games, stopped buying Braves paraphernalia, stopped watching TBS, that's a reason to get rid of Rocker. The public would have voted with their pocketbooks.

The other part is his teammates. If a large group of them went to the Braves and said, "We don't want to play with this guy, either get rid of him or us," or if they (heaven forbid) didn't play as hard when he was in the game, so the team was losing because of Rocker's presence, that would also be a good reason to get rid of him.

But you have to let that happen. Rocker's continued employment by the Braves is based on the premise that he helps them win and make money. If that's not longer the case, fire him. That's not some baseball god putting a limit on free speech, it's society punishing wrongful actions. In those cases, Rocker has no one to blame but himself.

But the reality is that fans don't care that much. When Boggs was introduced Opening Day after the Margo scandal, he got a standing ovation. So we'll see how much fans really care about this. But let the marketplace decide.

SCHINSKI: I think that last point you brought up was a good one, Bill. My take on the whole thing is this. Private citizens have their own opinions. To express those opinions while representing another body, like the company you work for, I think should be subject to disciplinary action by that body. But to just express those opinions outside of that should not be. The problem that professional athletes have is when can they be considered not representing their teams. I haven't seen Rocker's interview so I don't know the circumstances behind it. But from what I gather the article was an interview of Rocker as a private citizen who just happens to be professional ballplayer. As such, I don't think he should be subject to disciplinary action by baseball. I agree with David that the market should decide what if any action is taken.

SKELTON: If Ethan were to make racially hateful comments on ESPN radio, we should all be calling for some form of punishment, if not his resignation. Because we are his private employer and he was acting as a representative of STATS, we would have every right to punish him.

We tend to forget that Major League Baseball is a privately owned and operated entity because we all go out to watch the games. However, it's no different from STATS, Inc. in that it's privately owned, has a slew of employees and a CEO (Bud Selig in MLB's case). It is different in one aspect, and for good reason, because no one comes to watch us work.

Because baseball is privately owned, Bud Selig reserves the right to punish his employees as he so chooses. Since John Rocker used *Sports Illustrated* as his forum, we can, in good conscience, consider Rocker a representative of his employer(s), the Atlanta Braves *and* Major League Baseball. Due to his comments, John Rocker's presence at future Braves games (home or away), will likely create a hostile work environment. Call it harassment. You cannot harass your co-workers for their ethnicity anymore than you can sexually harass them. Imagine taking a job as public-relations director for the NAACP then wearing a white hood and sheet to your first day on the job. Do you think your right to free speech is going to protect your sheet-headed antics?

I have yet to hear this argument, but what you are saying, Bill, is that Pete Rose's ban from baseball, handed down by Commissioner Giamatti, should be lifted because it violates his right to privacy and freedom of expression because he has been punished for gambling on his own free time. Or perhaps his and Rocker's punishments should stand simply because their behavior was and is "detrimental to baseball."

JAMES: I wasn't arguing with him; I was just trying to understand what he was saying. But two points:

1. Bud Selig is *not* John Rocker's employer, as you explicitly stated that he was. Selig did not fire or suspend his own employee, which would be one thing. He instituted a ban prohibiting Rocker from working in the profession.

2. Designating someone as your spokesman, speaking for the company, is a clever ruse to deny the employee the right to speak his own thoughts. In the case of a professional athlete, since everything he does is extremely public, when *isn't* he acting as a spokesman for the company? In the privacy of his bathroom, perhaps? For all practical purposes, he's a 24-hour-a-day, 365-day-a-year spokesman for the company.

Is their anything good to say about racism or xenophobia? Nothing.

I would rather live with bigots than large, multinational companies that are empowered to tell me what I can say and what I cannot.

MATERN: My dad recalls reading that Judge Landis suspended a player for speaking in public in a way somehow embarrassing to the game. Does this ring a bell with anyone out there? I asked him for more details, but he said he'd have to dig it up and that may take awhile. In the meantime, I said that I'd bring it up and see if there is anyone else with more info. Let me know what the precedent here is.

JAMES: Responding to Matern's query, he could be referring to Jake Powell, who worked offseason as a cop in. . . it seems like it was Columbus, Ohio. Powell said in a radio interview in. . . I want to say 1936, but I haven't checked, that his offseason job was "hitting niggers over the head with a billy club." Powell may have suspended breifly by Landis; I think he was.

GREENBERGER: Selig's in a tough position. If he'd come out with a strong version of "I may not agree with what he says, but I defend to the death his right to say it," it would have made a small group of people happy, but a larger group would have accused him of copping out. In the current situation he looks like Ted Turner's butler, taking the heat for the Braves because, in essence, they want to play Jackie Robinson and still keep Dixie Walker.

Not that I give a damn about how tough a position Selig's in.

February 11—Bud Ball

PINTO: I think offense will be up this season. I saw this on the wires today:

(AP) - Get ready for Bud Ball this season. With no more league presidents, commissioner Bud Selig's signature will be on baseballs used for all major league games during the regular season. Through 1999, the signatures of the American and National league presidents were on the balls used for games in their circuits. In the 1990s, as part of a stepped-up marketing campaign, baseball began using balls with the commissioner's signature for the All-Star game and World Series. Baseball owners voted last month to eliminate the league offices and consolidate all power in Selig. The new ball will be unveiled by baseball and Rawlings on Thursday during the Super Show in Atlanta.

I can just see hitters using baseballs as a surrogate for Bud's head and bashing the ball even harder.

COOPERSON: How in the world would it help marketing to have the commissioner's name on all the baseballs?

February 12—Solo Homers

JAMES: Chipper Jones this year hit 45 homers—33 with the bases empty, 12 with men on base. I wonder if this is the highest solo shot percentage of the season? I'd bet it is, among guys who hit 25 or more homers, maybe a leadoff man or somebody.

STILLWELL: Chris Hoiles had a remarkably high percentage of solo shots for the Orioles a few years back, in one of the years when he hit a bunch.

PINTO: Here's your list for 1999:

Highest Percentage of Solo Home Runs—1999

Player	HR	Solo	Pct
Brady Anderson	24	20	.83
Al Martin	24	19	.79
Ruben Rivera	23	18	.78
Damion Easley	20	15	.75
Glenallen Hill	20	15	.75
Preston Wilson	26	19	.73
Chipper Jones	45	33	.73
David Bell	21	15	.71
Lee Stevens	24	17	.71
Bret Boone	20	14	.70

(min 20 total HR)

It's interesting to note the difference between Jones and Ramirez in solo home-run percentage. Ramirez is as low as Chipper is high (Manny, 18 solos in 1999). They had a difference of 55 RBI between them, with similar overall stats (Ramirez did have a better slugging percentage). Twenty of those RBI come from Manny having more runners on base for his homers. Just shows the importance of having good leadoff men in front of your sluggers.

JAMES: No, that's not right. Jones had 302 at-bats plus walks with men on base; Ramirez had only a few more (334). The far larger difference is not opportunities with men on base, but in home-run rates with men on base. Jones homered half as often with men on base as he did with the bases empty (adjusting for PA); Ramirez homered more often with men on base. Jones also hit .306 with men in scoring position; Ramirez hit .386.

PINTO: Bill, actually, opportunities did have a lot to do with it. If you look not at the number of times up with men on base, but the actual number of men on base, you see the difference:

Chipper Jones vs. Manny Ramirez—1999

Situation	Jones	Ramirez
Men on	395	507
Men on per PA	1.0	1.2
Men in Scoring Pos	202	305
Per PA	.76	.91

So in fact, Ramirez had a lot more opportunities to drive in men, simply because there were more to drive in. Granted, Ramirez performed a lot better than Jones in these situations, but he would have driven in more runners even if he had hit the same as Jones, just because they were on base.

Jim Henzler's
STATS Focus

March 5, 1999—1998 New York Yankees

We're already a couple weeks into spring training, and the exhibition schedule already has begun. But before we get too far into the 1999 mode, I'd like to take yet another look at the remarkable accomplishment of the 1998 Yankees.

As you're more than aware, the Yankees won 114 regular-season games last year, the second-most in major league history. If we include the Pinstripers' 11 postseason victories, New York triumphed 125 times, seven more than the next-best total, compiled by the 1906 Cubs.

For now, though, let's just concentrate on the regular season. New York's 114-48 record translates to a winning percentage of .704. But that torrid rate could use a little perspective.

The last team to exceed such a pace was the 1954 Indians (111-43, .721). And in the 44 years since 1955, a grand total of seven clubs have managed to play even .650 ball. So the Yankees were clearly defying the laws of gravity in 1998. But it goes even a little bit deeper than that.

In essence the Yankees turned the rest of the American League into a bunch of cellar dwellers. Their overall record compares respectably to what we reasonably should expect the league's best team to compile against the league's worst squad in any particular season.

I went back to the end of World War II and studied the overall record in these "David and Goliath" matchups—the best versus the worst in each league each season. For example, the Yankees themselves were 11-1 (.917) against the Tampa Bay Devil Rays last year, the club with the poorest winning percentage in the American League. The Braves, meanwhile, were just 7-5 (.583) against the Florida Marlins.

Combining the logs of all such "mismatches" since 1946, we discover that first-place teams compiled a 1,328-521 record versus the last-place clubs. That's a winning pecentage of .718, not much better than the Yankees' overall mark in 1998.

And the Bronx Bombers' percentage actually was comfortably higher than the overall mark in meetings between the top teams and those with the second-worst records. Here, I'll show the entire list based on the winning percentage of the top team's opponent.

League's Top Team vs. Opponent—1946-98

Versus	W-L	Pct
Worst	1,328-521	.718
2nd Worst	1,360-633	.682
3rd Worst	1,323-700	.654
4th Worst	1,282-774	.624
5th Worst	1,298-725	.642
6th Worst	1,239-832	.598
7th Worst	1,164-848	.579

It doesn't make any sense to go any deeper than the seventh-worst record, since there were only eight teams in each league until the early '60s. Because of the changing number of francises over the years, a case could have been made to limit the number of seasons studied.

But no matter which time frame you would use, you'd probably arrive at the same conclusion—the 1998 Yankees were a team for the ages.

March 12—Joe DiMaggio

Joe DiMaggio passed away this week at age 84. A lot has been written about the legendary center fielder, and I don't have much to add.

DiMaggio was voted the game's greatest living player in 1969, and since I never saw him play, with the exception of highlights, I'm in no real position to dispute his election.

There is one quick list I'd like to present. DiMaggio retired after the 1951 season at age 36. That would seem to be a relatively young age. And it's possible he could have hung on for a couple more years at an acceptable level of performance.

In the two seasons before his retirement, the Yankee Clipper had totaled 44 homers and 193 RBI, certainly respectable figures. In fact, only 10 players in baseball history have mustered at least 40 homers and 150 RBI in the two-year span preceeding their retirement:

Players With 40-Plus Home Runs and 150-Plus RBI in 2 Seasons Before Retirement—All Time			
Player	**Years**	**HR**	**RBI**
Hank Greenberg	1946-47	69	201
Bobby Doerr	1950-51	40	193
Joe DiMaggio	**1950-51**	**44**	**193**
Tony Horton	1969-70	44	152
Rico Carty	1978-79	43	154
Greg Luzinski	1983-84	45	153
Dave Kingman	1985-86	65	185
Doug DeCinces	1986-87	42	160
Larry Parrish	1987-88	46	152
Kirby Puckett	1994-95	43	211

Now, DiMaggio really didn't have that great a season in 1951. And New York also had a pretty good center fielder by the name of Mickey Mantle ready to succeed DiMaggio as a Yankee legend.

Still, it's interesting to note that DiMaggio may have accumulated even more impressive career stats had he only allowed himself to perform at anything less than his customary standards.

March 19—Kerry Wood

The big news this week was Kerry Wood's damaged elbow, an injury which will require surgery and end his 1999 campaign. The second-guessing of Cubs manager Jim Riggleman regarding his use of the 1998 National League Rookie of the Year began soon after the announcement was made.

At first glance, Wood didn't appear to be overworked last year. He threw five innings at Triple-A before pitching 166.2 innings for the Cubs. That hardly would seem like an abusive total. Eighty-seven pitchers threw more innings in the major leagues alone last year. But none was as young as Wood.

And that's the issue—whether Wood should have been handled more gently because of his youth. Conventional wisdom today posits that the typical pitcher's arm really doesn't mature until his mid-to-late '20s. Before then, a heavy workload might only beckon impending injuries.

Until relatively recently, innings pitched were just about the only tool we could use to measure a hurler's workload. But in the last decade or so pitch counts have become increasingly available.

The advantage of pitch counts is obvious when we consider that Wood needed 2,838 pitches to record his 166.2 innings last year. Brian Anderson, on the other hand, needed only 2,819 pitches to throw over 40 more innings (208.0). Clearly, Wood expended much more energy per inning than Anderson did.

STATS has been tracking game-by-game pitch counts for a while now. Unfortunately, similar information isn't readily accessible before the mid-80s. But that doesn't mean we can't do something to try to estimate those pitch counts. Given more than a decade's worth of information, you would think we could come up with some kind of formula that would provide a certain degree of accuracy.

So I looked at the average number of pitches that were required to generate three simple events in the 11 seasons since 1988—strikeouts, walks and hits. Here are the results:

Event	Pitches Per Event
Strikeouts	4.813
Walks	5.137
Hits	3.272

Keeping these rates in mind, it's possible to then compute the average number of pitches required to record all other non-strikeout outs. In other words, subtract all the pitches thrown while recording strikeouts, walks and hits from total pitches thrown, and then divide by (innings pitched minus strikeouts). By such a convention, we arrive at 3.1556 pitches per recorded non-strikeout out.

Thus, to estimate the number of pitches thrown by Bartolo Colon last year, we really need only four of his stats:

Event	Num	Rate	Pit
Strikeouts	158 *	4.813 =	760
Walks	79 *	5.137 =	406
Hits	205 *	3.272 =	671
Other outs	454 *	3.1556 =	1,433
Total			3,270

In actuality, Colon threw 3,285 pitches in 1998, a difference of 0.5 percent. Not all estimates are that close to reality, however. Greg Maddux, for instance, would have been expected to throw over 3,600 pitches in order to compile his statistical line. In point of fact, however, he required only 3,291, a difference of 9.5 percent.

Maddux is a rather unique case, though. He's such an efficient hurler that the pitch count formula consistently overestimates his workload. In fact, since 1995, four of the five largest formula discrepencies involved Maddux:

20 Largest Estimated Pitch Difference—1995-98

Player	Year	Est	Act	Diff
1) Greg Maddux	1996	3,484	3,029	15.0
2) Greg Maddux	1997	3,253	2,838	14.6
3) Greg Maddux	1995	2,884	2,621	10.0
4) Terry Mulholland	1996	3,072	2,805	9.5
5) Greg Maddux	1998	3,603	3,291	9.5
6) Esteban Loaiza	1995	2,729	2,502	9.1
7) Bob Wells	1996	2,090	2,296	-9.0
8) Mark Portugal	1998	2,520	2,314	8.9
9) Andy Ashby	1998	3,424	3,145	8.9
10) Bob Tewksbury	1996	3,119	2,872	8.6
11) Brian Meadows	1998	2,759	2,545	8.4
12) Aaron Sele	1996	2,689	2,927	-8.1
13) Wilson Alvarez	1996	3,562	3,863	-7.8
14) Rocky Coppinger	1996	2,076	2,249	-7.7
15) Paul Quantrill	1996	2,239	2,423	-7.6
16) Dave Mlicki	1995	2,526	2,732	-7.5
17) Sean Bergman	1998	2,609	2,427	7.5
18) Al Leiter	1997	2,554	2,758	-7.4
19) Fernando Valenzuela	1996	2,706	2,922	-7.4
20) Darren Dreifort	1998	2,835	2,640	7.4

(minimum 2,000 estimated pitches)

The total combined pitch count difference, at least for pitchers throwing a minimum of 2,000 estimated pitches in a season since 1995, was 0.7 percent. The average individual difference for this group, in absolute terms, was 3.1 percent. Not perfect, but seemingly reasonable.

There's a danger in placing too much confidence in the formula for previous generations of baseball history. I'm not sure if the rates discussed above can be applied to pre-DH eras. I'm also guessing there are ways to make the formula even more precise if we included more categories. But not all pitching categories are available for every season, and there's some advantage to keeping the formula rather simple.

I feel the formula can provide some insights on usage patterns in the past, and I'll likely be addressing those insights in the coming weeks. Maybe I'll even get around to using the information to discuss Kerry Wood's unfortunate injury.

March 26—Estimated Pitches Thrown

Last week, you might recall, I devised a formula that we can use to estimate the number of pitches thrown by hurlers during a season.

Now, pitch counts haven't become readily available until relatively recently. But STATS has been keeping track of them for over a decade. And since 1988, with a sample size consisting of hundreds of thousands of events, we've determined the average number of pitches resulting in these three outcomes:

Outcome	Pitches Per Outcome
Strikeouts	4.813
Walks	5.137
Hits	3.272

Knowing these rates, it's possible to then compute the average number of pitches required to record all other non-strikeout outs—3.1556.

Well now, if these rates are truly reliable from a historical perspective, they present a tremendous opportunity to gain insight on pitch counts through the years.

I want to be clear about that, and caution you about the uncertainty of what I've just measured. We really don't know (at least I don't) if these rates have remained constant throughout the various eras of baseball history.

Do we really think these rates were the same in the days before the DH? How about during the power-pitching dominated mid-60s? The offensive explosion of the 30s? The deadball era?

Well, I don't have an answer. I have no evidence to support the contention that the rates have remained constant. On the other hand, I have no evidence to indicate they definitely haven't.

So, for the sake of argument, and for the pure fascination of it, let's assume these rates *are* relatively accurate. What that would mean? Since the rules regarding three strikes and four balls didn't settle at those figures until 1889, we'll study only those decades since 1890.

As the first chart indicates, estimated pitches per nine innings remained fairly constant for the six decades between 1930 and 1989. In the 1990s, however, they've jumped a few pitches per game. But it's interesting to note how the rate of pitchers throwing at least 3,000 pitches per season has paradoxically decreased in recent years:

Pitchers Per 100 Teams by Estimated Pitch Count

Years	Est Pit / 9 IP	3000+	3500+	4000+	4500+	5000+
1890-1899	140.0	291.3	241.3	203.6	160.1	110.9
1900-1909	131.9	332.2	250.0	156.6	72.4	26.3
1910-1919	134.2	286.4	189.2	102.3	35.8	10.8
1920-1929	137.9	295.6	176.3	71.3	19.4	2.5
1930-1939	139.9	265.0	158.1	55.0	13.1	0.6
1940-1949	138.9	219.4	100.0	37.5	7.5	1.9
1950-1959	140.1	214.4	105.0	31.9	5.0	0.0
1960-1969	138.5	239.4	131.3	46.0	9.1	0.0
1970-1979	139.3	253.7	152.4	61.8	19.9	4.5
1980-1989	139.7	198.5	85.8	18.8	0.8	0.0
1990-1999	142.7	170.2	49.2	2.8	0.0	0.0

As you can see, the 1970s saw a big jump in the number of heavy workload occurrences. Pitchers threw at least an estimated 5,000 pitches in a single season on 11 occasions during the decade. That total exceeded the number reaching the 5,000 mark in the other 69 years since 1920 combined.

And 1970s hurlers dominate the list of the highest estimated pitch counts since the end of World War II. Here, I'll show the top 10:

Most Estimated Pitches—1946-98

Player	Year	Est
Bob Feller	1946	5,784
Mickey Lolich	1971	5,642
Nolan Ryan	1974	5,518
Wilbur Wood	1973	5,446
Phil Niekro	1977	5,435
Nolan Ryan	1973	5,332
Wilbur Wood	1972	5,329
Gaylord Perry	1973	5,272
Phil Niekro	1979	5,180
Nolan Ryan	1977	5,092

Nine of the 10 highest estimated pitch counts since 1946 occurred during the 1970s. Clearly, that kind of heavy workload has gotten rarer since that era. But even the burden carried by pitchers in the '70s would seem rather light compared to the workload bore by hurlers at the turn of the century:

Most Estimated Pitches

Decade	Entire Decade	Year	Single Season
1890-99	Kid Nichols (58,094)	1892	Bill Hutchison (9,250)
1900-09	Cy Young (45,933)	1904	Jack Chesbro (6,258)
1910-19	Walter Johnson (48,044)	1912	Ed Walsh (5,711)
1920-29	Burleigh Grimes (42,275)	1923	George Uhle (5,327)
1930-39	Red Ruffing (37,199)	1938	Bobo Newsom (5,575)
1940-49	Hal Newhouser (38,289)	1946	Bob Feller (5,784)
1950-59	Robin Roberts (43,124)	1953	Robin Roberts (4,983)
1960-69	Don Drysdale (38,791)	1965	Sandy Koufax (4,882)
		1969	Gaylord Perry (4,882)
1970-79	Phil Niekro (43,737)	1971	Mickey Lolich (5,642)
1980-89	Jack Morris (37,479)	1980	Steve Carlton (4,609)
1990-99	Greg Maddux (31,351)	1998	Curt Schilling (4,126)

To give you an idea about the grain of salt you may want to take with these figures, Roger Clemens actually has thrown the most pitches since 1990, with 32,073. Schilling really threw 4,213 pitches in 1998, not the 4,126 estimated here. Yes, that's a lot, but Clemens actually threw a decade-high 4,260 pitches in 1996.

Irregardless, Schilling's and Clemens' figures are both dwarfed by the season Bill Hutchison compiled in 1892. "Wild Bill" chucked an estimated 9,250 pitches while toiling a whopping 622 innings that year. No, his arm didn't fall off, but his effectiveness sure did. The next season, his ERA jumped by two runs, while his strikeout-walk ratio deteriorated from 312-190 to a pathetic 80-156.

He never really recovered, either, apparently becoming one of the very first victims of pitcher burnout.

April 3—Wohlers' Wildness

The story of Mark Wohlers has to be one of the most compelling of recent memory.

Four years ago, in 1995, Wohlers emerged as the closer for the World Champion Atlanta Braves. He saved 25 games during the regular season and another four in the postseason, including the deciding game of the World Series.

Three years ago, in 1996, Wohlers improved to 39 saves. He featured one of the best heaters in baseball, and fanned 11.6 batters per nine innings.

Two years ago, 1997, was more of the same—33 saves and 11.9 strikeouts per nine innings. But foreboding indicators loomed under the surface. Wohlers was much less effective in the season's second half, with his ERA jumping from 2.17 to 5.06 after the All-Star break. He was much more hittable too, as his average allowed rose from .172 to .278. Worse, his manager, Bobby Cox, seemed to lose confidence in him.

Wohlers got off to a deceptively decent start last year, saving his first seven opportunities while sporting a 1.93 ERA. But his control was precarious; he had walked nine batters and launched five wild pitches in only 9.1 innings. And then he went on the disabled list with a strained oblique muscle.

When he returned, Wohlers was a mess. His control had evaporated. He ended up walking 24 batters in his last 11 innings with the Braves. He also spent time at Triple-A Richmond, trying to somehow sort things out. Instead, he walked 36 in 12.1 innings there.

Not yet giving up, Wohlers came to spring training this year hoping to recapture the form that had made him so dominant such a short time ago. His progress has held continual drama this March and April. It seems like an ongoing soap opera. Almost every outing has been reported with his most important details—innings, walks and wild pitches.

One day Wohlers appears to have turned the corner and found his lost control. The next day he'll appear to be utterly clueness where his next pitch is going.

In his last outing, Wohlers walked five of the seven batters he faced and found the plate on only eight of his 31 pitches. This disheartening performance occurred only a day or two after Cox had implied that Wohlers would begin the season as the Braves' closer.

To be honest, I'm pulling for Wohlers to succeed. Nobody deserves the kind of torture he must be going through. It's gotta be a living hell to suddenly be unable to do the very thing which used to come so easily, a talent that had placed you among the best of your craft.

But the simple fact of the matter is, the odds don't appear to be in Wohlers' favor. The track record for pitchers who've suffered the kind of meltdown Wohlers has with his control is less than exemplary.

There really haven't been that many cases in baseball history which resemble Wohlers'. In fact, there have now been 11 instances in which an established big league hurler (minimum 250 previous career innings) has seen his walk rate increase by at least 150 percent from one season to the next. Wohlers' actually increased by 196 percent. To qualify, the pitcher had to work at least 15 innings both seasons, and he had to issue at least seven walks per nine innings in the year he collapsed.

There are a lot of numbers on this list. The first two lines for each player detail their walk rates in the year right before and the year of their control problems, as well as the ratio between the two walk rates. The next two lines for each pitcher are their career records before and after the year in question, with innings, W-L record, ERA, saves and walk rate included:

Walk Rate Increases by 150 Percent From One Year to the Next—1876-1998

Player	Age	Year	IP	BB	BB/9	BB/9 Ratio
Ferdie Schupp	26	1917	272.0	70	2.3	
	27	1918	33.1	27	7.3	3.15
Pre-1918:	496.0	31-10	2.10	2 Sv	2.7 BB/9	
Post-1918:	524.2	30-28	4.20	4 Sv	5.0 BB/9	
Jumbo Elliott	27	1928	192.0	64	3.0	
	28	1929	19.0	16	7.6	2.53
Pre-1929:	392.0	15-29	3.79	4 Sv	3.1 BB/9	
Post-1929:	795.2	47-43	4.41	8 Sv	3.0 BB/9	
Ewald Pyle	33	1944	164.0	68	3.7	
	34	1945	20.0	22	9.9	2.65
Pre-1945:	250.1	11-20	4.60	1 Sv	4.6 BB/9	
Post-1945:	0.0	0-0	—	0 Sv	— BB/9	
Ernie Broglio	28	1964	169.2	56	3.0	
	29	1965	50.2	46	8.2	2.75
Pre-1965:	1224.1	74-62	3.48	1 Sv	3.7 BB/9	
Post-1965:	62.1	2-6	6.35	1 Sv	5.5 BB/9	
Bill Parsons	23	1972	214.0	68	2.9	
	24	1973	59.2	67	10.1	3.53
Pre-1973:	458.2	26-30	3.53	0 Sv	3.2 BB/9	
Post-1973:	2.0	0-0	0.00	0 Sv	13.5 BB/9	
Rob Gardner	27	1972	97.0	28	2.6	
	28	1973	20.0	17	7.7	2.94
Pre-1973:	311.0	13-17	4.11	1 Sv	3.4 BB/9	
Post-1973:	0.0	0-0	—	0 Sv	— BB/9	
Steve Blass	30	1972	249.2	84	3.0	
	31	1973	88.2	84	8.5	2.82
Pre-1973:	1503.2	100-67	3.24	2 Sv	3.0 BB/9	
Post-1973:	5.0	0-0	9.00	0 Sv	12.6 BB/9	
Joe Decker	27	1974	248.2	97	3.5	
	28	1975	26.1	36	12.3	3.50
Pre-1975:	598.1	33-33	3.87	0 Sv	4.2 BB/9	
Post-1975:	85.1	2-8	4.96	0 Sv	6.9 BB/9	
Jim Palmer	37	1983	76.2	19	2.2	
	38	1984	17.2	17	8.7	3.88
Pre-1984:	3930.1	268-149	2.83	4 Sv	3.0 BB/9	
Post-1984:	0.0	0-0	—	0 Sv	— BB/9	
Dave Righetti	34	1993	47.1	17	3.2	
	35	1994	20.1	19	8.4	2.60
Pre-1994:	1334.0	79-76	3.33	252 Sv	3.7 BB/9	
Post-1994:	49.1	3-2	4.20	0 Sv	3.3 BB/9	
Mark Wohlers	27	1997	69.1	38	4.9	
	28	1998	20.1	33	14.6	2.96
Pre-1998:	365.1	31-21	3.33	104 Sv	4.1 BB/9	
Post-1998:	0.0	0-0	—	0 Sv	— BB/9	

(minimum 15 IP both years; 7.0 BB per 9 IP in second year; 250 IP before suffering wildness)

126

As you can see, of the last eight pitchers before Wohlers that appear on this list, *not one* pitched another 100 innings in the majors. Steve Blass probably is the most famous example. A year after appearing in the All-Star game he completely lost his effectiveness and would work in only one more big league game. Today of course, we refer to the malady from which Wohlers suffers as "Steve Blass Disease."

We remember Ernie Broglio mostly as one of the guys traded by the Cardinals to acquire Lou Brock in 1964. But Broglio's wildness in 1965 was one reason he won only three more games after turning 29.

Righetti and Palmer were both near the end of the line when their struggles occurred, but how about the cases of Joe Decker and Bill Parsons? Both were at ages in which they should have been entering their prime. Decker had won 16 games for the Twins in 1974, while Parsons won 13 games in each of his first two seasons with last-place Brewer clubs. Maybe they were hiding or pitching through injuries, but there's no denying the fact they simply couldn't seem to throw the ball over the plate. And their promising baseball careers were never the same.

To find the last pitcher on that list who subsequently enjoyed a successful career, you have to go back to Jumbo Elliott. Again, I'm not sure if Elliott had an injury in 1929, got too fat or just lost his control, but he did manage to rebound. He actually shared the National League lead with 19 victories in 1931.

Nevertheless, it's clear Elliott, and to some extent Schupp, were exceptions to the rule. We should keep that in mind as we witness the travails of Wohlers this season. Perhaps we shouldn't expect him to ever again be a dominant closer. For now, I'd simply settle for him being able to once again throw the ball and not having to worry about where it was going.

April 9—Assault on Aaron

This past Thursday we observed the 25th anniversary of the breaking of one of baseball's most cherished records.

At one time Babe Ruth's record of 714 lifetime homers looked like it might stand forever. But on April 8, 1974, Hammerin' Hank Aaron clubbed his 715th. Ever since, Aaron's total, which eventually reached 755, has looked just as insurmountable as Ruth's had.

But recent history has taught us that no home-run record is truly safe, especially in this tater-happy time.

It would probably be greedy to expect someone to break the single-season record this year, as Mark McGwire did in 1998 with his 70 roundtrippers. Still, McGwire and his compatriots are closing in on Aaron's total. And while they're all still a considerable distance from 755, it isn't too early to start preparing for the full-fledged assault.

In the most recent edition of the *STATS Baseball Scoreboard*, Bill James discussed this very topic. He estimated that there's an 83 percent chance that some active player will break

Aaron's record. I'm not going to present the same argument James did in his essay (if you haven't yet read his article, it's fascinating), but I will approach the topic from a different (simplified) angle.

The plain fact of the matter is that today there appears to be more players making impressive progress up the home-run charts than ever before. One simple way to measure this is to look at the number of players who have accumulated a certain amount of homers by a particular age.

For this study, I'll use this straightforward formula:

(age - 19) * 20   [minimum 20]

to check if a player has mustered a minimum number of homers at a certain age. For example, McGwire played last year at seasonal age 34. To qualify for inclusion at that age, he would have had to reach at least 300 career homers by the end of the '98 campaign ((34-19)*20 = 300). He actually finished with 457.

Proceeding the same way with every player last year, 22 sluggers managed to gain admission:

Career Home-Run Rate Qualifiers—1998

Player	Age	HR
Mark McGwire	34	457
Barry Bonds	33	411
Jose Canseco	33	397
Joe Carter	38	396
Cal Ripken Jr.	37	384
Fred McGriff	34	358
Ken Griffey Jr.	28	350
Albert Belle	31	321
Cecil Fielder	34	319
Rafael Palmeiro	33	314
Juan Gonzalez	28	301
Matt Williams	32	299
Frank Thomas	30	286
Sammy Sosa	29	273
Mo Vaughn	30	230
Jeff Bagwell	30	221
Gary Sheffield	29	202
Mike Piazza	29	200
Jim Thome	27	163
Manny Ramirez	26	154
Alex Rodriguez	22	106
Andruw Jones	21	54

((age - 19) * 20 and minimum 20)

It's apparent that some of these players have no chance at Aaron's record. Joe Carter has retired. Cal Ripken and Fred McGriff clearly are slowing down. Others, like Alex Rodriguez and Andruw Jones, have a long way to go before they start becoming serious threats. Nevertheless, those considerations exist every year. But never before have so many players, 22, qualified for the list. Until 1955, the high-water mark had been seven. Since then, it's gotten as high as 19, but the current level of 22 more than doubles the figure in 1984:

Career Home-Run Rate Qualifiers by Year

Year	Num	Year	Num	Year	Num	Year	Num
1959	15	1969	17	1979	13	1989	13
1960	14	1970	17	1980	11	1990	13
1961	15	1971	19	1981	10	1991	14
1962	14	1972	16	1982	10	1992	15
1963	15	1973	18	1983	9	1993	15
1964	16	1974	15	1984	10	1994	15
1965	17	1975	12	1985	12	1995	16
1966	16	1976	11	1986	12	1996	17
1967	16	1977	12	1987	14	1997	18
1968	16	1978	13	1988	13	1998	22

If you'd like to compare the class of 1971, the previous top group, with the current crop of contenders and pretenders, here's 1971's complete list:

Career Home-Run Rate Qualifiers—1971

Player	Age	HR	Final
Willie Mays	40	646	660
Hank Aaron	37	639	755
Harmon Killebrew	35	515	573
Ernie Banks	40	512	512
Frank Robinson	35	503	586
Willie McCovey	33	370	521
Al Kaline	36	366	399
Frank Howard	34	360	382
Orlando Cepeda	33	354	379
Billy Williams	33	319	426
Ron Santo	31	300	342
Boog Powell	29	259	339
Carl Yastrzemski	31	257	452
Willie Stargell	31	244	475
Dick Allen	29	234	351
Willie Horton	28	180	325
Tony Conigliaro	26	164	166
Reggie Jackson	25	132	563
Johnny Bench	23	114	389

As you can see, Ernie Banks retired in '71. Frank Howard, Orlando Cepeda and others were slowing down. Tony Conigliaro's tragic career would soon end. And Johnny Bench couldn't sustain his impressive start, worn down in part by the demands of catching.

Nevertheless, out of that group would emerge the eventual home-run champ—Hank Aaron. Now, Hank clearly had an advantage, having blasted 182 more homers through 1971 than McGwire had through 1998. On the other hand, Aaron was also three years older.

The class of '98 also boasts better "young" contenders. The 1971 group doesn't have anyone in the prime of their careers who were setting the kind of pace that Ken Griffey (age 28, 350 HR), Juan Gonzalez (28, 301) and Sammy Sosa (29, 273) now are. And those are the players, along with McGwire, who will likely make the most serious push at 600 homers and beyond. So yes, we salute Aaron on the anniversary of his tremendous achievement. And it'll be fun over the next few years to witness others trying to make history.

April 17—Sosa's Mastery

Evidently all Sammy Sosa needed to get back on track was a close encounter with the Brewers. He sure got healthy in a hurry in his first matchup against Milwaukee. Sosa entered Friday's opener against the Brewers with just five hits in 28 at-bats (.179) this year. But he nearly doubled that hit total when he went 4-for-4 in a 9-4 Cubs victory in Game 1.

Included in the hitting spree was Sosa's second homer of the season, a blast hardly surprising considering the power display he unleashed on Milwaukee pitching last year. In case you don't remember, Sosa was an absolute terror against the Brew Crew in 1998, clubbing 12 homers in 45 at-bats. He slugged a whopping 1.178, and his isolated power (slugging minus batting average) was an even .800.

In the last dozen years, no player ever has generated the kind of offensive fireworks against one team that Sosa produced versus Milwaukee:

Highest Isolated Power Average vs. One Team, Season—1987-98

Player	Year	vs.	Iso
Sammy Sosa	**1998**	**Milwaukee**	**.800**
Jay Buhner	1995	Minnesota	.778
Jose Canseco	1994	Boston	.731
Lee Stevens	1998	Seattle	.720
Dante Bichette	1996	Cincinnati	.718
Jeff Bagwell	1994	San Francisco	.714
Barry Bonds	1994	Cincinnati	.710
Tim Salmon	1998	Cleveland	.707
Rickey Henderson	1987	Cleveland	.704
Reggie Jefferson	1996	Detroit	.694

(minimum 25 AB)

If Sosa's performance last year, which he extended on Friday, is any indication, it could be a long weekend for the Brewers.

April 23—Mike Caruso

One of the nicest surprises of last season was the way rookie Mike Caruso seized control of the White Sox shortstop position. After having never played above the Class-A level before 1998, Caruso performed better than we realistically should have expected, batting .306 and scoring 81 runs in 133 games.

Despite the auspicious debut, there were clear warning signs that Caruso might experience growing pains in his sophomore season.

First, he looked at times as though he could have the bat knocked out of his hands. His isolated power ranked as one of the lowest in the American League—a puny .084.

Even worse, he showed an alarming lack of patience. He walked a grand total of 14 times in 555 plate appearances, the poorest rate among qualifiers.

Although he still managed to hit .300 last year, you would think opposing pitchers would eventually catch on to Caruso's anemic plate discipline, and begin to work him accordingly. Sure enough, Caruso has gotten off to a tough start in '99, though it's dangerous to read too much into just two or three weeks.

Nevertheless, I thought it might be interesting to see how other players in Caruso's situation have fared in the past. To qualify for inclusion, the player had to accumulate at least 500 plate appearances in his first full big league season. He also had to hit .300 or better that year, and walk fewer than once every 20 plate appearances.

Caruso was actually the 11th such player since 1940:

First-Year Players With a .300 Average and a Walk Rate No Higher Than .050—1940-98

Player	Year	Avg	BB Rate	Yr+1 Avg	After 1stYear
Bama Rowell	1940	.305	.035	.267	.268
Phil Rizzuto	1941	.307	.049	.284	.270
Dale Mitchell	1947	.316	.044	.336	.310
Al Dark	1948	.322	.041	.276	.287
Orlando Cepeda	1958	.312	.045	.317	.295
Tony Oliva	1964	.323	.047	.321	.302
Bob Bailor	1977	.310	.033	.264	.255
Benito Santiago	1987	.300	.028	.248	.256
Doug Glanville	1997	.300	.047	.279	.281
Nomar Garciaparra	1997	.306	.048	.323	.320
Mike Caruso	**1998**	**.306**	**.025**	—	—

(minimum 500 PA; maximum 100 previous PA)

As you can see, Caruso's limited plate discipline in his first full season doesn't necessarily doom him to a mediocre career. Phil Rizzuto and Orlando Cepeda have both been elected to the Hall of Fame. Tony Oliva might eventually.

But not everyone on the list has succeeded. Like Caruso, Bama Rowell and Bob Bailor complemented a weak walk rate with limited power. And neither one managed to ever match his rookie batting averages, though Rowell's career was interrupted by World War II.

Furthermore, three of the other 10 players on the above list saw their batting average decline in Year 2. In fairness, however, it's not necessarily easy to improve on a .300 average.

I find it interesting to note that players at the other extreme aren't guaranteed long and illustrious careers, either. Here's the list of those players since 1940 whose first full season was accompanied by not only a .300 average, but also a walk rate of .100 or better:

First-Year Players With a .300 Average and a Walk Rate No Higher Than .100—1940-98

Player	Year	Avg	BB Rate	Yr+1 Avg	After 1stYear
Stan Musial	1942	.315	.116	.357	.331
Richie Ashburn	1948	.333	.113	.284	.306
Larry Doby	1948	.301	.108	.280	.283
Billy Goodman	1948	.310	.140	.298	.299
Roy Sievers	1949	.306	.128	.238	.264
Minnie Minoso	1951	.326	.116	.281	.296
Jim Finigan	1954	.302	.114	.255	.247
Richie Hebner	1969	.301	.100	.290	.274
Thurman Munson	1970	.302	.108	.251	.291
Greg Gross	1974	.314	.112	.294	.282
Fred Lynn	1975	.331	.102	.314	.278
Mitchell Page	1977	.307	.132	.285	.253

As good as Stan Musial, Richie Ashburn and Larry Doby were, Jim Finigan, Greg Gross and Mitchell Page didn't enjoy particularly impressive careers. And interestingly, only Musial managed to improve his batting average in Year 2.

Even when Caruso batted .300 last year, it was an empty .300, with no power or walks to accompany it. If he does indeed struggle in 1999, it may be difficult to justify his spot in the lineup.

April 30—April Shellackings

Toronto Blue Jay righthander Roy Halladay entered Thursday night's start against the Anaheim Angels sporting a pristine ERA of 0.00. The Blue Jay rookie had not yet allowed an earned run through his first 20 innings of work this season.

But boy, how quickly things can change.

Halladay could barely survive a first-inning barrage by the Angels, surrendering seven runs on five hits, two walks and a hit batsman. By the time Randy Velarde smacked a three-run homer in the third, Halladay had seen 11 Angels cross the plate and his ERA balloon to 4.43. Now, that's just the kind of outing we've come to expect from Mel Rojas. Check out the disturbing trend with Rojas' ERA the past few years:

Mel Rojas' ERA by Year

Year	ERA
1992	1.43
1993	2.95
1994	3.32
1995	4.12
1996	3.22
1997	4.64
1998	6.05

With the exception of 1996, that's not the kind of progression which engenders much career security. And sure enough, Rojas began this season with the Dodgers, his fourth organization in the past four years.

He lasted all of five innings with the Dodgers, getting rocked for three homers and a 12.60 ERA before LA cut its losses and sent him packing to Detroit. In the American League for the first time, Rojas emerged unscathed through his first three appearances.

But then came Thursday night.

The Seattle Mariners abused the righthanded reliever with 11 runs in just 1.2 innings. Ken Griffey Jr. clubbed two homers himself, as Rojas' ERA exploded to 17.47.

While it's possible to see those kind of offensive fireworks anytime Rojas takes the mound, it's also true that such an outing appears more likely early in the season. Since 1994, there have been 21 occasions in which a pitcher has allowed at least 11 runs in one game. Ten of those performances have occurred during the month of April:

Pitchers Allowing 11-Plus Runs in One Outing—1994-99

Month	11+ Runs
April	10
May	3
June	1
July	3
August	4
September	0
Total	21

Now, it may seem that these results are skewed a little bit by the fact that we've now had six Aprils since 1994, as opposed to five of each of the other months. And, in fact, there was no September, and only half of August, in strike-shortened 1994. Then again, almost all of April was wiped out in 1995. So the numbers above appear valid.

There may be a number of factors which have contributed to this condition. Just speculating, but it's possible that managers are less reluctant to allow their pitchers to absorb a beating early in the season, in an effort to spare a pitching staff whose stamina may not yet be in midseason form.

I remember Mike Busby of the Cardinals absorbing a 13-run pounding at the hands of the Braves in April of 1996. The Cardinal bullpen had worked over 17 innings in the previous three games, including two extra-inning affairs. And Tony LaRussa used Busby as a sort of sacrificial lamb.

It's possible that a "short" bullpen isn't quite as big a concern later in the season, at least not in September, when rosters expand to 40 players. Sure enough, no pitcher has allowed 11 runs in a September appearance in the 12 years since STATS began compiling the data.

It might just be dumb luck, too, that so many miserable performances have occurred in April. Nevertheless, whatever the reason, it appears April and Mel Rojas are a volatile combination.

May 7—Billy Wagner

This past Wednesday, Billy Wagner delivered the kind of performance any team would like from its closer. He entered the fray with two outs in the eighth inning, trying to protect a 5-4 lead against the Mets.

The Mets were threatening, having put runners on first and second. But Wagner quickly doused the fire. Four batters. Four strikeouts.

The last hitter, Roger Cedeno, swung and missed at three straight pitches. Good morning. Good afternoon. Good night.

All told, Wagner threw strikes with 12 of his 15 pitches. Seven of them resulted in swinging strikes. Any pitcher is virtually guaranteed to be successful with that kind of swinging-strike-to-ball ratio.

As it turns out, Wagner isn't even the major league leader in this category, though he's close. Robb Nen of the San Francisco Giants ranks first on the list:

Highest Swinging Strike-Ball Ratio—1999

Pitcher	Swing & Miss	Ball	Ratio
Robb Nen	54	74	.730
Billy Wagner	**50**	**74**	**.676**
Ugueth Urbina	42	72	.583

Pitcher	Swing & Miss	Ball	Ratio
Armando Benitez	45	81	.556
Trevor Hoffman	26	48	.542
Scott Elarton	51	97	.526
Dan Plesac	42	81	.519
Rudy Seanez	26	53	.491
Jon Lieber	41	84	.488
Randy Johnson	141	297	.475

(minimum 10 IP)

Most of the hurlers on the above list are fireballing relievers, which shouldn't be too surprising. Their task usually consists of throwing as hard as they can for relatively brief bursts. A reliever who can't throw strikes is quickly replaced, while those who can make opposing batters miss often become closers.

With that in mind, Randy Johnson's ranking becomes even more impressive. The Big Unit has already made batters swing and miss 141 times this season. That's 28 percent greater than the next-highest total, registered by Pedro Martinez (110). No other pitcher is above 89.

At the opposite end of the spectrum are these hurlers. Opposing batters rarely fail to get some kind of wood on their offerings, especially in proportion to the number of balls off the plate:

Lowest Swinging Strike-Ball Ratio—1999

Pitcher	Swing & Miss	Ball	Ratio
Kirk Rueter	17	226	.075
Jay Witasick	11	125	.088
Jim Pittsley	13	134	.097
Jose Santiago	8	81	.099
Jim Mecir	15	148	.101
Scott Karl	25	241	.104
Mike Lincoln	21	202	.104
Jeff Suppan	23	215	.107
Mike Busby	10	93	.108
Alex Fernandez	13	115	.113

Considering that the major league average this year is .232, you can see how low these pitchers rank. Rueter's rate is roughly one-third of "normal."

While it isn't out of the question for pitchers with weak ratios to be successful, it's unlikely we'll find them saving many games, either. For that particular task, the responsibility usually falls to Wagner, Nen & Co.

May 14—Tony Gwynn

Sometime in the next month, assuming he stays healthy, Tony Gwynn almost certainly will reach the 3,000-hit plateau. Gwynn entered this weekend sitting on 2,970, just 30 shy of the magical mark.

In last week's issue of *The Sporting News*, Gwynn confessed that he won't necessarily be satisfied with becoming only the 21st player in major league history to lash 3,000 hits (or 22nd, depending on your interpretation of Cap Anson's final total). "I'll be thinking about 4,000," is what Tony was quoted as saying.

And who's to say 4,000 is unattainable? He certainly shows few signs of slowing down. He hasn't hit below .309 since 1982. He's won four of the past five National League batting titles. And he's off to another hot start in 1999, chugging along at a .365 clip.

But let's take a realistic look at Gwynn's chances. He finished last year at seasonal age 38 (he just turned 39 on May 9) with 2,928 hits. Only 13 other players in MLB history had generated more by the same age:

Career Hits by Age 38

Player	Age	Year	Hits
Ty Cobb	38	1925	3,822
Hank Aaron	38	1972	3,391
Pete Rose	38	1979	3,372
Tris Speaker	38	1926	3,292
Stan Musial	38	1959	3,203
Robin Yount	37	1993	3,142
Eddie Collins	38	1925	3,096
Roberto Clemente	37	1972	3,000
Sam Crawford	37	1917	2,961
Paul Waner	38	1941	2,956
Willie Keeler	38	1910	2,932
Eddie Murray	38	1994	2,930
Rod Carew	38	1984	2,929
Tony Gwynn	**38**	**1998**	**2,928**
Willie Mays	38	1969	2,926

As you can see, Gwynn is far behind the pace that was being set by the only other players who wound up getting to 4,000. Pete Rose (3,372) was at least two years ahead, having collected 444 more hits at the same age. And Ty Cobb (3,822) was in another area code, having produced four to five more seasons worth of hits (894) by age 38.

That doesn't necessarily preclude Gwynn from dreaming of 4,000, as long as he keeps producing. But if he truly has 1,072 hits left in his bat after seasonal age 38, he'll certainly set a new standard for life as a "golden oldie."

No other player in MLB annals ever collected even 1,000 hits after 38, so Gwynn clearly would be bucking history:

	Career Hits After Age 38			
Player	**Age 38**	**Final Tot**	**Dif**	**Final Age**
Cap Anson	2,016	2,995	979	45
Pete Rose	3,372	4,256	884	45
Sam Rice	2,237	2,987	750	44
Luke Appling	2,081	2,749	668	43
Jim O'Rourke	1,674	2,304	630	53
Honus Wagner	2,812	3,415	603	43
Carlton Fisk	1,767	2,356	589	45
Dave Winfield	2,548	3,110	562	43
Carl Yastrzemski	2,869	3,419	550	43
Paul Molitor	2,789	3,319	530	41
Deacon White	1,155	1,619	464	42
Joe Start	574	1,031	457	43
Stan Musial	3,203	3,630	427	42
Darrell Evans	1,825	2,223	398	42
Rabbit Maranville	2,211	2,605	394	43
Hank Aaron	3,391	3,771	380	42
Ty Cobb	3,822	4,190	368	41
Willie Mays	2,926	3,283	357	42
Nap Lajoie	2,892	3,242	350	41
Bob Boone	1,501	1,838	337	42

Gwynn has his work cut out for him in his quest for 4,000. While I wouldn't put the accomplishment past him considering his remarkable talent, he might want to savor the moment when he arrives at 3,000. It more than likely will be the last round number he gets to.

May 21—Greg Maddux

Has there been a more surprising development this season than the confirmation of Greg Maddux' mortality?

After winning four Cy Young awards and averaging 18 wins a year since 1992, Maddux has gotten off to a sputtering start in 1999. His ERA has more than doubled since last season, climbing to an alarming 5.02.

But if you really want to be shocked, check out the National League trailers in average allowed:

Highest Batting Average Allowed, NL—1999

Player	IP	H	AB	Avg
Greg Maddux	**57.1**	**88**	**251**	**.351**
Chris Peters	30.1	46	133	.346
Carl Pavano	39.1	56	164	.341
Chris Holt	34.1	46	139	.331
Jason Bere	31.1	40	123	.325
Kirk Rueter	43.2	59	185	.319
Rafael Roque	34.0	43	135	.319
Sean Bergman	43.0	53	168	.315
Stan Spencer	32.2	42	137	.307
Brian Meadows	53.1	68	222	.306

(minimum 30 IP)

And even this doesn't convey the struggles Maddux has endured in recent outings. He had looked like his usual dominating self when he opened 4-0 with a 2.73 ERA in April.

But May has been anything but merry for him, as he seemingly has turned into Jaime Navarro overnight. Maddux has gone winless in four starts this month, posting an ERA of 8.14 and surrendering 45 hits in 24 innings. In other words, he's turned the typical batter he's faced into the 1941 version of Ted Williams, since the league is hitting .409 against him in May.

But let's put that .351 overall average into even greater perspective. Remember, the league hit only .220 versus Maddux in 1998. So the typical hitter has gone from being Charles Johnson one year to Tony Gwynn the next, improving by 131 points.

That would almost be unheard of, should Maddux continue to struggle like this all season. Opponent at-bats are available for every pitcher since 1916. And since then, only one other hurler has ever lost his effectiveness in a one-year span to the degree that Maddux has:

Batting Avg. Allowed Increase From One Season to Next—1916-99

Player	Years	Yr1	Yr2	Diff
Jim McDonald	1954-55	.213	.345	.132
Greg Maddux	**1998-99**	**.220**	**.351**	**.131**
Terrell Wade	1996-97	.227	.349	.122
Red Ruffing	1946-47	.171	.290	.119
Mike Torrez	1983-84	.271	.388	.117
Moose Haas	1986-87	.218	.335	.117
Danny McDevitt	1957-58	.238	.355	.117
Steve Comer	1979-80	.252	.367	.116
Joe Genewich	1928-29	.249	.359	.111
Tony Kaufmann	1926-27	.262	.371	.108

(minimum 8 starts both seasons)

Now, it would be a huge upset if Maddux continues to scuffle as he has. Whatever changes the umpires have made to the strike zone may be contributing to Greg's troubles. But you've gotta believe a player with his pitching smarts eventually will make the necessary adjustments.

In the meantime, it'll be interesting to see how one of the truly all-time greats reacts to and attempts to overcome his first real encounter with adversity in roughly a decade.

May 28—Mike Lieberthal

We're nearly two months into the season, so we've had plenty of time for players to accumulate enough at-bats so that their stats now mean something. But that doesn't necessarily imply that their stats aren't misleading.

Some players are hitting over their heads, while others still are trying to overcome slumps. Among players in the former category, Mike Lieberthal may be the most extreme example. His OPS is 324 points higher this year than last:

Biggest OPS Improvement—1998-99

Player	1998	1999	Diff
Mike Lieberthal	**.703**	**1.028**	**.324**
Sean Casey	.782	1.105	.323
Fred McGriff	.815	1.102	.287
Fernando Tatis	.744	1.021	.277
Luis Gonzalez	.816	1.091	.276
Butch Huskey	.707	.957	.250
Charles Johnson	.670	.915	.245
Ed Sprague	.683	.919	.235
John Flaherty	.534	.767	.233
Jose Canseco	.836	1.063	.227

(minimum 300 PA in 1998 and 100 PA in 1999)

Now, it's unclear how many of the players on the above list may actually have achieved a new level of ability. Guys like Casey and Tatis may, in fact, be something close to this good. But others, like McGriff and Sprague, are likely to eventually come crashing down.

At the other extreme is Ben Grieve. Last year he was a rising star. Today he's experiencing a horrific sophomore slump:

Biggest OPS Decline—1998-99

Player	1998	1999	Diff
Ben Grieve	.844	.526	-.318
Gary Gaetti	.852	.592	-.259
Tony Clark	.880	.620	-.259

Player	1998	1999	Diff
Greg Vaughn	.960	.720	-.240
Charlie Hayes	.770	.536	-.234
Otis Nixon	.705	.482	-.222
Mark McGwire	1.222	1.010	-.212
Albert Belle	1.055	.850	-.205
Scott Brosius	.843	.641	-.202
Sean Berry	.895	.695	-.200

How about McGwire? He's suffered a 212-point dip in his OPS, yet it's still above 1.000. That's the kind of slump all players should be so fortunate to have.

And what about Brosius? It's an odd year, so I guess that means he's due for a poor campaign.

It'll be interesting to see how many of these players right their ships by the end of the season. Something tells me Grieve won't finish with an OPS that would make Rey Ordonez blush.

June 10—Rickey Henderson

Rickey Henderson has made it known in the past that one of his career goals is to set the all-time runs scored record.

He's already one of only six players in major league history to cross the plate 2,000 times. And Ty Cobb's mark of 2,245 runs is within his sights. Nevertheless, if Rickey hopes to catch the Georgia Peach, Henderson better pick up the pace.

The Mets left fielder scored 101 runs for the A's last year. That increased his total to 2,014 entering the 1999 campaign. But at age 39, the "Favorite Toy" or "Career Projections" pegged Rickey's chances of passing Cobb at just 12.6 percent:

Chance of Reaching 2,246 Career Runs				
Player	Age	Thru 1998	Rate	Chance
Ken Griffey Jr.	28	940	122.5	15.7%
Alex Rodriguez	22	383	118.3	13.5%
Rickey Henderson	**39**	**2,014**	**96.8**	**12.6%**
Barry Bonds	33	1,364	121.3	11.9%
Derek Jeter	24	352	119.5	6.8%
Chuck Knoblauch	29	830	120.8	5.5%
Craig Biggio	32	997	129.0	1.6%

As you can see, Rickey's recent run rate has fallen beneath 100. And as he nears the end of his fabulous career, the Career Projections figured he enjoyed only a 1-in-8 chance of surpassing Cobb.

Henderson can certainly defy those odds, but he needs to stay healthy. He's been dogged by injuries throughout his career, and spent time on the disabled list with a sore knee this spring.

As a result, Rickey has played in only 32 of the Mets' 59 games this season, and has scored only 18 runs. If he maintains that pace all year, he would wind up with a total of 49. A sum like that would erase him from the above chart.

So he needs to put the pedal to the metal.

Another record that Henderson is chasing is career walks. But there, he's putting on an impressive finishing kick.

He entered 1999 with 1,890 career free passes, well within range of Babe Ruth's lifetime total of 2,057. Career Projections gave him roughly a 50-50 shot at catching the Bambino:

Chance of Reaching 2,057 Career Walks

Player	Age	Thru 1998	Rate	Chance
Rickey Henderson	**39**	**1,890**	**112.2**	**50.7%**
Barry Bonds	33	1,357	138.5	39.0%
Frank Thomas	30	989	109.5	11.5%
Jeff Bagwell	30	736	119.3	4.2%
Mark McGwire	34	1,052	134.0	3.3%
Gary Sheffield	29	656	111.5	1.7%
Jim Thome	27	519	105.0	1.2%

Henderson always has been able to draw walks, and his batting eye hasn't diminished as he's gotten older. He led the American League with 118 free passes last year, and has drawn 32 walks in 32 games in 1999.

Assuming he continues to play and draw walks at the same rates, Henderson will finish the campaign with 88 of each, just 78 walks behind Ruth's total. Player Projections would boost Rickey's chances to 76 percent.

While Henderson surely would welcome holding yet another record, he might enjoy a relatively brief tenure as history's greatest walk man. Barry Bonds actually was ahead of Henderson's pace at age 33, so he clearly has a chance of eventually owning the record himself.

June 18—Cleveland Indians

Just yesterday, it seems, the Cleveland Indians were a pennant-race afterthought.

Pennant fever? Cleveland fans never caught the bug. Instead, the Indians were infected with a virulent case of "The Curse of Colavito."

Rocky Colavito, a fan favorite in Cleveland, was traded to the Tigers just before the beginning of the 1960 campaign. In the 34 years immediately thereafter, the Indians managed to finish within 10 games of the lead on only one occasion. And that was in 1981, when a strike divided the season into two halves.

Between 1960 and 1993, the Indians finished a combined 767.5 games behind their league or division winners. That was the worst performance by any team over the same period:

Greatest Cumulative Trail—1960-93

	Team	Years	Trail
	Indians	1960-93	-767.5
#	Senators/Rangers	1961-93	-750.5
	Cubs	1960-93	-632.0
#	Mets	1962-93	-611.0
#	Angels	1961-93	-575.5

(#—expansion team)

A typical Indian summer consisted of the Indians falling out of contention around the 4th of July, and ending the season over 22 games out of first place.

Ah, the bad old days. They're now a distant memory. Today, the Indians are the big, bad bullies of the American League Central Division.

The Tribe has captured its division championship each of the past four seasons. They've rarely been challenged, winning the titles by 30, 14.5, six and nine games in successive years.

Cleveland jumped into another commanding lead in 1999, pushing its advantage to double digits by June. When we combine their margins the past five years, the Indians boast a whopping 69.5-game cushion over their respective second-place challengers. No other team in baseball history has compiled such a log over a five-year span:

Teams Enjoying Greatest Cumulative Lead Over a 5-Year Period—1951-99

Team	Years	Lead
Indians	**1995-99**	**69.5**
Braves	1995-99	60.0
Indians	1994-98	58.5
Braves	1994-98	50.0
Orioles	1969-73	49.0
Reds	1972-76	40.0
Athletics	1971-75	39.5
Braves	1993-97	33.0
Yankees	1960-64	32.5
Braves	1992-96	32.0
Orioles	1970-74	32.0

As you can see, the Indians haven't yet cemented their grasp on the top spot of this chart, since the Braves continue to hold a virtual death-grip on the National League East Division lead. But Atlanta either will have to pick up the pace, or Clevelend will have to slow down, in order for the Braves to overtake the Indians.

Now, you surely noticed how many teams of recent vintage reside on the above list. Clearly, when the American and National Leagues both split into two divisions in 1969, and then again into three in 1994, it reduced the competition for the very best teams.

Instead of having to outperform the second-best club in their league, teams today only have to outdistance the second-best club in their division. To give you an idea what that means, let's refigure the above numbers, this time comparing teams from a full league perspective.

Going back to the turn of the century, one team dominates the top 10:

Teams Enjoying Greatest Cumulative League Lead Over a 5-Year Period—1900-99

Team	Years	Lead
Yankees	1936-40	57.0
Yankees	1935-39	56.0
Yankees	1939-43	54.5
Yankees	1937-41	54.5
Yankees	1938-42	50.5
Cubs	1906-10	44.5
Cardinals	1942-46	33.5
Yankees	1960-64	32.5
Yankees	1934-38	32.0
Yankees	1940-44	31.5

Beginning in 1936, the Bronx Bombers won 22 of the next 29 American League pennants. And judging by the above chart, they earned them.

Where are the 1995-99 Indians? Nowhere to be found. And the descendent of those great Yankee teams is a big reason why.

While the Indians' 89-73 record last year was good enough to outdistance the White Sox by nine lengths, it paled in comparison to the Yankees' 114-48 ledger. In fact, the Indians have been a cumulative 15 games back since 1995, hardly an estimable figure.

The Yankees actually have surpassed Cleveland over the same period, rating a combined 8.5 games back since 1995. But even that is dwarfed by Atlanta's performance. The Braves are a combined 23 games *ahead* of the National League over this timespan, and it's conceivable they could enter the top 10 with a terrific 1999.

So as far as the Indians are concerned, while it looks like 1999 will be yet another season in which they capture the AL Central going away, they probably shouldn't get overly excited. Until they prove otherwise, the Indians just might be big fish in a small pond.

June 25—National League Rookie of the Year?

As we approach the end of June, no National League rookie has emerged as the obvious favorite to capture Rookie of the Year honors.

J.D. Drew was the frontrunner entering the season, but injuries and a defective batting stroke have landed him back at Triple-A Memphis.

Other rookies like Florida shortstop Alex Gonzalez, Montreal catcher/third baseman Michael Barrett and St. Louis utilityman Joe McEwing have enjoyed promising beginnings to their careers.

But if a lefthander recently promoted by the Phillies can continue to pitch as effectively as he's started out, the NL Rookie of the Year will be a foregone conclusion.

The Phillies selected Randy Wolf in the second round of the 1997 draft, and he ripped through the minors in less than two years. But even the most optimistic Phillies fan couldn't have expected such an impressive debut:

Daily Pitching Log for Randy Wolf

Date	Opp	W-L	IP	H	R	ER	BB	SO	ERA
6/11/99	Tor	1-0	5.2	6	1	1	3	6	
6/16/99	@SD	1-0	8.0	5	2	1	2	7	
6/22/99	Pit	1-0	7.0	4	2	2	3	8	
Totals		3-0	20.2	15	5	4	8	21	1.74

You certainly can't complain about those pitching lines. Wolf came within one out in his initial appearance from having tossed three straight quality starts. And his peripheral stats have been impressive, too, with more strikeouts than innings pitched and a .200 opponents' batting average allowed.

Wolf's coming out party ranks among the finest by any pitcher over the last decade. Using "gamescores" as the measuring stick, Wolf has fashioned scores of 56, 71 and 66 in successive outings. That's an average of 64.3, and only 14 other hurlers have surpassed that mark in their first three starts since 1987:

Best Pitching Performance in First 3 Games—1987-99

Player	Year	Gm 1	Gm 2	Gm 3	Avg
Bob Milacki	1988	80	65	89	78.0
Pat Combs	1989	65	66	81	70.7
Orlando Hernandez	1998	68	83	61	70.7

Player	Year	Gm 1	Gm 2	Gm 3	Avg
Tim Wakefield	1992	76	63	72	70.3
Joe Magrane	1987	60	63	82	68.3
Jack McDowell	1987	72	55	77	68.0
Dennis Cook	1988	63	48	89	66.7
Randy Tomlin	1990	77	65	55	65.7
Rene Arocha	1993	68	64	65	65.7
Kirk Rueter	1993	81	64	52	65.7
Sam Militello	1992	77	63	56	65.3
Jimmy Haynes	1995	68	68	60	65.3
Erik Hanson	1988	63	75	56	64.7
Aaron Sele	1993	71	48	75	64.7
Randy Wolf	1999	56	71	66	64.3

(based on gamescores; all appearances must be starts)

I find this list rather surprising, for two reasons:

1) the presence of Milacki in the No. 1 spot, and

2) the absence of truly dominant hurlers.

No one really is even close to Milacki. Considering his rather pedestrian career, you'd be forgiven if you had forgotten about his sensational start. But he was one of the biggest highlights during the Orioles' miserable 1988 campaign.

Baltimore was already 51-95 when Milacki made his major league debut on September 18. He held the Tigers to only one hit over eight innings in a 2-0 victory. He wasn't quite as dominant in his next start, but he was still good enough to limit the Tigers to five hits and two runs in a 5-4 Oriole triumph. And he was at his best in his third start, striking out 10 while permitting just three hits in a 2-0 complete-game win over the Yankees. Those three victories were the only ones Baltimore registered in their final 20 contests.

Add it up, and Milacki had averaged a gamescore of 78. Unfortunately, it was generally downhill from there. Milacki would reach 10 strikeouts on only one other occasion, and he never again would produce a gamescore above 83.

But Milacki's experience certainly was not unique among the other pitchers on the above list. As the following chart shows, many of them subsequently endured mediocre if not downright disappointing careers:

Best Pitching Performance in First 3 Games—1987-99

Player	Year	1st 3 Avg	Rest of Year	Rest of Career
Bob Milacki	1988	78.0	0-0, —	37-47, 4.50
Pat Combs	1989	70.7	2-0, 4.32	15-17, 4.52
Orlando Hernandez	1998	70.7	10-4, 3.45	18-10, 3.71

Player	Year	1st 3 Avg	Rest of Year	Rest of Career
Tim Wakefield	1992	70.3	6-1, 2.55	74-62, 4.35
Joe Magrane	1987	68.3	7-7, 3.91	55-67, 3.86
Jack McDowell	1987	68.0	1-0, 3.52	125-83, 3.84
Dennis Cook	1988	66.7	0-1, 12.27	50-37, 3.80
Randy Tomlin	1990	65.7	3-3, 2.82	29-30, 3.49
Rene Arocha	1993	65.7	8-8, 4.06	15-17, 4.28
Kirk Rueter	1993	65.7	7-0, 3.44	60-32, 4.14
Sam Militello	1992	65.3	1-3, 3.99	2-4, 4.53
Jimmy Haynes	1995	65.3	0-0, 0.00	22-27, 5.61
Erik Hanson	1988	64.7	1-1, 4.74	88-82, 4.18
Aaron Sele	1993	64.7	6-2, 3.07	63-49, 4.54
Randy Wolf	1999	64.3	0-0, —	0-0, —
Totals			**52-30, 3.61**	**653-564, 4.15**

How many of those pitchers developed into stars? Jack McDowell probably comes the closest, having won a Cy Young Award, but even he would be stretching the definition. While Orlando Hernandez has a chance for a fine career, it's still too early to determine his ultimate value.

Kirk Rueter actually has generated the top career winning percentage (other than Hernandez and Wolf) among the hurlers represented on the chart, but he hardly qualifies as a staff ace.

Oh by the way, not one of those pitchers finished higher than third in Rookie of the Year voting. So Wolf must clearly continue his dazzling pitching before we should get too excited.

July 2—Pythagorean Theorem

The 4th of July marks the approximate midway point of the 1999 campaign. It's a decent opportunity to try to separate the contenders from the pretenders in Major League Baseball. By now, every team has at least 75 games in the books. That sample size is more than enough to get a pretty good handle on a team's relative strength.

One of the best ways to assess the true level of ability for any team is to look at its runs scored and allowed. Bill James long ago recognized the simple relationship between those two simple statistics and the two most important ones: wins and losses.

Bill found that a club's winning percentage is usually close to the ratio of the square of runs scored to the sum of squares of runs scored and allowed. He dubbed that relationship the Pythagorean Theorem. Here's the formula:

$$\text{Winning Pct.} = \frac{(\text{Runs})^2}{(\text{Runs})^2 + (\text{Runs Allowed})^2}$$

So if a team has scored 100 runs and allowed 80 in 15 games, we would expect a winning percentage of .610:

$$\frac{100*100}{100*100 + 80*80} = .610$$

In 15 games, that translates to nine wins.

When we apply the method to every team this season, we discover that the best club in baseball may not even lead its own division right now:

Expected Record Based on Pythagorean Theorem

Team	R	OppR	Pct	Proj	Actual	Diff
Astros	401	313	.621	48-29	44-33	-4
Indians	505	404	.610	47-30	51-26	4
Diamondbacks	438	360	.597	47-32	43-36	-4
Yankees	410	341	.591	45-31	47-29	2
Red Sox	395	330	.589	46-32	45-33	-1
Reds	384	327	.580	43-32	44-31	1
Braves	400	342	.578	46-33	48-31	2
Mets	413	355	.575	45-34	45-34	-0
Giants	432	399	.540	43-36	44-35	1
Pirates	417	393	.530	41-36	40-37	-1

Though the Astros recently have fallen behind the Reds in the National League Central, Houston continues to boast the best Pythagorean winning percentage in baseball. The Indians may have the game's most prolific offensive attack, but the Astros feature the game's stingiest pitching staff.

In a more perfect world, the Astros currently would lead the Reds by three games, instead of trailing them by one. But then, this sort of the thing has happened to Houston the last two years, though they still were able to overcome the vagaries of Pythagoras and capture the NL Central on both occasions.

In 1998, for instance, the Astros fell six games shy of their expected win total, the largest deficiency in baseball. Incredibly, over the last two seasons combined, the Astros' Pythagorean record is only a half-game behind the World Champion Yankees. But while the Astros have come up 10 games short of expectations, the Bronx Bombers have exceeded their's by five lengths.

And in 1997, the Astros fell a whopping 10 games off their expected pace. Clearly, this has been a trend during the Larry Dierker era. Whether the law of averages finally will catch up is an open question.

A couple of other points before I leave:

1) The law of averages *have* caught up with the Royals. Last year they exceeded expectations by an major league-high 10 games. This year, they've fallen seven games short, the largest discrepency in baseball.

2) The team with the worst 1999 Pythagorean winning percentage is the Twins, at .389. The Marlins actually may have a poorer record, but their Pythagorean mark of .398 edges Minnesota.

July 9—Extreme Baseball

The writer Lafcadio Hearn once lectured on the value of extremes, maintaining he was "Quite sure that all progress. . . has been obtained only with the assistance of extremes."

Well, the baseball gods must have re-read those words recently, because we're certainly living in an age of extremes on Major League Baseball fields.

We know about the phenomenal offensive numbers being compiled in recent years. All the homers and all the runs have made this the most prolific offensive era since the 1930s.

But amidst this hitting explosion, a few pitchers have made their mark.

Greg Maddux and Roger Clemens have continued their Hall-of-Fame march by capturing still more Cy Young Awards.

Randy Johnson has remained arguably the greatest strikeout artist since Nolan Ryan, fanning at least 290 batters in three of the last four seasons.

And Pedro Martinez simply looks to be a freak of nature. Is there any question he's now the best pitcher in baseball, if not its Most Valuable Player?

As if you needed additional proof, I'll offer one more stat that will try to provide some kind of perspective on Martinez' ability.

Pedro has been, shall we say, disinclined to allow many baserunners this season. He's permitted only 104 hits and 24 walks in 132.2 innings. As a result, Martinez has turned opposing hitters into a scaled-down version of Mike Caruso, allowing a puny .254 on-base percentage.

But wait, Martinez has a killer complement to his aversion to baserunners: strikeouts. He's already whiffed 184 this year, an average of 12.5 per nine innings. If he can maintain that pace, he'll have posted the second-highest rate (Kerry Wood, 1998) in history among pitchers with at least 100 innings.

Even better, Martinez has fanned 1.44 batters for every runner he's put on base via a hit or walk. No one has generated a better rate while working 100-plus innings:

Best Strikeout-Hit-Plus-Walk Ratio, Season—1900-99

Player	Year	IP	K	H	BB	K/(H+BB)
Pedro Martinez	**1999**	**132.2**	**184**	**104**	**24**	**1.44**
Bruce Sutter	1977	107.1	129	69	23	1.40
Pedro Martinez	1997	241.1	305	158	67	1.36
Sandy Koufax	1965	335.2	382	216	71	1.33
Randy Johnson	1995	214.1	294	159	65	1.31
Randy Johnson	1999	145.2	200	113	40	1.31
Randy Johnson	1997	213.0	291	147	77	1.30
Mariano Rivera	1996	107.2	130	73	34	1.21
Mike Scott	1986	275.1	306	182	72	1.20
Curt Schilling	1997	254.1	319	208	58	1.20

(minimum 100 IP)

We'll return to Martinez in a moment. But first, I want to present another chart, illustrating the apparent extremes we're witnessing as we approach the end of the millenium.

Remember, runs are scoring at a greater rate per game this season than in any year since 1936. Yet Martinez tops the previous list, and Randy Johnson sits at No. 6 with a rate of 1.31.

And if we decrease the minumum to 30 innings, four other hurlers from 1999 rank among the top five since 1900:

Best Strikeout-Hit-Plus-Walk Ratio, Season—1900-99

Player	Year	IP	K	H	BB	K/(H+BB)
Billy Wagner	1999	39.0	70	16	9	2.80
Armando Benitez	1999	44.0	72	17	22	1.85
Jeff Zimmerman	1999	50.1	46	18	9	1.70
Dennis Eckersley	1990	73.1	73	41	4	1.62
Troy Percival	1999	32.0	35	14	8	1.59
Dennis Eckersley	1989	57.2	55	32	3	1.57
Mike Jackson	1994	42.1	51	23	11	1.50
Troy Percival	1995	74.0	94	37	26	1.49
Bryan Harvey	1991	78.2	101	51	17	1.49
Tom Henke	1987	94.0	128	62	25	1.47

(minimum 30 IP)

Wagner almost surely will obliterate the previous mark, set when Dennis Eckersley refused to walk anyone in 1990. If Wagner's line still doesn't overwhelm you, perhaps it would have greater impact if it were reduced to rates per nine innings:

Billy Wagner, Per 9-IP—1999

IP	H	BB	K
9	4	2	16

That, my friends, is throwing serious heat. But Wagner clearly has two things working in his favor:

1) The role he fills, and

2) The era in which he pitches.

Because he's a reliever, Wagner has the luxury of throwing as hard as he can for as long as he can. And because he's working in the '90s, he has the advantage of toiling during the most strikeout-happy decade in history.

Martinez has taken advantage of the era, too. Still, it's likely he would have been successful during any period of baseball history.

As it is, he's the only hurler to work 1,000 innings in his career while accumulating more strikeouts than hits plus walks allowed:

Best Strikeout-Hit-Plus-Walk Ratio, Career—1900-99

Player	IP	K	H	BB	K/(H+BB)
Pedro Martinez	**1,278.2**	**1,405**	**994**	**397**	**1.01**
Randy Johnson	2,124.0	2,529	1,636	983	0.97
Sandy Koufax	2,324.1	2,396	1,754	817	0.93
Nolan Ryan	5,386.0	5,714	3,923	2,795	0.85
Roger Clemens	3,356.2	3,230	2,821	1,047	0.84
Curt Schilling	1,652.0	1,547	1,446	442	0.82
Sid Fernandez	1,866.2	1,743	1,421	715	0.82
Lee Smith	1,289.1	1,251	1,133	486	0.77
David Cone	2,510.0	2,330	2,070	946	0.77
Sam McDowell	2,492.1	2,453	1,948	1,312	0.75

(minimum 1,000 IP)

Eight of the 10 pitchers on the above chart worked at least four seasons in the 1990s, yet another testament to the current era.

So while we celebrate the enormous offense being exhibited in major league ballparks, remember, there still are pitchers out there surviving and thriving.

And somewhere, Lafcadio Hearn is smiling right now.

July 16—Safeco Field

Well, the Seattle Mariners christened Safeco Field with a 3-2 loss to San Diego Thursday night. Ken Griffey Jr. didn't homer, either.

Is the score, or Griffey's performance anyway, a sign of what we should expect in the future? *Sporting News* senior writer Michael Knisley, for one, has gone so far as to contend the new ballpark might cost Griffey up to 10 home runs per year.

Well, anything's possible, of course. We won't know for sure what effect Safeco will have until we have a few more games in the books. But 10 home runs a year strikes me as a bit alarmist.

Now, I'll concede that the Kingdome was a good home-run park. Nevertheless, it wasn't close to being the best longball venue in baseball. We all know Coors Field carries that title. Furthermore, the Kingdome didn't even rank among the top two or three homer havens in the majors. In fact, since 1996, the Kingdome's home-run index was a rather modest 107. Still high, the seventh-highest in the majors, but hardly indicative of a bandbox.

Seattle Mariners—1996-99

Category	Home	Road	Index
AB	18,363	18,456	
HR	764	715	107
LHB-HR	312	293	107
RHB-HR	452	422	108

(excluding interleague games)

Let's assume the typical hitter collects 600 at-bats each season, and that they're split evenly between home and road. The Kingdome's index of 107 would amount to approximately one extra home run per year.

Hitters actually have averaged 12.48 home runs per 300 at-bats at the Kingdome since 1996, while they've blasted 11.62 per 300 at-bats in Mariners road games. While the two figures both round to 12, you get the point.

However, there's no denying the fact that Griffey is not your typical hitter. To simplify things, I'll use whole numbers and include interleague games. Since 1996, Griffey has smacked 54 home runs per 600 at-bats. His rates per 300 at-bats at home and on the road are 28 and 26, respectively.

So for Knisley's prediction to come true, Griffey would be dropping to approximately 18 home runs at home each season. And if Junior's numbers are any indication, Safeco Field would thus boast a home-run index of roughly 70.

As you can see, such an index would mean the Mariners almost certainly would feature the worst home-run park in the majors. Since 1996, no other team has had a home-run index of less than 81:

Lowest Home-Run Indexes—1996-99

Team	Home Games HR	AB	Road Games HR	AB	Index
Astros	425	18,369	523	18,391	81
Marlins	425	18,020	497	18,022	86
Mets	462	18,178	531	18,145	87
Brewers	554	18,073	648	18,688	88
Diamondbacks	240	7,904	264	7,759	89
White Sox	577	18,323	640	18,251	90
Dodgers	483	17,785	544	18,279	91
Blue Jays	574	18,632	607	18,014	91
Indians	623	18,570	667	18,196	92
Expos	486	18,214	507	17,535	92

(excludes interleague games)

Again, it's possible that Safeco Field will have such a dampening effect on home runs. I wouldn't count on it, though. If it did, Safeco soon would become known as the anti-Coors.

July 23—Randy Johnson

So is this the year another cherished single-season record is broken? Last year, of course, it was Mark McGwire swatting a breathtaking 70 home runs. This year, will it be Randy Johnson striking out 384 batters?

The Big Unit still is a long way away from shattering Nolan Ryan's long-standing record of 383, set way back in 1973. But if Johnson can maintain his current pace, he stands a fairly decent chance of challenging Ryan's mark.

Entering Friday's (July 23) action, here's where things stood: Johnson had started 22 of the Diamondbacks' 97 games this season, and he had whiffed 229 batters in 169.2 innings.

If he continues to start one of every 4.4 Arizona games, Johnson will wind up with 37 starts this season. And if he can maintain his current pace of 10.4 strikeouts per game, he'll finish with 385 strikeouts, just enough to establish a new single-season mark.

It's true that Ryan's strikeout record hasn't lasted as long as Maris' home-run standard. But we also seemed better prepared for the possibility that Maris' record was in jeopardy.

The 50-home run mark had been reached on five separate occasions between 1995-97, with Ken Griffey Jr. and McGwire blasting 56 and 58, respectively, in '97. With that in mind, the awesome totals generated by McGwire and Sosa last year didn't seem quite so shocking.

By comparison, Ryan's strikeout record has been virtually impenetrable. In fact, outside of Ryan himself, no one since 1973 had fanned more than 320 batters in one season until Johnson K'd 329 last year. Johnson's total ranked as the seventh-highest since 1900:

Most Strikeouts, Season—1900-99

Player	Year	IP	SO
Nolan Ryan	1973	326.0	383
Sandy Koufax	1965	335.2	382
Nolan Ryan	1974	332.2	367
Rube Waddell	1904	383.0	349
Bob Feller	1946	371.1	348
Nolan Ryan	1977	299.0	341
Nolan Ryan	1972	284.0	329
Randy Johnson	**1998**	**244.1**	**329**
Nolan Ryan	1976	284.1	327
Sam McDowell	1965	273.0	325

So Johnson's 1999 campaign appears to be one of the few real threats Ryan's record has faced. But for Johnson to actually surpass 383, he'll need two things:

1) He must maintain his current strikeout pace, and

2) He must stay healthy.

Keep in mind, the Big Unit already has thrown 169.2 innings this year. Should he make 15 more starts (to reach 37) and continue to average nearly eight innings per outing, Johnson will finish with roughly 285 innings.

To pitchers of a generation ago, 285 innings may not seem like much. But only two hurlers since 1985 have endured that kind of workload in one season:

Most Innings Pitched, Season—1985-99

Player	Year	IP	SO
Bert Blyleven	1985	293.2	206
Charlie Hough	1987	285.1	223
Roger Clemens	1987	281.2	256
Dwight Gooden	1985	276.2	268
Dave Stewart	1988	275.2	192
Mike Scott	1986	275.1	306
John Tudor	1985	275.0	169
Fernando Valenzuela	1985	272.1	208
Oil Can Boyd	1985	272.1	154
Mark Langston	1987	272.0	262

Again, all this assumes Johnson will make 15 more starts this year. Should he only make 14, or even 13, more starts, his chances of breaking Ryan's record obviously diminish.

Then again, Johnson actually has *increased* his strikeout pace in recent outings, fanning 72 in his last six games. If he can maintain that torrid pace, he'd wind up surpassing Ryan's total even with 13 more starts.

It could be another historic September.

July 30—Hot Batting Averages

Don't know what the weather's like in your neck of the woods, but here in mid-America, it's absolutely scorching. The mercury climbed to 103 in the St. Louis area on Thursday, and any way you slice it, that's hot.

But as uncomfortable as triple-digit temperatures are to the average fan, imagine what they must feel like to major league pitchers. Talk about working up a good lather! It certainly isn't hard to break a sweat trying to pump fastballs past hitters.

And judging by data compiled this decade, it appears the pitchers are at a distinct disadvantage during the worst of the "dog days." The hotter the temperature gets, the higher opposing batting averages rise:

Batting Avg. by Temperature—1990-99

Temp	G	Avg
35-39	53	.257
40-44	131	.253
45-49	274	.257
50-54	553	.261
55-59	861	.257
60-64	1,639	.258
65-69	2,247	.259
70-74	6,334	.263
75-79	3,008	.264
80-84	2,646	.267
85-89	1,805	.269
90-94	810	.274
95-99	244	.280
100-104	28	.281
105-109	2	.284

The chart includes only those contests where the temperature at the *start* of the game was at least 35 degrees. I'm not sure if we can read too much into what the data is telling us when temperatures are beneath 55, but there appears to be no denying the trend above that figure.

The composite batting average rose in every five-degree increment above 55 degrees. Starting at .257 when the gametime temperature was between 55-59, batting averages steadily increased all the way to .280 when the thermometer read somewhere between 95-99.

At 100 or above, the sample size is so small that it would be dangerous to draw a definite conclusion, but it would appear that even at those lofty temperatures, the hitters are still heating up.

So when the sweat rolls down your back the next time the summer swelter turns your local ballpark into a sauna, remember, it could be worse. That could be you out there on the mound getting toasted by opposing hitters.

And melting into a puddle in the process.

August 6—Going the Distance

I received a question from Jayson Stark this week, the writer for the *Philadelphia Inquirer* whose work also appears in *Baseball America* and on ESPN. The Phillies had not had an opposing pitcher toss a complete game against them since last September. Jayson was interested in knowing whether the Phillies' streak was the longest current one in baseball.

Well, yes. Through Thursday's 9-3 victory over the Marlins, it was 130 games and counting since an opposing pitcher had gone the distance versus Philadelphia. The last time that occurred was way back on September 2, 1998, when the Dodgers' Carlos Perez tossed a two-hit shutout.

But in reality, the Phillies' streak is far greater in historical stature. STATS has been tracking game-by-game starts since 1987. Over that period, no team can match the Phillies' current streak:

Streaks Without a Complete Game Against—1987-99

Team	Stk	First Game	Last Game
Phillies	**130**	**9/4/1998**	**8/5/1999 ***
Mariners	125	8/24/1998	7/19/1999
Astros	118	6/24/1997	5/5/1998
Giants	112	9/21/1998	7/31/1999
Phillies	110	6/28/1997	4/28/1998
Marlins	101	7/16/1997	5/3/1998

(*—active)

Wait. Even this chart probably doesn't put the Phillies' streak in its proper historical context.

Consider the complete-game trend through the years. Complete games have decreased almost without exception since the beginning of baseball. Here's the rate per 100 starts since 1880:

Complete Games Per 100 Starts	
Decade	**CG/100**
1880-89	93.7
1890-99	85.3
1900-09	79.0
1910-19	56.8
1920-29	49.6
1930-39	44.6
1940-49	42.6
1950-59	33.5
1960-69	25.2
1970-79	25.3
1980-89	15.6
1990-99	7.5

As you can see, the rate this decade is less than half of what it was during the 1980s. And it shows no sign of recovering, either. This year's rate is 4.55 per 100 starts, the lowest in history. It's less than one-half of what it was only seven years ago. It's a quarter of what it was as recently as 1981. And it's one-tenth of what it was at the end of World War II.

So it's highly unlikely that any team ever generated a stretch prior to 1987 that even remotely resembled the Phillies' current streak.

How unlikely?

Well, let's assume complete games are a random event, with a probability of 0.0455 (this year's rate). Then the odds that a team will go 130 games without facing a complete game are roughly 1 in 426.

However, the rate in 1986 (the year before we have data) was 0.1377. The odds that a team would go 130 games without facing a complete game using that rate are approximately 1 in 231 million. In other words, extremely remote.

OK, let's go to the 1975 rate of 0.2720. The chances there would be 1 in 8.37 to 17th power. That's 1 in 837 *quadrillion*.

I won't even go back to the 1920s, when one in every two starts resulted in a complete game.

The bottom line: the Phillies' streak is almost without question the longest in history. Nevertheless, I'd be surprised if it lasted more than a couple years.

Complete games are becoming so rare that some day soon some team may go the entire season without facing a complete game. Who knows? The Phillies may accomplish that feat this year.

August 14—Three-Bagger

As you're undoubtedly aware, Mark McGwire snapped one of the longest streaks in baseball a couple weeks ago.

A triple isn't usually an historic event, but on August 2, it was. That's when McGwire connected for a three-bagger, his first in 4,618 at-bats without one.

McGwire's triple-less streak was the longest ever. And by ending it he moved down the chart of lowest triple rates in history:

Lowest Triple Rate—All Time

Player	3B	H	Per100
Jim Leyritz	1	634	0.16
Joe Oliver	2	756	0.26
Chris Hoiles	2	739	0.27
Willie Aikens	2	675	0.30
Rich Dauer	3	984	0.30
Mike Piazza	4	1,156	0.35
Scott Servais	2	570	0.35
John Flaherty	2	505	0.40
Mark McGwire	**6**	**1,460**	**0.41**
Paul Sorrento	4	864	0.46
Ron Kittle	3	648	0.46

(minimum 500 H)

McGwire has now averaged 0.41 triples per 100 career hits. And among the 1,936 players with at least 500 career hits (through Friday, August 13), McGwire's rate now ranks ninth-lowest.

Had he not legged out his sixth triple, his rate would actually be the worst among players with at least 1,000 career hits.

So McGwire clearly is not the speediest of runners. Another way to see how lumbering he is on the bases is to look at the next chart. It considers two other categories that indicate how fast a runner might be—stolen bases and runs minus homers:

Lowest 3B+SB+R-HR Rate—All Time

Player	3B	SB	R-HR	H+BB	Per100 H+BB
Gus Triandos	6	1	222	1,394	16.43
Clay Dalrymple	23	3	188	1,097	19.51
Milt May	11	4	236	1,276	19.67
Spud Davis	22	6	311	1,698	19.96
Ernie Lombardi	27	8	411	2,222	20.07

Player	3B	SB	R-HR	H+BB	Per100 H+BB
Frank Howard	35	8	482	2,556	20.54
Harmon Killebrew	24	19	710	3,645	20.66
Mark McGwire	**6**	**11**	**522**	**2,607**	**20.68**
Bruce Benedict	6	12	196	1,024	20.90
Boog Powell	11	20	550	2,777	20.92

(minimum 1,000 H + BB)

McGwire has generated six triples, 11 stolen bases, and 522 runs minus home runs in his career. That sum ranks as one of the lowest of all time when compared to his total of 2,607 hits plus walks.

Most of the players in the top 10 are catchers, just as we'd expect, since we're looking for some of the slowest players in history.

Of the four non-catchers—Howard, Killebrew, McGwire and Powell—all of them were prodigious power hitters, with nearly 1,800 career homers between them.

Clearly, that quartet's home runs more than compensated for its lack of footspeed. And McGwire's home-run rate, the best in history, obviously overshadows his low triple rate.

August 20—Craig Biggio

Every year about this time, it seems I'm always amazed by the kind of season Craig Biggio is having. He appears to constantly improve at least one facet of his game from one year to the next, taking those facets to new or higher levels.

Consider Biggio's career growth:

- Between 1988 and 1991, he improved his batting average from .211, to .257, to .276 and to .295 in successive campaigns.

- In 1992, he made the almost unheard of career switch from catcher to second base. Not only that, he also became the Astros' leadoff hitter. And he made both transitions with remarkable flair, leading the National League with 162 games, topping NL second basemen with 344 putouts, and raising his career high in walks from 53 to 94.

- In 1993, he added power to his game, setting new career highs with 41 doubles and 21 homers. He also paced NL second basemen with 447 assists.

- In 1994, he added speed, leading the National League with 39 stolen bases while getting caught only four times. Oh, he also became a .300 hitter (.318) and shared the league lead with 44 doubles.

- In 1995, he started perfecting the art of getting hit by a pitch, getting plunked 22 times, the first of three consecutive HBP titles. More important, he led the majors with 123 runs.

- While 1996 was a year of consolidation, all he did was play 162 games, score 113 runs, steal 25 bases in 32 attempts, lead the majors with 27 HBP, and top NL second basemen in assists and putouts.

- In 1997, he scored 146 runs, the highest single-season total so far in the second half of the 20th century. He also stole 47 bases and for the first time led NL second basemen in range factor.

- And in 1998, he became a 50-50 man—51 doubles and 50 stolen bases. He also topped 200 hits (210) for the first time, and set a career high with a .325 batting average.

Whew. That's quite impressive. It'll be hard for Biggio, at age 33, to continue his career growth.

But here we are, closing in on the end of August, and Biggio stands a pretty good chance of accomplishing something that no player has done since 1936. That season, Joe Medwick and Charlie Gehringer swatted 64 and 60 doubles, respectively. And no player has reached the 60-double plateau since.

Yet with 39 games remaining in the 1999 campaign, Biggio already has collected 49 two-baggers. If he can maintain that pace, he'll wind up with roughly 65. Only one player in history ever produced more—Earl Webb of the 1931 Red Sox. And if Biggio can accelerate his pace, Webb's one-year total of 67 is very much in danger.

In fact, Biggio virtually has lapped the field this year with his 49 doubles. Nobody else has more than 35. That spread of 14 is currently the second-greatest in history:

Biggest Spread Between Top Two Major League Doubles Totals

Year	Leader	Next	Diff
1931	Earl Webb—67	Dale Alexander—47	20
1999	**Craig Biggio—49**	Five players with—35	14
1950	George Kell—56	Red Schoendienst—43	13
1934	Hank Greenberg—63	Charlie Gehringer—50	13

Remember, Biggio legged out 51 doubles last year, so his two-year doubles total now sits at an even 100. And only two other hitters since 1940 have reached the century mark over a two-year span:

Most Doubles in Two-Year Span—1940-99

Player	Years	2B
Edgar Martinez	1995-96	104
Don Mattingly	1985-86	101
Craig Biggio	**1998-99**	**100**
Stan Musial	1943-44	99
Wade Boggs	1988-89	96

It's possible Biggio might challenge Medwick's two-year record total of 120 (1936-37), though Craig probably will have to settle for posting one of the five best marks ever.

But Biggio's excellence isn't just about doubles. It may be time he gets his due as one of the greatest leadoff hitters of this or the last generation. He's well on his way to achieving his fifth straight 100-run campaign, with 92 runs scored entering action on August 20. If he can cross the plate just 17 more times in the next 39 games, he'll have produced the best five-year stretch since 1960:

Most Runs in Five-Year Span—1960-99

Player	Years	R
Rickey Henderson	1982-86	613
Bobby Bonds	1969-73	613
Willie Mays	1961-65	613
Willie Mays	1960-64	602
Craig Biggio	**1995-99**	**597**

As I implied last year in this column, a case can be made that Biggio is the most under-appreciated player in the game today. He's rarely gathered much MVP support, ranking in the top 10 on only three occations, and never rising higher than fourth in the voting.

It's hard to believe he'll fare well in this year's balloting, either. The fine season teammate Jeff Bagwell is enjoying will drain some of Biggio's support, and '99 has been rather ho-hum by Craig's standards. But let's keep his season in perspective. It's still mighty impressive:

- He's hitting .308.

- His on-base percentage is .394.

- He's scored 92 runs, with 39 games to play.

- He leads major league second basemen with 95 double plays, and ranks second in the National League in range factor.

- He's enjoying one of the greatest doubles seasons in major league history.

We should all be forced to "endure" such a terrific campaign.

August 28—Hitting Streaks

Vladimir Guerrero's hitting streak finally ended at 31 games Friday night (August 27). Nevertheless, he already had become only the ninth player since 1987 to stroke hits in 30 or more consecutive contests.

The rarity of Guerrero's accomplishment provides some indication of just how great an achievement his hitting streak truly was. But let me try to provide just a little more perspective.

For the sake of this discussion, let's consider only those games in which a batter makes at least three plate appearances. Let's say Guerrero grounded out twice and drew a walk in one particular game. That game would be included in this study. But had he made one pinch-hitting appearance and then left, that game would have been excluded. Make sense?

Well, since 1987, batters who've accumulated at least three plate appearances in a game have managed to hit safely in 65.9 percent of those contests. In other words, if a batter made at least three trips to the plate, he enjoyed roughly a two-in-three chance of collecting at least one base hit.

Let's do a little math now. What are the odds that a batter will hit safely in 30 straight games, using the criteria and data outlined above?

It turns out to be roughly 1 in 270,000. But that's for an average hitter, and Guerrero has demonstrated he's quite a bit better than major league average.

In fact, among active players, only five other hitters have collected base hits in a greater percentage of those games in which they made at least three plate appearances:

Player	Gms	1+ H	Pct
Nomar Garciaparra	421	338	80.3
Mike Piazza	893	700	78.4
Tony Gwynn	1,628	1,275	78.3
Derek Jeter	597	459	76.9
Doug Glanville	390	299	76.7
Vladimir Guerrero	371	284	76.5
Alex Rodriguez	585	447	76.4
Kenny Lofton	1,033	781	75.6
Mark Grace	1,669	1,255	75.2
Roberto Alomar	1,637	1,228	75.0
MLB Average			**65.9**

Percentage of Games With 3-Plus Plate Appearances and at Least One Hit—1987-99

(active players; minimum 250 three-PA games)

Guerrero has managed to hit safely in 76.5 percent of those games in which he went to the plate at least three times. At that rate, his odds are about 1 in 3,000 that he'll hit safely in any 30-game stretch.

It's interesting to note that Garciaparra, the guy who tops the above list, is one of the other eight players with a 30-game hitting streak since 1987. He and most of the other players in the top 10 don't have abnormally high walk rates, a condition which seemingly provides them greater opportunities for delivering base hits.

These stats tend to indicate that Nomar may have the best chance of anyone right now of challenging Joe DiMaggio's fantastic 56-game hitting streak. But don't hold your breath. Using Garciaparra's rate of hitting safely in 80.3 percent of those games with three or more plate appearances, his odds of stringing together 56 games with hits is pegged at 1 in 219,000.

I wouldn't count on it.

September 3—Rafael Palmeiro

With the calendar now reading September, it's clear there isn't much baseball left to be played in the 1990s. Pretty soon we'll be hearing about voting for "Players of the Decade." And when we do, it's unlikely that Rafael Palmeiro will have received much support or attention for those kinds of awards or honors.

A week ago, we talked about Craig Biggio, another player who sometimes seems overlooked in these types of discussions. But Palmeiro actually may give Biggio a run for the money when looking for the most underappreciated stars of the game.

Really, the way Palmeiro is going, will there be any way to keep him out of the Hall of Fame in 10 or 15 years? Yet he's a guy who has never finished among the top five in Most Valuable Player voting.

Consider this. No player has generated more total bases this decade than Rafael Palmeiro:

Most Total Bases—1990-99	
Player	**TB**
Rafael Palmeiro	**3,077**
Ken Griffey Jr.	3,074
Barry Bonds	2,909
Albert Belle	2,878
Frank Thomas	2,803
Fred McGriff	2,742
Juan Gonzalez	2,671
Dante Bichette	2,622
Matt Williams	2,586
Sammy Sosa	2,581

I'm not sure how many people would have guessed that Palmeiro's total would surpass superstars such as Griffey, Bonds, Belle and Gonzalez. True, Griffey might overtake Palmeiro tomorrow, but Palmeiro will almost certainly be one of only two players to reach 3,000 total bases this decade.

Here's another one for you. With 41 homers already this season, Palmeiro has now clubbed 38 or more in each of the past five seasons.

Do you know how many other players in baseball history can say they've accomplished that feat? Five. And only Babe Ruth can boast a longer such streak:

Streaks of 38-Plus Home Runs

Player	Strk	Years
Babe Ruth	7	1926-32
Ralph Kiner	5	1947-51
Duke Snider	5	1953-57
Willie Mays	5	1961-65
Rafael Palmeiro	**5**	**1995-99**
Mark McGwire	5	1995-99

This is one of those lists that can be manipulated to fit one's argument. Palmeiro, for instance, has just managed to squeak by the 38-homer plateau in each of the last five years (39, 39, 38, 43, 41). McGwire, on the other hand, has blasted 50 or more longballs in each of the past four seasons.

Additionally, while Palmeiro's home-run barrage rates high from an historical perspective, it isn't necessarily out of the ordinary in the power-charged '90s.

You can see what I mean when you realize that not once has Palmeiro ranked higher than fourth in his league in either home runs or RBI. And as his mediocre performance in MVP balloting would indicate, he's rarely been judged one of the best players in baseball.

Nevertheless, it'll be hard to argue, once Palmeiro's career is over, that he doesn't deserve enshrinement in Cooperstown. After all, here's a guy who already possesses more than 2,100 hits, 350 home runs, and 1,200 RBI.

He's headed for 50 homers and 150 RBI this year alone, but let's assume he doesn't play another game in 1999, and finishes with 41 homers and 130 RBI. Using the logic employed by the "Favorite Toy," Palmeiro would figure to ultimately wind up with roughly 520 homers, 1,700 RBI, and 2,800 hits.

How the heck are you going to keep a guy with those kinds of numbers out of the Hall of Fame? Furthermore, how could you justify not enshrining him the very first year he's eligible?

Yes, I know Palmeiro's name doesn't resonate with the same legendary timbre as the Ruths, Cobbs or Aarons. True, Palmeiro's batting surge has coincided with one of the greatest offensive eras in history. And it's a fact that Palmeiro has not yet led his league in any category other than hits, doubles and runs scored.

But my goodness, 500 home runs and 2,800 hits have to count for something, don't they? At his current pace, he figures to ultimately rank among history's top 25 or 30 in terms of doubles, homers and RBI. And it's not inconceivable that he'll crack the top 15 in home runs.

Well, let's take a look at the players who've been the most similar to Palmeiro through this point in his career. He'll turn 35 later this month, meaning his seasonal age is now 34:

Most Similar Players to Rafael Palmeiro Through Seasonal Age 34

Player	Pos	H	HR	RBI	Avg	Slg	Score
Rafael Palmeiro	1B	2138	355	1,209	.297	.513	—
Orlando Cepeda	1B	2169	358	1,261	.298	.507	951
Billy Williams	OF	2231	356	1,199	.298	.510	916
Eddie Murray	1B	2352	379	1,373	.294	.494	892
Jim Rice	OF	2275	364	1,351	.302	.513	885
Fred McGriff	1B	1782	358	1,088	.285	.514	883
Ernie Banks	1B	1935	404	1,227	.280	.521	870
Will Clark	1B	1964	253	1,106	.302	.494	867
Dick Allen	1B	1807	346	1,088	.293	.539	859
Dave Winfield	OF	2083	305	1,234	.286	.479	853
Reggie Jackson	OF	1874	410	1,231	.273	.514	852

(thru 9/2/99)

Of the 10 players most similar to Palmeiro through age 34, four of them have either already been first-ballot inductees (Banks, Jackson), or likely will be (Murray, Winfield).

But here again, there's a difference. Banks and Jackson both earned MVP honors at some point in their careers. Murray finished second twice, and Winfield ranked in the top five on three occassions. Palmeiro's never been that close.

Conversely, four players on the above list (Rice, McGriff, Clark and Allen) may not ever be enshrined. And Cepeda, the player most similar to Palmeiro through age 34, had to wait for the Veterans Committee to elect him, though perhaps extenuating circumstances contributed to Cha Cha's delay.

It's possible that Palmeiro will become the "Don Sutton of hitters," one whose sheer weight of numbers is counterbalanced by the prevailing notion that he was never one of the best players in the game.

I'm one of those guys who feels if a player is good enough to make the Hall of Fame, he's good enough to make it on the first ballot. The question is whether enough voters feel the same way. In the meantime, Raffy continues to pile up numbers that will demand attention.

September 10—American League Batting Race

One of the hottest races coming down the stretch this season figures to be the struggle for the American League batting title. Entering Friday's (9/10) action, only a fraction of a percentage point separated the leader, Nomar Garciaparra (.3532), from the man in closest pursuit, Derek Jeter (.3529). The fact that the sparring partners are both shortstops, who also happen to play for the Red Sox and Yankees, respectively, only adds to the drama.

The exploits of Garciaparra and Jeter this season may have overshadowed the accomplishments of the third great young shortstop in the American League. But Alex Rodriguez is once again enjoying a remarkable campaign in his own right.

To begin with, Rodriguez has clubbed 36 homers this year. Remember, he missed more than a month early in the season following knee surgery. So those 36 homers have been swatted in just 416 at-bats (11.6 AB per home run). Only Mark McGwire (8.6) and Sammy Sosa (9.1) have generated better rates.

Perhaps even more remarkably, Rodriguez has scored 98 runs. Now, let's put that figure in greater perspective.

A-Rod has reached base 172 times this season via either a hit (124), walk (45) or hit by pitch (3). So his runs scored total represents 57 percent of that particular sum.

That's a very high rate in historical terms. In fact, since 1940, only one other player who reached base at least 150 times in a season via hits, walks and HBP has mustered a higher mark:

Runs Per Times on Base, Season—1940-99

Player	Year	H+BB+HBP	R	Pct
Robin Yount	1980	206	121	58.7
Alex Rodriguez	**1999**	**172**	**98**	**57.0**
Al Dark	1953	228	126	55.3
Jim Edmonds	1995	218	120	55.0
Zoilo Versalles	1965	230	126	54.8
Barry Bonds	1999	152	83	54.6
Johnny Mize	1947	255	137	53.7
Wally Post	1956	175	94	53.7
Marquis Grissom	1994	179	96	53.6
Eric Davis	1987	224	120	53.6

(minimum 150 times on base)

This is the kind of list where you might expect to see players who fit the mold of the classic leadoff men. Instead, we find hitters who usually had their names penciled lower in the lineup.

Prior to 1987, we don't have the details on Yount, Dark, Versalles, Mize and Post. But of the other five, only Grissom saw considerable action in the leadoff spot during the season in question.

Bonds and Davis usually hit third, while Edmonds typically hit second during their listed campaigns. Rodriguez has split this year roughly equally between the second and fourth spots in the order. It's hard to imagine sluggers such as Post and Mize helped set the table in the No. 1 hole, either.

Yet they all scored a considerable number of runs, at least when compared to the number of times they reached base. In some cases, the players' relatively low walk rate (Yount, Dark, Versalles) helped reduce their factor in the denominator (times on base), raising their run-scored rate. In other instances, the players either drove themselves in via home runs, or had teammates who hit the longball (Mize, Post, Davis).

In Rodriquez' situation, his walk rate (45 walks in 416 official at-bats) is not exceptional. His 36 homers rank sixth in the American League, and the Mariners as a team lead the majors with 215 roundtrippers.

These conditions are not really new for A-Rod, either. They help explain why his career run rate currently stands at 48.4.

Now, 1,636 players have reached base at least 750 times via hits, walks and HBP since 1900. And of all those players, only one, Red Rolfe, boasts a higher career run rate than Rodriguez:

Runs Per Times on Base, Career—1900-99

Player	H+BB+HBP	R	Pct
Red Rolfe	1,930	942	48.8
Alex Rodriguez	**993**	**481**	**48.4**
Jack Smith	1,657	783	47.3
Pepper Martin	1,609	756	47.0
Earle Combs	2,553	1,186	46.5
Joe DiMaggio	3,050	1,390	45.6
Woody Jensen	861	392	45.5
Tommy Leach	2,839	1,280	45.1
Sammy Sosa	1,846	831	45.0
Oddibe McDowell	1,018	458	45.0

(minimum 750 times on base)

There's no denying that Garciaparra and Jeter are both enjoying exceptional seasons. With averages hovering above .350, they deserve whatever accolades they receive.

Still, it's interesting to note that Rodriguez, despite playing fewer games, beats Garciaparra and Jeter in the other two Triple Crown categories. It's clear A-Rod is again enjoying another spectacular season.

September 15—Frozen Ropes

It's a simple concept, really. Hit line drives, collect base hits.

Simple in concept. Difficult in execution.

Batters are hitting a robust .751 this season whenever they attach a line drive to the end of their swings. That's good.

The problem is, only one in every six at-bats has resulted in line drives.

So it's clear the guys who possess the peculiar talent of consistently hitting the ball on a line—avoiding strikeouts, flyballs, popups and grounders—will enjoy a greater likelihood of success. And it's yet another reason to marvel at Tony Gwynn.

Gwynn is rolling along with a .327 average this season (entering Wednesday, 9/15). That's a mark which to him is nothing particularly special. Yet he continues to make the most consistently solid contact in baseball.

Almost 28 percent of Gwynn's at-bats have resulted in line drives in 1999. No other hitter (with at least 300 at-bats) has a rate higher than .251:

Line-Drive Percentage—1999

Hitter	Pct	Avg
Tony Gwynn	**.277**	**.770**
Alex Arias	.251	.797
Darryl Hamilton	.241	.734
Sean Casey	.240	.792
Mark Grace	.233	.691
Joe Randa	.233	.750
Rafael Palmeiro	.232	.765
Joe McEwing	.232	.646
Jeff Cirillo	.230	.797
Jeff Conine	.229	.703
MLB Average	**.167**	**.751**

(minimum 300 total AB; through 9/14/99)

There's a very strong correlation between healthy line-drive rates and robust overall batting averages. Of the 10 players on the above list, eight of them boast .300 batting marks this season.

While the overall average is .751 when hitters stroke line drives, it falls all the way to .256 when they hit flyballs. It falls even further, to .236, on grounders. And it plummets all the way to .074 on popups.

It's also clear that the best way to be successful hitting flyballs is to blast them a long way. The average is actually only .119 when flyballs don't result in home runs.

So which pitcher is most successful in preventing line drives? The answer may surprise you:

Line-Drive Percentage Allowed—1999

Pitcher	Pct	Avg
Wilson Alvarez	.113	.787
Tim Hudson	.119	.755
Doug Jones	.121	.773
Keith Foulke	.124	.744
Ramiro Mendoza	.126	.839
Derek Lowe	.127	.617
Bartolo Colon	.130	.789
Mike Trombley	.131	.878
Pedro Martinez	.132	.769
Ryan Rupe	.133	.735

(minimum 300 total opponent AB; through 9/14/99)

I'm not sure what this says about which type of pitcher allows the fewest line drives. True, there are some hard throwers on the list, but Doug Jones tosses three speeds of slow, and Wilson Alvarez, the hurler topping the chart, could hardly be described as a flamethrower.

It is, however, yet another opportunity to appreciate the remarkable season Pedro Martinez is having.

September 24—Tribe Taters

Each fall, we at STATS Inc. produce three of the best baseball books you can buy—the *Major League Handbook*, *Minor League Handbook* and *Player Profiles*. If you're not familiar with them, you should be. And the great thing is, they're each available within weeks of the World Series.

However, it takes time to prepare these books, and that time is looming on the horizon. So this may be my last "STATS Focus" for awhile.

But before I go, I just wanted to make a quick point about the Indians. Their potent offense has been a subject of discussion for much of the season.

The Tribe has averaged roughly 6.2 runs per game this year. And if it can maintain that pace for its last nine games, Cleveland will become only the seventh team since 1900 to score 1,000 runs in a single season.

The Indians have slowed down a bit as the year has progressed. They've averaged 5.9 runs per game in September, which is actually .3 runs higher than their rate in August. But at that pace, the Tribe would score 53 runs in its next nine games, which would boost it to exactly 1,000. So it appears the race for the millennium mark will come down to the wire.

Clearly, the Indians offense is a beautiful thing to behold, at least if you're not an opposing pitcher. Still, you might wonder if it would be even more potent if it hadn't lost some of the players on this list through trades or free agency:

Player	1999 HR
Brian Giles	39
Jay Bell	37
Albert Belle	36
Sean Casey	24
Eddie Taubensee	20
David Bell	20

Each of these players made his first major league appearance as a member of the Indians. And they've each clubbed 20 or more homers this season while playing for other teams.

Remember too, the Indians have three other homegrown power hitters—Manny Ramirez (40), Jim Thome (33) and Richie Sexson (31)—still blasting homers for them. And the thing is, the six castaways would fit quite nicely into the other six positions to fill a lineup which almost surely would have blown away the single-season home-run record.

Eddie Taubensee could work behind the plate. David and Jay Bell could form the middle infield. Albert Belle still could play left field, while Brian Giles has performed well in center with Pittsburgh this season. Third base is the only place where the Indians may be thin, but Thome could slide back to the position he played when he arrived in the big leagues. That would allow Sean Casey and Richie Sexson to split the first base and DH duties.

Add it all up, and we're talking 280-plus homers. Truly scary.

Then again, the Tribe has survived quite nicely using the players it still has, thank you very much. I'm sure the Indians would rather have Roberto Alomar at second base than David Bell, and shortstop Omar Vizquel is vastly superior to Jay Bell defensively. Kenny Lofton and David Justice also are enjoying decent seasons.

So it's a bit misleading to look at those homers the Indians have let get away and say they'd be better off if Cleveland still had them. But the simple fact is, no other team has had its former players (based on first big league team) hit as many homers for other clubs in 1999:

HR by Former Players—1999

Team	HR
Indians	**221**
Athletics	192
Brewers	191
Rangers	174
Yankees	160

(based on first major league team)

The high rank of the Athletics may not be surprising, considering Mark McGwire (59) broke into the big leagues with them. But how about those ex-Brewers? Greg Vaughn (42), John Jaha (34), Gary Sheffield (29), B.J. Surhoff (28) and Troy O'Leary (28) would provide a pretty strong power core for a team that ranks 12th in the National League in home runs right now.

We also should point out that three teams on the above list—the Indians, Rangers and Yankees—currently lead their respective divisions, while the Athletics remain alive for the wild-card berth. So they've clearly found more than capable replacements.

Still, as the Indians make their push for 1,000 runs, you can't help but wonder if they'd have cleared the hurdle already with the players they've let get away.

Mat Olkin's
Fantasy Baseball Advisor

February 16, 1999—Offseason Winners and Losers

Last week I stopped in at the Seven-Eleven to pick up something to drink. The can of Diet Coke ran me 78 cents, and I handed the clerk a pile of coins I'd mined from the floorboards of my car. He dropped most of it. Then, as the pennies rolled under the cooler, it hit me: this guy was a dead ringer for Kevin Reimer.

Who knows—maybe it really was Reimer. I was too embarrassed for him to ask. No one seems to know what Reimer's up to these days. I mention him only because he's the player the Rockies traded to Milwaukee for Dante Bichette.

For Reimer, the trade was just another bend in the road on the way to oblivion. But for Bichette, the deal made him a star. Ensconced in the best hitters' park of all time before rabid expansionite fans, Bichette became a bigger run-producer than anyone could have dreamed. The value of his actual production has been hotly debated, of course, but from a fantasy standpoint, he's been a fine player to own.

The Rockies haven't acquired any hitters of note this offseason, but there have been several transactions that could turn out to be unduly beneficial or harmful to the players involved. I thought it might be fun to make a list of the five biggest winners and losers—the players who we can expect to feel the biggest impact from their new surroundings.

It's fairly clear to me that the winter's biggest winner is Texas' new first baseman, Rafael Palmeiro. The Ballpark in Arlington is a haven for lefthanded hitters, and Palmeiro's been a holy terror in the 22 games he's player there: a .342 average with nine home runs, 22 RBI and a .772 slugging percentage. Will Clark's power got quite a boost from the Ballpark, and he doesn't have half the pop of Palmeiro. What's more, Palmeiro has something to prove. He's always felt slighted that the Rangers let him walk in order to sign Clark, and nothing would give him more pleasure than to show the Rangers what they've been missing.

An easily overlooked winner is Arizona's center fielder, Steve Finley. Qualcomm Stadium has been one of the most pitcher-friendly ballparks in baseball over the last few years, and no Padres hitter was hurt more by it than Finley. During his four years in San Diego, Finley has hit almost .300 and slugged close to .500 on the road, while hitting .260 and slugging only .418 at home. The park has cost him about 18 homers over that time. I had expected Bank One Ballpark to be a hitters' park, and it has been, although not to the extent I'd expected. That could change; one season isn't nearly enough time to get a good read on a park's overall effects. Anyway, Arizona should help him to some extent, and compared to San Diego, he'll feel like he's taking BP.

New Pittsburgh left fielder Brian Giles moves into a much more promising situation, for reasons that go beyond the change in ballparks. In Cleveland, he had to wage a daily battle just to hang onto a platoon role. And no matter how well he hit, he almost never saw a lefthander or batted any higher than sixth in the order.

Now, the Pirates are talking about playing him every day, against all types of pitching. He should be able to handle it; he hit lefties well in Triple-A, and while he hasn't hit for power against them in the majors, he's shown he can handle them by hitting for average and maintaining a good strikeout-walk ratio. Not only will he play full time, but he'll also move up into the heart of the Pirates' order, batting either third or fifth.

On top of all that, the Pittsburgh park should help him more than the Jake, which never did much for his numbers. His line-drive bat is much better suited for the fast turf at Three Rivers Stadium.

Another winner is Jon Lieber, who finally escaped Pittsburgh after toiling for the hapless Pirates for five years. With a decent offense and defense behind him in Chicago, there's no reason he can't be a consistent winner. From an effectiveness standpoint, there isn't a heck of a lot of difference between him and a pitcher like Kevin Tapani.

Someone else who'll be happy to come to Wrigley is catcher Benito Santiago. Provided that he's fully recovered from the injuries he suffered in last year's car wreck, Santiago could enjoy hitting at Wrigley more than any other home park he's ever had. In 44 career games at Wrigley, he's hit .298 with nine home runs, 28 RBI and a .563 slugging percentage. Tyler Houston is a decent bench player, but he's not talented enough to keep a halfway-decent hitter like Santiago out of the lineup.

One of the biggest losers is sure to be Brant Brown, who leaves the Cubs for Pittsburgh. Though the Pirates are talking about making him their full-time center fielder, Brown is neither a full-timer nor a true center fielder. In 96 career at-bats against lefthanders, he's batted under .200. He came through the minors as a first baseman, and while he managed to survive for a few months in center field last year, it was his first extended trial in the outfield. His defensive shortcomings may become much more apparent now that he'll be playing in a carpeted ballpark. He'll miss Wrigley too, the park where he's hit two-thirds of his big league home runs.

Mo Vaughn could hit in a dark warehouse, but the move from Fenway to Anaheim will cost him some singles and doubles. His career home/road splits read: .327 with 121 doubles in Boston, and .281 with 78 doubles everywhere else. The pre-renovation Anaheim Stadium used to be one of the best home-run parks in the majors, but the new configuration has been much less forgiving—especially for lefthanded hitters like Mo.

Devon White is another hitter who'll have to fight an uphill battle just to break even. With his speed and gap power, he's always been a better turf hitter, batting 32 points higher on carpet for his career. Now he'll be dealing with the natural grass of Dodger Stadium, one of the worst hitters' parks in the majors.

Robby Alomar may regret his decision to leave Baltimore for Cleveland. He liked to hit at Camden Yards, batting .337 with 31 home runs there over the last three years, compared to .288 with 19 homers on the road. Now he'll be trying to reach the fences at the Jake, something he has yet to do in 27 games.

Finally, there's the biggest loser of all: Brian Bohanon, of Coors.

March 9—The High Strike

Catchers are not about to shed their masks, most pitchers continue to throw overhand, and the Braves have not announced any plans to move back to Milwaukee. There is one vestige of old-time baseball that appears to be on the comeback trail, however: the high strike. If you believe what you read, the umpires have grudgingly conceded to the Commissioner's Office, and apparently will make some sort of effort to call the high strike this season.

Of course, we have every reason to remain skeptical. Exactly the same sort of rumblings were heard in the spring of 1996, and if there was any real change in the strike zone that year, it escaped the notice of Brady Anderson's bat. Up until now, the umpires have outright refused to abide by the league's directives on this matter, so it wouldn't be surprising if they now were paying mere lip service to the idea of an altered strike zone.

But let's suppose for a moment that they *aren't* lying. If the strike zone is called differently this season, the effects could be substantial, and perhaps more severe than most people would anticipate. As anyone who watched the 1997 NLCS will agree, a small change in the size of the strike zone can have a large impact on the balance of power between the pitcher and the hitter. If the legitimacy of belt-high pitches is restored, which pitchers figure to benefit the most?

The most obvious answer is "pitchers who pitch up in the strike zone." STATS doesn't record the location of each *pitch*, but we do record the distance and direction of each batted ball. Generally speaking, pitchers that work up in the zone give up the greatest proportion of flyballs, so we may infer that extreme flyball pitchers are the ones who would reap the most benefit from the "new" strike zone. (Admittedly, the argument requires a few leaps of logic, but if all of this comes to pass, you should come out several leaps ahead of your competition).

The following starting pitchers were the most extreme flyballers in baseball last year: Eric Milton, Rick Helling, Woody Williams, Tim Wakefield, Hideki Irabu, Denny Neagle, Brett Tomko, Brian Anderson and Mark Gardner. I'm not so bold as to predict that each and every one of them will improve this season, but I would be willing to bet that they'll improve as a group. Or, to put it another way, I think each of them is more likely to improve than decline.

I haven't seen enough of Eric Milton to say whether or not he's ready to turn the corner, but speaking from personal experience, I will say that Wakefield is a high strike away from being the pitcher he was in '92 and '95. Tomko should improve, even without a more generous strike zone, as should Brian Anderson (especially if he gets out of Arizona). Williams is the only one I'd be leery (Leary?) of; his arm was overworked last year. Irabu may have the most to gain, since he was the one member of the group who had the most trouble throwing strikes.

Ball-strike data becomes less absolute the more you study it. One fundamental problem is that every pitch a batter swings at is automatically deemed a "strike." This muddies the waters quite a bit; many pitchers, like Steve Carlton, made their living by getting batters to swing at pitches that were *out* of the strike zone. For this reason, I decided to examine the results of only those pitches that were *taken*. The results tell us which pitchers are able to both fool the hitter and get the call.

Of the nine most extreme flyball pitchers, Irabu got a called strike on 28.2 percent of all pitches taken, the lowest percentage of any pitcher in the group. Williams was second-lowest at 28.8 percent, and Milton followed with 29.5 percent.

The pitch-count data turned out to be more fun than I'd expected, and I eventually forgot all about the original idea for this essay. After calculating taken-strike percentages for a few dozen pitchers, I suddenly realized that the data—however enlightening—would be all but impossible to work into the essay as I'd planned it.

So much for the plan. I'll take good info over good writing any day of the week.

Here's what I found. (I might have missed someone, but I know I got most of the important names.) The following pitchers get the highest percentage of called strikes: Greg Maddux (37.5 percent), Rick Reed (37.1), Tom Gordon (36.9), Keith Foulke (36.2) and David Wells (36.1). But do you know who got the highest percentage of strikes of all of them? Doug Jones, 41.3 percent. It just goes to show that even pinpoint control isn't enough when you can't break the speed limit.

I also noted the pitchers who threw the *lowest* percentage of strikes. If you're counting on Matt Anderson for some saves, you may not need both hands—he got the call on only 23.3 percent of pitches taken. Dennys Reyes (24.0) also looked like a guy who needed some more seasoning. Jose Mesa showed no signs of rebirth with a dismal percentage of 23.2 (he was around 30 percent in his salad days back in '94 and '95) and young Blake Stein must have felt squeezed (23.4). One of the only successful pitchers who got the call less than a quarter of the time was Al Leiter (24.9). He may continue to get by with it, though—he's a lefthander who throws hard with excellent movement, and that was the Carlton formula.

March 16—Fringe Players

You may have noticed that I seldom devote much space to fringe players. "They just don't matter all that much," I'd tell people. "You may feel like a roto-Einstein if you snag a dollar-dude who isn't completely useless, but the fact of the matter is that those guys comprise only a tiny proportion of your roster's value. It's the full-time players that win and lose pennants."

I'd make that argument in earnest, but the truth of the matter is that I just didn't care. No matter how hard I tried, I couldn't get all that interested in trying to figure out who was more likely to steal three bases—Tomas Perez or Alex Diaz.

I'm coming around, though. Participating in leagues where the talent is less watered-down has heightened my awareness of minimum-bid candidates. I guess it's one of those things people like to call an "acquired taste."

Steve Moyer is the one who's always had an eye out for unknowns. He used to work for STATS, and we got to hang out a few weeks ago at the LABR draft in Tampa. The fact that I was in the AL and he was in the NL made it easier for us to swap ideas. We were bee-essing with Ron Shandler and Gene McCaffrey when I said, "Hey, Steve. I've got a one-dollar catcher I know you'd just love." "Who?" "Brian Banks."

That set him off. He'd come in with the perfect sleeper up his sleeve, and I'd blown his cover. To hear him tell it, he'd been planning his whole draft around Banks. It's true that Banks is a decent pick for a scrub—a decent hitter who is out of options, qualifies at catcher, and could see some time in the outfield—although Steve ultimately found a way to construct a Banks-less team. Not that you could tell; the haranguing continued all weekend. Anyway, in Steve's honor, I've decided to devote an entire column to the least unworthy dollar drafts.

David Lamb is a fairly anonymous Rule 5 draftee. The Devil Rays are trying to find room for him on the roster; otherwise they'll have to offer him back to Baltimore. Lamb has no power, but he's a switch-hitter who can hit for a decent average and hold his own at shortstop. If he's able to fill in a little at second and third, he could be this year's David Berg.

We also have the Torey Lovullo of pitchers, Steve Karsay. This guy has gone under the knife so often that his arm has no original parts left. Still, he insists that he feels better than he has in years, and is poised to take over Chad Ogea's swingman role. Performing in that capacity would allow for his occasional DL stints while giving him a chance to pick up a few wins for a strong team.

McKay Christiansen is waging a spirited battle to wrest the White Sox' center-field job from Brian Simmons. He probably won't stick, but if he does, he's sure to swipe a few sacks. Offensively, he's little more than a young John Cangelosi, which is ironic, since Cangelosi will be backing up the winner of the competition. Simmons has more power, but Christiansen has much better long-term potential.

Mike Simms' injury may give Scott Sheldon his long-awaited chance to make the show. He's a power-hitting shortstop, but the Rangers may need him to DH against lefties and caddy for Rafael Palmeiro at first base. He qualifies at third, which makes him somewhat useful, and he may be able to pop a few homers.

Remember Vincente Palacios? He's been AWOL—south of the border—for three years, but he may be coming back—north of the border. After Palacios put together a super season pitching out of the bullpen in Mexico, his agent convinced the Blue Jays to take a flier on him. No team's bullpen is more wide open than Toronto's, so it wouldn't be out of the realm of possibility for Palacios to pick up a few saves. At least Palacios has proven he can get hitters out at the major league level; Tom Davey can't claim that.

You'd better grab Butch Henry while he's still between injuries. There's something to be said for a guy who pitches well whenever he's able to pitch. Remember, his most recent physical challenge was a knee injury, not an arm problem; the most demanding thing his arm has done in the last 10 months is channel-surf.

Can you believe that the Orioles are talking about carrying Willis Otanez? This, from a team that's so overloaded with 1B-DHs that Calvin Pickering can't even find a spot on the bench. They say they need a righthanded bat, though, and it seems that Chris Hoiles may be totaled. Otanez is a Geronimo Berroa-type, waiting for the rest of the DHs to get hurt.

Jeff Suppan might have pitched horribly enough last year to knock him down into the bottom of the pool. Although he's stuck with a rebuilding franchise, there's enough left between the youth and the Triple-A stats to merit a minor bid.

In Montreal's kaleidoscopic left-field situation, the current favorite is converted infielder Jose Vidro. He flunked a trial at second base last year, but that makes him all the more valuable, as he still qualifies at the keystone. He didn't show much last year, but he's still very young, and he began to tap into his power in winter ball. Felipe Alou is excited about his offensive potential, and that should say something.

John Halama is making a bid to take his Triple-A, soft-tossing, pick-'em-off-first act to Seattle. It would be hard for the M's to call in Halama and try to explain why they were sending him back down, what with Jamie Moyer playing Nintendo a few feet away.

That's it. Have fun at draft day, and remember not to discuss these guys in front of the competition.

March 23—Spring Training Stats

Generally speaking, spring training stats aren't worth a damn. No one is really trying all that hard to win, so it's hard to take a team's won-lost record seriously. Individual players' stats often are impossible to accept at face value. The veteran pitcher with the 13.50 ERA may be an MRI away from reconstructive surgery, or perhaps he's just working on a new pitch. The kid outfielder from the California League with the .455 batting average may be the next phenom, or perhaps he's hit a few grounders in "B" games that have skidded through the rock-hard infields of Arizona.

Besides, spring training is only four weeks long. It's hardly a stretch to say that *anyone* good enough to be on a major league roster could hit .300 in a given four-week stretch. Even Garth Brooks, who's 1-for-13, is only a four-hit game away from the magic .300 mark.

We may rest assured that Chad Allen eventually will go back to where he belongs and resume playing like Chad Allen should. This doesn't mean we should entirely ignore spring training stats, however.

In certain situations, spring stats can be quite telling. Sometimes a player's performance—even in a limited number of games—can tell us something we need to know.

Take William VanLandingham. Here's a guy who suffered a complete meltdown in '97, losing his spot in the Giants' rotation by walking 59 batters in 89 innings. They sent him down to Triple-A, where he started four games and walked 21 more in only 17 innings. Then they sent him home.

Last year was even *worse*. He pitched nine games for Triple-A Vancouver, going 0-6 with an 11.23 ERA and allowing 48 hits and 44 walks in 33.2 innings (his average line was: L 3.2 5 5 5 5 1).

This year, the Brewers invited him to camp—perhaps to sharpen their hitters' reflexes. To everyone's astonishment, he's gotten it back together, walking only a single batter in 9.2 innings. In fact, he's pitched so well that he may make the club as a swingman.

The point is not that we should rush out and sign VanLandingham. We can be fairly sure, though, that he's conquered whatever psychological or mechanical demons that were plaguing him, and that he won't end up working on Sam Militello's highway crew.

Ricky Bottalico is another pitcher who's showed significant progress. A premature return from elbow surgery last year caused his ERA to soar and his strikeout rate to plummet. This spring, in eight innings he has fanned six hitters without walking anyone.

Now look at the contrast between two of the White Sox' starters, James Baldwin and Jim Parque. Baldwin is a fastball-curveball pitcher, and he absolutely must be able to get his curve over in order to succeed. He can lose faith in his bender for months at a time, and his career has been, predictably, a continuous series of hot streaks and long dry spells.

He went 12-6 in Triple-A in '94. The next year, he dropped to 5-9 and his ERA approached 6.00. The year after that, he went 11-6 with the White Sox. He went 15-18 over the next year and a half, before righting himself and talking 10 of 13 decisions over the second half last year.

Many people are gambling that his hot second half will carry over to this season, but his spring record suggests that isn't likely. In 15 innings, he's walked nine men and fanned only four. This, from a pitcher who posts a 2-1 ratio going the other way when he's on.

On the other hand you have Jim Parque. After the Chisox had first called him up last year, he tried to be too fine, and walked far too many hitters in his first seven starts. He improved in the second half, posting a strikeout-walk ratio better than 2-1 over his last 14 starts.

His performance this spring tells me that he may continue to improve steadily. In 15 frames, he's notched a dozen strikeouts and only one walk. This could be either an aberration, or the first sign that he's turned the corner. I won't take my eye off him until I know for sure, one way or the other.

Other potentially significant developments involve Philadelphia catcher Mike Lieberthal and Toronto shortstop Alex Gonzalez. Lieberthal went down last year with an injury that apparently defied description or treatment. (It might have involved friction between his pelvic bones; I don't know for sure and I don't think I want to.)

Anyway, Lieberthal's status was uncertain in the beginning of camp. Now, after hitting .560, slugging .920 and playing without pain in his first 11 games, he's looking good as new. Considering the dearth of 20-homer catchers out there, he could be one of this year's best pickups.

Kansas City is the next-to-last place you'd look for a pitcher, but they may have a sleeper this spring: Erik Hanson. Don't laugh; he's finally healthy, and this is a guy who's made a career out of recovering from arm problems. He's had a decent spring, and the Royals would like to have him around to buy beer for the rest of the staff.

Finally, we have the perennially disappointing Alex Gonzalez. He came up a few years ago with Shawn Green and Carlos Delgado. Since then, the latter two have blossomed into stars, while Gonzalez has produced the most consistently mediocre stats since Mookie Wilson.

Things may be different this year, however. Over the winter, he got married—which may or may not make a difference—and he hired a personal trainer and put on seven pounds of muscle, which may help him enormously. He's also altered both his batting stance and his approach at the plate, lowering his hands and working on becoming less pull-conscious. As a result, he's batting .361 and slugging .639 this spring. Ultimately, he may wind up hitting .239 like he always does, but if he breaks out, his spring numbers will have been the first giveaway.

March 30—A Royal Future

Few teams can be as frustrating to watch as the Kansas City Royals. This observation comes from a fan of the Milwaukee Brewers, mind you. The Brewers' mediocrity is a bit more tolerable. The yearly editions of the Brewers are so interchangeable and uniformly boring that a Brewers fan is apt to be lulled to sleep, secure in the knowledge that nothing interesting will happen until the new stadium opens.

The Royals, on the other hand, lurch from one ill-conceived plan to another, tearing apart last year's groundwork while furiously implementing today's diametrically-opposed and equally-doomed design. Last year, en route to a 72-89 finish, they "rebuilt" around Bush-era favorites like Terry Pendleton, Luis Rivera, Scott Leius and Chris Turner. They gave those four relics a total of nearly 400 at-bats, and got what they deserved: a cumulative .239 average, with three home runs and 40 RBI. (Question: How many Kansas City Royals front office executives does it take to fly a plane? Answer: Two—to fight over the controls.)

Things may be changing, though. The Royals have completed their usual offseason overhaul, and while their moves include the normal quota of head-scratchers, they've done a few things that suggest that they finally may be moving in the right direction.

This may prove to be a moot point if they continue to change direction every couple of months, but for the time being, there are some reasons for optimism. The most promising development is their strong commitment to two of their best young players, center fielder Carlos Beltran and second baseman Carlos Febles.

Beltran is an athletic center fielder who got a short look last September. So far, his journey to the majors has been similar to Johnny Damon's. As Damon had three years before, Beltran began the year at Double-A at age 21, and hit his way to the big leagues by the end of the season. Like Damon, he has the speed to steal bases, the athleticism to cover center field, and the potential to hit for both power and average.

Ironically, Beltran has displaced Damon as both the center fielder and the leadoff man. Damon has been moved to left, and his developing power has earned him a spot in the middle of the batting order.

It's tough to get a read on Beltran's offensive abilities because of his lack of experience in the high minors. He didn't hit all that well in A-ball, but in his defense, he played in tough hitters' parks and was younger than most of his competition. In 47 games at Double-A Wichita last year, he hit .352 and slugged .687. There's no way anyone could keep up that kind of pace for a full season, but at the very least, it tells us that Beltran probably can out-hit a Jermaine Allensworth.

I've seen all sorts of projections for Beltran. The least enthusiastic ones have him hitting around .270 with a decent number of steals. The most optimistic ones see him as a fully-developed star, complete with a .300 batting average, tons of steals, and legitimate extra-base power.

I'm not ready to call him another J.D. Drew on the basis of what he did in only 47 games at Double-A, but from everything I've seen, I'm confident that he'll equal or surpass what Damon did in his first full season. In other words, I'm looking for a batting average in the .280s with single-digit home-run power and a couple dozen sacks.

Carlos Febles may be even more of a sleeper. He also has the ability to hit for power and steal bases, but the club has de-emphasized his offense by slotting him into the nine-hole. There's little doubt that they're committed to him, however.

Last year, second baseman Jose Offerman was one of their top players. He became a free agent at season's end, and it would have been all too easy for the Royals to talk themselves into shelling out millions to keep him. They made a much more courageous decision, opting to turn over the second-base position to a player who'd played only 11 games for them, Carlos Febles.

Although he's never played above Double-A, Febles played so well last year that he could be one of this year's biggest surprises. A .290 batting average and 30 stolen bases wouldn't be out of the question, and if he is able to avoid an early slump, the Royals might consider moving him up to the No. 2 spot in the order.

If outfielder Jeremy Giambi's hamstring ever heals, the Royals could wind up with *three* legitimate Rookie-of-the-Year candidates. Giambi, like his brother Jason, is a .300 hitter with line-drive power and minimal defensive skills.

Of course, the free-agent defections of Offerman and Dean Palmer will be a lot to overcome. The youngsters' development may not outweigh those losses, but at least the Royals are recognizing and cultivating the players who someday might lead them back into contention.

New third baseman Joe Randa and shortstop Rey Sanchez will do nothing for the offense, but the pair may have a considerable impact on the Royals' young starting pitchers. Last year, the left side of the Royals' infield was a disaster area. Palmer brought his spectacular immobility to third base, and shortstop was manned by a series of ne'er-do-wells like Felix Martinez, Shane Halter and Mendy Lopez.

Both Randa and Sanchez are top-notch defenders, and may help youngsters like Jose Rosado, Jeff Suppan and Glendon Rusch—pitchers who must throw strikes and allow the hitter to put the ball in play in order to succeed.

Beltran's emergence strengthens the outfield defense too, albeit indirectly. Damon will cover more ground than any other left fielder in the league. No longer will players like Hal Morris and Jeff Conine be allowed to embarrass themselves in the outfield.

Of course, things have not turned around completely. Chad Kreuter was signed and immediately named the No. 1 catcher, on the strength of his "ability to work with young pitchers." (The documentation of this alleged ability remains purely anecdotal.)

The Royals' refusal to commit themselves to young catcher Mike Sweeney is difficult to understand, and frankly annoying. Somehow, manager Tony Muser has become convinced that Sweeney doesn't call a good game. Early last year, he cited a statistic that showed that the Royals' staff had a better ERA with Sal Fasano behind the plate than with Sweeney. By the end of the year, the difference between the two had shrunk to eight-one-hundredths of a run, but never mind; Muser wasn't about to reverse himself.

There's also the lingering black hole named Jim Pittsley. He was a super prospect before blowing out his arm in '95. Since then, the Royals have been in complete denial, and have kept promoting Pittsley as if the injury never had occurred. They've been strangely oblivious to the fact that he hasn't gotten anyone out in three years.

Still, these are only minor annoyances in the greater scheme of things. The more important point is that the Royals have some good young players, and they've realized it before burying them or trading them away. They may not see the bright side of .500 for a while, but at least they won't be playing Hal Morris in left field any more.

April 6—Expos on the Rise

Felipe Alou has no patience for pretense. Last year, when it was clear that the Expos were going nowhere, he didn't offer hollow optimism. When asked about his goals for the season, he simply said he hoped to teach his young player to play ball. This year, he's telling people he's got the strongest Montreal club since the '94 juggernaut was broken up. We'd do well to listen.

Granted, it's hard to imagine that this year's Montreal club—which is coming off a 97-loss season—could outperform, say, the '96 club, which won 88 games. But that's nitpicking. Alou's point is obvious: *this club could surprise a lot of people.* And while the game's best manager needs no validation from an outside columnist, this one would heartily concur.

It's clear that this year's club is more comparable to the '94 club than to last year's sorry collection of stragglers. Let's compare them to the '94 team, position by position.

The '94 team wasn't any stronger behind the plate. Darren Fletcher was the regular, with Lenny Webster contributing in a backup role. Current starter Chris Widger is comparable to Fletcher—he has about as much power, hits for a lower average, and has a much better throwing arm. Second-stringer Bob Henley is a good defensive catcher and an easily-over-looked asset.

Five years ago, the club's first baseman was a rookie named Cliff Floyd. He batted .281 but hit only four homers and drove in only 41 runs (they only played about two-thirds of the schedule that year, but that excuse only goes so far). Brad Fullmer is an inferior defender, but he could match Floyd's average and add four home runs a month. He's also shown that he can keep his glove out of the way of oncoming baserunners.

At first glance, it wouldn't seem that Wilton Guerrero could contribute as much as Mike Lansing used to. It's important to remember that the '95 version of Lansing was the pre-weightlifting version. At that point in his career, Lansing wasn't anything special at the plate. His on-base percentage that year was .299, and his slugging percentage was .392. Wilton Guerrero's career averages are superior in both categories, and he's only 24 years old. Guerrero's come a long way in the field, although the '95 version of Lansing probably was better on the pivot. Overall, there's no clear advantage either way.

Third base is one of the key positions for this year's Expos. Alou has made the gutsy decision to bench incumbent Shane Andrews in favor of rookie Michael Barrett. Andrews is no star, but he is a sure fielder and a proven run-producer on a team that needs all the power it can get.

The decision makes sense though, because Barrett is better. He can handle himself in the field, and his production last year at Double-A suggests that he's got what it takes to hit in the majors, right now. Alou's ability to evaluate talent allowed him to see that Barrett was the better player, and his faith in his own judgment gave him the courage to bench the proven veteran in favor of the rookie fresh out of Double-A.

Hopefully, Andrews can be dealt for something more useful. If Cal Ripken's back problems are as serious as they seemed to be when he came out of the game last night, the Orioles may be interested. The Reds and Royals are other clubs that could use a power-hitting third baseman.

Meanwhile, Barrett has a good chance to do more than Andrews did last year or Sean Berry did in '94. Berry's .261 average and medium-range power is equivalent to a middling-to-pessimistic projection for Barrett. More likely, the kid will flirt with .300 and contend for Rookie-of-the-Year honors.

The shortstop position features two completely dissimilar players, Wil Cordero and Orlando Cabrera. Cordero was one of the best offensive shortstops in the league, but one of the worst glove men at the position. In '95, his last year as a shortstop, he finished next-to-last in the majors in both fielding percentage and range factor. Cabrera could hit for an acceptable average, but has no real offensive strengths. His fielding has drawn raves. Overall, it's tough to weigh Cordero's offense against Cabrera's defense, but we'll give Cordero the benefit of the doubt.

The '94 Expos' biggest strength was their outfield unit of Moises Alou, Marquis Grissom and Larry Walker. Both Alou and Walker batted well over .300 with plenty of power, and Grissom hit .288 and won a Gold Glove.

This year's Expos may not be able to match that, but with Vlad Guerrero and a healthy Rondell White, they may come close. White will begin the year in left field to save wear and tear on his knees, and once he moves back to center, Orlando Merced may see a lot of time in left. Merced's ability to reach base may prove useful in the No. 2 hole, especially with the notoriously impatient Wilton Guerrero batting leadoff. In any event, Merced and a platoon-mate should be able to improve upon Ryan McGuire and Derrick May's sorry performances.

Taking the offense as a whole, it's hard to see how the Expos could *fail* to improve. Last year's club scored fewer runs than any team in baseball, but as we've seen, this year's lineup may not be all that much worse than the '94 club's.

The biggest challenge will be for Felipe Alou to develop several young pitchers. That's one of the hardest things for a manager to do, but Alou has a better track record in that respect than just about anyone else.

He'll have a lot of work to do to build a staff like the one he had in '94. Ken Hill had his best season (16-5, 3.32), leaving Pedro Martinez (11-5, 3.42) as the No. 2 starter. Lefthanders Jeff Fassero (8-6, 2.99) and Butch Henry (8-3, 2.43) were outstanding.

In the bullpen, he had two legitimate closers, with John Wetteland (2.83 ERA, 25 saves) and Mel Rojas (3.32 ERA, 16 saves). He also had three solid middle relievers, with Tim Scott (2.70 ERA), Gil Heredia (3.46) and future closer Jeff Shaw (3.88).

Right now, Alou's staff already has the two most important ingredients: the ace, Dustin Hermanson, and the closer, Ugueth Urbina. Hermanson has everything you look for in a young pitcher; he gets strikeouts, he's tough to hit, he has good control, and his arm hasn't been abused. It's a testament to his ability that he was able to post a winning record with such a weak supporting cast last year. He's every bit the pitcher Pedro Martinez was in '94, and if he gets the run support that Ken Hill did that year, he'll be a strong Cy Young candidate.

Many things will need to break right for the rest of the rotation to jell. There is plenty of potential for improvement, though. Carl Pavano is as good a bet to improve as any pitcher in baseball. He pitched awfully well last year, considering that he was a rookie on a losing club. He overcame early-season shoulder tendinitis, and finished with less than one hit allowed per inning and a strikeout-to-walk ratio of almost two-to-one. He could become a 15-game winner and a solid No. 2 starter.

It's difficult, but not impossible to have hope for a pitcher with a 5-15 career record and a 6.06 ERA. Javier Vazquez didn't do the job last year, but it was a case of a raw, young pitcher doing his learning at the major league level. Steve Avery, John Smoltz and Andy Ashby are just a few of the pitchers who've had similar experiences and lived to tell. At age 21, Vazquez was one of the youngest players in the majors last year. Both his stuff and his minor league record are excellent. His performance this spring (23 innings, zero walks, 13 strikeouts) suggests that he may have turned the corner.

Mike Thurman and Miguel Batista are two more development projects. The chances are that the youngsters won't all come at once, but on the other hand, the talent here is just as impressive as the '91 Braves had.

Urbina could use some help in the bullpen. Lefthander Steve Kline was surprisingly tough last year, and Alou will need to get something out of veterans Mike Maddux and Anthony Telford.

No, this year's club isn't anything close to the machine Alou assembled in '94. But are they strong enough to be a factor in the NL Wild-Card race? You bet. It says right here that the Expos will be this year's most successful small-market franchise.

April 13—First Impressions of a New Season

Impressions from the first week of the season:

A few weeks ago, I mentioned that the Kansas City Royals' improved infield defense would help their young pitchers. Let me amend that: it's going to help their young pitchers *immensely*. Joe Randa, Rey Sanchez, Carlos Febles and Jeff King form KayCee's best infield defensive unit since George Brett, Freddie Patek, Frank White and John Mayberry were together.

Yesterday, they defused two Cleveland rallies with twin-killings while protecting a 2-0 lead. They eventually lost in extra innings, but it was clear that last year's defenders would have lost the game in nine, easily. Kansas City has turned 14 double plays, four more than any other team.

The Royals also have excellent speed in the outfield, with Johnny Damon, Carlos Beltran and Jermaine Dye. With that kind of defense behind them, Jose Rosado and Jeff Suppan could be two of this year's most "improved" pitchers.

Has Raul Mondesi finally learned to lay off bad pitches? Since the beginning of spring training, Dodgers manager Davey Johnson has been on a mission to teach Mondesi the virtue of patience. So far, the results have been phenomenal. In seven games, Mondesi already has drawn seven walks—almost one-quarter of last season's total—and has been named NL Player of the Week.

Johnson's used some interesting psychology in his attempt to get through to his sometimes-enigmatic right fielder. Early in the spring, when Mondesi asked to bat third, Johnson said he would grant the request only if Mondesi were able to curb his free-swinging ways.

Mondesi put forth an earnest effort, and finished the spring with eight walks in 62 plate appearances—a far better ratio than he'd ever posted during the regular season. Johnson, perhaps sensing that giving in too easily might encourage Mondesi to lapse back into hacker mode, refused to let Mondesi have the carrot. Johnson told Mondesi that he's made good progress, but that it wasn't enough. Mondesi has remained in the No. 4 hole, pressing on for his "promotion" to the third spot, and his walk rate has continued to climb. It isn't often that a free-swinger is able to learn patience overnight, but Sammy Sosa showed similar signs early last year, and look where he ended up.

Keep an eye on Oakland's second-base situation. Tony Phillips has started four of the A's first seven games there. Second base always has been his best position, and it's odd that more managers haven't used him there.

It's been assumed from the beginning of the spring that Phillips would be used in left field and that Scott Spiezio was secure at second base. That began to change after Matt Stairs came into camp with his throwing shoulder repaired and his physique firmed up. It quickly became apparent that Stairs was better suited to play right field than Ben Grieve, who was dug up and replanted in left. That left Phillips without a place to play, as the DH spot was taken by John Jaha, who currently is between injuries.

Somebody had to lose out, and Howe quite properly selected Spiezio to sit. Although Spiezio generally is regarded as a youngster on the rise, the truth is that he isn't all that young—26 year old—or that good. His range afield is subpar, and at the plate, he's no more of a threat than Mark Lewis.

An injury to any one of a number of players could start a chain reaction, one that could land Phillips back in the outfield at any time. But on the other hand, it won't be long before Phillips has logged enough time at the keystone to qualify there, something that would greatly enhance his fantasy value.

In his quest to prove that he isn't *exactly* Steve Ontiveros, Butch Henry is back—alive and pitching. To be fair, there is one significant difference between Henry and guys like

Ontiveros, whose arms break down twice a year. Henry's last significant injury was a *knee* injury, and in one sense, that's a positive. The injury wiped out almost all of last season for him, and prevented him from being overworked when he was coming off an elbow reconstruction.

Now, he's not only healthy, but also well-rested. We might even consider him something other than a poor injury risk. That's important, because whenever he pitches, he pitches well. In his last eight starts (spread over three seasons, admittedly) he's gone 3-1 with a 1.75 ERA.

Abandoning switch-hitting has worked for Luis Castillo—so far, at least. Swinging from his natural side, the right, he batted .345 this spring to beat out Craig Counsell for the Marlins' second-base job. In seven regular-season games, he's hit .296 and struck out only once in 27 at-bats, after fanning 132 times in 580 at-bats over the previous three seasons.

Is something really wrong with Francisco Cordova? He usually throws in the low-90s, but when he faced the Cubs a few days ago, he couldn't get out of the mid-80s. The Cubs cuffed him around, and the Pirates pulled him in the third. Later, they said he "couldn't get loose."

Suck it up, Frankie. You'll be plenty loose once that ligament snaps.

April 20—Blue Jay Way

Even though Tim Johnson no longer is around to fire up the troops with the story of how he stormed the Bastille, the Blue Jays remain anything but boring. Last week alone, their Opening Day cleanup hitter gave up switch-hitting and sustained a potentially serious wrist injury on the same day, one of their top starting pitchers went down with a shoulder injury while a young hurler stepped into his rotation spot and pitched a gem, and their beleaguered bullpen was strengthened by the return of their stopper—a 29-year-old with a 5.25 ERA and seven career saves. Who needs a Canseco?

Ah, the bullpen. The nether regions where Mike Timlin toiled in obscurity, relegated to mostly middle relief by Cito Gaston for an alleged lack of "guts." The place where the formerly-dominant Randy Myers suddenly developed an advanced case of mediocrity. Late last year, having disposed of both Timlin and Myers, the Jays decided to turn over the closer role to Robert Person, who'd never saved a single game in the majors.

Person trained for the job by closing at Triple-A for a few weeks, where he pitched decently. He was brought up to Toronto in September and continued to perform creditably, saving six games in eight chances. A hamstring injury delayed his start this year, but when he came off the disabled list last week, he found that his job was ready and waiting for him.

To have any hope of making a run at a wild-card spot, the Jays need Person to succeed; there simply isn't anyone else in the bullpen who's qualified to close out games. Veteran lefthander Dan Plesac is a useful setup man, but will tell you himself that he hasn't had closer's stuff for about 10 years. Graeme Lloyd is a one-out specialist who's had little success when asked to do anything more than face selected lefthanded hitters. Tom Davey and Peter Munro are rookies and converted starters.

Can Person do it? On one hand, there's no obvious reason to think he'll be a good closer. He's thrown almost 300 innings in the majors, and hasn't found consistent success in any capacity. There's nothing in the numbers that indicates he's better suited for short relief. (When Tom Gordon was sent to the bullpen, we were able to predict success because he'd always been so strong one time through the order as a starter. Person, however, has been uniformly unimpressive from start to finish). Pitchers with lifetime ERAs over 5.00 seldom are entrusted with ninth-inning leads.

On the other hand, it's easy to overestimate what it takes to save 30-odd games a year. First, you need to be the stopper, and second, you need to have talent. The former is far more important than the latter.

It's entirely possible for a mediocre pitcher to save a ton of games; it happens all the time. The essence of pitching is to prevent batters from doing the things that create runs, like getting on base and hitting for power. If we examine pitchers by their opponent on-base-plus-slugging (OPS), it's clear that just about any half-decent pitcher can compile enough saves to hold onto the closer's job for a season or five.

Last year, Rod Beck saved 51 games, and Jeff Montgomery saved 36. Neither of them pitched well. Beck's opponent OPS was .745, two points higher than Montgomery's. People look at their save totals and get the impression they pitched well, but consider how their opponent OPS compare to some other pitchers'. If Beck and Montgomery had posted similar numbers as starters, they would have come in right around Steve Woodard (.734), Orel Hershiser (.741) and Mark Clark (.743). Would anyone consider Mark Clark closer material?

So, if the question is whether Person can pitch as well as Mark Clark, the answer is "probably." And if that's the answer, then Person probably can save 30-something games. I'm not saying he *will*, mind you; I'm just saying he *can*.

One more thing Person has going for him is the presence of manager Jim Fregosi, who got three big-save seasons out of Mitch Williams while the Wild Thing was walking more than six batters per nine innings. Let's just say that Person won't necessarily exhaust Fregosi's patience if he pitches himself into a few tight spots early on.

Then you have Dave Hollins, the season-opening cleanup hitter and currently disabled DH. He drove in one run in his first nine games before Fregosi came to him with a bold idea: give up switch-hitting.

I'd been waiting for that for a long time. For years, Hollins has been one of the most imbalanced switch-hitters in baseball. From the right side—his natural side—he's a monster, with a lifetime batting average over .300 and slugging percentage over .500. From the left, he'll do whatever he can to get on base, including drawing a walk or dropping down a bunt (honest), but he just isn't the same hitter: .240 average, .375 slugging.

It's been obvious for quite a while that Hollins would have little to lose from going righthanded all the way. If you looked at other righthanded hitters who hit lefties the way Hollins does, you'd find that very few of them drop off so dramatically against righthanders. Besides, in recent years there have been a number of lopsided switch-hitters who've improved markedly after committing to their strong side (the list includes Mariano Duncan, Orlando Merced, Rich Becker and Reggie Jefferson. This year, Luis Castillo and J.T. Snow are trying it).

So I was excited to hear that Hollins had dropped switch-hitting. Then, in his first game batting strictly righthanded, he was plunked on the wrist. He's currently headed for the DL and the Blue Jays are expecting to hear that he's broken a bone.

Oh well. At least the Jays will be able to platoon Willie Greene and Geronimo Berroa. Greene is hopeless against lefties, but quite powerful against righties, and it's odd that he didn't draw more interest this winter. He was born to be the lefthanded part of a DH platoon.

Out at shortstop, Alex Gonzalez continues his quest to join his friends Carlos Delgado and Shawn Green as full-fledged stars. The three of them came up together and persevered through Cito Gaston's hazing. Delgado broke out in '96, and Green exploded last year, but Gonzalez remained stuck in neutral.

Gonzalez got himself in much batter shape over the winter, and overhauled his plate approach this spring. The results were a .324 average in spring training and a .346 average so far this season.

In the outfield, Shannon Stewart and Jose Cruz Jr. are on the verge of becoming Green-magnitude stars. Stewart doesn't get the recognition he deserves, probably because he's a speed guy at a power position. Has anyone noticed that what he did last year (.279-12-55, 67 walks, .417 slugging) was very comparable to what Bernie Williams did at the same age (.268-12-68, 53 walks, .400 slugging)? It was the following year that Williams broke into the upper echelon of major league outfielders, and Stewart has shown signs of doing the same so far this year.

In center, Junior Cruz has shown signs of maturing, drawing a league-high 18 walks. The turnaround actually started last year when he was sent down in midseason. He got it back together in Triple-A and continued to hit from the time of his recall until the end of the season. His recovery wasn't well noted because his first-half stats kept his numbers down all year. He won't have that problem this season.

And in the rotation, you have—thanks to Joey Hamilton's shoulder injury—Roy Halladay, who's allowed three earned runs in his first 30 major league innings. With Chris Carpenter and Kelvim Escobar, the Jays have three of the best young power arms in the majors.

Will this collection of prodigies and curiosities be able to drag their veteran baggage into the wild-card race? I say, sure—why not? Like before, I'm not saying they *will*; I'm saying they *can*.

April 27—The New Strike Zone

If the umpires are properly enforcing the "new" strike zone, the effect hasn't been quite what we'd expected. In fact, it's been just the opposite.

Pitchers weren't the only ones who lauded the return of the belt-high strike. To many observers—especially broadcasters who pitched or caught in the majors during the 1960s—everything from the belly button to the knees rightly belonged to the pitcher. To them, the renewed emphasis on the high strike signaled the reversal of a gradual, three-decade-long lowering of the strike zone.

The accompanying elimination of the off-the-outside-corner strike call was seen as nothing more than an incidental adjustment. Perhaps the rest of the league wanted to see the Braves try to throw to a real strike zone, but for whatever reason, there was very little grumbling about it. From everything you heard, it sounded like the pitchers would be gaining a lot more above the waist than they'd be losing off the outside corner. It all seemed consistent with Major League Baseball's stated goal of speeding up games.

It hasn't worked out as planned. For whatever reason, the balance of power has continued to shift from the pitcher to the hitter. *Fewer* pitches are being called strikes, not more. As a result, batters are seeing more pitches than ever before, and walks are up by a whopping 13 percent. This has led to a slight increase in scoring, even though batting averages and home-run production remains level.

So, if last year was the year of the home run, will this year be the year of the walk? Will this summer feature Mark McGwire's assault on Babe Ruth's bases-on-balls record? McGwire drew 162 free passes last year, eight shy of Ruth's all-time single-season mark. Right now he has 17 in 16 games and is on pace to draw 162 walks for the second straight year.

McGwire isn't leading the majors in walks, though; he isn't even close. Through Monday, Jose Cruz Jr. had drawn a major league-high 22 bases on balls, putting him on pace for 178. This, from a player who'd drawn a total of 98 walks in two previous seasons.

Cruz isn't the only one who's found the new strike zone to be much more workable. Chicago second-sacker Ray Durham is threatening to unseat Frank Thomas as the White Sox' most patient hitter. He's taking more pitches and working deeper counts, and his walks are up almost 50 percent. Waiting for his pitch may be helping his power too, as he's slugging close to .600.

Meanwhile, Braves wunderkind Andruw Jones is on pace to walk 115 times, almost three times as often as he did last year. Jones' newfound command of the strike zone hasn't yet paid off in an improved batting average, but it's early.

Reggie Sanders has made a terrific adjustment to the No. 2 hole in San Diego. Utilized more as a run-producer in Cincinnati, Sanders has drawn 14 walks and scored 14 runs in 17 games.

Although he's only batting .235, his .409 on-base percentage is higher than any he's ever posted, and he's already socked four home runs.

Oddly, Bernie Williams and Matt Lawton have been much more aggressive this year. Williams has gone after the first pitch almost half the time, more often than any other hitter in the AL and almost twice as often as he did last year. There's no obvious explanation for the change in his approach. (It's hard to imagine that he's been carrying around an undiscovered weakness for belt-high pitches.) He's managed to keep his average up, but he's only gone deep once and has walked only four times.

This spring, Lawton was told that he'd gotten too many hits off fastballs last year and that pitchers would make him hit the breaking ball this year. This may explain his sudden willingness to hack at anything. Perhaps Lawton is looking for first-pitch fastballs in order to keep pitchers from getting to the breaking ball. Whatever the reason, the adjustment hasn't hurt his production. Last year's dramatic increase in his strikeout-walk ratio indicated continuing improvement, and Lawton's still on target to post his best season yet.

May 4—Reading Fast and Slow Starts

Buying low and selling high—it's a concept that's easy to espouse but difficult to practice. The biggest problem is overcoming the natural aversion to slumping players. When Delino DeShields is batting .155, the head says it's the perfect time to trade for him, but the stomach disagrees. There's a nagging fear—often justifiable—that the player really has gone off the deep end.

Luckily, we have a tool that helps us to distinguish normal early-season slumps from the kind of struggles that signal a real change in ability: the STATS in-season projection system.

Creating an in-season projection is a rather simple process. All we do is take the player's preseason projection, add it to the player's current stats, and prorate the totals over the remaining schedule. Then we add in the player's current stats to get full-season totals.

The beauty of it is that the system recognizes an important truth: just because Luis Gonzalez is batting .383 on May 5 doesn't mean he'll be batting .383 on October 1. The system will give him "credit" for getting off to a hot start, but it will rely much more heavily upon his preseason projection, which only has him hitting .274.

His projected batting average for the *remainder* of the season will be much closer to .274 than .383—.280, to be exact. When you add that to his 31-for-81 start, you come out with a season-ending batting average of .295.

As the season goes along, the player's current stats gather more and more weight, relative to his preseason projection. If Gonzalez is still batting .383 in mid-June, then there will be good reasons to suspect that he's become a significantly better hitter. Right now, there's no reason to think that he has; his in-season projection has him batting .295, and he's done that before.

What the system does very well is alert us when a player has either: 1) established a new level of ability, or 2) dug himself such a deep hole that he'll *never* be able to climb completely out of it by October.

Fernando Tatis is the most obvious example of the former. His in-season projection has him batting .283 with 26 home runs and 93 RBI. The system is telling us, essentially, that with nine home runs already, Tatis couldn't possibly finish with anything close to last year's total (11). It's also properly recognizing that his power numbers in '97 (both in the majors and the minors) suggested that he'd hit with more power. At any rate, it's a safe bet that he'll finish with better numbers than Robin Ventura.

Another true gem is Brian Giles. His projection is even better than Tatis': .283-31-97, with 97 walks thrown in for good measure. That's a reflection of both his hot start and the fact that he's finally playing full-time.

Sean Casey is someone else who's established that he's going to do a lot more than he did last year. Coming off a .272 season, Casey gets an in-season projection of .325-16-100 with a whopping 47 doubles.

For some others, the system tells us not to get too worried about their early struggles. Todd Walker projects at .294 with similar power numbers to last year's. Johnny Damon showed too much last year to slide this far, this fast, and comes in at .272-12-60. Todd Helton's forecast calls for another solid season (.314-21-92), and even DeShields comes out OK (.252, which isn't bad, considering where he's at right now).

Not all slumps can be written off so easily, though. The system tells us that Tom Glavine's noted difficulties are more than a hiccup. He's projected to go 13-11 with a 3.53 ERA, his worst season in years.

Barry Larkin's been in a terrible skid for three weeks. The system recognizes that he still has power, but predicts that this will be the first year in a while where he won't come close to .300. It has him batting .265 with 20 homers and 69 RBI.

Even Sammy Sosa comes down to his pre-1998 levels, checking in at .263 with 44 homers and 121 RBI. I happen to concur with this one wholeheartedly—Sosa's lost a lot of the plate discipline that made him such a monster last year.

We also get confirmation that Greg Vaughn's back to normal (.229-34-98). This one, I'm not so sure about. Despite Vaughn's anemic batting average, he's maintained an uncharacteristically good strikeout-walk ratio. To me, this suggests a much greater possibility of recovery. But on the other hand, walks are way up this year (more than 12 percent) and the system may be right. We'll find out eventually.

May 11—Sniffing For Arm Trouble

Sometimes you can see an arm injury coming.

For example, it was fairly apparent that there was something wrong with John Smoltz in 1997. Of course, you wouldn't necessarily be able to detect it by looking only at his conventional stats. Although his won-lost record dropped off from 24-8 to 15-12, his ERA remained right around 3.00, and he fanned a total of 241 batters. Nothing in those numbers suggested that he was anything other than a dominant pitcher.

What gave him away was an in-game pattern that he followed consistently throughout that season. Game after game, Smoltz would start strongly but tire noticeably after the fifth inning.

The contrast is obvious when his opponent batting line is split into totals through 60 pitches and after 60 pitches. Opponent batting lines have no all-encompassing stat like ERA, so it's useful to summarize them by presenting opponent average/on-base percentage/slugging percentage.

In 1996, Smoltz' Cy Young season, he held batters to an Avg/OBP/Slg of .216/.260/.331. In '97, he was equally effective over his first 60 pitches: .210/.255/.278. After reaching the 60-pitch mark, his numbers deteriorated significantly: .279/.328/.454.

Of course, there are many pitchers who lose a little something as they get deeper into a ballgame. Even so, Smoltz' record was abnormally schizophrenic. His early-game opponent batting line was consistent with an ERA around 2.20, while his late-game opponent batting line suggested an ERA more than twice that high.

Sure enough, after the season ended, Smoltz admitted that he'd been pitching with an elbow problem. He had surgery over the winter and has posted a 22-4 record since his return.

Any time you see a pitcher who's effective early on but consistently loses his edge at a certain point in the game, you have to suspect that his problem may be physical. There already are several pitchers who are raising warning flags this year.

Carlos Perez is one of the most extreme cases. His late-inning meltdowns already have drawn attention. Still, it's shocking to see the extent of his late-game struggles.

Although he sports an ugly 5.65 ERA, through his first 60 pitches, he's been even tougher than he was last year, when he posted a fine 3.59 ERA in 241 innings. His opponent batting line through 60 pitches is .200/.264/.325, compared to his overall numbers from last year, .264/.312/.395.

After that, he loses it, like only a Perez brother can: .486/.526/.886. This is not a misprint. After Perez has reached the 60-pitch mark, hitters have gone 17-for-35 against him with six doubles, a triple and two homers.

What's going on here? Is it his arm? It can't be his head; Perez is just as "colorful" in the seventh inning as he is in the first.

Another pitcher to worry about is Seattle southpaw Jamie Moyer. First, you have the fact that he averaged nearly 105 pitches per start last year, far more than the string-bean lefty ever had averaged in any previous season. Then you have his disastrous performance so far this year. He came into Tuesday with an ERA approaching 8.00; as I write this, the Red Sox are ripping line drives off him left and right—most of them right at people, so far. But again, the most damning detail has been his in-game deterioration.

If you can believe it, he's actually been more effective than last year, at least through his first 45 pitches: .253/.270/.333, compared to .256/.295/.408 for all of last season. And as you may guess, he ultimately and completely loses it.

He does it in two steps. Over his *next* 45 pitches, his opponent batting line jumps to .319/.397/.493. As if that's not bad enough, he suffers a Perez-like meltdown after the 90-pitch mark: .500/.581/.806 (18-for-36).

It doesn't help that he's probably going to be left out on the mound to wilt many more times this season. The Seattle bullpen's 5.64 ERA doesn't give Lou Piniella too many options. It's 500,000,000 of one or a half-billion of the other.

The last lefty with a potential DL stint in the cards is Al Leiter of the Mets. Like the others, he's been just as effective as last year up to a certain point. Through 90 pitches, he's held hitters to .210/.301/.348, compared to .216/.298/.306 for all of last year. And like the others, he's shown a consistent pattern of late-game blowups. After hitting the 90-pitch mark, his opponents' numbers zoom to .432/.490/.773.

Let me be clear: none of this means that these pitchers necessarily are suffering from arm problems. All we're saying is that they're showing a pattern that's consistent with that of a pitcher who isn't fully healthy. But that's enough for me to steer clear of them.

May 18—Buying Low

Here are eight slumping hitters who could come cheaply in a trade:

Tony Clark, Detroit. Right now, he's batting .217 with four home runs and 20 RBI in 35 games. My advice: ignore his numbers. We all know that Clark runs hot-and-cold. He goes through a dry spell like this every year but always manages to finish with good numbers. He had equally barren 35-game stretches in 1996 (.198-7-15), '97 (.256-3-18) and '98 (.230-4-19) but still averaged .275-31-97 over that three-year period. He's been drawing more walks recently—a good sign.

Todd Helton, Colorado. With a .263 average, he appears to be struggling, although he's on pace to both score and drive in well over 100 runs. Due to a scheduling quirk and the Columbine High School tragedy, the Rockies have played 22 of their first 34 games on the road, so their hitters haven't gotten their usual Coors boost yet. With a more even split,

Helton's average would be right around .300. He'll be in the thick of the batting race by year's end.

Eric Chavez, Oakland. Olmedo Saenz is a competent, useful player, the type that can help a team off the bench, but he's no more qualified to play ahead of Eric Chavez than he is to be the United States' Ambassador to China. Chavez seems to have hit his way back into the starting lineup, and in light of his considerable offensive abilities, he ought to be able to hit enough to remain there for quite a while. It will be an uphill climb, but he should be able to finish with a batting average in the .280s and respectable power numbers.

Travis Lee, Arizona. His numbers are stuck in Tony Clark territory (.230-3-22), but there are some positive signs as well. The biggest one is the fact that he's cut his strikeout rate by over 50 percent—a dramatic development that promises to yield big returns in the near future.

Delino DeShields, Baltimore. It's been said many times, but it's true: the thumb injury that delayed the start of his season effectively turned the month of April into his spring training. Now that he's played his way into shape, his bat has started to come around, and the O's have begun to rotate him back toward the top of the lineup. He should wind up there eventually, since he's much more qualified to bat second than Mike Bordick. Batting ahead of B.J. Surhoff and Albert Belle, DeShields ought to score a lot of runs.

Barry Larkin, Cincinnati. Sure, he's only batting .231, but he's also got more home runs and RBI than any other NL shortstop except for Rich Aurilia. And for once, he isn't being dragged down by nagging injuries.

Brian McRae, New York Mets. McRae never hits in April, and this year was no different. His numbers at the same point last year were nearly identical (.237-2-14 last year, .235-3-11 this year) and he wound up with the best power numbers of his career.

J.D. Drew, St. Louis. After slugging .972 in 14 games at the tail end of last season, Drew has stumbled from the gate and suffered with various aches and pains. Despite batting only .230 while being regarded as one of the season's biggest disappointments, he's continued to draw walks and hit for power. With an on-base percentage of .337 and a slugging percentage of .459, it is, as Kevin Goldstein says, "the kind of slump that stars have."

May 25—The Middle Men

I'm no biblical scholar, but I know there's something in there about the meek inheriting the earth. The crazy thing is that it's actually starting happen—in baseball, at least.

The long reliever, traditionally *persona non grata* in the fantasy realm, is becoming an increasingly important member of the pitching staff, both in real and fantasy baseball. This is a subtle but significant result of the continuing rise in offensive levels.

From a pitching standpoint, compiling victories always has been the domain of the starting pitcher. Modern closers rarely get the chance to pick up a significant number of wins. Middle and long relievers rarely get the chance to win enough games to make them very useful in fantasy.

This year, however, the balance between starters and relievers has begun to shift. With so many starting pitchers getting knocked out early in the game, many teams have had to find a long reliever of decent quality. Some of these long men have been getting quite regular work.

Not only have the long man been making more appearances and throwing more innings than ever, but they've also had more chances to pick up victories than ever before. In previous years, a long man worked mostly when his team's starter had been shelled and the club was hopelessly behind. This season, with more runs than ever being scored, it seems that no deficit is insurmountable. More importantly, there have been more *two-sided* slugfests this year than ever before. Now long men regularly are brought into games where their club trails by only a few runs or even holds a lead.

Last year, starters earned 71.6 percent of all victories; relievers accounted for the remaining 28.4 percent. This year, relievers' share of the victories has swelled to 31.2 percent, an increase of 11 percent over last year. And bear in mind that the relievers' gain results in a corresponding loss for the starters. As I said, these changes are subtle, but when everything is added up, their impact can be significant.

So while we have fewer starters with quality stats than ever before, we also have a new wave of long relievers who are downright useable. The best example is Cleveland's Steve Karsay. If we were to construct a scenario in which a long reliever could win 20 games, it would have to mirror Karsay's situation with the Indians.

For a long reliever to have a shot at winning 20 games, a number of conditions must apply. First, he'd need to be a quality pitcher, of course (Karsay fits the bill). Second, he'd need to pitch for a team with a good offense (this Indians team has a shot to score more runs than any team in the 20th century). Third, the team would have to have starting pitchers that were fairly decent but didn't work deep into ballgames all that often (the Indians' starting staff's ERA is 5.21, which is slightly above-average for the American League. They've thrown only a few more innings than the average staff).

Karsay satisfies all the conditions. The Indians have gone to him early and often, and as a result, he owns a 4-1 record. At this rate, he'll win 15 games, something a reliever hasn't done in a long time.

We all know that probably won't happen, though. Even if he stays healthy all year, which is something Karsay rarely does, his luck will have to hold up for him to win even 12 games.

But if he *does* win a dozen, think what that will mean. Compared to a starter with a dozen wins, Karsay won't be just a *little* more valuable—he'll be *much* more valuable. First, he won't have nearly as many losses. He's rarely brought into a game where the Indians are leading, and on those rare occasions when he is, he's usually pulled for a setup man before he has a chance to lose it. And second, he'll have a much lower ERA. Right now, the average AL starting pitcher's ERA is 5.33. Karsay's is barely above 2.00, and even if he finishes in the mid-threes, it will more than offset his lower innings-pitched total.

The most amazing thing is the number of pitchers who've been slotted into Karsay-type roles. Up in Milwaukee, the most valuable member of their entire pitching staff has been long man David Weathers. The Brewers' starters have been getting shelled so regularly that Weathers has been on call as something of a sixth-starter, ready to pitch several innings every second or third day. He's gone 4-0 with a few saves thrown in for good measure.

Sean Lowe has filled a similar position for the White Sox, whose starters are forced to early showers as regularly as anyone's. Half of Lowe's 14 appearances have been for two innings or more, and he's registered a fine 2-0 record and 2.87 ERA. Bill Simas' promotion to co-closer may mean that Lowe will be called upon even more frequently in the middle innings.

Cincinnati's starters have tossed a major league-low 221 innings, which has left plenty of work for Cincinnati's bullpen. It's been fun to watch Scott Williamson, Danny Graves and Ron Villone jockey for position in the closer derby, but the real yeoman's work has been turned in by sidearmer Scott Sullivan. In 31.2 innings, he's got a 2-0 record and a sub-2.00 ERA. Earlier in the year, it was Williamson who handled the long relief chores. After winning three games in that capacity, Williamson has begun to edge toward the closer's role, leaving long relief for Sullivan, a strong first-half pitcher.

Mets lefthander Dennis Cook was the first pitcher to win five games this year, but that was little more than a string of good luck. The most likely candidate to pick up wins out of their bullpen is Allen Watson. With Al Leiter hobbling on a gimpy knee, Bobby Jones struggling with a sore arm, and Jason Isringhausen trying to re-establish himself in the major leagues, Watson's services are sure to be needed. Manager Bobby Valentine likes Watson in the long role so much that he opted to have Isringhausen promoted rather than insert Watson back into the rotation.

Watson has another thing going for him in his long-relief role: his bat. As one of the best-hitting pitchers in the majors, Watson is more likely to help himself—and less likely to be lifted for a pinch-hitter—than any other pitcher around.

Other long men who stand a chance to win a decent number of games in relief are Boston's John Wasdin, Montreal's Bobby Ayala, Oakland's Brad Rigby and San Diego's Brian Boehringer.

June 1—The New ERAs

The earned-run average is obsolete. This year's numbers—particularly in the American League—are so far outside the normal range that customary standards no longer apply.

An ERA of 5.00 used to be the hallmark of futility. No more. The average ERA for an AL starting pitcher this year is well over 5.00, at 5.31. This represents a jump of over one-half of a run compared to last year. It also amounts to an increase of nearly *one-third* compared to the ERA of the average AL starter 10 years ago.

In other words, for an AL starter, an ERA of 5.00 no longer is bad—in fact, it's pretty good. A 5.00 ERA is about five percent below the league average for starters. Back in 1990, AL starters posted a collective ERA just over four; a starter with an ERA five percent better than average would have had an ERA around 3.82.

That year there were seven AL starters (minimum 162 innings) with an ERA within one-fifth of a run of that 3.82 mark. All seven were quality pitchers. Three still are active (Tom Candiotti, Randy Johnson and Tom Gordon), three have retired (Greg Harris, Teddy Higuera and Scott Sanderson), and one is trying to make it back (Jack McDowell). Get this: all seven of them had winning records, and all seven won at least 11 games. The average won-lost record for the seven was 14-10. The point is that there are going to be several pitchers who will wind up with similar won-lost records this year; they will have pitched just as well, but their ERAs will be around 5.00.

Like the new $20 bills, it's going to take a while before people will be able to look at the "new" ERAs without doing a double-take. Try one yourself: 14-10, 5.07. See? It' just doesn't *look* right. Thirty years of scanning the backs of baseball cards has programmed the "stats" portion of your brain to sound the alarm bells whenever it comes across the combination, "14-10, 5.07."

We're going to have to get over this. The fact of the matter is that there are plenty of quality pitchers in the American League with ugly ERAs. In order to see the quality, we're going to have to learn to see past the ERAs.

No AL starter's ERA is more misleading than that of the Yankees' Orlando Hernandez. With an ERA approaching 5.00, it looks like he's taken a huge step back from his super rookie season of a year ago. It looks that way, but he hasn't.

Effective pitching almost always translates into the prevention of runs. The "almost" applies to the rare exception like Hernandez, who has retired hitters effectively this year but has been scored upon anyway.

Last year he allowed a .222 batting average, a .299 on-base percentage and a .341 slugging percentage. This year, his opponent batting numbers are nearly identical: .217/.296/.354 (and all three marks are among the top six in the AL).

It's hard to explain how such fine pitching could result in such an ugly ERA. Sure, his 4.92 ERA is well below the league average, but that only goes so far. A bigger factor has been his tendency to give up hits at the most crucial moments. For some reason, the only time he's been truly hittable this year has been when there have been runners in scoring position. Perhaps he's tipping his pitches while pitching from the stretch. More likely, it's the sort of quirk that will even out in time. Don't be surprised if his record for the remainder of the season mirrors what he did last year.

Like Hernandez, Anaheim's Chuck Finley has been saddled with a mediocre record despite pitching about as well as he did last year. He got off to a slow start after a back injury prevented him from fully working into shape during spring training. He's still pitched well overall, and doesn't deserve anything like the 5.15 ERA he's been stuck with. He'll probably get it into the low-fours by the end of the year, and get the 13-to-15 wins he usually finishes with.

Charles Nagy's resurgence has been largely obscured by his 4.16 ERA. Still, he's made a significant recovery after a tater-plagued 1998. He's allowed only five homers, cutting his home run-allowed rate by about 50 percent. Opponents have slugged only .385 against him, the 10th-lowest mark in the league. Put in its proper context, his ERA actually is quite good, and he has the best offense in baseball behind him. If he keeps pitching this well, he could be on his way to his first 20-win season.

Detroit's Brian Moehler is another unheralded hurler. The only attention he's gotten has been for allegedly bringing a piece of sandpaper to the mound. He's been fairly effective, and those who would maintain that his success is the product of cheating should note that he hasn't lost much since returning from his suspension. He's a durable, reliable pitcher, and his ERA is about a half-run higher than it ought to be. With better luck, he could be within reach of the AL's top 10 in ERA. If Luis Polonia is able to cure the Tigers' dysfunctional offense by getting on base at the top of the lineup, the Tigers could score enough runs to get Moehler 15 victories.

Who's been the Orioles' most effective starter? Most would pick Mike Mussina (7-2, 4.21), but the fact is that youngster Sidney Ponson (5-4, 4.37) has been distinctly superior. Opponents have batted over .300 against Mussina, who's lucky to have an ERA below 5.00. Meanwhile, Ponson has held opponents to a .257 average and .315 on-base percentage, placing in the AL's top 20 in both categories. Since moving into the Baltimore rotation one calendar year ago, Ponson has gone 13-11 with a 4.70 ERA in 29 starts. Which reminds me. . . it's a good thing Charles Johnson is such a wonderful handler of pitchers, or else the Orioles' staff would be having a *really* bad year.

June 8—Closer Jobs Up For Grabs

Starting pitchers' win totals and earned-run averages may continue to deteriorate, but at least one important pitching category will weather the offensive onslaught: the save. It's more important than ever to watch for changes in teams' bullpen roles.

After Baltimore's Mike Timlin blew three games in 10 days in mid-May, Ray Miller lost confidence in him. When Miller gave Arthur Rhodes two save opportunities during the last week of May, it looked like Rhodes had been given at least half of Timlin's job.

That may have changed after last Saturday, when Miller called on Rhodes with a two-run lead in the ninth. Rhodes promptly walked the bases loaded on only 13 pitches (one above the minimum). Miller was forced to go back to Timlin, who allowed a run-scoring double play and a two-run homer to put the O's behind. Baltimore ultimately came back to win the game, but Rhodes' and Timlin's respective roles remained as unclear as ever.

While the Orioles' save opportunities may be distributed according to Miller's day-to-day frustrations, Timlin has at least one major advantage over Rhodes: the ability to work on consecutive days. Due to a chronically fragile elbow, Rhodes always has needed at least one day off between appearances.

Admittedly, this is a minor point—especially since the Orioles look like they may never win consecutive games again. Still, it guarantees that Timlin is likely to retain at least *part* of the closer's job. And besides, Timlin hasn't pitched all that badly. He's been guilty of serving up some ill-timed gopher balls, but his overall performance hasn't been as bad as his 6.33 ERA might suggest.

It's impossible to tell who the Royals' closer is right now, since they Royals haven't had any games to save in weeks. Manager Tony Muser has announced that Jeff Montgomery no longer will be the sole finisher, but no one else has had the chance to take over, since the clubs' dropped 12 of their last 13 games.

The most likely candidate to get the first crack at Montgomery's job is rookie righthander Jose Santiago. He's hardly a typical short reliever, being a groundballer rather than a strikeout artist. He's pitched well, but hasn't been all that sharp over the last couple of weeks.

The sleeper here is the recently-promoted Orber Moreno. Although he's only 22 years old and has been pitching out of the bullpen for little over a year, he's got the mid-90s fastball of a future closer. In his first seven major league appearances, he's allowed only three hits in 24 at-bats. He could be the kind of rookie short reliever who seemingly comes out of nowhere, the way John Rocker did last year.

Still, there's no guarantee that either Santiago or Moreno will get a real chance to take over for Montgomery. The Royals are paying Montgomery a lot of money, and they may feel compelled to keep giving him save opportunities in the hope that a contender will pick him up for the stretch run. Muser's comments were made in frustration, and he may not completely follow through; he's always been intensely loyal to Montgomery, who would have lost his job years ago under many other managers.

In order to avoid any misunderstandings, let me preface the next few paragraphs with the following disclaimer: Mike Jackson is the Indians' closer. There are no published reports to the contrary.

With that said, you'd still be well advised to keep an eye on the situation. Jackson admitted he was suffering from shoulder tendinitis last month, and was rested for five days. Even after the layoff, he hasn't been himself. Last year, he allowed four home runs and 13 walks; he's already given up six dingers and 11 walks this season. Last year, he fanned 7.7 batters per nine innings, his lowest strikeout rate in over a decade; this year, he's whiffed only 5.3 men per nine.

So if Jackson's tendinitis resurfaces, or he pitches himself into middle relief, do what the Indians did when he went down last month—turn to Paul Shuey. Since his recall in early May, Shuey has worked in 13 of the Indians' 23 games. His longtime weakness, control, hasn't been a problem, as he's issued only six unintentional walks in 26.2 innings.

Shuey earned his fourth save last Sunday when Tribe manager Mike Hargrove passed over Jackson, who'd worked each of the previous two games. If Jackson and his iffy arm continue to require careful handling, Shuey may scoop up the spare saves even if Jackson remains the nominal closer. The only sure thing is that there will be plenty of save opportunities to go around.

For weeks, the team with the most muddled closer situation of all has been the Cardinals. When Juan Acevedo was removed from the closer role and inserted into the starting rotation in early May, fantasy owner watched to see how the save opportunities would be divided between Rocky Bottalico and Scott Radinsky. Soon thereafter, Manny Aybar and Rich Croushore emerged as viable candidates as well.

Lately, it's been all Bottalico. As Tony La Russa's confidence in him has grown, his control problems have evaporated. Over his last eight appearances, Bottalico has converted four of five save opportunities while walking only one batter in 12.2 innings.

Radinsky hasn't come close to breaking out of his specialist role. Even in Acevedo's absence, Radinsky hasn't been used for more than four batters at a stretch. Manny Aybar has bagged a couple of saves, but each of them have been of the two-inning variety. It's clear that Bottalico now is La Russa's man when the game is on the line.

Each of the Chicago clubs has major questions in the bullpen. The White Sox began the year with Bobby Howry closing, but he pitched himself out of the job with a wild streak in mid-May. Bill Simas took over but soon befell a similar fate. Now Howry may be on the verge of reclaiming the job.

Up at Wrigley, Rick Aguilera has been as awful as Rod Beck had been before succumbing to arm surgery. Aguilera had been pitching very well for the Twins before being traded, so his problems probably aren't physical. Terry Adams has been the resident closer-in-waiting for years, but the Cubs have made it clear on several occasions that they'd rather commit themselves to a fading veteran than entrust meaningful innings to Adams. As long as Aguilera is able to stand without a cane, he'll probably continue to close for the Cubs.

June 15—President Jackson Reporting?

(Mat Olkin was unavailable this week due to a severe case of turf toe. Sitting in is Andrew Jackson, who regularly appears on the twenty-dollar bill.)

With home attendance down to less than 9,000 a game—only a few hundred more than the Senators averaged during their final season in Washington—the Expos' migration south of the border is growing increasingly inevitable. Proponents of a new downtown complex are having a hard time maintaining that a 10-minute ride on the Metro is what's keeping thousands of fans away from the game every night. Once the club finds a home where hockey is not the No. 1 sport, they'll be able to resume the task of building a perennial contender. For all that's gone wrong for them this year, a lot has gone right. Michael Barrett has established himself as a future star either behind the plate or at third base, Jose Vidro has grown into a rare switch-hitting second baseman with power, and Miguel Batista has learned to attack the strike zone with his power arm. With cornerstones like Vlad Guerrero, Rondell White and Dustin Hermanson in place, and Peter Bergeron and Ted Lilly in the pipeline, all the Expos need to do is find a venue that will provide enough revenue for them to lock some of their players into long-term deals. . . After getting stuck behind Chad Curtis, Curtis Pride and Melvin Nieves in Detroit, and Rich Butler and Paul Sorrento in Florida, Bubba Trammell finally has outlasted the competition. The Devil Rays have seen enough catchable balls fall in front of Paul Sorrento to give up hope that he'll ever develop outfielder's instincts. Now they want to see if Trammell can pound the ball the way he's done in the minors. Remember, Trammell hasn't exactly been a flop in the bigs, with a slugging percentage close to .500 in over 300 at-bats. . . Lance Johnson's constant aches and pains have the Cubs so exasperated that they bit the bullet and placed him on the DL when he begged off before a big game against the crosstown White Sox last weekend. Now they'll begin to explore other options in earnest, possibly including shifting Jose Hernandez to center field and reinstalling Jeff Blauser as the everyday shortstop. Blauser's made it through an entire season without a major injury only once in the last five years. Hmmmm. . . The trade of Tony Batista opens up Arizona's shortstop position for Andy Fox, one of Buck Showalter's favorite players. Fox doesn't have Batista's youth, range or power potential, but the Diamondbacks see him as a lefthanded-hitting Jay Bell. . . The Ruben Mateo Era began this week in Arlington when the heralded prospect was promoted and handed the center-field job. Scouts say he has "electric stuff," a compliment usually reserved only for pitchers. At the time of his callup, Mateo was in the top five in all three of the Pacific Coast League's Triple Crown categories. This, at age 21 and without help from an Albuquerque-type bandbox for a home park. . . Jason Christiansen was uncommonly wild early this season, walking 13 batters in his first 15.1 innings. The problem was traced to Christiansen's sore neck. After three weeks of inactivity, Christiansen has returned with seven scoreless innings over four appearances, with six strikeouts and one walk. . . The Red Sox are concerned that the MRI of Tom Gordon's elbow will reveal a season-ending injury—so much so that Tim Wakefield has been named interim closer. Can a knuckleballer be trusted in the late innings of a close game with men on base? Hey, ask Hoyt Wilhelm. . . Duquette and company feel they can stay close in the wild-card race, even without Gordon. With Pedro Martinez, Bret Saberhagen and Brian Rose, all they need to do is plug the fourth and fifth rotation spots until Ramon Martinez is able to return. Mark Portugal's unretirement has helped. . . The Angels could be the sleeping dogs of the AL West. Consider this fact: despite all their problems, they've allowed the second-fewest runs in the AL. The problem is offense, but things will turn around once Mo Vaughn gets healthy and Darin Erstad gets going. . . Scouts say that even after all he's been through, Alex Rodriguez still is one of the youngest players in the league.

This is Andrew Jackson, STATS, Inc.

June 22—The Finale

Caution: you are about to read my last column.

I'm outta here—off to Washington to work for *Baseball Weekly*. Soon, another STATS expert will take over this column. But in the meantime, I'm left to try to cram an entire season's worth of predictions into one essay (and even if I manage to do it, I still have to finish packing). Anyway, here goes.

Carlos Beltran will edge teammate Carlos Febles in the AL Rookie-of-the-Year balloting, although most serious analysts will give the nod to Febles. Some time around September, people will wake up and realize that Beltran and Febles are the best rookie teammates since Lynn and Rice.

Speaking of rookies, 1999 will go down as the best rookie crop in history. The Royals' pair of gems are part of a stellar class that includes present and future stars like: Jeff Weaver, Jeff Zimmerman, Gabe Kapler, Michael Barrett, Warren Morris, Eric Chavez, Alex Gonzalez, Bruce Aven, Benny Agbayani, Joe McEwing, Brian Daubach, Carlos Lee, J.D. Drew (he'll merit inclusion with a big second half), Preston Wilson, Brian Rose, Freddy Garcia, Scott Williamson, Billy Koch and Byung-Hyun Kim.

The Mariners shatter the single-season home-run record with a total of exactly 300 round-trippers. Junior Griffey leads the league with 60, and six more Mariners hit 25 or more. Brian Hunter is the only leadoff hitter in baseball who's the worst hitter in the batting order.

The Indians will set a modern record for runs scored with 1,068—one more than the 1931 New York Yankees. Manny Ramirez will drive in 171 runs. Both Robby Alomar and Kenny Lofton score more than 150 runs.

Cleveland minor-league slugger Russ Branyan leads the American Association with 45 home runs. He also fans 227 times.

Pittsburgh's Brian Giles breaks the century mark in runs, RBI and walks.

San Diego's Ruben Rivera bats .212 with 13 home runs. The Padres respond by announcing that they're going to make it a priority to find out if Rivera can play.

In August, with the club 37 games out of first place, the Brewers finally relent and call up former No. 1 draft choice Kyle Peterson. In his first major league start, Peterson hurls a six-hit shutout. In his next start, he tears his rotator cuff.

In order to weed out unqualified candidates and provide proper motivation, Seattle manager Lou Piniella implements a new policy: every starting pitcher allowing more than three runs in a game will be sent either to the bullpen or to the minor leagues. Within a week, Seattle has a 12-man bullpen and no starting rotation.

J.D. Drew returns to St. Louis and has a red-hot second half. Rick Ankiel joins the team in August and fans 36 over four starts to run his season total to 235.

The Marlins lose 105 games and post the worst record in baseball for the second straight year. On the last day of the season, Livan Hernandez blows out his elbow during a 159-pitch complete-game defeat. Manager John Boles says, "This would have happened a long time ago if we'd overworked him like Jim Leyland did last year."

Pokey Reese reverts to form in the second half and finishes with a .249 batting average.

Adrian Beltre and Eric Chavez finish with virtually identical batting stats, something that seemed all but impossible back in June.

Sean Casey bats .339 with 49 doubles. Todd Helton overcomes a slow start to hit .338.

When Joe Girardi's batting average slips below .180, the Yankees send him to a psychologist for testing. The doctor concludes that Girardi's veteran presence and leadership skills have seriously eroded, but may recover if his batting average gets back up over .250.

After posting a 2-10 record over the first half of the season, Reds righthander Brett Tomko reaches his breaking point. In an emotional, three-hour meeting with manager Jack McKeon, Tomko comes to the realization that his genteel demeanor is nothing more than a mask he's created to conceal his insensitive, macho nature. The meeting ends when Tomko punches out McKeon, steals his cigars, and drives over a squirrel on his way out of the players' parking lot. Tomko wins his next eight starts, but soon is suspended for the rest of the season. A Tomko pitch knocks Jose Canseco unconscious; Tomko, irate at Canseco's "crowding," rushes to the plate and tries to body-slam the now-unconscious ballplayer. McKeon says of Tomko: "We'll miss him. I respect the hell outta that guy."

Don Zminda's
Zee-Man Reports

February 12, 1999—1999 Training Camps

Thoughts as the camps open:

THE CLEMENS TRADE. It's no shock that he wound up with the Yankees, but didn't you think the Jays would get more than this for him? David Wells is a very fine pitcher, but he's about to turn 36, and his value in SkyDome is nowhere near as high as it is in Yankee Stadium, where Wells in 27-7, 3.30 in his career. Homer Bush and Graeme Lloyd are modest talents who don't figure to play nearly as well in 1999 as they did in '98. Couldn't the Jays have received at least one top-level prospect in a Clemens deal—if not a team's first- or second-best prospect, then at least someone with down-the-road potential? I don't get it. As Jim Callis put it, Gord Ash must have been thinking like a guy in a Strat-o league: "Yeah, I lost Clemens, but I got a guy who went 18-4 *and* a pitcher with a 1.67 ERA *and* a .380 hitter!" If they could play this season using the '98 cards, Toronto would look good for a playoff berth.

ALEX FERNANDEZ. The Marlins are saying that Alex (or "Young Alex," as Hawk Harrelson always called him) will be their Opening Day starter after missing all of 1998 while recovering from rotator-cuff surgery. That might be rushing things, but if you're looking for a late-round sleeper pick in your fantasy draft, you might want to look at Fernandez. Alex has always had a beautifully compact delivery, and he's always been a hard worker (albeit with a tendency to put on weight). If anyone can make a quick comeback from serious arm problems, he's the one.

GABE KAPLER. I like Kapler very much as a prospect, but over the past few weeks I've expressed doubts as to how much he'll get to play this year with the Tigers apparently set on a Higginson-Hunter-Encarnacion outfield. Now the Tigers are saying that they want to try Kapler in center, probably in preparation for a trade of Hunter. The only question is whether Kapler—a decent but not great corner outfielder with only adequate speed—can handle center field. I'd say no, but if he can't, maybe Encarnacion can. The point is, it looks like Kapler might wind up with more major league playing time this year than I originally thought. He can play, so you might consider picking him up in your fantasy draft.

TIM McCARVER AND BOBBY VALENTINE. I'm not much of a McCarver fan—he talks too much—but I admire his honesty, and I've liked him better on Mets broadcasts than I have on the network games. The Mets apparently didn't agree and replaced him with Tom Seaver (McCarver quickly signed with the Yankees' broadcast team). Bobby Valentine says he had nothing to do with McCarver's firing, but nobody's buying that. My sense is that Valentine's tactlessness and sensitivity to criticism are wearing very thin, and that he'll be gone by midseason if the Mets aren't strongly in contention. Davey Johnson's a bit of a jerk, too, but there's a difference: Johnson wins pennants.

DEREK JETER AND MARIANO RIVERA. If there are any clouds on the Yankees' horizon, it's that they decided to go to arbitration this year with Derek Jeter and Mariano Rivera. STATS does a good bit of work on arbitration cases, so I know quite a bit about the process; in fact, assisting in the preparation of arbitration cases is one of my major offseason jobs. With each passing year, arbitration is becoming more and more of a "court of last resort": the process can easily become antagonistic, and it's often in the best interest of both player and club to reach a compromise prior to the hearing. It's also more common these days for budget-minded teams to simply release players who are apt to win good-sized awards in arbitration; that's what happened to Pat Meares of the Twins this year. As a result, there are a number of general managers in the game today who have never had a case go to arbitration.

The Yankees, of course, can afford to pay Jeter and Rivera. But rather than lock up both players with multi-year deals or compromise on a one-year pact, they chose to go to the mat with them (in fairness to the Yankees, they did discuss a multi-year deal with Jeter but could not reach an agreement with him). Jeter, who's remarkably poised for a 24-year-old, seemed to take the arbitration process—and the negative comments from the team that are an inevitable part of the presentation—in stride. Of course, it helped that he won his case. If he'd lost, it might have been different. All I'm saying is, I don't see how it's in a team's interests to risk antagonizing one of its best players, no matter how young or old the player might be. But then, George Steinbrenner often does things that are difficult to understand.

I have one first-hand story about the Jeter case. I was down in Tampa while the case was being heard, and I was talking with some people about a hundred feet or so from the arbitration room. One of the people was an absolute drop-dead blonde named Mary Ann, who was assisting on some of the cases. She looked like Jennifer Aniston, only better. . . a really beautiful woman, maybe 23-24 years old. Nice, too, a really sweet person. (Working in baseball has its occasional perks.) Anyway, Mary Ann kept talking about how she *had* to meet Derek Jeter, and how her friends were telling her that she couldn't come back from Tampa until she'd done so. So during one of the breaks, she offered to assist another woman who was carrying some equipment over to the arbitration room.

A few minutes later, she came back, looking a little pale. "I saw him," she said softly. "I saw Derek Jeter. We made eye contact. I MADE EYE CONTACT WITH DEREK JETER! He's *so* gorgeous." I thought she was going to faint.

No wonder Jeter didn't sweat the arbitration process. In my next life, Lord, make me good-looking, athletic, incredibly talented, a nice fella. . . and worth $3.2 million even if I "lose."

February 25—Baseball Movies

One of my rituals of spring is to get in the mood for baseball by viewing a few of my favorite baseball movies. I have most of the good ones on video, and a couple of them are even available in DVD, which is the way to go if you can afford a unit. I thought I'd update a column I wrote a few years ago on my favorite baseball movies. Here's the Zee-Man's Top 10:

1. "Bull Durham." To me, this movie still has the best feel for the game of any baseball movie ever made. It's funny, it has a point, it rings true, and the game scenes look realistic (except for Tim Robbins' girlish pitching). I have the DVD of this film, and it's fabulous, with an alternate soundtrack featuring scene-by-scene commentary from the director, former minor league player Ron Shelton.

2. "Field of Dreams." Also available in the DVD format with commentary from the director and cinematographer (among other features). I highly recommend it, and of course I love the movie. The story is sappy and a little unbelievable (I have a great wife, too, but I don't see her letting me plow up the crops to build a ballfield because I was hearing these voices). . . but it works.

3. "The Natural." I've told this story before, so forgive me if you know it. I was talking to Bill James at a SABR convention a few months after "The Natural" came out, and he asked me what I thought of it. Before I could answer, he said, "I thought it stunk." I guess Bill preferred the novel, which is dark and very different in tone from the film. But the movie worked just fine for me, Hollywood ending or not. The game sequences are very good, and Robert Redford *looks* like a good hitter. Also, Randy Newman's score is one of the best movie soundtracks ever made.

4. "It Happens Every Spring." Dumb but effective black-and-white classic from the early '50s. Ray Milland plays this chemistry professor who accidentally invents a substance which repels wood. . . meaning that when it's rubbed on a baseball and thrown at a guy swinging a bat, it'll jump right over it! Milland immediately becomes the greatest pitcher in baseball and hurls the St. Louis Browns to a pennant. There are some pretty stupid things in this movie; for instance, his girlfriend and her family never discover that he's playing ball, even though he's become the most famous player in the world. Doesn't matter. . . it's great.

5. "Long Gone." A somewhat-obscure HBO movie about a minor league team called the Tampico Stogies. Another movie with a nice feel for the game. It features a great performance by William Peterson, a Chicago-based character actor who's one of the best pure actors around (check him out in the non-baseball movies "Manhunter" and "To Live and Die in LA").

6. "Major League." The sequels were pretty bad, but the original "Major League" was funny enough to overcome some hokey ballfield scenes, especially the game-winning rally, which was totally unbelievable. But the cast—Charlie Sheen, Tom Berenger, Wesley Snipes, Corbin Benson and Bob Uecker doing his "*Just* a bit outside. . ." shtick more than makes up for it.

7. "Bang the Drum Slowly." Like "The Natural," it's not as good as the book, a classic by Mark Harris. But it's a great story, and the acting of Robert DeNiro and Michael Moriarty more than make up for their awkwardness in the game scenes.

8. "Eight Men Out." I'm a big fan of John Sayles, the director of "Eight Men Out." I don't think this is one of his greater flicks, but the story of the 1919 Black Sox scandal is enough of a grabber to make up for its weaknesses. After reading the book and watching the movie, however, I always ask myself: Were the 1919 Sox so great that they could only lose a game if they were dumping it? Seems pretty farfetched to me.

9. "Soul of the Game." Another HBO movie, this one about the duel between Satchel Paige, Josh Gibson and Jackie Robinson to become the first black player to perform in the majors in this century. I'd rank it higher, but they make Paige and Gibson so good that the movie starts to lose credibility. They even finish by reporting, as fact, the totally unsubstantiated claim that Gibson hit more than 900 homers.

10. "Pride of the Yankees." A classic, though somewhat overrated. To me, the awkward and clumsy Gary Cooper just doesn't catch the essence of Lou Gehrig, who of course was powerful and athletic. And there are way too many corny scenes. But Cooper *is* touching and powerful as the dying Gehrig, and that more than makes up for the movie's weaknesses.

March 4—Veterans Committee Selections

The Veterans Committee met this week and elected Orlando Cepeda, Smokey Joe Williams, Nester Chylak and Frank Selee. Some comments:

CEPEDA/20TH-CENTURY MAJOR LEAGUERS. How good was Cepeda? Let's compare him with two players who have thus far not gathered a lot of Hall of Fame support, Jim Rice and Dale Murphy (Murphy was on the ballot for the first time this year but received only 96 votes out of 473 cast). I include both their offensive career stats and the "black-ink test": significant awards won and categories in which they led the league:

Player	G	AB	H	2B	3B	HR	R	RBI	BB	SB	Avg	OBP	Slg
Cepeda	2124	7927	2351	417	27	379	1131	1365	588	142	.297	.350	.499
Rice	2089	8225	2452	373	79	382	1249	1451	670	58	.298	.352	.502
Murphy	2180	7960	2111	350	39	398	1197	1266	986	161	.265	.346	.469

Player	Awards, Led League
Cepeda	ROY 1, MVP 1, HR 1, RBI 1
Rice	MVP 1, H 1, 3B 1, HR 3, TB 4, RBI 2, RC 1, RC/27 1, SLG 2
Murphy	MVP 2, GG 5, HR 2, TB 1, R 1, RBI 2, BB 1, RC 4, RC/27 1, SLG 2

ROY = Rookie of the Year; GG = Gold Glove

Cepeda's career stats are very similar to Rice's and generally better than Murphy's. But the black-ink test helps Rice and Murphy, who was easily the best defensive player among the three.

So if Cepeda got in, why are Rice and Murphy having such a hard time? The answer, of course, is that Cepeda got voted in by a different group of people than Rice and Murphy are currently dealing with. Cepeda was on the writers' ballot for 15 years, and he never got more than 50 percent of the votes until year 13, when 57 percent of the writers put his name down.

He improved to 60 percent in year 14 and then got 74 percent—missing election by seven votes—in his final year of eligibility. Both Rice and Murphy are getting more votes at this point on their path to the Hall of Fame than Cepeda was at a similar point. One would think that if they don't get elected in their 15 years on the writers' ballot, they'll come close enough to make it when the Veterans Committee reviews their case. This is what happened with Jim Bunning, Nellie Fox and now Cepeda in recent years.

If that happens, I'm fine with it. Cepeda, Rice and Murphy all won MVP awards; they were all considered to be among the very best players in baseball for significant portions of their playing careers, and all of them have received (or undoubtedly *will* receive, in Murphy's case) significant support from the Hall of Fame writers during their years on the ballot. These guys are clearly a cut above people like Phil Rizzuto, who never got more than 38 percent of the vote from the writers, or Dom DiMaggio—supposedly a hot Veterans Committee candidate this year—who never polled more than 11 percent in any election. To sum it up: I'm happy for Cepeda.

SMOKEY JOE WILLIAMS/NEGRO LEAGUERS. If you know anything about the Negro Leagues, you have to wonder why it took Smokey Joe so long to make the Hall of Fame. He was clearly considered one of their greatest pitchers and eminently worthy of the Hall of Fame, by all accounts. One negative comment: I wish reputable newspapers wouldn't write stuff like, "Smokey Joe went 41-3 in 1914 and struck out 20-plus batters in more than 20 games." The only way that could be true is if they counted barnstorming games against town teams and sandlotters. I'm sure that if Jaime Navarro faced the STATS, Inc. All-Stars, he'd strike out *at least* 20 of us. But that doesn't make him a Hall of Famer. So skip those outlandish Negro League stats, guys; meaningful statistics from those glorious leagues only exist in sketchy, incomplete form, and you don't need them to prove Smokey Joe Williams was a great player.

Williams' election was the last in a five-year period in which the voters could pick one former Negro Leaguer each year. I'm fine with that, and I wish they'd continue doing this for a few more years. From what I know about the Negro Leagues, there are a number of solid candidates still out there. I can think of two off the top of my head: Biz Mackey and Turkey Stearnes.

FRANK SELEE/19TH-CENTURY GREATS. Selee's election was a surprise, but he belongs: he won five pennants, had a .598 career winning percentage, and he's credited with the development of a number of great players. As was the case with the Negro Leaguers, his election came as part of a five-year plan in which one 19th-century figure could be elected each year. I think there are a few more worthy candidates out there, but I'd like to see this get wrapped up in some sort of orderly way. Why don't they draft a committee of 19th-century experts and give them a few years to close the book on the era? Then they could do the same with the deadball era. It's 80 years since 1919, and there's hardly anyone alive who actually remembers the players of that day. Do the homework, induct the remaining candidates who are clearly worthy (no Vic Willises, please), then close the books. I'd give the Negro League people another decade, then wrap that one up also.

NESTER CHYLAK/UMPIRES. There are a few umpires in major league history who were clearly legendary figures in the game's history, and for that reason worthy of Hall of Fame consideration: Bill Klem, Tommy Connally and Bill McGowan come to mind. I'll buy Doug Harvey from the current era, also. But. . . Nester Chylak? As best I can figure it, Chylak got in because Ted Williams liked him, and the committee wanted to give Ted a consolation prize for Dom D not making it. Whatever; this seems like a bogus selection to me.

March 11—Thoughts on Spring Training

I found this great CD in a bargain bin last weekend: "Ricky Nelson: All My Best." Wow, it was like being beamed back to the late fifties or early sixties, watching "Ozzie and Harriet" and getting ready for the next sock hop. "Travelin' Man." "Hello Mary Lou (Goodbye Heart)." "Poor Little Fool." "Stood Up (Broken Hearted Again)." And it tore me up when Rick broke into:

> *Some people call me a teenage idol*
> *Some people say they envy me*
> *Guess they got no way of knowing*
> *How lonesome I can be. . .*

All this is a roundabout way of saying that while I probably have to be considered an old-guy sportswriter—I'm about to turn 51—I just didn't feel what most old-guy sportswriters guys seem to be feeling about Joe DiMaggio dying. Great player? Without question. American icon? I can buy that. But I never saw him play, and his passing just didn't move me the way it will when Ted Williams—whom I saw perform many times—finally passes on. My personal experience with Williams, and my lack of experience with DiMaggio, is part of it. The heroes of your youth are always a little bit more vivid than the heroes of someone else's.

There's also this: DiMaggio was one of the last baseball superstars whose career was basically over before the age of television. The fact that not many people saw him play wound up adding to his mystique. In that sense, it's really true that there will never be another one like him, a hero who exists mostly in stories and a few grainy film clips. I'm not going to dispute DiMaggio's greatness, but it's a lot harder to be a legend in 1999.

On to the current game. It's still early in spring training, but not too early to monitor the progress of pitchers who are coming back from injury. A brief rundown:

KEVIN APPIER. Looking good thus far, with no runs and only two hits allowed in five innings. The only negative is that he's only struck out two batters. Still, Appier has shown enough to get some teams interested in trading for him. Is he a good gamble for another major league club, or for your fantasy team? Only if the price is fairly low, I'd say. Even if he makes it through the year healthy, I don't see him working a lot of innings in 1999.

ALAN BENES. Hasn't pitched yet, and probably won't before May or June. He had surgery in December, and he's a very risky pick for '99.

ALEX FERNANDEZ. Still looking good, with only one run allowed in four innings. Supposedly the Marlins are thinking about trading him, but how many teams will risk dealing for a high-salaried pitcher who just missed an entire season? I think he'll work more innings than Appier this year, but I'll bet most if not all of them will be in a Florida uniform.

JEREMY GONZALEZ. Still hasn't pitched yet, and definitely won't be ready for the start of the season. Pretty risky at this point.

CHRIS HOLT. Making a nice comeback, with two runs allowed in five innings thus far. Larry Dierker seems to be a whiz at handling pitchers, and I'm betting that Holt wins 10-12 games this year, and possibly more.

DONOVAN OSBORNE. Seems to be progressing nicely, with no runs allowed in three spring innings. Thirty starts, 10 wins seem about right to me.

DAVID WELLS. Having back problems, which often happens to players who are carrying around too much weight. I'm not too worried—I think he'll make his usual 30-plus starts this year—but he's not going to be anyway near as effective as he was in 1999. He's still a good pitcher. I'm predicting Wells will be dealt in late July or August, and help some contending club make the playoffs.

PAUL WILSON. Remember him? Back from the dead, with five scoreless innings this spring. Only one strikeout, however. Wilson may open the year in the Met bullpen, with a chance to move into the rotation in May or June. Should be available cheap, and worth a gamble.

MARK WOHLERS. Well, he's not walking everybody any more, but he still has a long way to go, with an ERA of 18.00 thus far. I don't expect much of a comeback; in fact, I can picture him in the Northern League in 2000, trying to convince some major league team that he can make it back.

KERRY WOOD. Arm seems to be OK, but who really knows? He's been out with a nasty virus, and hasn't worked in any games yet. The Cubs are already saying that they're going to baby him in 1999, and he might not work 200 innings this year. Maybe that's just as well. Should be sensational again when he finally toes the hill; just don't expect Dwight Gooden, 1985.

March 18—Kerry Wood

Kerry Wood: what a shame, even if you're not a Cub fan (and I'm not).

Now the finger-pointing begins. ESPN.com had an on-line poll yesterday, asking readers to answer yes or no to this question: "Are the Cubs to blame for Kerry Wood's injury?" Thus far there have been more than 21,000 responses, and more than 40 percent of the readers have answered, "Yes." That surprised me, given the fact that, though they were locked in a tight race for a playoff spot last year, the Cubs seemed to go out of their way to avoid high pitch counts for Wood. They also shut him down completely at the first hint of elbow tenderness late in the season. A lot of people, including some of Wood's teammates (notably Kevin Tapani), thought they were being *too* cautious. A few critics went so far as to say the Cubbies were babying Wood.

So who's to blame for Kerry Wood's injury? This is not an easy question to answer. Shortly after Wood's 20-strikeout game last year, Bill James wrote these comments on our e-mail network (this is excerpted from the latest edition of the *STATS Diamond Chronicles*, which will be available shortly):

JAMES (5/8/98): "The Kkkkkkkkkkkkkkkkkkkkkerry Wood game is fascinating because, on the one hand, it is so exceptional that it leaves little doubt that Wood will be one of the better pitchers in the league this season. Nobody can be that dominant in a game unless he is legitimately good; it's a classic example of signature significance.

"There's an adjustment to come. Obviously a lot of the strikes in that game were on balls out of the strike zone, and some hitters will learn to recognize that big sweeping curveball earlier and lay off, but then, Wood will learn to take advantage of that, too. Anyway, he's going to be good this year.

"But I think it is also very well documented that early success with an immature arm almost always leads to arm injuries by mid-career. It's such an extreme case that it's hard to know how to balance them. But if I was a betting man, I'd bet that he doesn't win 100 games in the majors."

Bill was right on the money (actually, a little early) about the arm injury; we'll have to wait and see about the less-than-100-win prediction. But I don't think he would blame the Cubs, necessarily, for Wood breaking down. John Sickels, who used to work for Bill and is now the author of our annual *STATS Minor League Scouting Notebook*, offered this perspective when the news about Wood's elbow came out:

SICKELS (3/16/99): "I've been warning people about Kerry's elbow since he was drafted. His high school pitching coach made him throw both ends of a doubleheader once."

Good point; we tend to forget that arm abuse can begin long before a pitcher begins his professional career. That said, what *should* a team do when it has a young pitching talent like a Kerry Wood? I'm all for being cautious, but it's hard to imagine a major league club getting away with yanking an overpowering pitcher like this after 100 or 110 pitches every time out until he's 25 or so, just to protect him from getting hurt. To put it bluntly, the pressure to win is too great. So most teams would do what the Cubs tried to do: use him, but try to be cautious about it.

Complicating the issue is the fact that, despite what you may read or hear, there's *not* an automatic relationship between throwing a lot of pitches at an early age and coming down with serious arm problems within a few years. Using a formula to estimate pitches thrown in a season based on strikeouts, walks and hits allowed, Jim Henzler of my staff generated a long list of pitchers since 1969 who had had Wood-like workloads at age 20 or 21 (2,700 or more pitches in a season). A lot of them broke down, like Jose Rijo and Juan Nieves and Richard Dotson. But a lot of them didn't, including several pitchers who had Wood-like talent. Dennis Eckersley, who threw more than 2,700 pitches at both age 20 and 21, was on the list, and he pitched forever. Bert Blyleven was on the list, also. In fact, Blyleven threw over 4,000 pitches at both age 20 and 21, before going on to win 287 games. Vida Blue worked 312 innings and threw an estimated 4,500 pitches at age 21 in 1971, and he won 209 major league games.

Baseball has changed since the early 1970s, and maybe we need to be more careful than ever in the care and feeding of young arms. However, I thought one of the more perceptive comments on this issue came from our own Jim Callis, one of the leading experts in the country on amateur and minor league players. This is Jim in response to the John Sickels comment quoted earlier:

CALLIS (3/16/99): "I'm not going to say that throwing both ends of a doubleheader is good for anyone, but I think it's a little simplistic to blame the arm injury on that. The guy blew major league hitters away for five months last year, then got hurt. I can't imagine he was pitching hurt the whole time.

"Everyone has theories about how much a young pitcher can take. There's no set answer. Virtually every pitcher has a serious injury at some point in his career, often early in his career. That's just a fact of life."

I think Jim is right; pitchers, and not just young pitchers who have been worked very hard, break down all the time. Fortunately we're in an era in which the treatment of pitching injuries has advanced dramatically over even 10 or 15 years ago. As baseball fans, we can all hope that Kerry Wood is able to recover within a couple of years, and resume his brilliant pitching.

March 25—Headliners

In the news:

METS OUTRIGHT NOMO. How the mighty have fallen. The Mets have apparently concluded that Hideo Nomo can't help them enough to justify his $2.9 million salary. Given the way Nomo pitched last season and thus far this spring, that seems like a reasonable conclusion. Some other club will undoubtedly given him another chance; the question is, can he help them? Given the critical shortage of starting pitchers, I think he's worth a gamble. I don't think it's unreasonable to think that he'll win 12 games with an ERA around 4.50. You could do worse than that.

METS SIGN HERSHISER. Obviously the Mets don't believe that Nomo will "win 12 games with an ERA around 4.50" because they've just signed Orel Hershiser, who was 11-10, 4.41 last year. For '99, Hershiser seems like a safer bet. Supposedly he wants the 10 wins he needs to get 200, which would increase his Hall of Fame chances. Hershiser's had a nice career (190 wins, .588 winning percentage, 3.33 ERA), but I don't think of him as a Hall of Famer. Do you?

"RED SOX DOCTOR UPBEAT ABOUT GARCIAPARRA'S RECOVERY." When I read this story on ESPN.com today, the first thing I thought was, "Consider the source." Dr. Arthur Pappas, the Red Sox team physician, has been sued in the past by former Sox players Marty Barrett and Butch Henry for allegedly misdiagnosing injuries. In fact, Barrett won a $1.7 million judgment against Pappas. According to *Sports Illustrated*, Barrett claims that Pappas failed to disclose the extent of a torn ACL, and Henry told a similar story. The story also says that two other Sox players, Reggie Jefferson and Lou Merloni, played with stress fractures that Pappas described as a strain (Jefferson) and a bone bruise (Merloni). So when Pappas assures people that Nomar's elbow injury will be "just fine," I don't feel a great degree of comfort. An elbow injury to a shortstop is not a good thing, and we'll just have to wait and see.

DENNY NEAGLE. Suffering from shoulder soreness which is "not believed serious," according to the Reds. He'll open the season on the DL but isn't expected to miss too much time. I have no reason to doubt the diagnosis, but I get nervous when a pitcher is diagnosed with an injury like a weak shoulder. Neagle has pitched a lot of innings over the last four years, and I'd consider him a risky fantasy pick at this point.

ADRIAN BELTRE. Having a big spring for the Dodgers, hitting .459 the last time I looked. Prior to this I was a little nervous that Beltre might get off to a bad start and prompt the Dodgers to bring back Tim Wallach or something. Now I'm more much optimistic.

PAUL KONERKO. Also having a big spring (.829 slugging average) for the White Sox. This time for sure!

TROY GLAUS. Another young infielder tearing it up in Arizona, with 17 RBI in 16 games. Like Konerko, I think he's the real thing.

Speaking of the Angels, I can't believe they still haven't traded off one of their outfielders for the help they need (second base, catcher, starting pitching). All winter long, Angels players were bad-mouthing Jim Edmonds, yet he's still hanging around saying stuff like, "I know they all hate me and I hate them too, but I'm going to get past that and have a great year." Yeah, sure. What are the Halos waiting for?

THE ROYALS. Sorry, but I still don't believe they're for real.

April 1—Zee-Man's Baseball Predictions

Fearless predictions:

NL EAST. Braves again. They won't be as good as last year, but they don't need to be.

NL CENTRAL. Astros. Also not as good as last year, but it's a weak division, and I believe in Larry Dierker.

NL WEST. Dodgers. They have some problems, but Kevin Brown's terrific, and Davey Johnson is one of the best managers ever.

NL WILD-CARD. Wide open. Could be the Mets, and I'm a bit tempted to go with the Reds. But Dusty Baker always manages to get the most from his team, so I'll go with the Giants.

AL EAST. Who else but the Yankees?

AL CENTRAL. Indians, of course. This year might not be as easy.

AL WEST. Rangers. I liked the Angels until I heard that DiSarcina is going to be out for four months.

AL WILD-CARD. I think the Angels will be just good enough to sneak in here.

NLCS. Braves over Dodgers. They're due to make it to another World Series.

ALCS. Yankees over Indians again.

WORLD SERIES. Big upset: Braves in seven. I never give up with this, do I?

AL MVP. Alex Rodriguez. He's due.

AL CY YOUNG. Mike Mussina. Ditto.

AL ROOKIE OF THE YEAR. Eric Chavez, A's.

NL MVP. Jeff Bagwell.

NY CY YOUNG. Randy Johnson. Just a hunch.

NL ROOKIE OF THE YEAR. J.D. Drew, Cardinals.

AL HOME-RUN CHAMPION. Albert Belle with 58.

NL HOME-RUN CHAMPION. Mark McGwire with 63.

AL BATTING CHAMPION. Derek Jeter.

NL BATTING CHAMPION. Larry Walker.

.400 AVERAGE. Once again, no one will come close.

FIRST MANAGER FIRED. Phil Garner.

FIRST TEAM TO ANNOUNCE THEY'RE MOVING. Montreal Expos, followed closely by the Minnesota Twins.

Remember, you heard it here first.

April 8—"The Jack Clark Game"

Another season underway. Nothing startling thus far, except maybe for the injury to Alex Rodriguez. Bummer, but I didn't see the Mariners going anywhere with that bullpen.

I always prepare for the season by watching some of my favorite baseball movies, plus maybe a game or two from my collection of baseball broadcasts. Last weekend I happened to put in the tape of Game 6 of the 1985 NLCS, known to most people as "The Jack Clark Game." With the Cardinals trailing 5-4 in the top of the ninth, Clark hit a three-run homer off Tom Niedenfuer to put St. Louis in the World Series.

This game was played 14 years ago—not that long ago—but a lot of things have changed in baseball, and in baseball broadcasting, in that time. A few examples:

1. The Dodgers brought in Niedenfuer, their closer, to relieve Orel Hershiser with one out in the top of the seventh inning. Tommy Lasorda expected Niedenfuer to finish the game, and he did work the last 2.2 innings. What manager would do *that* any more?

2. Echoing this, Whitey Herzog brought in the man who by then had become the Cards' closer, Todd Worrell, to relieve Joaquin Andujar in the bottom of the seventh. Worrell worked two innings and undoubtedly would have finished the game had he not been lifted for a pinch-hitter.

3. The game turned on Lasorda's decision to have Niedenfuer pitch to Clark with men on second and third and two out rather than walk Clark and pitch to Andy Van Slyke. It was a defendable decision: Niedenfuer had struck out Clark with men on in the seventh, and he'd been far more effective against Clark to that point of his career (4-for-17, 0 home runs) than against Van Slyke (3-for-5 with a homer). But one option Lasorda apparently never considered was something a 1999 manager would be ready to do in an instant: walk Clark and bring in a lefty to pitch to pitch to Van Slyke, who had batted .111 (6-for-54 with no homers) against lefties in 1985. Herzog had a couple of righties left on the bench (Brian Harper and Tom Nieto) but neither was the caliber of a Clark or a Van Slyke (vs. righties anyway). Why didn't he bring in a lefty? Because the Dodgers had only one lefty reliever available, Carlos Diaz, plus a couple of lefty starters who'd been pounded in the Series (Rick Honeycutt and Jerry Reuss). Lasorda apparently didn't think enough of Diaz to trust him in a pressure situation. What current-day division winner would be without a viable lefty in the bullpen in the late innings?

4. The NBC broadcast, featuring Vin Scully and Joe Garagiola, was very simple by 1999 standards. No reporter on the field. Relatively simple graphics. No major second-guessing of the decision to pitch to Clark. No interview with Clark after the game (they did talk briefly with Herzog in the clubhouse). Just a nice, clean broadcast. Pretty refreshing, actually.

I was reminded again of the difference between then and now when I checked out the 1999 MLB totals this morning. There have been 78 games started by major league pitchers through Wednesday. . . and no complete games. Zip. Zero. And nobody thinks anything of it. We've basically reached a point where anything past six innings by a starting pitcher is considered a bonus, except for the elite starters like Maddux, Brown and others of their ilk. And even those guys don't go nine very often. I'm not criticizing modern-day pitchers for this; the game has changed a lot even since 1985, and pitchers go all-out from the first pitch to the last. It takes its toll. But when it becomes the norm for three or four pitchers to work a game even for the winning teams, the value of each individual pitcher declines. Which means that, however good they are, even a Maddux or a Brown *can't* have the impact on their teams that the great starters of even 15 years ago had. Which is why I consider it a stretch when people argue that Maddux is the greatest pitcher of all time. Simply put, he's not as valuable to his team as Bob Gibson or Steve Carlton were. Can't happen. He doesn't work enough innings.

On to other matters, quickly:

BASEBALL ON THE INTERNET. Several people have e-mailed me this spring, asking how they can listen to games on their PCs. There are a number of sites which list a menu of broadcasts; the one I like is www.fastball.com, since it lets you pick the individual team whose announcers you want to listen to. The official MLB site, www.majorleaguebaseball.com, also has a menu of games, but they make the choice of broadcasters for you. That isn't as good. There are some other sites as well which let you pull in games; I'm sure our readers can help here.

FROM ABBA DABBA TO ZORRO: THE WORLD OF BASEBALL NICKNAMES. This, believe it or not, is the first baseball book I've written all by myself. It's not a stat book; it's meant to be a fun look at some of the great nicknames in baseball history, with my usual irreverent comments.

April 15—Early-Season Notes

In the news:

POWER SURGE. If this seems like an especially big-hitting season thus far, it is. This chart compares the first 11 days of 1999 with the first 11 days of '97 and '98:

MLB (First 11 Days of Season)

Year	Avg	R/G	HR/G
1997	.258	9.31	1.88
1998	.270	10.15	1.85
1999	.271	10.29	2.29

I have stats back to 1987 on this, and the overall batting average in '99 is the highest over the 13 seasons in the study. The home-run rate is the second highest (just below the 2.30 HR/G in 1994) and the scoring rate is the third highest next to 1994 and 1995, a season which we probably shouldn't consider because it started much later due to the strike settlement. So it's shaping up as an even bigger-hitting year than the last few, which is saying something.

What's even more interesting is how these figures break down by league:

American League

Year	Avg	R/G	HR/G
1997	.277	11.10	2.24
1998	.274	10.64	1.93
1999	.281	11.10	2.19

National League

Year	Avg	R/G	HR/G
1997	.240	7.63	1.55
1998	.267	9.77	1.78
1999	.262	9.58	2.37

The intriguing thing is the power surge in the NL; it's basically off the map. Is this a result of the "new" strike zone? I think it's too early to tell; these numbers could change a lot as the season wears on, and I haven't monitored enough games to detect how much the strike zone has changed, if at all. But it sure is interesting.

J.D. DREW. Currently hitting .130, and not making my Rookie of the Year prediction look very good. I still think Drew is the real thing, but he's very inexperienced in professional baseball, and a period of adjustment ought to be expected. It's even possible he might have to return to the minor leagues for a little while.

I cast no aspersions on Drew for his decision to reject the Phillies' offer in 1997 and go back into the draft. His decision wasn't any more greedy than the actions of a lot of other people in baseball, on both sides of the labor/management fence. Basically it was an economic decision. But I think it was a *bad* economic decision. Had he signed with the Phillies in '97, he'd have an extra year of experience in professional ball by now, and be that much closer to the big payouts a major league star can cash in on. In baseball the really big money starts coming in when a player approaches free agency, and by holding out on the Phillies, Drew may have delayed that process by a year. Doesn't make a lot of sense to me.

PAUL KONERKO. Not setting the world on fire, either, with a .200 average thus far. It's only 20 at-bats, and I still believe in him. What I don't understand is why the White Sox aren't playing him every day until it's clear that he *can't* play. They've already sat him down twice in favor of Jeff Liefer, a decent prospect but someone who a) has yet to play in Triple-A and b) has nowhere near the potential that Konerko has. Where are the White Sox going this year that they can't give a month or two of steady play to someone who's been regarded for several years as one of the best prospects in baseball?

THE RED SOX. Off to a great start, which surprises some people including me. I really have to hand it to Jimy Williams; he doesn't have the greatest talent going for him (just look at that outfield), but he makes the most out of what he has. A very impressive managing job.

DARRYL STRAWBERRY. You don't want to condemn somebody until all the facts are in, but this doesn't look very good, does it? Strawberry's always been his own worst enemy. After last year, I thought he'd gotten past all that. So did a lot of other people. Let's hope we were right.

April 22—Prospects Report

I thought I would devote this week's column to monitoring how some of the more promising young players are doing:

CHAD ALLEN. Spring-training star has hit with some power (three HR) but has two walks in 15 games. Not a bum, but I don't see him as much more than major league journeyman.

MARLON ANDERSON. Hasn't done much thus far (.250 OBP, .264 SLG). He's better than this, but his lack of plate discipline makes me downgrade his chances.

CARLOS BELTRAN. Hitting .288 thus far, but with no power, and he has one walk in 14 games. I had my doubts about him prior to the season; I still have 'em.

ADRIAN BELTRE. Looking very solid at .321-.449-.556. I was worried he'd get off to a bad start and get sent back to the minors. I guess I don't need to worry now. Should be solid this season and one of the best players in the majors within two years.

KRIS BENSON. After three starts he's been OK (1-1, 4.96, 14 Ks in 16 innings), but not overpowering. Benson has really struggled during his minor league career, and I have my doubts about his ability to continue pitching as well as he did in spring training. Still has a great arm. I like him more as a long-term pick than I do for '99.

LUIS CASTILLO. Playing everyday with the Marlins and looking very solid, with a .377 OBP and five stolen bases. I've always liked Castillo and think he's going to put up very solid numbers this year.

ERIC CHAVEZ. Struggling at .175. The A's will be patient—why wouldn't they be?—but if Chavez continues to have problems, they might feel forced to send him to the minors to find his stroke. He's only 21 and hasn't had a full year of Triple-A yet, so that wouldn't be the end of the world. I'm starting to waver on my Rookie of the Year pick, but I think Chavez will put up quality numbers before the year is out.

MATT CLEMENT. Has made three starts thus far, looking fine in one and horrible in the other two. I think he's going to be OK and win in double figures this year.

J.D. DREW. I talked about him last week, so I won't spend a lot of time on him. Currently hitting .220 but slugging 200 points higher. I'm still predicting that he'll win the Rookie of the Year Award.

SCOTT ELARTON. After being sent to the Astros' bullpen to start the year, he's been sensational, pitching nine scoreless innings with 15 Ks and only three hits allowed. Whether he moves into the rotation depends mostly on Houston's other starters. I think it's 50/50 he'll remain in a setup role this year, which could be nice for the Astros while making him a lot less valuable to fantasy players.

CARLOS FEBLES. Off to a really nice start, hitting .292, slugging .500 and going 4-for-4 on the bases. I like him a lot and see him as a .280 hitter with good peripheral stats this year. Potential Rookie of the Year.

FREDDY GARCIA. Looking good after three starts (2-0, 3.54), but Lou is pushing his pitch counts to avoid using that horrible bullpen. I don't know if this will result in arm problems this year, but Garcia could weaken from fatigue in the second half.

TROY GLAUS. Currently hitting .382, and 14 of his 21 hits have been for extra bases. He's not going to keep doing that all year, but he's "the rill thing," as Little Richard once put it.

CRISTIAN GUZMAN. "Riding the Interstate" with some horrid stats: .158-.179-.184. Only 21 and will be back in the minors shortly. Has some potential, needs to work on his plate discipline.

ROY HALLADAY. Looking as good as he did late last year (2-0, 0.00 and a save in 16 innings), and basically forcing himself into the Toronto rotation. I really love the guy and think he could win 12+ games as a rookie.

DOUG MIENTKIEWICZ. Doing very nicely for the Twins with a .404 OBP and .479 SLG. Sort of a poor man's Mark Grace. I like him.

PAUL KONERKO. I've written about him plenty already, insisting that he'll be fine if they just put him in the lineup and leave him alone. He's beginning to make my confidence waver a little, but it's early. Be patient, Jerry Manuel; what have you got to lose?

MITCH MELUSKEY. Hasn't played a lot, but has done reasonably well (.259 with .410 slugging). I expect him to be a good hitter, but doubt that he'll get more than about 300 at-bats this year.

TROT NIXON. Off to a 2-for-31 start, and Pawtucket beckons. Could be back; his best chance to play will happen if the Red Sox drop out of the race.

JEFF WEAVER. He's only started two games thus far, but he looks awfully good (2-0, 0.82). He's a fine prospect, but I wouldn't go overboard on him for 1999. Like a lot of teams, the Tigers got scared by Kerry Wood and are holding Weaver to a very rigid pitch count thus far (less than 100). What this means is that he's probably going to miss out on several wins he would have gotten otherwise. I like him in the long run, but there are a number of better pitching prospects out there.

April 29—Prospects Report, Part II

Judging from the comments I received regarding last week's column, the readers want evaluations of more young players. And I always aim to please. Here's some guys I left out last week:

MICHAEL BARRETT. Off to a great start for the Expos. Won't draw many walks, but I see him hitting for both power and average this year. I love him, and I'm hardly alone. Rookie of the Year candidate if J.D. Drew falters.

SEAN CASEY. No longer a rookie, but a lot of people have been asking whether his hot start is for real. I don't see him as a big-time power hitter, but Casey hit well over .300 everywhere he played in the minors, and he could certainly hit .320 or higher this year. I wouldn't expect more than about 15 homers, but he's a big guy, and sometimes players start hitting more homers after reaching the major league level. He's a good one.

McKAY CHRISTENSEN. Interesting player. A former No. 1 draft choice of the Angels, Christensen took two years off to do a Mormon mission, so he hasn't played above Class-A prior to this year. Has great speed, can handle center field, and is off to a .314 start at bat. He's still so inexperienced that it's hard to know quite what to expect, but I don't see him as much more than a .260 hitter with little power, at least for this year.

ALEX GONZALEZ (MARLINS). After struggling in his big league debut last year, Gonzalez is off to a good start in '99, hitting .266. Has some power and offensive potential, plus his glove should keep him in the lineup. For this year, I see him around .240 with 10-15 homers.

RICHARD HIDALGO. Another non-rookie that several people have asked me about. The consensus seems to be that he was playing over his head when he batted .304 last year. I tend to agree. A .280 average wouldn't surprise, but his peripheral stats will probably be unexceptional (few walks, 10-15 homers).

BOB HOWRY. Now firmly established as the White Sox closer. Big guy, throws hard, very competitive. Likely to get 30-plus saves, with good stats across the board.

JOSE JIMENEZ. I will avoid bad jokes about the name (and anyway, you need to be close to 50 years old to appreciate them). Got rocked in his last start, but still has nearly a 6-to-1 strikeout/walk ratio. I think he can stay in the Cardinal rotation but don't see him as anything special. I'd guess 11 wins and a 4.40 ERA.

GABE KAPLER. Back with the Tigers after the trade of Brian Hunter, and presumably their center fielder unless he shows he can't handle the job. As many of you know, I'm very high on Kapler as a hitting prospect, and he continued to hit very well during his stint at Triple-A Toledo this year (.315-3-14 in 54 AB). Even if he has defensive problems in center, I think the Tigers will find a way to keep his bat in the lineup. Over a full season, I'd expect something like .280-20-80.

JOE McEWING. Now here's a weird case. After spending three years in Double-A doing basically nothing, McEwing went crazy last year, hitting .354 at Arkansas and .334 after moving up to Triple-A Memphis. He's continued to tear the cover off the ball with the Cardinals this month, though he's yet to hit a homer. McEwing's MLEs show him as a .315 hitter with 10-15 homers, but that's all based on his big '98 season; he's 26 years old, and there's nothing else in his past to indicate he could suddenly turn into a star. It makes you start thinking steroids or corked bats or something, though there's absolutely no evidence of that in this case. If I were a gambling man, I'd bet McEwing will hit at least .280 this year, with so-so power. A .315 average or something like that would surprise me.

WARREN MORRIS. Trying to move up from Double-A, he hasn't done a whole lot thus far (.241 average). I see him as a .300-hitting second baseman with good power in a couple of years, but I don't think he'll be anywhere near that good as a rookie. Second basemen who can hit like him are hard to find, however, so he's definitely worth a gamble.

WILLIS OTANEZ. Minor league veteran is taking advantage of Ripken's absence, hitting .283 with two homers in 46 at-bats. Not a great hitter for average, but could hit 25 homers if he played every day. Worth a risk.

ODALIS PEREZ. Winless after three starts, but his peripheral stats aren't too bad. Perez is still very young (21); he has a lot of talent, but I'm betting that he'll be out of the Braves' rotation by June.

ARMANDO RIOS. Should get a chance to play with Bonds out. Has the potential to hit 20 homers or so as an everyday player, but he doesn't excite me much.

RUBEN RIVERA. Currently hitting .148 with no home runs. I don't know about you, but I'm ready to give up on the guy.

RANDALL SIMON. Getting a little playing time for the Braves and doing very well, hitting .379 for 29 at-bats. He has some power and could surprise, but I don't see him as much more than a marginally productive bench player.

May 6—Teams in the News

A month into the season, let's talk about some teams in the news:

WHITE SOX. My favorite team is doing better than expected, 13-12 as I write this, which at least theoretically puts them in wild-card contention. When a young team such as this starts surpassing expectations, there's a tendency to get impatient with its struggling young players. The Sox are already doing this, hinting that they might have to do something about Paul Konerko (.213) and Jeff Abbott (.158). I think that would be a big mistake; when you're building for the future, you *have* to give guys with minor league records like Konerko's and Abbott's more than a month to show what they can do.

ATHLETICS. Similar to the Sox at 14-15, they're pondering what to do with Jason McDonald (.230), A.J. Hinch (.177), Eric Chavez (.227) and last year's Rookie of the Year, Ben Grieve, who's hitting .129. So far I think Art Howe is handling this right, sitting guys down now and then but not abandoning them. The tricky thing will be what to do with Chavez, who faces competition from 28-year-old rookie Olmedo Saenz, who's been tearing the cover off the ball (.359 with 14 ribbies in only 39 at-bats). Saenz, who was in the White Sox system for a number of years, could go .280-20-80 without much trouble; he's so eager to show what he can do in the majors that he might just do a lot better than that this year. It wouldn't bother me to see them farm out Chavez, who is only 21 with just 47 games of Triple-A experience, and let Saenz play for awhile. But they have to make room for Chavez before very long.

TWINS. Also going with youth, with mixed results. Doug Mientkiewicz (.280) and Corey Koskie (.302) are hitting, Torii Hunter has been so-so (.245), Chad Allen (.237) and Cristian Guzman (.205) are having problems. I don't think much of Allen, and Guzman's plate discipline problems (18 strikeouts, one walk) make me think he belongs back in the minor leagues. I'd stick with the rest of the guys, which isn't a difficult choice for Tom Kelly. They might finish last, but isn't this team a lot more fun than the Otis Nixon/Mike Morgan team they had out there last year at this time?

ORIOLES. I didn't expect them to be *this* bad, but I'm not feeling very sorry for them. The Baltimore front-office guys who tried comparing Albert Belle to Frank Robinson as a team leader should spend some time reading Frank Robinson's book and reviewing Robinson's career both on and off the field. Belle can hit, but if he's a team leader, I'm Will Shakespeare.

ANGELS. Well, they didn't trade Jim Edmonds, and now he's on the shelf for four months. Edmonds' teammates love him so much that they're even grumbling about his injury; they thought he should have had surgery on his shoulder last winter. "I don't have a reaction," said Darin Erstad, one of the most-highly respected players on the Angels, when asked about Edmonds. "I have nothing to say. It's his life. He does what he wants to." Sounds like a real fun clubhouse the Halos have when Edmonds is around. This will continue to be a problem when Edmonds returns; what in the world were the Angels thinking of last winter, when they had four regular outfielders and needs to fill?

CUBS. Jim Henzler just did a study for me which showed that, weighted for usage, the '99 Cubs are one of the two oldest National League teams since 1920. The other was the 1983 Phillies, who went to the World Series. After watching Rod Beck throw a few times this year, I don't think lightning is going to strike twice. But *old* is not necessarily *bad* when you're fighting for a playoff spot. Remember that.

GIANTS. Dusty Baker continues to amaze me; now he's winning without Barry Bonds. Yesterday's starting outfield for the Giants was Stan Javier, F.P. Santangelo and Marvin Benard. This can't last. . . can it?

DODGERS. After a slow start, Davey Johnson is doing what he always does, leading the Dodgers toward the postseason. I have a feeling that the Dodgers will pass the Giants next week, and that will be that. We'll see, won't we?

May 13—Teams in the News, Part II

Continuing what we started last week, let's review some more teams:

DIAMONDBACKS. After all the money they spent last winter, it's not a shock to see the Diamondbacks in wild-card contention. The shock is *how* they've gotten into contention—the pitching's been OK, but they're winning primarily because they've been tearing the cover off the ball. Jay Bell? Luis Gonzalez? Matt Williams back from the dead? What's going on?

As you may have suspected, the ballpark has a bit to do with the Diamondbacks' surprising numbers. Bank One Ballpark is starting to play like the hitters' park we expected it to be:

Bank One Ballpark Park Indexes

	1998	1999
Avg	105	108
R	102	131
HR	91	108

I haven't computed '99 park indexes for all teams, but based on past experience, the BOB is looking like one of the best hitters' parks in the NL. The interesting thing, however, is that while the park seems to be helping Jay Bell a lot, Williams and Gonzalez have been as potent on the road as they've been at home. Meanwhile, the Diamondback pitchers have actually performed better at home than they have on the road in the early going. I don't know how this will play out the rest of the way, but I'm betting that the BOB will soon rank as the best hitters' park in the NL next to Coors Field. That's something to remember when considering Arizona players for your fantasy team.

BLUE JAYS. A couple of readers have written to me asking who's going to close for the Blue Jays, now that they've given up on Robert Person. The most intriguing candidate is Billy Koch, the former No. 1 draft pick who's made an amazing recovery from Tommy John elbow surgery. Koch can throw extremely hard, but he's been a starter for most of his professional career, and I think the Jays are more likely to break him in as a middle reliever. If you want to gamble on a young Toronto reliever, you might consider Tom Davey, who's had more experience closing games in the minors than Koch has. Davey throws hard, also, but I think it's more likely the Jays will pick a veteran like Graeme Lloyd to close, or go with a bullpen-by-committee approach. But I would grab Koch if I had the chance; talent like this is hard to find.

ROYALS. I will admit I was wrong about Carlos Beltran, who's been driving the ball a lot more consistently than he was early in the season. But I still like Carlos Febles as a long-term prospect more than I do Beltran. I also like Mike Sweeney, who is making the most of an opportunity to play after the Royals were about ready to give up on him. He can hit.

MARLINS. Terrible, as expected, but they have a lot of young players. Some random comments:

Kevin Orie. I always thought he could hit in the majors, and he's finally coming through with the Marlins after flopping with the Cubs. I don't see him as a star, but he can provide adequate offense at third.

Mark Kotsay. Not showing much in the early going of '99, but I still expect him to develop into a star.

Luis Castillo/Alex Gonzalez. I've talked about them before, so I won't devote much time to them. I think Gonzalez will hit around .240 with a little bit of power this year, and I think Castillo will be a good top-of-the order hitter.

Derrek Lee/Preston Wilson. Low average, a little bit of power, few walks, many strikeouts. This combination doesn't excite me much.

Matt Mantei. Awesome in the early going. Throws really hard, but he's had injury problems every season of his career. I don't trust him, but if you're in a gambling mood. . .

REDS. I've previously mentioned my affection for Sean Casey, who continues to slug away. But Pokey Reese, .320 hitter? Don't be fooled by this; the man has never hit higher than .269 in his professional career. Pokey's not a total slug offensively, but he'll be lucky to hit .260 this year, and his peripheral stats will be lousy.

TIGERS. Gabe Kapler's done quite well since his recall from the minors, hitting with the kind of power Brian Hunter can only dream about. He'll draw some walks, also. Juan Encarnacion is also off to a decent start, but beware: he has 23 strikeouts, two walks, and it's practically impossible to succeed in the majors with that kind of strike zone judgment. The other Tiger I wanted to mention was Frank Catalanotto, who's taken advantage of some injuries to get a little playing time. Catalanotto could be a good offensive player in the majors if he got a chance to play, but I don't see him getting that chance with the Tigers. Injuries or a trade are his only chance.

May 20—Cleveland and Other Offensive Explosions

In the news:

THE INDIANS. The Tribe scored 13 runs in each of their three games against the White Sox, who were leading the American League in team ERA going into the series. For the year, the Indians are hitting .310, slugging .525 and averaging 7.4 runs a game, which would be a 20th-century record. Pretty amazing stuff.

Can they keep it up? I don't think any team can keep hitting quite like this, but I wouldn't be surprised if the Tribe becomes the first team since the 1950 Red Sox to score 1,000 runs in a season. The '50 Red Sox were also the last team to bat .300 for an entire season, but I doubt the Indians will be able to maintain that high an average. Still, they look like they could wind up with the best offensive numbers we've seen from a team in nearly 50 years.

Which begs a question: can the Indians go all the way without trading for a No. 1 starter like Curt Schilling? I'd say yes, especially if Bartolo Colon and Jaret Wright can start pitching a little better. Pitching's important, but despite what you always read, there's no credible evidence that "good pitching beats good hitting in a short series." A study we did several years ago in the *STATS Baseball Scoreboard* (based on some excellent work done by a SABR researcher named Don Coffin) showed that in 29 postseason matchups between hitting-dominant teams and pitching-dominant teams, the hitting-dominant clubs won 18 times. This is typical of all the research I've seen on the subject.

Still, after falling short of a World Championship in each of the last four seasons, I expect the Tribe to make *some* kind of a deal for a quality starter between now and the end of July. I think the current team is good enough as is, but a quality arm won't hurt.

LARRY WALKER. Currently hitting .431, and it's not just a Coors thing: he's batting .432 at home, .431 on the road, and his overall numbers are actually better on the road than at home. I've been skeptical about anyone hitting .400 for a full season, but if anyone can do it, Walker can. Despite his impressive road numbers, playing in Coors is a tremendous advantage for any hitter. Here's another advantage: Walker, who draws some walks and gets hurt now and then, will probably wind up without an excessive number of at-bats for the year (I'm assuming he'll qualify for the batting title). I think you can prove statistically that the more at-bats a player has, the less likely he is to hit .400, since averages tend to normalize over longer periods of time. So Walker has got a lot going for him. I personally don't think he'll make it, but I'll be rooting for him.

OFFENSIVE LOG. An update of a chart I run now and then to monitor the overall level of offensive performance:

Through 46 Days (May 19)

	Avg	R/G	HR/G
AL	.275	10.78	2.47
NL	.269	10.04	2.18
MLB	.272	10.39	2.32

We've been keeping this log since 1987, and for both leagues and MLB as a whole, the '99 figures are the highest on record *in every category*. Going back farther:

1. The overall batting averages for both the NL and MLB, if maintained for the full season, would be the highest full-season marks since the 1930s (highest for the NL since 1937, highest for MLB since 1939). The .275 AL mark would be the second-highest since 1939; the AL hit .277 in 1996.

2. The scoring level for the AL, NL and MLB would also the highest since the 1930s (AL since 1936, NL and MLB since 1930), if maintained for the full season.

3. The home-run rate would be a new record for all three (AL, NL, MLB).

Already this season, there have been 119 games in which one of the two teams has scored at least 10 runs in a game, or more than one double-digit score for every five games (21.9 percent). We've also had nine games already in which *both* teams have scored in double figures. I love hitting as much as the next man, but doesn't it get to be a bit much sometimes?

Of course, it's still pretty early in the year, and a lot could change between now and October. But I think we can say that this "new strike zone" thing doesn't seem to be having the desired effect. I'll also say that if the final-season numbers are anything like this, we may see some more drastic action taken to help the pitchers during the offseason. Like it or not.

PAUL KONERKO/VON JOSHUA. Well, my hero's finally starting to hit the way I thought he would, hitting .333 and slugging .574 thus far in May. The Sox have given a lot of credit to hitting coach Von Joshua, who's urged Konerko to stand closer to the plate and hit the ball to the opposite field more often.

Fine and good; that seems to be working. On the other hand, Konerko has drawn exactly one walk all month, and five for the season in 118 at-bats. I think he's going to have trouble slugging .574 doing *that*. I looked up Joshua's major league record in our *All-Time Major League Handbook*, and he had exactly 108 walks in a 2,234 at-bat career. . . 20 of them intentional. How can you be a good hitting coach if you have no understanding of the value of ball four?

CONSPIRACY THEORY. From this morning's *USA Today*: "OF Paul Sorrento hit a 491-foot home run over the grassy knoll in center field, the longest in the history of The Ballpark in Arlington." As of now, the Devil Rays are insisting that Sorrento "acted alone," but I'm not buying it, for several reasons:

1. Eyewitnesses interviewed after the game reported seeing a second batsman hidden in the grassy knoll.

2. Sorrento could never have hit a ball that far. He's not that good a marksman.

3. Did you see the replay? A kid jumped out and made a great dive to beat another kid for the baseball. Reliable sources have told us that the kid was working for the CIA; he grabbed the ball so that nobody else could get a chance to examine the evidence.

4. Only a "magic baseball" could have taken that trajectory.

Or maybe a 1999 baseball.

May 27—Down on the Farm

A lot of readers have been asking about how some of baseball's top prospects are doing in the minors thus far this year, so we'll call this column our "Down on the Farm" edition.

The following players were all ranked among the 20 best prospects in baseball prior to the season by either John Sickels (in our *Minor League Scouting Notebook*) or Jim Callis (in *The Scouting Notebook*).

RICK ANKIEL, LHP, CARDINALS. After getting off to a 6-0, 0.91 start at Double-A Arkansas, Ankiel has won his first two starts (with a 2.38 ERA) for Triple-A Memphis. Ankiel, who won't turn 20 until July 19, has clearly established himself as the No. 1 prospect in baseball. The Cardinals have indicated that they want to keep him in Triple-A, but if he keeps pitching like this, I don't know how much longer they can keep him in the minors. I agree that Ankiel is an awesome prospect, but I don't see how he could be much help to your fantasy team this year. If they bring him up, they're going to be really, really cautious about his pitch counts, and that's going to greatly decrease his value for 1999. He's also risky as a long-term prospect because of the chance for injury. As a prospect, Ankiel is sort of like an Internet stock: he might pay off big, but he also could get seriously hurt and turn out to be relatively worthless. I can't wait to see him pitch, however.

RUBEN MATEO, OF, RANGERS. Currently hitting .324-14-49 at Triple-A Oklahoma, solidifying his reputation as the top hitting prospect currently in the minor leagues. He's also very fast and considered a pretty good center fielder. Mateo's only 21, and as is the case with Ankiel, the Rangers would like to leave him be and give him a full year in Triple-A. But Tom Goodwin's struggling, and if that continues it's pretty likely that Mateo will be playing center for the Rangers in another month or two. Grab him if you can.

NICK JOHNSON, 1B, YANKEES. Another outstanding hitting prospect, Johnson is tearing it up at Double-A Norwich (.286-7-32 with a .486 OBP). He won't turn 21 until September, and the Yankees are in no hurry to move him along. The most likely scenario would be for Johnson to stay in the minors for another year; Tino Martinez' contract expires at the end of the 2000 season, and the Yankees could either move Martinez this winter or deal him sometime next year, making room for Johnson. On the other hand, if they win another title, they might decide to give Martinez a long-term contract. If you're a Johnson fan, you'll need to be patient.

PAT BURRELL, 1B, PHILLIES. Sort of the consolation prize to the Phillies after they failed to sign J.D. Drew, Burrell is hitting .343-5-13 in 102 AB at Double-A Reading, with a .472 OBP. I agree with Jim Callis that Burrell is nowhere near the prospect that Drew is, but I expect him to be a solid major league hitter. How soon? That's a good question. The Phillies are in wild-card contention, and they also have this delusion that Rico Brogna is a useful player. I expect Burrell to move up to Triple-A very soon, but I don't think he'll get much major league playing time before next year.

JOHN PATTERSON/BRAD PENNY, RHP, DIAMONDBACKS. Patterson is 21, Penny 20, and they both throw serious heat. Both are struggling in their first exposure to the Double-A level: Patterson is 2-3, 5.60 in nine starts, Penny 1-3, 5.09 in eight starts. I wouldn't be too discouraged; El Paso is one of the toughest places in the minors to pitch, and both pitchers are averaging more than a strikeout an inning. They remain outstanding prospects, but given the Diamondbacks' depth in starting pitching, I don't think we'll see either of them in the majors before about midyear 2000.

DERNEL STENSON, 1B, RED SOX. Stenson, who will turn 21 on June 17, is a big first baseman who's eventually supposed to make up for the loss of Mo Vaughn. The operative word here is "eventually." Stenson isn't setting the world on fire at Triple-A Pawtucket (he's currently .245-5-24 for 143 AB), so the Sox will probably keep him in the minors for the rest of this year, at least. He's a good bet for next season, however.

RUSSELL BRANYAN, 3B, INDIANS. Currently at Triple-A Buffalo and looking like a young Rob Deer: in 155 at-bats, Branyan is hitting .200 with 14 homers and 81—that's right, 81—strikeouts. Branyan has always had huge strikeout totals, but this is a little ridiculous. Branyan is only 23, he's coming off a wrist injury that limited him to 43 games last year and this is his first exposure to Triple-A baseball, so there's time for him to get straightened out. If I were Travis Fryman, I wouldn't be too worried at the moment.

RYAN ANDERSON, LHP, MARINERS. The Next Unit has had some problems after moving up to the Double-A level, going 3-4, 6.37 in his first eight starts for New Haven. Control has been his problem, but he's averaging over a strikeout an inning. Anderson won't turn 20 until July 12, so he's got plenty of time to get things straightened out. Anderson is 6-10, 215 and still growing, and my gut feeling is that if he can fill out and put on 20 pounds or so, his size and strength will make him less of a candidate for serious arm trouble than is the case with Ankiel, who is 6-1 and 210. We'll see.

LANCE BERKMAN, OF, ASTROS. A switch-hitter with excellent power and a good batting eye, Berkman has been bothered this year by knee problems. When he's played, he's done very well, going .290-2-18 in 62 AB for Triple-A New Orleans. The knee is a concern, and Berkman, who's 23, will probably spend the whole year in Triple-A unless the Astros get desperate for more hitting help.

PABLO OZUNA, SS, MARLINS. Only 20 years old, Ozuna is playing well at Double-A Portland, going .294-4-17 in his first 180 at-bats. The only concern is his lack of discipline: only six walks. With Alex Gonzalez playing pretty well at shortstop for the Marlins, I don't expect Ozuna to reach the majors for at least another year. But he's a solid prospect.

CALVIN PICKERING, 1B, ORIOLES. The massive (6-5, 283) Pickering got a brief trial with the Orioles earlier this year, but now he's back at Triple-A Rochester, going .247-3-12 for 73 at-bats. Pickering is only 22, and he has great power and a good batting eye. If I were the O's, I'd try to unload Will Clark and bring Pickering up immediately. But the O's aren't that sensible.

JEREMY GIAMBI, 1B-OF, ROYALS. With the retirement of Jeff King, a lot of people thought the Royals would immediately bring up Giambi, who's recovered from some early injuries to go .337-7-15 in 86 at-bats at Triple-A Omaha. Unfortunately, Tony Muser has decided he needs Larry Sutton's glove in the lineup. This is what happens when you give your managerial job to a first baseman who could field but not hit. This can't last; Giambi should be up soon, and he's going to give the Royals another good young hitter.

MATT RILEY, LHP, ORIOLES. Still only 19 (he turns 20 on August 2), Riley got off to a good start for Frederick in the Carolina League (3-2, 2.61), so the O's have moved him up to Double-A Bowie. He had a no-decision in his first start there. He throws very hard and has a wicked curve, but he's still a long way away from the majors. Especially pitching in the Oriole system.

June 3—Recent Baseball Books

I was unavoidably detained yesterday, so this is a day late. I thought I'd devote this week's column to a few baseball books which have come out recently:

You're Missin' a Great Game, Whitey Herzog and Jonathan Pitts

While I don't always agree with him, I've always had a lot of admiration for Whitey Herzog. He comes across like a good guy to sit around with, having a couple of beers and talking baseball. That's basically the tone of this book. Whitey doesn't like a lot of what's happening in baseball—to name three things, he's against divisional play, he doesn't like interleague games, and he thinks the home-run epidemic has gotten out of hand—but his arguments are usually thoughtful and well-reasoned, and it's obvious that he genuinely cares about the game. Even when he falls off the deep end completely, this book is a lot of fun. For instance, there's a section where he starts talking about Game 6 of the 1985 World Series, and right off the top he says that if he had to do it all over again, he'd act differently. "Good," I thought. "Whitey's finally grown up and accepted the fact that bad umpiring calls are just part of baseball." But that's not how he would have acted differently. What Whitey says is that after Don Denkinger made his infamous safe call at first base to begin the Royals' game-winning rally, he should have taken his Cardinals off the field and risked forfeiting the game, thus shaming baseball into looking at a replay of the call. In other words, if he had to do it all over again, he would have acted like even *more* of an eight year old. Well, that's Whitey, unrepentant to the last. Good book.

Total Baseball Sixth Edition, John Thorn, Pete Palmer, Michel Gershman and David Pietrusza

Total Baseball is a competitor of our *STATS All-Time Major League Handbook* and *STATS All-Time Baseball Sourcebook,* and I'm naturally a little prejudiced: I just think you find a lot more in-depth information in our two volumes than you can in *Total Baseball's* one. But there's a lot of good stuff in this book, as always. For instance, there's a section on baseball in Japan with the yearly pitching and hitting leaders, plus the all-time leaders in a number of categories. Pretty cool stuff. There's a section on baseball movies which lists the director and cast of virtually every baseball movie ever made. I like that, also. Of course, by trying to squeeze in stuff like this *and* the player register into one volume, something has to give. The result is that *Total Baseball* dispenses with a lot of the stats you'll find in our books. The biggest missing element is fielding stats: we give you every official stat for every player year by year, they just have fielding average and games by position. How can you truly evaluate a player with only partial information? I'm not knocking *Total Baseball* for this;

they had to make a choice, and they chose to dispense with a lot of the statistical matter. That limitation understood, it remains a fine book.

The International League: Year-by-Year Statistics, 1884-1953 The American Association: Year-by-Year Statistics, 1902-52 Marshall D. Wright

If you like minor league history, these are wonderful books to have. Wright's books are set up like the *Sports Encyclopedia: Baseball* series, going through each season on a team-by-team basis with the essential stats for every International League or American Association player. If you want to study the great Baltimore Oriole minor league dynasty of the early 1920s or track the players on the St. Louis Cardinals' Triple-A teams in the '30s, these books are perfect. The only thing I didn't like is that Wright ended them in the early 1950s; I guess he felt they would have been too bulky otherwise. That said, both books are gems, and I'm hoping he gets to the Pacific Coast League soon. Both are published by McFarland, a publisher which produces a lot of really nice baseball books. I recommend checking them out at www.mcfarlandpub.com.

The Cultural Encyclopedia of Baseball, Jonathan Fraser Light

Also published by McFarland, and another wonderful book. This is an offbeat kind of baseball encyclopedia, with articles on subjects like advertising, superstitions, youngest players, all kinds of stuff. If you look up "pennant races," you'll find rundowns of the best pennant races of all time. There are sections on each major league franchise, biographical sketches of all Hall of Famers, and much more. Light, whom I met at the SABR convention last year, is a terrific writer, and this book is a lot of fun to just browse. I highly recommend it.

From Abba Dabba To Zorro: The World of Baseball Nicknames, Don Zminda

Well, it's finally out, the first book I've ever written completely on my own. This is a STATS book, but not a "stat" book; instead it's a fun look at the world of baseball nicknames from all kinds of angles. The key word here is fun. There's a section with all-nickname teams for each major league franchise, a section with the best animal nicknames, one on the most politically incorrect nicknames, about 20 different chapters in all. I try to tell the story about how the player got his nickname, and tell a little bit about his career as well. (My favorite story is about how a 19th-century umpire named John Kelly got his nickname, Honest John.) To top it off, each chapter ends with a "favorite nickname" list from people like Bob Costas, Ernie Harwell, Jim Palmer, Gary Carter and Tommy Hutton. Not to toot my own horn too much, but this is really a neat book, and I think you'll enjoy it. Only $9.95, and you can buy it on our web and AOL sites.

June 10—Up-and-Comers

Let's talk about some players I haven't previously reviewed:

BENNY AGBAYANI, METS. Who is this guy with the .409 average and eight homers in his first 66 MLB at-bats? Well, prior to this year, Agbayani had never hit more than 11 homers in any *full* season during his professional career. So this is a fluke. He's not a terrible player, but put him out there for a full season, and you'd be lucky to get a .260 average with 15 homers. Enjoy it while you can, Benny.

MATT ANDERSON, TIGERS. After a solid start (0.90 ERA in April), he fell apart so badly in May that the Tigers have sent him to Triple-A Toledo to get his act together. The Tigers think he needs to work on a breaking pitch, but his biggest problem has been lack of control. He's walked 19 batters in 23.2 innings, and he's also given up five home runs—a result, no doubt, of laying pitches down the middle in an effort to get some strikes. Some people are second-guessing the Tigers because they didn't give him more innings in the minors prior to bringing him up last year. It's even been suggested that they should have let him start as a minor leaguer in order to get him professional innings more quickly. I think this is classic second-guessing; there were no complaints last year, when Anderson pitched extremely well for the Tigers after being recalled in midseason. He still has that awesome fastball, and I expect him to get back on track pretty quickly.

BRUCE AVEN, MARLINS. Starting to get some playing time and tearing the cover off the ball, hitting .351 with .596 slugging and 29 RBI in only 94 at-bats. He's not that good, of course, but Aven has pretty good power and surprising speed for a guy who's short and stocky. He missed most of 1998 after undergoing Tommy John surgery, but our '98 MLE for him was .275-15-72 for 425 AB. You could do worse.

RON BELLIARD, BREWERS. Injuries to Fernando Vina have given him an opportunity to play, and he's been outstanding, going .305-.452-.488 in 82 AB. He's a good fielder, also. I like Vina, but I'm amazed the Brewers didn't trade him last winter and open up a spot for Belliard, who could almost certainly hit .290 or better, with solid peripheral stats. I still think a Vina trade is likely between now and July 31, so if you have a chance to grab Belliard, please do.

MIKE DARR, PADRES. A former second-round draft pick of the Tigers, Darr has an interesting array of skills: he hits for average, he has some power, he's fast, he draws some walks. He can also handle center field, though he's not considered an outstanding glove man. Only 23, he's younger than Ruben Rivera and Gary Matthews Jr., and he hasn't played in Triple-A prior to this year. But since Rivera hasn't done much and Matthews may need more experience, there might be an opportunity for Darr. John Sickels rates him a B+ prospect; I'd call him a good, solid B, and well worth taking a chance on.

BRIAN DAUBACH, RED SOX. Described last winter by John Sickels as "one of the better hitters currently trapped in the minor leagues," Daubach finally attracted some interest when he went .316-35-124 with 80 walks last season for the Marlins' Charlotte farm club, earning Triple-A Player of the Year honors. The Marlins somewhat surprisingly released him after the season, but he was picked up by the Red Sox, who were desperate for lefthanded hitting after losing Mo Vaughn to free agency. Given a shot as a platoon player against righthanders, Daubach has batted .324 and slugged .637 in 102 AB. Though this is his 10th year of pro ball, he's still only 27, and I see no reason why he couldn't fashion a John Lowenstein-type career.

JOHN HALAMA, MARINERS. One of three players the M's received from Houston in last year's Randy Johnson deal, Halama started out in the bullpen this spring, but has recently moved into the rotation with good results thus far. Tall and thin, he's your typical lefty finesse pitcher, with no great fastball but good command and a fine changeup. John Sickels thinks he's as good as Jamie Moyer, but I doubt that. He might be as good as Moyer was 10 or 11 years ago, however, and he could fashion a similarly lengthy career.

CARLOS LEE, WHITE SOX. Off to an impressive start with the White Sox, hitting .314 with power for his first 105 at-bats. Lee is going to be a quality major league hitter; the only concerns were about his defense, and he looks a lot more comfortable since being moved to left field.

MIKE LOWELL, MARLINS. Lowell would have been the Marlins' Opening Day third baseman, but he was diagnosed with testicular cancer and had to go on the DL. The cancer was treated in time, and he's back and off to a decent start. If he's healthy Lowell should be an above-average hitter for a third baseman, producing some power along with a decent average. He could become a Travis Fryman type, which ain't bad. The only thing is, I'm not sure he's got all his strength back yet. He might not pay immediate dividends, but he's a good bet for the future.

GARY MATTHEWS JR, PADRES. Sarge's son is a switch-hitting outfielder who can field, run, hit with power and draw some walks. Unfortunately he's been slowed by wrist injuries, and he was hitting only .234 at Triple-A Las Vegas when the Padres recalled him last week. He might get a chance to play with Reggie Sanders on the shelf, but he's competing with Darr and Owens for playing time, and chances are that he'll be sent back to the minors pretty soon to get some more experience. I like him, but I'll be surprised if he sees much major league action this year.

KEVIN MILLAR, MARLINS. So lightly regarded that he had to begin his professional career in the Northern League after going undrafted, Millar signed with the Marlins and has been a steady .300 hitter in the minors, with good power. At 27, he's finally getting his first major league chance, and he's making the most of it, hitting .333 with a .455 OBP for his first 63 AB. I really like this guy and would recommend taking a chance on him.

HERBERT PERRY, DEVIL RAYS. Prior to this season, Perry had hardly played since 1996, when he tore up his left knee while playing for the Indians' Buffalo farm team. Now 29, he's come back with the Devil Rays and is hitting very well (.357-.434-.500 for 70 AB).

If the knee holds up, Perry can hit .290 with decent power, but I don't know how much playing time he's going to get. An intriguing long-shot.

CHRIS SINGLETON, WHITE SOX. A one-time second-round draft pick of the Giants, Singleton wound up being the White Sox' regular center fielder after Brian Simmons got hurt and McKay Christensen proved too inexperienced. Singleton is fast and a pretty good fielder, but he's currently hitting .252 with only three walks in 127 AB, and he'll be lucky to hit .230 if the Sox keep him out there. The Sox would be far better off recalling Simmons, who seems to be in the doghouse for some unknown reason. Unlike Singleton, Simmons is a real major league prospect.

DARYLE WARD, ASTROS. A big guy who's primarily a first baseman, Ward is a major league-caliber hitter, but there's a guy named Bagwell in his way. His best hope is that the Astros will package him in a July deal for some stretch-run help. If you can afford to have a little patience, he's not a bad pickup.

JEFF ZIMMERMAN, RANGERS. Two years ago, Zimmerman was a 25-year-old, undrafted former college pitcher who was working for Winnipeg of the independent Northern League. You can't get much more obscure than that, but Zimmerman got a shot in the Ranger farm system in '98, and since then he's been absolutely dazzling, posting a 1.28 ERA in two minor league stops last year and a 1.15 ERA in 24 games thus far this year for the Rangers. I don't see how this can possibly continue, but the guy is definitely a good pitcher.

June 17—Hall of Fame

Let's bring back a game I introduced last season: which active players would make the Hall of Fame, without question, if their careers ended today? This eliminates the Derek Jeters and Alex Rodriguezes, because you need at least 10 seasons in the majors to qualify for the Hall. Here's my current list of active players:

HALL OF FAME SURE THINGS: Wade Boggs, Barry Bonds, Roger Clemens, Ken Griffey Jr., Tony Gwynn, Rickey Henderson, Greg Maddux, Mark McGwire, Cal Ripken.

That's nine players, not a lot, but I wanted to limit this list to the players who will be automatic selections. However, there are a number of others who are arguably Hall of Famers based on what they've accomplished thus far, and others who are very close to being automatic. Here's a "Hall of Fame Watch" for players who have at least 10 years in the majors, listed in the order of how close I think they are to being sure things. If a player needs five or six more years of decent production to reach the point where he'd be considered an automatic choice, I ranked him lower than a guy who needs two or three more good years. Also, keep in mind that I'm primarily talking about which players *will* be in the Hall, rather than whether or not they *should* be. In addition, keep in mind that is this is done in fun, and not very scientific; please don't nit-pick because I had player A one slot above player B or something like that:

CLOSEST TO THE HALL (10 OR MORE MLB SEASONS):

FRANK THOMAS. Now in his 10th season, he has two MVP Awards, a .323 lifetime average, and he ranks sixth all-time in both on-base and slugging percentage, arguably the two most important stat categories for a hitter. He's also on track for his ninth straight season with both 100 RBI and 100 walks. He's very close, and getting the seven homers he needs for 300 would probably put him over the top even if he starts having some mediocre years, which would drag his percentages down.

JUAN GONZALEZ. Also has two MVP Awards, plus five seasons of 40-plus homers and six years with 100 or more RBI. I think one more big year ought to do it, and he's on track to have another such season in 1999.

JOSE CANSECO. A year ago, I would have considered him a long shot, but he had 46 homers in 1998, and this year he could threaten or break Maris' American League single-season record. He already has 423 lifetime homers and may be over 450 by the end of the year. If he hits more than 60 this year, I'd say he's in. Even if he doesn't, he's mighty close.

TIM RAINES. Many people think Raines is a Hall of Fame-caliber player, and I'm one of them. The question is whether the voters will agree. He's hurt by his drug problems and by the fact that most of his great years came early in his career; he's helped by his splendid lifetime totals, including his 804 stolen bases. I think he'll make it, but I also think it'll be tougher than it should be.

OREL HERSHISER. I wouldn't have given him a chance a couple of years ago, but he's only four wins away from 200 for his career; his lifetime winning percentage is excellent (.587), as is his career ERA (3.38); he's had great success in the postseason (8-3, 2.70); and he had that huge season in 1988. I still think he needs another 15 or 20 wins to get in, but I feel he's going to be a strong candidate.

JOHN FRANCO. Passed the 400-save mark earlier this year, and should challenge Lee Smith's major league record of 478 before he's through. Also has a splendid career ERA of 2.63. That's a lot in his favor; what works against him is the lack of 40-save seasons and the lack of a blow-'em-away pitch. Franco has a ton of "career value," but so did Don Sutton, and it took him forever to get in. Still, I think Franco has enough to make it.

ROBERTO ALOMAR. His revival after signing with the Indians has greatly increased his Hall of Fame chances. He's a .303 lifetime hitter with a lot of postseason appearances and a roomful of Gold Gloves. He may reach the 2,000-hit mark by the end of this year, and he's going to go well beyond that. Even with the spitting incident hanging over him, he's very close to the Hall of Fame right now. I'd say a good finish to '99 and another good year in 2000 ought to do it.

BARRY LARKIN. Doesn't get a lot of press, but as he adds to his impressive lifetime numbers, people are starting to realize that this is one of the best shortstops of all time. It would help if he kept his lifetime average over .300; he's at exactly .300 now, so that's going to be tough to do. His MVP Award and three Gold Gloves will help his cause; his lack of a 100-RBI season may hurt him. I personally think Larkin is close to being a Hall of Famer right now. We'll have to wait and see whether the voters agree.

TOM GLAVINE. Has two Cy Youngs and a splendid lifetime winning percentage of .612, but will probably need at least 200 wins. He needs 23 more; despite his problems this year, I think he'll have that by the end of next year and keep going on from there.

DAVID CONE. Very comparable to Glavine. Only 175 lifetime wins, but his career winning percentage is .648, which is awesome. I'd say he still needs the 25 wins to make it to 200 in order to get into the Hall, but I think he'll have that by the end of next season, and I don't think he'll stop at 200.

RANDY JOHNSON. His lifetime winning percentage is even better than Cone's at .652, and he's been so spectacular that he might be able to get in with a little less than 200 wins. He has 152 wins; I'd say three more good years, including 1999, would wrap it up for him.

KEVIN BROWN. Only 146 wins, but his lifetime winning percentage (.586) is good and getting better, and people are going to remember his great postseason performances. At his current pace, he won't reach 200 wins until the 2002 season, but I like his chances.

SAMMY SOSA. Going great. Sammy still only has 295 lifetime homers, but that's 295 with a bullet. I'm betting he'll make it to 500 in another four years or so, and go on to easy election to the Hall.

HAROLD BAINES. Still going strong at age 40, he has 359 lifetime homers, 1,523 RBI, 2,703 hits and a .292 lifetime average. There are a lot of guys in the Hall of Fame with stats not as good as that, but I think Baines is going to have a tough time unless he winds up with 3,000 hits or close to it.

RAFAEL PALMEIRO. His career started slowly, but Palmeiro is on track to hit at least 38 homers for the fifth straight season, and he passed the 2,000-hit mark earlier this year. With 333 lifetime homers, he still is a ways away, but Palmeiro is only 34 and still going strong. I'm betting that by the time he retires, he'll have 500 homers, close to 3,000 hits if not more, and that he'll sail in to the Hall of Fame. He's farther away from the Hall than guys like Baines, but he has much more momentum.

ALBERT BELLE. Bill James says that once a player is retired for awhile, the only thing that will matter are his stats. Belle will be a good test of that notion. His numbers say "Hall of Fame" already, but he's got a ton of negative baggage along with those great stats. With 332 lifetime homers, he wouldn't get in if his career ended today, but I think he'll have well over 500 before he's through. If he does that, I don't see how they can keep him out; if his career ends abruptly in the next couple of years, I think he'll have a tough time.

EDGAR MARTINEZ. Thanks to the thick-headedness of the Mariner brass, Martinez didn't start playing regularly until he was 27. That may cost him his chance to make the Hall of Fame. Edgar's a .318 lifetime hitter and his OBP (.425) and slugging (.521) marks are splendid as well, but with the late start, he has only 1,450 hits and 185 lifetime homers. At 36, he's running out of time, but if he can maintain those high percentages and make it to 2,000 hits and 300 homers, he's going to start looking pretty good.

FRED McGRIFF. Making a nice comeback this year. Has 374 homers; he'll need to get well over 400 to make it, maybe even 500. So it's going to take a few more good years. I'm not sure the Crime Dog has it in him.

MARK GRACE. Non-power-hitting first basemen face an uphill struggle, but Grace has a lot going for him. He has a .310 lifetime average and a .386 lifetime OBP, both of which are excellent. He's 55 hits away from 2,000, and he could challenge the 3,000-hit mark before he's through. He's also a Gold Glove fielder. I'd say he's going to need the 3,000 hits, and that's going to take six or seven more years.

WILL CLARK. Just recorded his 2,000th hit, and he has more power than Grace. But Grace is a better fielder and has managed to stay healthier. The Thrill is a long way away from Hall of Fame consideration.

TONY FERNANDEZ. Thanks to his splendid 1998 and 1999 (thus far) seasons, Fernandez is suddenly an arguable Hall of Fame candidate. He's won four Gold Gloves at shortstop, and his lifetime hit total of 2,172 is quite good for a middle infielder. He will probably need another good year or to be considered a serious candidate, and even then, it will probably be an uphill struggle.

DWIGHT GOODEN. His lifetime numbers (187-105, 3.38) are comparable to David Cone's, and he's nearly two years younger than Cone and more than a year younger than Randy Johnson. But that doesn't mean anything, since he hasn't won 15 games in a season since 1990. If Gooden could manage a comeback year or two and get up to 215 wins or so, I think he might make it. But if he gets to 200 with a couple of seven-win seasons and then hangs it up, it's going to be tough.

ANDRES GALARRAGA. Was starting to build some Hall of Fame momentum when he was stricken by cancer prior to this season. He'll get a lot of sympathy for that, but he only has 332 homers, and most of his best seasons came at Coors. He turns 38 tomorrow, and I think he's going to run out of time.

I'm sure I forgot a player or two, but before you write to remind me, remember that the discussion was limited to guys who have played at least 10 seasons in the majors.

June 24—Thoughts on Pitching

I'm off for the SABR convention in Phoenix early Thursday morning, so this will be briefer than usual, and a little earlier as well. A few odds and ends about pitching:

UNHITTABLE RELIEVERS I. Here's a list of the 1999 relievers with the lowest opposition batting averages:

Lowest Opp Avg, Relievers—1999

Pitcher, Team	Opp Avg
Jeff Zimmerman, Tex	.109
Billy Wagner, Hou	.113
Troy Percival, Ana	.116
Armando Benitez, NYM	.127
Pedro Borbon, LA	.143

(minimum 0.3 IP per scheduled game)

To put this in context: prior to 1999, only one pitcher in history had ever recorded an opponents' average under .150 in a season in which he worked at least 50 innings. That was Troy Percival of the Angels, who did it twice with a .147 mark in 1995 and a .149 average a year later. This season, *five* pitchers are on pace to break Percival's mark, led by rookie Jeff Zimmerman of the Rangers, who has been all but unhittable with an opponents' averages of .109. Billy Wagner and Percival aren't far behind, nor are Armando Benitez and Pedro Borbon. Zimmerman's been particularly amazing, since he's already worked 45 innings.

What makes this even more noteworthy is that it's happening in a season in which the hitters are more in control than ever. In fact the overall major league average of .272 would be the highest in 60 years, if it holds up. While the trends in baseball in recent years have greatly worked to the advantage of the hitters, there have been some extraordinary pitching performances as well. This is a by-product of expansion: as weaker players (both hitters and pitchers) enter the talent pool with expansion, the best performers (both hitters and pitchers) can take advantage of the weakened competition. OK, but that still doesn't explain Pedro Borbon to me.

UNHITTABLE RELIEVERS II. Billy Wagner of the Astros has faced 116 batters this year, and struck out half of them (58). This is amazing, even for Wagner. He's currently averaging 17.0 strikeouts per nine innings, which would dwarf his own record for most Ks per nine innings in a season (minimum 50 innings).

Most Strikeouts Per 9 Innings, Season—All Time

Pitcher, Team	Year	K	IP	K/9
Billy Wagner, Hou	1998	97	60.0	14.6
Billy Wagner, Hou	1997	106	66.1	14.4
Rob Dibble, Cin	1992	110	70.1	14.1
Rob Dibble, Cin	1991	124	82.1	13.6
Armando Benitez, Bal	1997	106	73.1	13.0

(minimum 50 IP)

In his career, Wagner has recorded 328 strikeouts in only 209 innings, an average of 14.1 Ks per nine innings. Among pitchers who have worked 200 innings in the majors, that's easily the best strikeout ratio of all time. Armando Benitez is No. 2 with 12.3 Ks per nine. Strikeouts aren't everything, of course, but this is still pretty cool.

CAN PEDRO CATCH NOLAN? These relief pitchers have nothing on Pedro Martinez, who has 161 strikeouts in 111.2 innings this year, an average of 13.0 Ks per nine innings. This would be a new single-season record for ERA qualifiers, breaking the mark of 12.6 set by Kerry Wood last year.

A more interesting question is whether Martinez has a chance to break Nolan Ryan's record of 383 strikeouts in a season. Martinez does have a chance, albeit a slight one. With 161 Ks in 15 starts, he's averaging 10.7 strikeouts per start. At that rate, he could break the record if given 36 starts, and come within seven or eight of the record with 35 starts. Last year the American League leader, Scott Erickson, made 36 starts, and four pitchers tied for the NL lead with 35. Unfortunately, Pedro has never started more than 33 games in season, and this year it looks like he'll get 34 or 35 at most. It's a long shot, but he could make it interesting.

Another amazing thing about Martinez is that his league-leading strikeout total is nearly twice as high as the No. 2 man, Chuck Finley of the Angels, who has 84. This would not be a record for dominating a stat category—just off the top of my head, I know that Maury Wills had more than three times the number of steals as the No. 2 man back in 1962 (104 to Willie Davis' 32)—but I don't think anyone has ever dominated the strikeout category like this. I hope he can keep it up.

July 1—All the Way to. . . Jose

Prior to last week's SABR convention in Scottsdale, AZ, there were two things I'd never experienced in my lengthy baseball-loving career:

1. I'd never gotten a baseball—either foul ball or home-run ball—as a souvenir.

2. I'd never seen a no-hitter in person.

This is no small feat, considering that I attend 25 or 30 games a year and that I've been going to major league games since 1954, when I was six years old. If you read the news, you've probably figured out that I was present for Jose Jimenez' no-hitter against the Diamondbacks last Friday night. More on that in a moment. But first, my foul ball story.

In my 46 seasons of attending major league games, I've become notorious for coming close to catching foul balls, but never quite getting one. I've had balls fly within inches of my outstretched fingers. I've had a ball bounce over my head, hit a wall, and then bounce over my head again. . . just out of reach both coming and going. One time I was at a game in Kansas City, and the guy sitting right next to me got *two* balls within a three-inning span. But not me. I'm so famous for this that I once spent 20 minutes on a radio show (the Chip Franklin show in Washington, DC) talking about my non-foul-ball-catching experiences.

Then came last Thursday, Bank One Ballpark, Cardinals vs. Diamondbacks. My friends— Rob Neyer, Mat Olkin and Pat Quinn—and I had great seats between home plate and third base, prime foul-ball territory. Travis Lee was up in the seventh, and he hit a mile-high popup in foul territory. We looked up—way, way up, almost up to the BOB's roof—as the ball reached its apex and started its downward descent. It picked up momentum, traveling faster and faster and looking bigger and bigger. It was coming right down toward us like a mortar shell. This was it! This time for sure!

At that moment, I just froze.

A week later, I can't completely explain this, even to myself, but I didn't even get out of my seat. I just sat there. Maybe it was fear of getting bonked by the ball. Maybe it was own fatalistic nature after 46 years of frustration, saying, "Something will happen. You won't catch it." And indeed, the ball's trajectory did change a little as it neared the end of its descent. It hit off the hands of someone in the row right in front of ours, bounced off the concrete, rebounded off the head of the lady sitting right in front of me (fortunately she wasn't hurt) and finally landed in the hands of an Oriental guy sitting two seats to her right. If I'd stood up and joined the scramble, I might have had a chance to pick it off as it was bounding around. But I didn't. . . I just sat there, frozen in place. I'll probably be repeating this scene in my head over and over for the rest of my life, like my own personal Zapruder film.

But what the heck, it was only a baseball. And there's always tomorrow.

"Tomorrow," as it turned out, was another Cardinal-Diamondback game at the BOB, Jose Jimenez vs. Randy Johnson. I was sitting with Steve Schulman, the Runs Prevented guy, in even better seats than Thursday, 10 rows behind the third-base dugout. No foul balls this night, but what a pitcher's duel. Neither side had a hit until the top of the fourth, when Joe McEwing led off the frame with a double. "Well, I guess if we're going to see a no-hitter tonight," I said to Steve, "we'll have to depend on Jose Jimenez." We both laughed; entering the game, Jimenez was 3-7 with a 6.69 ERA.

Johnson was awesome—he wound up with 14 Ks—and while the Cardinals threatened a couple of times, they couldn't score off him. To our great surprise, Jimenez didn't allow anything close to a hit until the sixth, when Andy Fox hit a sinking liner to right. Eric Davis dove and made a great catch. The next hitter, Johnson, also hit a sinking line drive, and Darren Bragg had to race in and catch the ball off his shoe-tops. When the final Diamondback hitter in the sixth, Tony Womack, hit a scorching grounder right to Edgar Renteria, Jimenez still had his no-hitter. But he looked like he was about to lose it.

Or so we thought.

With one out in the seventh Jimenez gave up his second walk of the game, but Mark McGwire got him out of the inning by starting a nifty 3-6-1 double play. Mark McGwire, nifty play? On Thursday Darren Oliver had Tony Womack picked off twice, but on both occasions McGwire had thrown wildly to second. Now here he was, looking like Keith Hernandez. You had to think something special was happening here.

Jimenez *was* a little lucky, but his pitches were moving like crazy, and he kept his poise despite some trying circumstances. One of them happened in the bottom of the eighth, when a fan ran onto the field. It took close to 10 minutes and about half a dozen security people to get that bozo off the field, with Jose standing and watching with the rest of the players. When the game resumed he calmly took the hill and completed another hitless inning. Three outs to go!

But it was still 0-0. I started thinking, "Oh, great, he'll pitch nine hitless innings but the Cards won't score, either, and then the bullpen will blow the no-hitter." I *am* a little fatalistic after all these years. But Johnson walked Bragg with one out in the ninth—the first walk he'd allowed all night—and then walked McGwire as well. He got Davis for his 14th strikeout, but with two out Thomas Howard—Thomas Howard?—hit a broken-bat single to left, and Bragg raced home with the first run of the game. McGwire was tossed out at third on the play to end the half-inning, and Jose took the hill one last time.

Andy Fox was the first hitter. The count went to three-and-two; then Jimenez threw a pitch that looked out of the strike zone. Fox started trotting to first, but plate umpire Bruce Froemming called it strike three. Replays indicated it was a bad call, but I was with Froemming on this one. You gotta swing the bat in a situation like that!

David Delucci pinch-hit for Johnson and hit another sinking liner to right. You probably saw the replays: Davis made another diving catch, this one even better than the one in the sixth. As he jumped up to show the ball and celebrate, it popped loose, but there was no doubt that he'd made the catch. Except to Buck Showalter, who came out to argue for a long, long time. Once more Jimenez had to stand there and cool his heels, one out away from history. It couldn't have been easy. Heck, it was driving *me* crazy.

Tony Womack was the final hitter. I thought about my foul-ball misses, including the one the night before, and all my no-hitter misses as well. I've had a few, including one (Dave Stieb) that was lost in the ninth. Was I cursed? I didn't think so. This time I didn't freeze in my seat; I stood up to watch and cheer with the rest of the 47,724 fans. And on the first pitch, Womack hit a nice, most routine grounder right to Joe McEwing at second. No-hitter!

What a sweet feeling.

I don't know if you've ever witnessed something like this in person, but take it from me: it's wonderful. It's great to witness history, and the more times you've been disappointed, the better it feels. The Diamondback fans were upset about losing the game, of course—especially after the way Johnson had pitched—but most of them did a really classy thing: they stood and applauded while the Cardinals mobbed Jimenez on the mound.

So did I.

July 8— Midseason Awards

Midseason awards from the Zee-Man:

AL MVP 1. Derek Jeter 2. Nomar Garciaparra 3. Manny Ramirez

Not that this means everything, but these three also lead the AL in on-base plus slugging, in that order. Ramirez' staggering RBI total has to be considered, but I'm more impressed by the fact that Jeter and Garciaparra are compiling these numbers while playing shortstop, a far more important defensive position than right field. Also considered: Rafael Palmeiro, Ken Griffey Jr., Shawn Green.

NL MVP 1. Jeff Bagwell 2. Sean Casey 3. Larry Walker

I don't have much doubt about Bagwell, and I think Casey deserves the runnerup spot. Walker's a problem. He leads the league in OPS by a good margin, but that's definitely a Coors-aided number: his OPS is 1.374 at home, .980 on the road. On the other hand, .980 is awfully good. Also considered: Sammy Sosa, Luis Gonzalez, Matt Williams.

AL CY YOUNG 1. Pedro Martinez 2. Troy Percival 3. Jeff Zimmerman

No contest here; Martinez has been so good that you could make a good argument for him as the AL MVP. The "will he win 30?" talk is a joke, however; Pedro has had a decision in every one of his 18 starts, and that's not going to continue. Even if it did, he'd have to go 15-1 or 15-2 the rest of the way, because he won't get more than 16 or 17 more starts. Ain't gonna happen.

If it weren't for Martinez, Percival would have to be considered very seriously for the Cy. He's 22-for-23 in save opportunities, and opposing teams are hitting .128 off him. And I really think you have to consider Zimmerman as well. Yes, he's a middle reliever, but he's 8-0 and that ain't a fluke; the guy has an 0.89 ERA and a .110 opponents' batting average. He's keeping the Rangers' shaky rotation afloat.

NL CY YOUNG 1. Randy Johnson 2. Curt Schilling 3. Billy Wagner

Johnson's "only" 9-6, but the Diamondbacks have stopped scoring for him. He leads the league in ERA, strikeouts, innings pitched, opponents' batting average and opponents' OBP. He also has a fighting chance at Nolan Ryan's strikeout record, though I don't think he'll get it. He's been awesome. Schilling continues to excel for a mediocre team, and Wagner's like Percival: 21-for-22 in saves, .110 in opponents' average. Can't pitch much better than that.

AL ROOKIE OF THE YEAR 1. Jeff Zimmerman 2. Carlos Beltran 3. Billy Koch

This is a fabulous year for AL rookies: there's also Jeff Weaver, Carlos Febles, Chris Singleton, Carlos Lee, Corey Koskie, Brian Daubach, Chad Allen, a few others. But I don't see how the award could go to anyone but Zimmerman, based on what's transpired thus far. This is shaping up to be a performance of historic proportions. Can he possibly keep it up?

NL ROOKIE OF THE YEAR 1. Scott Williamson 2. Alex Gonzalez 3. Ron Belliard

The NL rookies have also been outstanding: others include Joe McEwing, Warren Morris, Michael Barrett, Bruce Aven, Danny Graves. I don't know if he can keep this up, but based on the first half, I think Williamson has to get the nod. He's been the leader of Cincinnati's awesome bullpen, which has been the key to their first-half performance.

AL FLUKE OF THE YEAR 1. Kevin Stocker 2. Chris Singleton 3. Brook Fordyce

Not an official award, of course, though I think this one would be pretty nifty. Maybe they could call it the "Joe Charboneau Award." Two of these guys are members of my beloved White Sox, but I don't think the Sox are a fluke team. They have a lot of great young talent, and they're enormous fun to watch. It's just that Singleton and Fordyce can't possibly keep hitting like this. Can they?

NL FLUKE OF THE YEAR 1. Luis Gonzalez 2. Kent Bottenfield 3. Benny Agbayani

Luis Gonzalez is a wonderful human being, but he's no .356 hitter. Bottenfield looks like he's in line for the "Rick Helling Fluke 20-Game Winner" Award. Benny's bubble has already burst, but it was fun while it lasted.

July 15—Newsmakers

In the news:

MARLINS/DIAMONDBACKS TRADE. This is a fascinating trade: the Diamondbacks get the closer they think they need (Matt Mantei) for the steep price of Brad Penny, Vladimir Nunez and a player to be named later. There's no question that the Diamondbacks gave up a lot. The player to be named later isn't expected to be anyone special, but Nunez is a Cuban defector with outstanding stuff, and Penny is considered one of the best pitching prospects in the minors, despite some struggles at Double-A El Paso this year (2-7, 4.70 in 17 starts). El Paso is one of the toughest places in the minors to pitch, so that record can be discounted. Despite his home park, Penny had 100 strikeouts and only 25 walks in 90 innings for the Diablos prior to the trade. He also had surrendered only nine home runs, no mean feat in El Paso's bandbox park.

Is it worth this much to get a top closer? Given that a) late-inning relief has been Arizona's biggest problem this year, b) the Diamondbacks feel that they have a chance to go deep into the postseason this year, c) Mantei is only 26 years old and d) depth in starting pitching is one of the strengths of the Diamondbacks' organization—they had two other excellent pitching prospects at El Paso, John Patterson and Nick Bierbrodt—I'd say it's a gamble worth taking. . . *if* Mantei is indeed a top closer. I think there's still some room for doubt on this one, despite his 100-MPH fastball. While Mantei had 51 strikeouts in only 37.1 innings in the first half, his control (24 walks) was a problem at times, and he finished the first half with only 11 saves. The other negative about Mantei is that he's had a long history of injuries including a herniated disk in his back which required surgery in 1995 and shoulder problems that led to rotator-cuff surgery prior to the 1997 season. So. . . would I make this deal? I probably would, but it's anything but an easy decision.

THE UMPS RESIGN. For years, one of the biggest problems in baseball has been the insufferable arrogance of the major league umpires. I realize that players and managers can be abusive, but when you see an ump chasing after a player to provoke and prolong an argument—something which happens these days as a matter of course—it's too much for me. And don't get me started on the strike zone. There's no other sport in which the officials wield this much power; it's not even close.

Sandy Alderson, the former A's GM who's now serving as Bud Selig's right-hand man, is determined to bring the umps back under control, and this is his big chance. Of course, if he calls Richie Phillips' bluff, baseball may have to put up with some pretty inept umpiring for awhile. That's what happens when you bring in amateurs and minor leaguers. Pretty much every time this has happened in the past, the players and managers have bitched and whined so much about the replacement umpires that MLB has quickly caved in to Richie Phillips' demands. I think Alderson will hold out this time, but he's going to feel some heat. When it ends, I suspect you'll see a lot of the old umps back in action (though that may take a little while). . . this time with a lot of accountability for their actions. That can only be good for the game.

As for the suspension of umpire Tom Hallion—the issue which apparently pushed Phillips and his boys over the line—it was *not* unprecedented in baseball history, as some have said. Back in the old days, umpires were even more combative than they are now, and they sometimes paid a price for it. Probably the most famous umpire suspension happened in 1939, when Giant shortstop Billy Jurges and National League umpire George Magerkurth wound up in a fistfight after a dispute about a home-run call. National League president Ford Frick meted out the same punishment to both Jurges and Magerkurth: 10-day suspensions and $250 fines. Players, managers and umpires are a little more civilized now, but if a player can get suspended for bumping an ump, why can't an umpire get suspended for bumping a player?

ALL-STAR GAME/TOP 100 PLAYERS. Almost everyone agrees that the pre-game festivities overshadowed the game, but then, these were very special festivities. It's the sort of thing that baseball does best, right up to bringing out the ultimate mythological sports hero, Ted Williams. It got to me, like it did to almost everybody I talked to. Would people get tears in their eyes if Sammy Baugh came out to throw the first pass prior to the Pro Bowl Game? Of course not; that rich tradition is one of the strengths of baseball.

I did wonder about the whereabouts of some of the "living legends," like Yogi Berra and Willie McCovey and Willie Stargell, none of whom were present, to my knowledge. Where were they? But it was great to see the guys who *were* there. As for the contest to pick the top 25 players of the century from a list of 100, I'm sure it'll be fun. . . but I wouldn't take it too seriously. I hope to get to my own choices in a future column.

June 22—Cameron/Konerko Trade

One of the more intriguing trades of the offseason was the November deal which sent outfielder Mike Cameron from the White Sox to the Reds for first baseman Paul Konerko. Both were highly-regarded young players who had struggled mightily in 1998. In fact their batting, on-base and slugging averages were nearly identical:

	AB	H	HR	RBI	SB	CS	Avg	OBP	Slg
Konerko	217	47	7	29	0	1	.217	.276	.332
Cameron	396	83	8	43	27	11	.210	.285	.336

I liked both players despite their problems, but as many of you know, I was especially high on Konerko, who I considered one of the two or three best prospects in the minors prior to his disastrous 1998 debut. So I was squirming in my chair this April, when Cameron got off to a hot start with the Reds while Konerko was looking even worse than he had in 1998. Since then, Konerko has caught fire:

	G	AB	H	HR	RBI	Avg	OBP	Slg
Konerko thru 4/28	15	59	11	1	3	.186	.226	.271
Konekro 4/29 to 7/21	58	198	64	12	32	.323	.366	.566

Now *that's* the Konerko I expected to see. He's a fascinating hitter to watch. In the minor leagues he usually drew a decent number of walks, but thus far this year, he's walked only 16 times in 279 plate appearances. It hasn't been for lack of trying, as Konerko hardly ever swings at the first pitch—only 13 percent of the time this year, one of the lowest percentages of first-pitch swinging in the majors. He usually takes the second pitch as well, and the pitchers have been taking advantage of his passivity. I watch a lot of White Sox games, and for awhile, it seemed to me that every Konerko plate appearance was starting with a 0-and-2 count. That's an exaggeration, of course, but Konerko *is* getting into a deep hole more often than the average hitter; about 19 percent of his PAs have started out 0-2 this year, well above the league average of 15 percent.

So, how is he succeeding? One reason is that he's an excellent two-strike hitter, slugging more than 100 points higher with two strikes than the average AL batsman (.409 vs. 306). He's also moved closer to the plate, which seems to have given him better plate coverage. He's driving the ball now, hitting hard line drives and flyballs instead of the groundballs he was producing earlier. Konerko, who's painfully slow, was hitting into a ton of double plays for most of the first half of the season, but this month he has only one GDP in 50 AB.

I can think of another reason for Konerko's recent success: White Sox manager Jerry Manuel. Manuel is not a perfect manager by any means, but the more I see of the guy, the more I like him. He seems to be very good with young players; he shows a good amount of patience with someone who's struggling, and even when he feels compelled to sit a guy down for a little while, he doesn't bury him. This has worked wonders with Konerko, who seems visibly more relaxed in pressure situations than he did earlier in the year. I'll admit that Manuel hasn't been able to help Greg Norton or Mike Caruso very much, but he's had more hits than misses.

As for Cameron, he's performing back at his 1997 rookie level, and it's looking more and more as if 1998 was just a fluke bad season (yes, I know... Manuel couldn't help *him*, either, last year). Comparing the two through yesterday's game, this is clearly a deal which has helped both clubs:

	AB	H	HR	RBI	BB	SO	SB	CS	Avg	OBP	Slg
Konerko	257	75	13	35	16	32	0	0	.292	.335	.498
Cameron	324	87	10	41	44	91	28	6	.269	.358	.460

Overall, you'd have to rate Cameron as a little more valuable to this point because of his speed and defensive ability. But of course, the season's not over. One difference between the two is that Cameron has struggled mightily with two strikes, a big reason why he ranks among the NL leaders in batter strikeouts:

	AB	H	HR	RBI	BB	SO	GDP	Avg	OBP	Slg
Konerko	132	30	6	13	7	32	8	.227	.266	.409
Cameron	165	24	3	15	24	91	0	.145	.253	.261

Well, I like them both. Despite my affection for Konerko, I don't think the deal is a slam-dunk for the White Sox. One problem is that he really belongs on first base, and the Sox already have Frank Thomas. Another problem is that almost all the good Sox hitters—Thomas, Magglio Ordonez, Konerko, Carlos Lee—hit righthanded. The surprising Chris Singleton is the only exception, and I really don't think Singleton can keep hitting the way he has been. If Konerko keeps slugging away, it would not stun me to see the Sox trade Thomas, either prior to the July 31 deadline or (more likely) in the offseason... much as I would hate to see that happen.

Finally, Konerko's recent success is a reminder that even great hitters sometimes struggle when they first reach the majors. The rookie years of Ty Cobb, Mickey Mantle, Carl Yastrzemski, Willie Stargell and a number of other Hall of Famers were nothing special, compared with what came later. Will Konerko be a great hitter? He's only 23, but I like what I'm seeing. And if anyone out there wants to trade me J.D. Drew...

August 5—Stretch-Run Predictions

Let's look at some key teams heading into the last two months of the season:

METS. The clear winners of the late-July tradefest, the Metsies added Darryl Hamilton, Kenny Rogers, Billy Taylor, Chuck McElroy and Shawon Dunston without paying an excessive price. They were even with the Braves prior to making these moves, so you have to like their chances. The starting rotation doesn't do much for me, but the offense is very solid and the bullpen is deep and strong.

Two things I don't like about the Mets:

1. Bobby Valentine. Valentine manages a game very well, and he knows how to get the most out of a deep roster, which the Mets definitely have. But he also has—to say the least—an abrasive personality, and umpires, opposing teams and even a lot of his own players feel no affection for him. In a tight series down the stretch or in the postseason, all the bad blood he's stirred up might come back to haunt him.

2. Armando Benitez as closer. When Benitez fell apart for the second straight year in the 1997 playoffs, I thought —Calvin Schiraldi— and wrote the guy off. To his credit, he's come back and posted some amazing numbers this year, including 90 strikeouts and only 30 hits allowed in 55.2 innings. But he's also blown five saves in only 16 opportunities. I watched him last weekend against the Cubs at Wrigley, and he looked like the same old Armando: get him under pressure and he starts to lose his command. I don't think the Mets are sold on him, either, which is why they dealt for Billy Taylor. We'll see what happens, but among Benitez, Taylor (at least lately) and a John Franco coming back from injury, there's not a closer I really trust.

BRAVES. They didn't get Fred McGriff, who would have been a nice fit for them. They *did* get Jose Hernandez, a versatile player with a good bit of power, and Terry Mulholland, an aged veteran who's been awful since the end of May. Overall, I'm not impressed; they still have big holes at first base and behind the plate. I think the Braves are too good to miss the playoffs, but they're probably going to have to battle the Mets down to the wire to win the NL East. Despite my reservations about the Mets' closers, I'm going with New York.

REDS. They're not going to go away, are they? Juan Guzman—terrible in April, excellent since then—was a nice pickup, and Denny Neagle's back. This will take some strain off their overworked bullpen, which leads the National League in both relief ERA and relief innings. This is a good story, a relatively small-market team that spent money wisely, made some good deals and was able to contend. I don't think they'll beat out the Mets or Braves for the NL wild-card, but it could be close.

ASTROS. They didn't make any moves, but I'm not sure they needed to. Jeff Bagwell's the best player in the National League, and Craig Biggio isn't far behind. Moises Alou could be back for the last month, and Ken Caminiti should be back even earlier. And of course the Astros have Larry Dierker again. I think this may be the year Houston finally makes it to the World Series.

GIANTS. I'm not one of those guys who has a heart attack every time a manager lets a starting pitcher throw 120 pitches in a game, but Livan Hernandez. . . there's a guy whose arm has had a lot of mileage put on it the last couple of years. On the other hand, Hernandez should benefit from the challenge of pitching in big games again. I think he'll help San Francisco, but I don't see the Giants catching the Diamondbacks.

BLUE JAYS. Like the Reds, they keep hanging around. David Segui was a good pickup, but he's wasted as a DH. The Clemens trade looks a lot better now than I thought it would last March. And Shawn Green has become one of the top five hitters in the American League. I like the Jays to win the AL wild-card.

RED SOX. Gordon's gone for the year, Martinez is still hurting. Butch Huskey helps, but he can't pitch. I love the way Jimy Williams has kept this undermanned team in the race, and I'd love to see Tim Wakefield closing games in mid-October. But I don't think it's going to happen.

YANKEES. The King is back! It's a minor move, but Jim Leyritz was a perfect pickup for a team which still has just about everything. But what's with Clemens? He's starting to make me think I'd rather have David Wells.

INDIANS. They didn't get a No. 1 starter (again), but there wasn't a lot out there. I mean, would you part with Richie Sexson to get. . . Chuck Finley? (Now, *Mrs.* Finley. . . that's another story!) So they'll keep trying to bludgeon teams to death while hoping that Bartolo Colon continues to pitch like he did in July (4-0, 2.36). Still a very strong possibility to win it all.

A'S. Unlike the Reds, who've spent some bucks, this is a true small-market, low-budget team trying to contend. . . and succeeding, at least to a degree. Their late-July moves were fascinating: adding a solid second baseman (Randy Velarde), dumping a quality starter (Kenny Rogers) but then coming back and getting *two* pretty good starters in Kevin Appier and Omar Olivares. But the Billy Taylor trade bewilders me. Granted, he had a rough July (four blown saves, 7.50 ERA), but what did the A's have to replace him with? Not Doug Jones again! Whatever. . . this is fun.

My playoff picks, as of August 5:

NL DIVISION WINNERS: Mets, Astros, Diamondbacks. NL WILD-CARD: Braves. NL CHAMPION: Astros.

AL DIVISION WINNERS: Yankees, Indians, Rangers. AL WILD-CARD: Blue Jays. AL CHAMPION: Yankees.

WORLD CHAMPION: Yankees.

We'll see, won't we?

August 12—The Phillies, The Big Hurt and Bratwurst

A few people have pointed out that in my rundown of contending teams last week, I neglected to mention the Philadelphia Phillies. That was an oversight, as the Phils are definitely still in contention for the National League wild-card. I'd call them long shots: they can hit, but they don't have the pitching depth to match the Mets, Braves and Reds. I'd like them better if they had picked up another starting pitcher for the stretch run, but they didn't.

Speaking of the Phillies, I thought the whole J.D. Drew thing was totally disgusting. Boo the guy if you feel the need to, but throwing batteries and garbage? It's too much. And it isn't just battery-throwing, either. There was a sign in the upper deck at the Vet last night which said, "Plain and simple, J.D.: We hate you," and that pretty much summed up the atmosphere of the crowd. Think about those words, "We Hate You," and the emotions behind them. After what's happened in America the last few months, do we really need stuff like this? I'm sorry, but that really bothered me.

Enough of that. Here in Chicago, the big news is that Frank Thomas has basically decided that he doesn't want to play first base any more. "I've had my days at first," he told the *Chicago Tribune* Monday. "I know what position I should be playing, and that's DH. I feel good there. I feel comfortable."

The Big Hurt may feel comfortable as a DH, but he doesn't hit as well. Thus far this year, Thomas has batted .346 and slugged .553 when he's played first base; as a DH, he's hitting .287 and slugging .439. This is nothing new, as Thomas has shown this pattern during his entire career. And that's why Jerry Manuel wants Thomas in the field, despite Frank's obvious weakness with the glove.

Thomas' latest gaffe in the field was an error in Oakland on Sunday that helped the Athletics beat the Sox, 7-5. He's embarrassed by his awkward fielding, and he should be. But can he produce more runs with his bat at first base than he lets in with his glove?

I looked into this a couple of weeks ago, and there's no question in my mind that the Sox are better off with Thomas playing first. Based on his offensive numbers at first base vs. his production as a DH, I estimated that he would create 36 more runs as an everyday first baseman. How does that compare with the number of runs he lets in with his glove? Using zone ratings as a guide, I estimated that his lack of range and overall awkwardness around the bag resulted in about nine additional runs for the opposition over the course of a year (it might seem like more, but I think the estimate is quite reasonable). Thomas himself is not especially error-prone (his lifetime fielding percentage is .990), but he commits about three more errors per year than an average first baseman does. In addition, Thomas is pretty weak at scooping up errant throws, and as a result the other infielders commit more throwing errors with The Big Hurt playing first than they do with other first basemen. Compared to an average first baseman, Thomas' weakness results in about 6.5 more throwing errors for the other infielders over the course of the year. That's a total of 9.5 more errors per year with Thomas at first. How many runs would 9.5 errors lead to? Obviously it depends on when they occur, but a reasonable estimate is four or five. So he's producing 36 additional runs with his bat, letting in maybe 14 more runs with his glove.

You could quibble with my math, but everyone who's ever studied the subject has concluded that if you have a first baseman who can really hit, you'll take your chances with his glove. To put it another way, Dick Stuart played every day; Mike Squires usually sat on the bench until the ninth inning. The White Sox know this, which is why they want Thomas at first. But if Thomas is going to sulk and whine every time he has to play defense, how's that going to work?

It would be a lot simpler for everyone concerned if Thomas showed he was more comfortable as a DH by hitting a little better. Maybe he should talk to Harold Baines or something. In the meantime, I'm more convinced than ever that the Sox will try to trade Thomas this winter. But what's the market for a .280-hitting DH with sub-standard power who's making $10 million a year?

I went up to Milwaukee with my dad last Sunday for the Brewers-Reds game, the first time I'd been up there in several years. The idea was to get one last look at County Stadium before they closed it down for good. Though it now seems certain that County will be around for a good part of next season, if not all of it, after the July 14 crane accident that killed three ironworkers working on the Brewers' new stadium, it was good to be back in Milwaukee, one of the favorite haunts of my baseball youth.

I'll say it right off, however: old County isn't what it used to be. My dad and I started driving up to Milwaukee back in 1962, when the Braves were still in their glorious Aaron/Mathews/Spahn/Burdette years, and some of the seats look like they haven't been painted since the Braves left town. There are other signs that the Brewers are just playing out the string in this park. For instance, they didn't even have a live version of the National Anthem, just some canned orchestra music. For the seventh-inning stretch, they played more canned music, Kate Smith singing "God Bless America." A nice patriotic song, to be sure, but for the seventh-inning stretch? Back when County was rocking, the organ guy would go from "Take Me Out to the Ballgame" right into the "Beer Barrel Polka," and the whole place would go nuts. I miss that.

As for the rest of the experience:

1. The bratwursts with red sauce are as great as ever. Showing unusual restraint, I limited myself to two.

2. Miller Park, which was well under construction until the tragic crane accident, looms beyond the right-field bleachers. It is already an impressive structure, but there's nothing about it which says "Milwaukee"; in fact, it looks identical to Bank One Ballpark in Phoenix. Maybe they could erect a big statue of a bratwurst outside the place. . .

3. Hideo Nomo started for the Brewers and looked great—for the first four hitters. After that the Reds pounded him mercilessly; even Chris Stynes had a two-run homer. Nomo worked four-and-a-third innings, gave up eight hits and seven runs, and didn't throw more than two or three good fastballs the whole time. He's gotten pounded three starts in a row, and if he was on my fantasy team, I'd dump him immediately.

4. They have vendors selling Captain Morgan and Jack Daniels cocktails. I love Milwaukee!

5. In the Brewer third, Jeff Cirillo hit a medium gapper to left-center, a sure double eight times out of 10. Unfortunately, Cirillo stumbled halfway to first and needed a couple of steps to regain his balance. He foolishly headed for second anyway and got thrown out by 10 feet. Even good players make dumb decisions sometimes.

6. The obligatory fat-ex-player's barbecue stand at County Stadium is "Gorman's Grille," for Gorman Thomas. I'll bet Pete Vuckovich has a permanent table.

7. In the Reds' fifth, Greg Vaughn hit a three-run homer off Nomo on a 3-0 pitch. There have been 14 home runs hit in the National League on 3-0 pitches this year; Vaughn has three of them. Since the start of the 1996 season, Vaughn has hit 10 homers on 3-and-0 pitches.

8. In the Reds' eighth, the fans started doing The Wave. This would never happen in Chicago. In fact, I've been to games in about a half-dozen stadiums over the last three or four years, and I can't remember seeing one Wave. Do people still do this in your home park?

9. Stan Belinda pitched the final three innings for the Reds, and didn't allow a hit. It's nice to see Belinda, who was diagnosed with multiple sclerosis last September, back in action and pitching well. I credit Belinda with being one of the game's great, though uncredited, innovators: back when he was with the Pirates, he was the first player I can recall who wore his cap with the bill deeply curved like college kids always do. A true pioneer.

August 19—Players in the News

Players in the news:

BRIAN DAUBACH. With his dramatic game-winning double with two outs in the bottom of the ninth against the A's Monday night, Daubach is very much in the news. He's been unreal in August, hitting .450 with seven homers and 25 RBI in 16 games. In basically a half-season of work (79 games, 291 at-bats), Daubach is .337-19-68, with 29 doubles. Unreal.

A few things about Daubach:

1. He's probably hitting over his head, but he's not a fluke. Our MLE for him this year, based on his big 1998 season for the Marlins' Triple-A farm club, was .270-22-88 for 466 AB, with .502 slugging.

2. Though he's been pretty strictly platooned this year, Daubach *can* hit lefthanders. At Charlotte last season, Daubach went .280-10-35 vs. lefties in 157 AB. He's 11-for-35 (.314) against southpaws with the Sox thus far this year.

3. He's not a creation of Fenway Park; he's hitting .322 and slugging .664 on the road.

4. He's hitting .390 with runners in scoring position and .412 with runners in scoring position and two out.

5. Before getting his big chance this year, Daubach spent two seasons in rookie ball, three seasons in Class-A, two seasons in Double-A and two more in Triple-A. His resume includes 965 games and 3,383 at-bats in the minors.

6. Marlins GM Dave Dombrowski usually has a great eye for talent, but the Marlins released Daubach last November. I'm sure they regret it, even though Kevin Millar, who's the same age as Daubach (27), has been doing a fine job at first base for them.

ALEX RODRIGUEZ. A-Rod's knee injury took him out of the Seattle lineup for five weeks in April and May, so people aren't fully appreciating the season he's having. In only 87 games, Alex has 32 homers, 87 ribbies and 88 runs scored. Project those numbers to 162 games (he played in 161 last year), and you get 60 homers, 162 RBI and 164 runs. Wow. Could he do that for a full season? I believe he could, even with the move to SAFECO Field. I'm still not sure who will turn out to be the best overall shortstop among A-Rod, Derek Jeter and Nomar Garciaparra, but I'm pretty certain Rodriguez will be the best *hitter*, maybe even better than Honus Wagner.

Will he be doing all that hitting for the Mariners? The M's seem to feel that they can't afford to sign both Ken Griffey Jr. and A-Rod to long-term contracts, and of the two, Griffey seems the more likely to leave at this point (though it would obviously make a difference if his father becomes the Seattle manager). However, it's possible that they'll lose *both* players. That would be a shame, but that's the way baseball is these days.

RANDY JOHNSON. The Big Unit currently needs 99 strikeouts to equal Nolan Ryan's single-season record of 383. Can he do it? According to *USA Today*, Johnson figures to get nine more starts, so he'd need to average 11 strikeouts an outing. So far this year, he's averaging 10.5 Ks per start, but over his last 17 outings, his average has been 11.1 per game, enough to give him the record.

If you map out Johnson's last nine starts on the schedule, giving him four days' rest between starts, they look like this:

8/21, @Pit 8/26, @Fla 8/31, Pit 9/05, @Atl 9/10, Phi 9/15, Pit 9/20, Col 9/25, @SF 9/30, SD

It would be best for Johnson's chances at the record if the Diamondbacks stick to this schedule, rather than giving him an extra days' rest once or twice along the way while keeping the rest of the Arizona rotation intact. Holding to this schedule, Johnson's last scheduled start would be on the Thursday prior to the end of the regular season. That would give him four or five days' rest before the first game of the Division Series, depending on whether the Diamondbacks begin postseason play on Tuesday, October 5, or Wednesday, October 6. Perfect.

But let's say he gets an extra day's rest along the way, and his last scheduled start is Friday, October 1, with Arizona's first playoff game set for the following Tuesday. Unless the Diamondbacks *have* to win this game to get into the playoffs—unlikely, given their current comfortable lead—they would probably pull Randy after five innings or so, record or no record, to make sure he's rested and ready for his first playoff start. At this point, Buck Showalter isn't going to care beans about the strikeout record. . . his priority will be to have The Big Unit ready to go when the playoffs begin.

So it won't be easy. But Johnson's quest for the record should help liven up the last couple of weeks of the regular season.

August 26—J.D. Drew

Glutton for punishment that I am, I wanted to write a little more about J.D. (Booooo!!!!) Drew. I can understand Phillies fans being a little miffed at the guy, but how did J.D. become this national pariah, this universal symbol of greed? Drew gets booed even in Chicago, and about 95 percent of the newspaper and magazine columns I've read about him have had headlines like, "J.D. Deserves Your Scorn" . . . often written by people who have never met the man.

I've never met him, either, and in all honesty, J.D. Drew is *not* one of my heroes. But there's another side to this story, and simple fairness dictates that we look at it before deciding whether to condemn him. Let's start at the beginning. In the weeks leading up to the 1997 draft, Drew and his agent, Scott Boras, were very upfront about wanting a package in the $10 million range. That might seem like an outrageous amount of money, but in 1996, two amateur players had received packages in that precise price range. San Diego State first baseman Travis Lee got $10 million from the Diamondbacks, and Waynesboro, PA high school pitcher Matt White got $10.2 million from the Devil Rays.

To be sure, Lee and White were special cases: both players had been declared free agents through procedural errors made by the teams which had drafted them. As a result, major league teams were bidding against each other for their services. Other amateur free agents had gotten big money in the year prior to the 1997 draft. Cuban righthander Rolando Arrojo got $7 million from the Devil Rays; another righthander, John Patterson, received $6.075 million from the Diamondbacks; and the Devil Rays gave $3 million to lefthanded pitcher Bobby Seay. Patterson and Seay had been declared free agents via the same loophole that freed Lee and White (their drafting teams had failed to tender a contract offer within the 15-day time period specified in the Basic Agreement). Seay and White were Scott Boras clients; Lee and Patterson were not.

Given all that, it was a little disingenuous for the Phillies and other major league clubs to argue that J.D. Drew's demands were "outrageous" and that no drafted player was "worth" that amount of money. Was Drew as good a prospect as Travis Lee or Matt White? By all accounts, he certainly was. The only difference was the draft, a system which gives one team exclusive rights to negotiate with a player for a period of one year. Whatever benefits the draft may offer for maintaining competitive balance—I personally think the degree of benefit has been greatly overstated—there's no denying that it's a helluva way to keep the prices for amateur talent down. You don't want to sign for what we're offering you? Fine; go play in the Northern League.

Scott Boras is no fool, and neither are a lot of other big-name agents. They know that, given the draft system, their options are limited, but they also know that they *have* options. One is to look for loopholes in the draft, which they did successfully in the case of White, Lee, etc., and which Boras would try to do—unsuccessfully, and a little ridiculously—in the case of Drew. The more practical option is to announce, as Drew and Boras did, that they want X amount of dollars to sign, and that they're not going to play unless they get it. This tactic did not begin with J.D. Drew, and it didn't end with him, either. It's the reason that the early rounds of the baseball draft now revolve around "signability," with players who want a lot of dough often going later than their talents would dictate. You may consider these players greedy, but given the mechanics of the draft, what other kind of leverage do they have?

Boras has said that several teams had told him prior to the draft that they were willing to give Drew his $10 million. That may have been overstating things a little, but there's little doubt that several teams would have been willing to pay $7 million or more in guaranteed money to get Drew's name on a contract. Instead Drew was grabbed by the Phillies with the second overall pick. The Phillies made it clear from the first that they had no intention of offering Drew anything close to $10 million. "This kid is not a free agent," Phillies owner Bill Giles said, and stated that the Phillies' offer would be in the $2 million range that Kris Benson, the No. 1 overall pick in 1996, had received. Not surprisingly, things got ugly pretty quickly. The Phillies eventually increased their offer, ultimately offering a guaranteed $5.3 million plus incentives, according to *Baseball America*. But that came very late in the negotiations, and it wasn't enough to get Drew to sign.

What did the Phillies get out of all this? First of all, they wasted a valuable draft pick, one that they might have used to select Troy Glaus or Vernon Wells or any number of talented—and much more affordable—players who were available in the '97 draft. Heck, Rick Ankiel, another Boras client, was available; he lasted until the second round because he wanted, and got, an "outrageous" $2.5 million. Wasting their pick was bad enough, but the Phillies didn't even succeed in their self-appointed quest to hold the line against mega-dollar demands by draftees. When the 1998 draft arrived a year later, the Phillies, who had the No. 1 overall pick, selected University of Miami infielder Pat Burrell. The Cardinals, drafting fifth, selected Drew, who was back in the draft after an unsuccessful effort by Boras to get Drew declared a free agent. Drew, anxious to play and happy to be dealing with a club that acted like it wanted him, quickly signed for a package that guaranteed him $7 million, plus incentives—not $10 million, to be sure, but a lot more than the Phillies had ever offered him. The Phillies, the club which had insisted on holding the line with Drew, then signed Burrell to a deal with an $8 million guarantee. Doesn't that make Pat Burrell a greedy jerk who's trying to ruin the game, also? No, it doesn't work like that. The Phillies weren't seen as hypocrites, either; once Drew had received his cash, the Phillies could declare that "the market had moved" and that they had no choice but to give the No. 1 pick more money than Drew was getting. It was OK, see, as long as *they* didn't move the market. As David Rawnsley put it in his splendid review of the draft in *Baseball America's 1999 Almanac*, "Thus they (the Phillies) ended up paying Burrell, a lesser player by all accounts than Drew, significantly more than they had offered Drew less than two months before."

Sounds like a great way to run your franchise.

Here's my prediction. The first time Pat Burrell (a splendid prospect in his own right, by the way) steps up at the Vet in a Phillie uniform, he'll be cheered like a conquering hero. The cheers will continue up until he gets his first strikeout. Then he'll get a more traditional Philadelphia welcome. But whatever Burrell does or doesn't do from that point on, he'll never get booed the way J.D. Drew gets booed, either in Philadelphia or anywhere else. See, only J.D. Drew deserves your scorn. . . because he didn't want to sign for what the Phillies were offering him.

Maybe I'm dense, but I'm still trying to figure out why the Phillies drafted J.D. Drew in the first place. "We made it very clear to the Phillies the day before the draft, and even an hour before the draft, and they still picked me," Drew told *Baseball America* shortly after the 1997 draft. "We had things on the table that other teams would offer. And we let the Phillies know that if they weren't willing to match that, then don't draft us. There are other people willing to pay. We made that very clear to them, and they still drafted me." Yes, they did. To which I say: Booooooooooooooooooooooooo!

Before I go, I wanted to mention something about Brian Daubach and the Marlins. Jim Callis suggests that the Marlins' release of Daubach last fall was probably done as a favor to Daubach, so that he'd be able to land another job. At the time the Marlins were figuring that Derrek Lee would be their first baseman in 1999 and for many years thereafter, and they felt that they couldn't spare a spot for Daubach on their 40-man roster. In retrospect this looks like a colossal blunder, but hindsight is always 20-20.

As for Derrek Lee, he was hitting .289-16-64 in 289 at-bats for Triple-A Calgary the last time I looked. . . pretty good power numbers even in the PCL. His strikeout/walk ratio is still a problem (75 Ks, 23 BBs), however. Lee won't turn 24 until next month, so there's still hope for him, but I'm betting he never becomes much more than a low-average major league hitter with occasional power. I wonder if Lee is starting to think about the Japanese League, where his father Leon and his uncle Leron were long-time stars.

I will be off next week as I make a final pilgrimage to Tiger Stadium while I still have a chance. Who knows, maybe they'll ask me to umpire third base.

September 3—Baseball at the Corner

I wasn't going to do a column this week, but I was back from Detroit a little early, and there's a holiday weekend coming up, so why not? A few random comments:

TIGER STADIUM. I'd been to Tiger Stadium a couple of times prior to yesterday's game, but this was the first time I moved around the park, sitting in different places and checking things out. It's a wonderful old place, a real ballpark with lots of seats close to the action. And there's so much history there. Detroit people like to talk about "Baseball at the Corner," meaning the corner of Michigan and Trumbull where major league baseball has been played continuously since 1901. Cobb and Crawford. Greenberg and Gehringer. Kaline and Lolich. Whitaker and Trammell. And many, many others. That's a lot of history.

Tiger Stadium, of course, is noted for the distinctive upper deck which wraps around the entire stadium. The upper deck extends over the seats in the lower deck more than in any stadium I can think of, which is great in some ways but not so good in others. The problem is that when you're sitting far back in one of the lower-deck seats, you feel like you're sitting in the darkness looking out into the light. The first place I sat was behind home plate but quite a ways back, with the broadcast booth hanging down and blocking out even more of the sunshine. I couldn't even see the scoreboard. The effect was completely different from Wrigley Field, another stadium built in the same era. Wrigley seems open, light and airy; a lot of Tiger Stadium seems closed off, dark and a little confining.

Enough quibbling; overall it's a great place to see a game. Many of the seats in both decks are right on top of the action, to a degree that can't be matched by any of the newer parks. The fans are enthusiastic and knowledgeable; the staff is courteous and helpful (I've always loved Michigan people). And when you look up in the broadcast booth, you see Mr. Baseball History himself, Ernie Harwell. What a place. We're all going to miss it.

THE NORTHERN LEAGUE. In contrast to Tiger Stadium, baseball has been played at the corner (?) of Springinsguth Rd. and the Elgin-O'Hare Expressway since May of 1999, when the Schaumburg Flyers joined the independent Northern League. My dad lives in Schaumburg, and he's been to about a half-dozen games this year. I went there for the first time with him a couple of weeks ago, and the whole experience was really a lot of fun.

Independent leagues like the Northern, as you probably know, have no affiliation with Organized Baseball. The players tend to fall into two groups: ex-major leaguers or minor league veterans still hoping to get back to the big time, and younger players who either went undrafted or drew their releases after a season or two in the regular minor leagues. The game I saw was between the Flyers and the Fargo-Moorhead Red Hawks, and it included a couple of ex-major leaguers: Mike Busch for the Red Hawks, Jack Voigt for the Flyers. Both are interesting stories. Busch, who is 31, had some pretty good seasons in the Dodgers' farm system in the early and mid-'90s, but he batted only .220 in 100 at-bats with the big club. He did hit seven homers in those 100 ABs, however, and half his hits went for extra bases. At the time of the game he was leading the Northern League in home runs, and he's hanging on in hopes that some major league team will give him another chance. Voigt, who is 33, has played in bits and starts for four major league clubs, and while his lifetime average is only .235, his other stats aren't that bad: .324 OBP, .401 SLG, 20 homers, 83 RBI and 78 walks in 588 career at-bats. Both he and Busch are no worse than a lot of guys currently filling up major league roster spots, and they're undoubtedly better than many of them.

The indy leagues are full of stories like this, though most of the players have never been near the majors. The Flyers, for instance, have an outfielder named Jamie Lopiccolo, who, after going undrafted, batted .388 with good power in his minor league debut with Ogden of the Pioneer League in 1995. In four minor league seasons, Lopiccolo has a .315 career average, but he's never advanced higher than Class-A ball. At 26, he's probably never going to make it to The Show, but you have to admire the guy for hanging in there.

Two more things I liked about the Schaumburg Flyers: their manager is Ron Kittle, and their pitching coach is The Little Bulldog, Greg Hibbard. Cool! The caliber of play in the Northern League is a little ragged but not bad overall, and the games are very enjoyable to watch.

I was hoping to write a little about Randy Johnson and Sammy Sosa this week, but the holiday beckons. Happy Labor Day!

September 9—The Home-Run Race

In the news:

SOSA AND THE HOME-RUN RACE. As I'm writing this, Sammy Sosa has just hit No. 59, meaning that he needs 11 homers in his final 22 games to tie McGwire's record, 12 to break it. That would have been an impossible pace a few years ago, but not any more. Sosa has hit 12 home runs in his last 21 games, and that sort of pace isn't unusual for him. Pressure? Knowing Sosa, I don't think it'll be much of a factor. So it could happen, though the odds are obviously against him. Two problems he faces: a series this weekend in the Astrodome, a very tough home-run park, and six more games against McGwire's Cardinals, including a season-ending series in St. Louis. Think the Cards are just going to lay it in there for him?

Even if Sosa doesn't tie or break the record, he's going to come close, and that makes McGwire's 70 homers a little less amazing than they they seemed to be a year ago. Unless baseball does something to restore a little more balance between the batters and the pitchers, I think someone could hit 75 or even 80 homers before too long. Put a really big-time power hitter in a place like Coors Field, and it might not stop there.

Will it happen? I don't think so. I'm pretty sure MLB feels it needs to do *something* to help the pitchers, and its decision to go to war with the umpires was based in part on the umps' reluctance to call high strikes. (That was only one of the problems with the umps, of course.) If changing the strike zone doesn't work, I think they'll raise the mound. But something will happen to ensure that 70-homer seasons don't become commonplace.

SOSA FOR MVP? Crazy as it might seem, a few writers in Chicago are arguing that Sosa should repeat as National League MVP. Their argument is that he's been the league's dominant player by far, unlike 1998 when—according to them—Sosa had numbers comparable to McGwire's while playing for a contending team.

This is an absurd argument on both ends. To begin with, Sosa's 1998 numbers *weren't* comparable to McGwire's; overall, Big Mac's were clearly superior. And in 1999, the only category where Sosa is dominant is home runs. Look at on-base plus slugging, one of the best pure measures of offensive effectiveness. Sosa ranks fifth in the league in that category, behind Larry Walker, McGwire, Chipper Jones and Jeff Bagwell. I don't know how you could vote for Sosa over Jones or Bagwell, who produced their great numbers in the heat of a pennant race.

RANDY JOHNSON. With five starts left, he needs 55 strikeouts to tie Nolan Ryan's single-season mark, 56 to break it. Johnson has averaged 11.4 strikeouts per start over his last 15 starts, so it's definitely within his range. His projected starts for the remainder of the season based on four days' rest between starts: 9/10 PHI, 9/15 PIT, 9/20 @ COL, 9/25 @SF, 9/30 SD. As I wrote a few weeks ago, it would be ideal for Johnson if the Diamondbacks stick to this schedule, because it would mean Johnson's final start would come on the last Thursday of the season. That would give him four or five days' rest prior to the opening of the Division Series (depending on whether Arizona's first playoff game comes on October 5 or 6), and he could go all out for the record in his final start if he's close. However, the Diamondbacks have off-days scheduled on September 16 and September 23; if they stay in a five-man rotation rather than skip someone for Johnson, that would move his final start to October 1 or 2, which could force Buck Showalter into taking him out early to ensure that The Big Unit is properly rested for the playoffs. My hunch is that the Diamondbacks want Johnson to have a shot at the record, and that they'll adjust their rotation to keep him going every five days as long as it looks like he's got a realistic chance to break it. This could be very interesting.

RICK ANKIEL. After four starts, he's still looking for his first major league victory, but you can see why people are excited about him. The kid has a world of stuff, averaging more than a strikeout an inning thus far while holding opposing teams to a .345 slugging average.

I still don't think he'll be a big winner for a few years. After Kerry Wood's injury this spring, teams are paranoid about overworking their young pitchers, and Ankiel has yet to go beyond six innings or 110 pitches. It's hard to win a lot of games when you're on such a strict pitch limit.

September 16—The Pennant Races

Reviewing the pennant races and postseason possibilities:

YANKEES. They look strangely vulnerable, don't they? It's hard to believe the Yanks are going to blow their AL East lead, but even if they hang on, this team has a number of problems: Cone (1-4, 4.42 in 10 starts since the perfect game) and Clemens (0-3, 6.27 this month) aren't pitching well, the setup relief corps doesn't look anywhere near as good as it was in 1998, Knoblauch has 25 errors, etc. I still like their chances, but the key men for them could be Andy Pettitte, who is 8-4, 3.44 since the break, and Orlando Hernandez, who's had an outstanding year but who also has been worked pretty hard of late (four straight starts with at least 128 pitches). If Pettitte and El Duque pitch well in the postseason, it takes a lot of pressure off Cone and Clemens.

RED SOX. How does Jimy Williams do it? I don't know, but he's made a believer out of me; the Red Sox could conceivably win the East, and if not, they figure to take the AL wild-card. Of course, when the postseason comes along, Jimy may be reduced to Pedro in Game 1, followed by a couple of games of three-inning stints from Tim Wakefield, brother Ramon, Sabes, etc., until it's time for Pedro to start again. Knowing Williams, whatever he tries will have a good chance of working. And Trot Nixon (.367 over his last 18 games, 4 HR and 8 RBI in his last 5) is God!

BLUE JAYS. About out of it after a brave run, barring a miracle. It would have been nice to see Boomer Wells facing the Yankees in the postseason, wouldn't it? And I love that Green/Delgado combination.

INDIANS. The Tribe needs 97 runs in their final 17 games to become the first team since 1950 to score 1,000 runs in a season. Now that Kenny Lofton's back and looking healthy at last (5-for-14 in three games since his return), the Cleveland offense should be in top shape for the postseason. Will a top three of Bartolo Colon, Charles Nagy and Dave Burba be enough? And who will be the No. 4 starter? The current candidates are Jaret Wright, Chris (Mister) Haney and Doc Gooden. Ouch! Still, the offense is so good that the Tribe could make it to another World Series. But I don't think so.

RANGERS. Another team that can score; the Rangers need five RBI from Rusty Greer and 10 from Todd Zeile to become the second team in MLB history (after the 1936 Yankees) to have five players with 100 or more RBI (the Indians could also accomplish this feat with five more RBI from Jim Thome and 14 from David Justice; Harold Baines will probably top 100 also, but most of those came for the Orioles). However, the Rangers' pitching problems are even more severe than Cleveland's: Texas starters rank dead last in the league with a 5.67 ERA. The bullpen, which has been asked to carry an unreasonable load, has also been getting cuffed around lately (especially the once-unhittable Jeff Zimmerman, who has a 5.09 ERA since August 1). Once again, I don't see the Rangers getting past the Division Series.

A'S. Barring a collapse by the Red Sox or Yankees, they're probably not going to make it. Which is too bad, because I love this team. Matt Stairs! John Jaha! Rich Becker! Olmedo Saenz! Sounds like the "Steve Moyer All-Stars"!

BRAVES. Still hanging on for dear life, with the Mets breathing down their necks and six games remaining between the two teams. Those two September series could be better than the playoffs. The Braves have withstood every threat thus far, but right now I think the Mets have a better team and that New York is going to win the division. Even if that happens, the Braves' depth in starting pitching makes them dangerous in the playoffs. But then I look at their starting lineup and some of the September averages: Eddie Perez .200, Jose Hernandez .195, Bret Boone .178, Brian Jordan .160, Andruw Jones .244 with two ribbies in 13 games. This looks like "Chipper Against the World," and while that sounds like a nifty title for a TNT movie, my hunch is that it will end in tears for the Braves. . . again.

METS. Since all their wheeling and dealing ended at the July 31 trading deadline, the Mets have gone 28-14. The starting lineup features seven .300 hitters and three players who have surpassed 25 homers and 100 RBI. The defense has committed only 64 errors, 29 fewer than any other team in the National League. And Armando Benitez, a favorite Zee-Man whipping boy, is 10-for-10 in save opportunities while allowing exactly one run over his last 17 appearances. Hey, that's pretty good! This could be a very dangerous team in the postseason. . . but when I think about the October history of guys like Benitez, Kenny Rogers and Mike Piazza, I start to wonder. We'll see.

ASTROS. With all their injuries, the Stros should be stumbling down the stretch. Instead, they've run off a long winning streak and put a little distance between themselves and a very competitive Reds team. Houston has a very solid starting foursome heading into the playoffs: Hampton, Lima, Reynolds, Elarton are a combined 8-0, 2.25 this month. And despite all the injuries, the Biggio/Bagwell/Everett nucleus has gotten such a big September boost from guys like Ken Caminiti (.400-4-17 in 14 games) and Daryle Ward (.367-3-10 in 10 games) that the Stros are averaging seven runs a game for the month. Houston has had big problems beating quality teams for most of this season, but I still think this is their year. My fearless prediction: they'll be closing the Astrodome next month with a celebration on the mound, and the part of Joaquin "One Tough Dominican" Andujar (1982 vintage) will be played by Jose Lima.

REDS. Despite Houston's hot play, the Reds are only two games behind the Astros in the loss column, and they're just as much in the wild-card hunt. The bullpen is holding up pretty well despite Jack McKeon's heavy use—Danny Graves is 6-for-6 in save opportunities in September—and Greg Vaughn has been going slightly crazy, with 10 homers and 22 RBI for the month. This is another team I love, and I don't think they're going to go away.

DIAMONDBACKS. Barring a late collapse, the Diamondbacks have the NL West sewn up, and with the league's highest-scoring non-Coors offense and a pitching staff led by Randy Johnson, they should be formidable in the playoffs. But while I respect Omar Daal, Andy Benes and the other Arizona pitchers, most of it depends on Johnson, who's reporting a tender shoulder after a season in which he's thrown 3,859 pitches—nearly 400 more than anyone else in the majors. They'll forget about the strikeout record and take it easy on him the rest of the month, but how Big will The Unit be in October?

September 30—What If. . .

I'm back from New Mexico. Fabulous trip, though definitely a "non-sports" vacation. In eight days I saw only one brief snippet of one game, but my karma was definitely working on that one. I had to meet my stepson to drive over to a wedding in Albuquerque the first Saturday, and as I walked into his motel room, he said, "Come on over to the TV. Sammy's up." I sat down just in time to see Sosa hit his 60th homer. Pretty neat; I clicked off the set and proceeded to enjoy the rest of my vacation. Since then, Sosa's hit only two more homers in 12 days. Do you think he needs to have me watching?

I watched the Reds-Astros game last night, and on the surface, it was everything September baseball ought to be: two good teams fighting for a playoff spot, a big crowd, a tense game that the home team final broke open. But when I thought about it, the game also demonstrated everything that was *wrong* with September baseball, 1999 style, at least in my opinion. First of all, baseball's "balanced schedule" leaves us with far too few matchups between contenders, especially late in the year. The two-game series between the Reds and Astros this week was the first between those clubs since the fifth of July. When you get something like the home-and-home series between the Mets and Braves that took place last week and this, it's almost an accident.

Then there's the whole wild-card thing. How exciting can a late-season game really be when the loser—like the Mets in the East or the Houston/Cincinnati also-ran in the Central—can still qualify for the playoffs? I'm sorry, but it sort of spoils it for me. And I'm not even sure how great this system is for the fans of the wild-card winners or the first-place club in a weak division of four or five teams (can you hear me, Cleveland?). Finishing first in a group of seven or eight teams after a year-long struggle is an accomplishment, something to savor for years. "Making the playoffs," or finishing first in a bozo division like the AL Central, is something of far less consequence. That's why Dan Duquette is still under fire in Boston, and will be unless the Red Sox make it to the World Series.

Just for fun, let's rearrange the 1999 standings into two divisions in each league, split geographically:

AL East	W	L	Pct	GB
Cleveland	96	62	.608	—
New York	95	63	.601	1.5
Boston	91	67	.576	5.0
Toronto	81	77	.513	15.0
Baltimore	78	80	.494	18.0
Tampa Bay	68	91	.428	28.5
Detroit	67	91	.424	29.0
AL West	**W**	**L**	**Pct**	**GB**
Texas	94	64	.595	—
Oakland	85	73	.538	9.0
Seattle	78	80	.494	16.0
Chicago	72	86	.456	22.0
Anaheim	66	92	.418	28.0
Minnesota	63	94	.401	30.5
Kansas City	63	96	.396	31.5

This is interesting. In the East, we would have had a season-long battle between two powerful clubs, the Yankees and Indians—who would have been playing meaningful games all year long, for once—with the Red Sox in the thick of it until the very end, and the Blue Jays making some noise until September. All in all, a very memorable pennant race. The West wouldn't have been anywhere near as good, but it wouldn't be any worse than what we have now, and the A's would still be a good story.

Here's the NL:

NL East	W	L	Pct	GB
Atlanta	100	58	.633	—
Cincinnati	95	64	.597	5.5
New York	93	65	.589	7.0
Pittsburgh	77	80	.490	22.5
Philadelphia	75	83	.475	25.0
Milwaukee	72	85	.459	27.5
Montreal	66	93	.415	34.5
Florida	63	96	.396	37.5
NL West	**W**	**L**	**Pct**	**GB**
Arizona	97	61	.614	—
Houston	95	64	.597	2.5
San Francisco	84	74	.532	13.0
Los Angeles	75	83	.475	22.0
St. Louis	74	84	.468	23.0
San Diego	73	85	.462	24.0
Colorado	71	88	.447	26.5
Chicago	65	93	.411	32.0

The NL East would have been a classic three-team struggle between the Braves, Reds and Mets, until Atlanta finally pulled away in late September. The West would still be going down to the wire, with the Diamondbacks and Astros—two natural geographical rivals—duking it out to the very end. Isn't there a lot of appeal in that?

The two-division-in-each-league system existed from 1969 through 1993, and for my money it worked very well, producing numerous good pennant races and a lot of late-season excitement. In essence baseball has decided to muffle the excitement, to a considerable extent, for the sake of the Division Series, a third round of playoffs which has yet to catch on either with the public or the television networks.

I don't consider myself an old fart, and I *don't* want to live in the past: things change in baseball, just as they do in life. I'm not naive; some years you just don't have pennant races, and things like scheduling would remain a problem—especially in a league with two eight-team divisions. Still, I wonder about the wisdom of this particular change, the move to three divisions and a wild-card. Was it worth it? Is the game better or worse for the fans? I'd be interested in hearing what you have to say, particularly fans of teams which are benefiting from the wild-card structure, like the Red Sox and Mets. What do you people think? I'd like to know.

October 7—Amazing Stats From '99

Stat notes on the fascinating 1999 season:

PEDRO MARTINEZ of the Red Sox was 23-4 this year for an .852 winning percentage. That's the best winning percentage by a 20-game winner since Roger Clemens went 24-4 for the Sox in 1986. Good as Clemens was in '86, Martinez was better. Pedro's 2.07 ERA was 2.79 runs below the league average, the biggest margin ever between a pitcher and his league:

Biggest ERA Differential, Pitcher vs. League—1900-99

Pitcher, Team	Year	ERA	LgERA	Diff
Pedro Martinez, Red Sox	**1999**	**2.07**	**4.86**	**-2.79**
Greg Maddux, Braves	1994	1.56	4.21	-2.65
Greg Maddux, Braves	1995	1.63	4.18	-2.55
Roger Clemens, Blue Jays	1997	2.05	4.57	-2.52
Dazzy Vance, Dodgers	1930	2.61	4.97	-2.36
Lefty Grove, A's	1931	2.06	4.38	-2.32
Kevin Brown, Marlins	1996	1.89	4.21	-2.32
Pedro Martinez, Expos	1997	1.90	4.21	-2.31
Lefty Gomez, Yankees	1937	2.33	4.62	-2.29
Randy Johnson, Mariners	1997	2.28	4.57	-2.29

(minimum one IP per team G)

I didn't get a chance to have this checked, but I believe that the 1.37-run gap between Martinez and the Yanks' David Cone, who finished second in ERA, is also the biggest ever. You can see why Martinez is being talked about seriously as an MVP candidate. He was that dominant, and that important to his team.

MIKE MUSSINA of the Orioles, who went 18-7 for a sub-.500 club this year, is now 136-66 (.673) lifetime. Mussina's winning percentage is the fifth-best ever among pitchers who have had at least 200 major league decisions:

Highest Lifetime W-L Percentage—All Time

Pitcher	W-L	Pct
Dave Foutz	147-66	.690
Whitey Ford	236-106	.690
Bob Caruthers	218-99	.688
Lefty Grove	300-141	.680
Mike Mussina	**136-66**	**.673**

(minimum 200 decisions)

BILLY WAGNER of the Astros held opposing hitters to a .135 average this year. That's the lowest in history for a pitcher working at least 50 innings in a season:

Lowest Opponent Average, Season—All Time

Pitcher, Team	Year	Opp Avg
Billy Wagner, Astros	**1999**	**.135**
Troy Percival, Angels	1995	.147
Armando Benitez, Mets	**1999**	**.148**
Troy Percival, Angels	1996	.149
Rob Murphy, Reds	1986	.155

(minimum 50 IP)

Note the presence of **ARMANDO BENITEZ** of the Mets in third place. The fireballing Wagner fanned 14.9 batters per nine innings this year, breaking his own record for most strikeouts per nine innings by a pitcher working a minimum of 50 innings. Benitez was only a shade behind him at 14.8:

Most K/9 IP, Season—All Time

Pitcher, Team	Year	K/9
Billy Wagner, Astros	**1999**	**14.9**
Armando Benitez, Mets	**1999**	**14.8**
Billy Wagner, Astros	1998	14.6
Billy Wagner, Astros	1997	14.4
Rob Dibble, Reds	1992	14.1

(minimum 50 IP)

Pitcher usage notes: **SCOTT SULLIVAN** of the Reds worked 113.2 innings in relief this season, the most by a reliever since 1990. Teammate **DANNY GRAVES** was only a shade behind with 111.0 innings. **STEVE KLINE** of the Expos pitched in 82 games, the most by an NL pitcher since '90, when Juan Agosto worked the same number. And **RANDY JOHNSON** of the Diamondbacks pitched 271.2 innings, most in the majors since Dave Stewart's 275.2 in 1988. If Johnson continues to get cuffed around in the playoffs, there's going to be some second-guessing of Buck Showalter for not dialing back on Johnson a little earlier.

LARRY WALKER, who led the NL in hitting for the second straight year with a .379 average, is the first player to hit .360 or better in three straight seasons since Al Simmons, who batted .365-.381-.390 in 1929-31, and the first National Leaguer to perform the trick since Rogers Hornsby in 1927-29. But of course, he had a little help, in the form of Coors Field. Walker batted an amazing .461 at Coors this year, .286 on the road. His .461 average is the highest by far since we started compiling home/road splits in 1987:

Highest Home Average—1987-99

Player, Team	Year	Avg
Larry Walker, Rockies	**1999**	**.461**
Larry Walker, Rockies	1998	.418
Albert Belle, Indians	1994	.413
Eric Young, Rockies	1996	.412
Wade Boggs, Red Sox	1987	.411
Paul O'Neill, Yankees	1994	.409
Kirby Puckett, Twins	1988	.406
Tony Gwynn, Padres	1994	.403
Andres Galarraga, Rockies	1993	.402
Paul Molitor, Brewers	1987	.394

(minimum 200 PA at home)

Speaking of Coors Field and Colorado, the **COLORADO ROCKIES** led the National League in hitting for the fifth straight year with a .288 team average. Only one other team has led its league in hitting five straight years: the mighty Philadelphia A's of 1910-14, who played a little closer to sea level.

NOMAR GARICIAPARRA of the Red Sox led the American League in hitting with a .357 mark. That's the sixth-highest average for a shortstop since 1900:

Highest Season Average, Shortstops—1900-99

Player, Team	Year	Avg
Luke Appling, White Sox	1936	.388
Arky Vaughan, Pirates	1935	.385
Honus Wagner, Pirates	1905	.363
Cecil Travis, Senators	1941	.359
Alex Rodriguez, Marines	1996	.358
Nomar Garciaparra, Red Sox	**1999**	**.357**
Honus Wagner, Pirates	1903	.355
Lou Boudreau, Indians	1948	.355
Honus Wagner, Pirates	1908	.354
Joe Sewell, Indians	1923	.353

In case you're wondering, Honus Wagner batted .381 in 1900 and .353 in 1901, but that was before he became a full-time shortstop.

With 48 homers, **KEN GRIFFEY JR.** of the Mariners won his third straight home-run title. Griffey now has 398 homers through the age of 29, most ever for a player that age:

Most HR, Through Age 29

Player	HR
KEN GRIFFEY JR.	398
Jimmie Foxx	379
Mickey Mantle	374
Eddie Mathews	370
Hank Aaron	342
Mel Ott	342

Interestingly, Hank Aaron, the career leader, is only fifth on this list, tied with Mel Ott. Aaron stepped up the pace after the age of 30, while Ott, Jimmie Foxx, Mickey Mantle and Eddie Mathews all faded out relatively early (it may not be coincidental that the latter three were all known to be heavy drinkers). Still, Griffey could take the next two years off and still have the same career total through age 31 that Aaron did (398). You have to like Junior's chances to break the record.

And what about **MARK McGWIRE**? With 65 homers this year, Big Mac now holds the record for most homers in a two-year (135), three-year (193), four-year (245) and five-year (284) period. McGwire will be 36 years old next year and is still 233 homers short of Aaron, but when you're homering at such a prolific rate, you can make up ground amazingly fast. I'd say he's got a shot, as long as he can stay relatively healthy.

CRAIG BIGGIO of the Astros had 56 doubles, the highest doubles total since George Kell of the Tigers hit the same number in 1950. Earl Webb's doubles record of 67 has lasted since 1931, but it's being seriously challenged for the first time since the 1930s. That record could fall within a few years, if this remains a big-hitting era.

And speaking of big hitting, **DAVID DELLUCCI** of the Diamondbacks, who entered 1999 with a .257 career average for 443 AB, batted .394 in 109 at-bats this year before a career-threatening wrist injury put him out for the year. Believe it or not, that's the third-highest average since World War II by a hitter with at least 100 PA:

Highest Season Average—1946-99

Player, Team	Year	Avg
Ted Williams, Red Sox	1953	.407
Bob Hazle, Braves	1957	.403
David Dellucci, D'backs	**1999**	**.394**
Tony Gwynn, Padres	1994	.394
George Brett, Royals	1980	.390

(minimum 100 PA)

Wow, that's the first time I've seen Bob "Hurricane" Hazle's name in years. Seems like a good place to quit.

October 14—The Playoffs

I've been making an effort lately to remember my dreams, and I had a doozie last night. In the dream I was watching the deciding game of a playoff series between the Houston Astros and an unnamed opponent. Some symbolic team in black uniforms, I think. Anyway, Houston was losing, 1-0, in the bottom of the ninth with runners on second and third and two out. Then—would you believe it?—Jeff Bagwell singled up the middle to plate the tying and winning runs. The crowd went wild, and The Most Beautiful Girl in Texas threw her arms around me and gave me a big smack. I woke up all warm and glowing, if you know what I mean. Reflecting on my unfortunate prediction a couple of weeks ago that the Astros would win the World Series, I guess this adds new poignancy to the phrase, "In your dreams."

Let's talk about the playoffs, beginning with the National League.

BRAVES-ASTROS. The Astros are now thought of as worse choke-meisters than ever, but if it weren't for the incredible play made by Walt Weiss in the 10th inning of Game 3, Houston would have won that game, and quite possibly the series as well. That's baseball. The question is, where do the Astros go from here?

When a team comes up short like this several years in a row, there's a temptation to turn against your best players. This must be especially tempting in Houston after the repeated postseason failures of Craig Biggio and Jeff Bagwell. But baseball history is full of teams who have come up short in the postseason, often for years, before finally breaking through. To cite some examples, the Philadelphia Phillies lost three straight LCS in the late 1970s before winning it all in 1980. The Kansas City Royals of the same era lost three times in the LCS and once in the World Series before finally breaking through in 1985. The Toronto Blue Jays suffered through years of late-season collapses and playoff failures before winning back-to-back World Series in 1992-93. Even the mighty Cincinnati Reds of the mid-1970s lost the World Series in '70 and '72, lost in the LCS in '73 and blew a late-season lead to miss the playoffs in '74 before finally winning it all in 1975-76. The Astros appear to be of a mind to stay with Biggio and Bagwell and manager Larry Dierker as well. I think that's a good thing.

METS-DIAMONDBACKS. The Diamondbacks have their own supposed "choker" in Randy Johnson, who once again failed to come up with a victory in Game 1 of the playoffs. The simple truth is that Johnson has pitched pretty well in most of his postseason losses, and he kept Arizona in Game 1 against the Mets until the ninth inning, when fatigue finally got to him. While I'd rather have Kevin Brown, I'll take my chances with Randy Johnson in Game 1 of *any* series.

There's no need to shed any tears for the Diamondbucks, a well-run organization with enough wealth to be perennial contenders. Anyway, the Mets are a lot more fun. When the Metsies seemed about to go down for the count a couple of weeks ago, Phil Rogers of the *Chicago Tribune*—a writer whom I respect a lot—wrote a piece tracing the Mets' collapse to the frenetic style of Bobby Valentine, and then compared Valentine with the easygoing Jack McKeon of the Reds. He quoted Reds GM Jim Bowden saying, "The attitude of Jack and the coaches. . . they don't put pressure on the guys. I've never seen a team have this much fun."

Of course Valentine's Mets have been the ones having the fun lately, but I agree with Rogers on this point: when it comes to long-term success, the yelling-and-screaming type of managers have a lot tougher time succeeding than the guys who are more low-key. In baseball, where you play every day, it's harder to succeed while keeping the tension high than it is in football, where they play once a week. There are exceptions, like Earl Weaver and (for one-year intervals) Billy Martin, but those guys were certified geniuses. Bobby Valentine is no Earl Weaver, but he's sure got an entertaining team.

BRAVES-METS. Speaking of Bobby V., he admitted that he screwed up yesterday when he let Kenny Rogers stay in after Brian Jordan's two-run homer tied the game in the sixth inning. I'm pretty sure the Braves would have won anyway, and that they'll go on to win this series fairly easily (famous last words). I think this Atlanta team is stronger than most of the clubs they've had this decade, thanks to two pitchers: Kevin Millwood and John Rocker. Especially Rocker. I generally think closers are an overrated commodity, but their importance is heightened in the postseason, and Rocker is the best one they've had, an appealing mixture of cockiness and great stuff.

As for Bob Cox's other "innovation," using his starters in late relief, this is the sort of thing that was once very common in baseball—especially in the postseason. Now it's coming back, though the comeback really started in the 1995 Division Series between the Yankees and Mariners, when Randy Johnson and Jack McDowell took the hill in the late innings of Game 5. Cox, who used Maddux in relief last year (the Padres went to Kevin Brown), is being careful about it, only using his pitchers for an inning or less when they're in between starts and throwing on the sidelines anyway. So why not? He not only gets a good pitcher on the mound, he's saving wear and tear on Rocker, which should keep him fresh if the Braves reach the Series.

YANKEES-RANGERS. Like the Astros, the Rangers can't get past the first round of the playoffs, and this year they looked worse than ever, scoring only one run in three games. In truth the Rangers aren't as good as the Yankees—c'mon, Aaron Silly, Rick (S)helling and Esteban Louisiana as your three playoff starters?—but they ought to be able to score some runs and make a fight of it. Instead they died like dogs for the second year in a row. I think "team chemistry" is another overrated concept, but if I were Doug Melvin, I'd be tempted to shake up the Ranger mix a little bit this year—starting with trading one of their big bats for some pitching help. Think Juan Gonzalez would draw some interest?

RED SOX-INDIANS. Speaking of trading big bats for some pitching help, how about those Indians? In future years, people are going to be scratching their heads in wonder over how the Tribe managed to give up 44 runs in the final three games of this series to the Red Sox, who finished ninth in the American League in runs scored. Cleveland's pitching was so thin that after Dave Burba got hurt in Game 3, the whole staff fell apart. I can assure you that there were starting pitchers to be had before the July 31 trading deadline—someone good enough to give them a few respectable innings in middle relief in Game 3, someone who could have started Game 4 and given Bartolo Colon another day's rest. The Tribe apparently thought Jaret Wright was going to come back and solve the problem, but they were dead wrong. Cleveland *will* address this problem over the winter—but with the AL Central being in the state it is, we don't know whether the moves have helped until late October.

Though I'm not a big fan of the wild-card, I have to say I was happy for Jimy Williams and the Red Sox. Look at their roster from top to bottom, and you have to marvel at how they knocked off the Tribe with their Troy O'Learys and John Valentins. Of course the Red Sox have no chance against the Yankees. . . or do they?

YANKEES-RED SOX. Sometimes I'll be watching a game that goes into extra innings, and it'll be getting late and I want to go to bed and I'll just think, "*Somebody* score a run and get this thing over with so I can get some sleep." So when I saw Rod Beck enter the game last night, I looked up at the heavens and said, "Thank you." That said, the Sox played the Yankees tough last night, and they still have a chance to win the series. If Boston takes Game 2 tonight, they have Pedro ready for Game 3 (going against The Traitor, Clemens. . . cool!), and things could get really interesting. But the smart money is still with the Yankees, as it should be.

I don't have a huge rooting interest in this series apart from hoping I see some good baseball, but please, please spare me this "Curse of the Bambino" stuff. So you're cursed. . . get over it! And definitely spare me all this "long-suffering Red Sox fans" stuff. You want suffering? Try rooting for the Chicago White Sox. Better yet, try going to the last game of the season at New Comiskey Park between the Sox and the mighty Minnesota Twins—real hot matchup there, huh?—and it's cold as hell and it starts to pour and finally it's the seventh inning and you think, "Just nine more outs and we can go home," and then the Twins score a run to tie the game but you think, "Well, Konerko's comin' up pretty soon, we'll untie this thing and *then* we can go home," and right then good old Durwood Merrill, umpiring the last game of his career and bound and determined to make a production out of it, *calls a rain delay.* That's suffering.

I'm going to go dream about Ms. Texas.

October 21—Umpires

The Yankee-Red Sox series was over pretty quickly, thanks at least in part to some atrocious umpiring. Most of the bad calls went against the Sox, and it was no comfort to Boston fans that a couple of umps *admitted* they blew it. While it's difficult to say that bad umpiring cost the Red Sox the series, it certainly made things more difficult for them. The question before the house is, what—if anything—should we do about bad umpires' calls? Some options:

MORE UMPIRE CONFERENCES. Jimy Williams was screaming for this during the LCS, and it's hard to disagree with him. In the NFL, the officials *always* confer with one another before making a critical call, but in baseball it's like one ump is afraid to embarrass another by questioning a decision. More conferences would undoubtedly help overturn many bad calls, assuming that getting the decision right is the umps' No. 1 goal (sometimes it's hard to tell). But conferences would only help in a limited number of cases. Spread out as they are, the other umps are often in no position to help the guy who blew the call.

MECHANICAL UMPIRING DEVICES. In tennis, there are mechanical devices which can tell whether a serve was in or out. Could you do this in baseball? I don't see why not. The most obvious application would be to use electronic devices to call balls and strikes; then we could *really* have a "rule-book strike zone." You probably could also have some kind of sensors on and near the foul lines which could tell whether a ball was fair or foul. This wouldn't solve every issue—for one thing, you'd still have the checked-swing problem on ball-and-strike calls—but it could help get a lot of calls right, if properly designed. I don't see this sort of thing happening anytime soon, however; it would take awhile to develop the proper technology, and even then the skinflints who run baseball would bitch about the costs. And no matter how good the machinery, you still need human beings to make the vast majority of calls.

INSTANT REPLAY. This idea got a lot of support during the LCS, which is not surprising given that there were clear replays showing some of the calls were bad—like the phantom tag by Chuck Knoblauch in the late innings of Game 4. In that particular case, only a view of a replay would have convinced the umps to change the call. . . a conference among the umps probably wouldn't have helped, because only Tim Tschida was in any kind of position to see what happened. But if they had instant replay in baseball, what kind of mechanics would be used? You couldn't get away with reviewing all close calls; the games are too long already. The only workable system would involve:

a) some kind of limit on what sort of calls would be reviewable and/or

b) some kind of challenge system like the NFL has this year, with each team permitted to make only a limited number of challenges.

Option a) would probably work pretty well with issues like fan interference or questions about whether a ball cleared a home-run line. Those are very tough calls for the umpires, who often lack the proper viewing angle to make the correct decision. (Not coincidentally, those are also the kind of calls that the umps will most often get together and huddle about.) Would replay help? Yes, but there would still be numerous cases where even the replay wouldn't provide definitive evidence. You'd also have cases where the umps would look at the replay and still get it wrong; this happens way too often in the NFL.

If you expanded the scope of reviewable calls to include safe-or-out plays on the bases, fair-or-foul calls on balls hit down the line, checked swings, questions about whether a fielder truly had made a legal catch, etc., etc. . . well, the games could last forever without some limits on the number of calls that could be challenged. An NFL-type challenge system sounds nice, but without a penalty for asking for a replay on what turned out to be a correct call, you'd be inviting challenges even in bogus cases. You also bump into the time-of-game issue again. It's not an easy issue to decide.

Of the three ideas, replay is the one which could get the most bad calls corrected, starting as soon as the idea was implemented. There would be many issues to overcome—especially the issue of adding even more time onto games that are already too long. But speaking of that, there's one way that baseball could immediately save time during disputes about umpiring calls: don't let the managers come onto the field to complain. Let them yell from the sidelines, like the managers and coaches do in other sports, and stop holding up the game complaining about decisions that aren't going to be overturned anyway. You'd lose the fun of a good Earl Weaver/Joe Brinkman jaw session, but that's no great loss; there are only a couple of managers left in baseball who can stage an entertaining argument.

Rest assured that even if replay was approved on a limited basis, there would still be a lot of complaining about bad calls, and there'd be a lot of bitching about the replay system itself. This is exactly what has happened in the NFL. But I personally feel that the NFL with a flawed replay system is a lot better off than the league was in 1998, when there were a number of ludicrously bad calls, often in crucial situations, with no system in place to review or overturn them. For that reason, I'd support the use of replay in baseball—on a very limited basis, to begin with. Would it be perfect? Of course not. Would it get more bad calls corrected? I don't see how it couldn't. But what do the fans think? I'm anxious to hear your thoughts.

October 28—Postseason Q&A

Well, the season's finally over. I, like most of you, was wishing for a more competitive World Series, something to rival the epic Braves-Mets struggle in the NLCS. Unfortunately this was not 1986, when two compelling LCS were followed by an equally compelling World Series. Bud must be a little disappointed by that, not to mention the folks at NBC. But my hat goes off to the Yankees, a truly great team.

Let's do a postseason Q&A:

WHAT DYNASTY IN HISTORY DO THE CURRENT YANKEES RESEMBLE MOST?

Talking to a Vancouver reporter yesterday, I suggested Casey Stengel's 1949-53 Yankee teams, in that the team was driven more by effective role players than stars and superstars. Looking at the Yankee starting lineup, the only really exceptional performers are Derek Jeter and Bernie Williams. The catchers are pretty nondescript. Tino Martinez is a below-average performer for an AL first baseman. Chuck Knoblauch's one of the better-hitting second basemen, but his defense drags him down. Scott Brosius is a below-average hitter for his position. Left field was a problem for the Yanks all year. Paul O'Neill is no longer one of the top right fielders, and the Yankee DHs were no great shakes this year, either.

All this is reminiscent of the early-'50s Yankees, where you had Yogi Berra and the developing Mickey Mantle surrounded by a bunch of Hank Bauers and Bobby Browns who always seemed to excel in the postseason. Of course the Yankee pitching *is* exceptional, which was the case with the early '50s team as well. And the role players don't just come through in October: the Yanks did, after all, score 900 runs, third-most in the American League. While they're not super-strong at every position, they're not really weak anywhere, either. From 1 to 25, just about everybody is a solid pro who doesn't make too many mistakes and who can handle the pressure of the postseason. They're a beautiful team to watch.

IS THE YANKEE DOMINANCE BAD FOR BASEBALL?

We heard this refrain in the 1930s, when the Yanks were winning flags with contemptuous ease, then cruising through the postseason the way they are now. We heard the same thing in the '50s, though that Yankee team usually had to withstand stiff challenges in both the regular season and World Series. In the '30s they even tried to restrict other teams from trading with the Yankees, not that this helped much.

The disparity between rich and poor teams existed in the '30s and '50s as badly as it does now, and it's a problem that baseball has yet to really address. It can't be much fun being a fan of an underfinanced, small-market team; these days, their poster boys are the Oakland A's, pluckily contending—unsuccessfully, of course—for a wild-card spot. On the other hand, the Yankees are hardly the only wealthy team, and I applaud them for using their wealth wisely. . . as opposed to the Dodgers and Orioles, to cite two obvious examples. In addition, one of the hardest things to accomplish in sports is to sustain success once you've reached the top. Thus far the Yankees have been able to keep their egos in check and stay focused on winning.

WILL THE YANKEES CONTINUE TO DOMINATE NEXT YEAR AND THE YEAR AFTER?

That's a good question. This spring the Yankees went to arbitration with their two best young players, Derek Jeter and Mariano Rivera. They lost both cases, and George Steinbrenner was hopping mad. If The Boss goes all out for arbitration victories again next spring, things could get nasty—especially after the way Jeter and Rivera performed this year.

The Yanks will also soon be faced with the issue of what to do with aging players who have been contributing to their championship teams, but who are now in decline: O'Neill, Martinez and Brosius, to name three. If the Yankees want to continue to succeed, they're going to have to make room for the Nick Johnsons and Alfonso Sorianos who are tearing up their farm system. What will happen to the "all for one" spirit if they dump Tino or Brosius to make room for a young hotshot? Lest you think the Yanks are too smart to screw things up, hearken back to this past winter, when only some miraculous last-minute events prevented the Yanks from letting Bernie Williams go, and replacing him with Albert Belle.

ARE THE BRAVES UNDERACHIEVERS?

Another good question. Knowing how difficult it is for a team to stay at the top year after year, it's hard to dump too much on the Braves. To put what the Braves have done into perspective: in 1991, when Atlanta reached the Series for the first time this decade, the Yanks were a fifth-place club going 71-91 under the immortal Stump Merrill. The Yanks didn't reach the postseason until 1995, by which time the Braves were playing in their fourth World Series of the decade.

That 1991 Braves team had an infield of Sid Bream, Jeff Treadway, Terry Pendleton and Rafael Belliard. Among the bench players were Lonnie Smith, Francisco Cabrera and Deion Sanders. The only guys still remaining from that '91 club are Tom Glavine and John Smoltz (Otis Nixon and Brian Hunter left and later returned). To change the cast almost completely while continuing to finish first every year. . . that's quite an accomplishment.

Still, there's something kind of weird about how the Braves just laid down and died in front of the Yankees this year. I kept wondering, where was the fire in their bellies? The Braves have often been compared with the Brooklyn Dodgers of the late 1940s-early 1950s, another great team which managed to win only one World Series. There are two differences, in my opinion: the Dodgers generally lost out to the Yankees, a club which most people felt was superior, and Brooklyn never lost without a fight to the death—Jackie Robinson wouldn't let them. I don't know, maybe I'm being too hard on the Braves. But there's some element that still seems to be missing at crunch time.

DID THE BRAVES LOSE BECAUSE OF BAD STRATEGY BY BOBBY COX?

I think Cox gets criticized way too much for his decisions. In my opinion, he did make a couple of bad mistakes in this postseason: he benched Walt Weiss and Bret Boone for Game 2 of the Series, replacing them with Ozzie Guillen and Keith Lockhart; and he stuck too long with Tom Glavine in Game 3. But those were defendable decisions, and I thought Cox did a lot of things *right* in the postseason, like using his starting pitchers in relief and being unafraid to leave John Rocker out there for two innings.

ARE YOU HAPPY THAT ROGER CLEMENS FINALLY GOT THAT POSTSEASON MONKEY OFF HIS BACK?

As happy as I can be for a self-centered jerk who doesn't have an ounce of loyalty in his body. The Rocket's a great pitcher, and I like seeing great performers rise to the occasion. I admire the man for his talent. That's as far as I'll go.

WHAT WILL YOU MISS THE MOST ABOUT THE 1999 POSTSEASON?

Really, I think it'll be the sight of George Steinbrenner in that dorky tan World Championship cap. I kept thinking, so *that's* what the Yanks were struggling for all these months! If I were Joe Torre, I would have turned to The Boss and said, "Hey, while you're at it, would you mind checkin' the oil?"

WHAT WON'T YOU MISS ABOUT THE 1999 POSTSEASON?

1. The Curse of the Bambino.

2. The MasterCard All-Century Team. Hey, did you notice there were no Native Americans on that team? And get this—*not one woman*. From now on, I'm only using Visa.

3. Any and all comments about Chuck Knoblauch's throwing.

4. Jim Gray talking to people.

5. People *not* talking to Jim Gray.

6. People talking *about* Jim Gray.

7. Anything having to do with Jim Gray.

8. Pete Rose, the Innocent Victim.

Maybe I'll write about old Pete next week. Or maybe not. For now, I think I'll go play cards with Rickey Henderson and Bobby Bonilla.

November 4—The Juan Gonzalez Trade

I was going to write about Pete Rose this week, but then the big Ranger-Tiger deal took place, and I think it deserves a column. We'll get to Pete in the near future. In the meantime, let's talk about the trade.

WHY DID THE TIGERS WANT TO MAKE THIS DEAL?

Economic considerations aside, any team would love to acquire a slugger the caliber of Juan Gonzalez. But the Tigers were more eager than most. A few years ago, they were a struggling team in a city that had finally agreed to build a new stadium. Like several other teams in this position, the Tigers decided to adopt the "Cleveland plan" that had been carried out so brilliantly by Indians general manager John Hart. The plan works roughly as follows:

1. Pour a lot of money into scouting and player development. 2. Sign and trade for as much good young talent as you can. 3. Nurture the best young players and wrap them up with multi-year contracts so that they're guaranteed to be around when the new stadium opens. 4. Open the new park with a club that's ready to contend.

A couple of years ago, the Tigers seemed to be carrying out this plan to perfection. The farm system was producing promising young players like Travis Fryman, Bobby Higginson, Tony Clark, Deivi Cruz, Justin Thompson and Brian Moehler. They'd added developing young stars like Damion Easley and Brian Hunter in trades. And the team had a bright young manager in Buddy Bell. In 1997, the club went 79-83 with no regular position players older than 29. . . and Juan Encarnacion, Gabe Kapler and Matt Anderson (a '98 draftee), perhaps the three biggest jewels in the Tiger farm system, hadn't even arrived yet.

Then it all fell apart. In '98, the Tigers regressed so badly (65-97) that Bell lost his job. Many of the players stalled in their development. The '99 season wasn't much better (69-92) despite the addition of a high-priced free agent in third baseman Dean Palmer. At the end of the year, Bell's replacement, Larry Parrish, got bounced also. Some way to open the new park next year, with a rudderless team still nowhere near contention.

Given all that, it's not surprising that the Tigers jumped at the chance to get Gonzalez, even though he'll be a free agent at the end of next season. Adding Gonzalez shows that the Tigers are "doing something," not just counting on the new ballpark to pull in fans. In a way this is an act of desperation. . . Plan A wasn't working, so they felt that they had to try something which was risky, but which had a potentially big payoff. How this trade will look depends on a) how Gonzalez performs for the Tigers and b) whether they're able to sign him to a multi-year deal. I think he'll perform; the big risk is b).

WHY DID THE RANGERS MAKE THIS DEAL?

There's two reasons. One is that the Rangers weren't winning *with* Gonzalez, and they felt a need to shake things up. But the biggest reason was money. Gonzalez is probably going to be a $15 million a year player when he signs his next contract, and that was a bit too rich for the Rangers' blood. Is it an ominous sign when a big-market team like the Rangers feels they can't afford to pay their biggest star, a two-time MVP? Yes, it is. As Peter Gammons put it, the Rangers figured that they would be paying Gabe Kapler, who came over in the Gonzalez deal, and Ruben Mateo, their hottest young prospect, around $15 million apiece over the next five years. That's a small amount of money to pay these days for two potentially very good players. The Rangers could then use some of the money they save on Gonzalez to sign a free agent pitcher or two. The end result? They still have a contending club while keeping their payroll within limits. That's baseball in the early 21st century.

Whether the Rangers continue to contend depends in good part on the players they got for Gonzalez and two guys who were basically throw-ins, Danny Patterson and Greg Zaun. We can skip Bill Haselman, a reserve catcher who isn't going to play much behind Pudge Rodrigruez. How about the other guys the Rangers got?

GABE KAPLER. I was among the many people who were high on Kapler this spring, and his rookie numbers for the Tigers (.245-18-49) were a little disappointing. The leading STATS experts on young players are split on Kapler: John Sickels is very high on him, ranking him 12th in his top 50 prospects this spring, while Jim Callis is a lot more restrained, ranking him at No. 45 in his own spring top 50. Even Sickels doesn't think Kapler will be a superstar, however. Kapler also goes from Tiger Stadium, where he did almost all his offensive damage last year (.301 with 12 homers at home; .183 with 6 homers on the road) to The Ballpark in Arlington, which is no bargain for a righty slugger. Right now I'd say Kapler looks like a productive regular who will be a good No. 5 or 6 hitter. Another Gonzalez? There's very little chance of that.

JUSTIN THOMPSON. After going 15-11 in 1997, Thompson has had injury problems and totaled only 20 wins in 1998-99. He could be very good, but he had shoulder surgery in

August (he also had elbow surgery after the '97 season). There's no telling how quickly or fully he'll recover. He's a gamble, but his upside is very good.

FRANK CATALANOTTO. Sickels thinks he could become the Rangers' regular second baseman in time. I think that's a stretch, but Catalanotto has some power and can play several positions. Guys like that can be very valuable.

ALAN WEBB. Didn't he play cornerback for the New York Giants in the early '60s? No, that was *Allan* Webb. This Webb is very young (20). Sickels says he doesn't throw particularly hard, and he's coming off a so-so year in Double-A (9-9, 4.95). I still think he's a pretty good prospect; he was very highly regarded coming out of high school, and Jacksonville can be a tough place to pitch for anyone, let alone a 20-year-old. He could be a rotation starter for the Rangers, though probably not in 2000.

FRANCISCO CORDERO. Very good prospect, only 22, throws 99 MPH, pitched pretty well for the Tigers in 20 games this year (3.32 ERA). His negatives are a history of elbow problems and the poor control he showed with the Tigers this year (18 BB in 19 IP). I'd still love to have him, and think he could be setting up John Wetteland next season.

The general consensus is that the Rangers did very well in this deal, given Gonzalez' contract status. I'm in complete agreement on that, even though I agree with Jim Callis that Kapler is probably somewhat overrated (I think I overrated him myself this spring). Will Texas be a better team in 2000, however? Not unless they use some of the money they're saving to add a quality starting pitcher or two.

As for the Tigers, this deal isn't going to put them in the playoffs next year; they still have too many holes to fill. It will only help them if they can sign Gonzalez to a long-term contract. Which is very possible. There's an old adage in trading that in a big multi-player deal like this, the club which gets the best player will wind up winning the deal. Given the chaotic economic situation baseball is going through, that adage might be less true now than it was a few years ago. But Juan Gonzalez is a tremendous player. If the Tigers manage to re-sign him, and if Gonzalez and the new park pull in the fans and help the franchise prosper, they could wind up having the last laugh. They're taking a big risk, but I have to admire their guts.

November 11—Salaries And Awards

The offseason is just beginning, and already we've seen three big trades: the Juan Gonzalez deal, the Green-Mondesi trade, now Andy Ashby going back to the Phillies. All these deals were predicated by money, with the Green trade being the most curious of all: a guy has his first great season, and his team's response is to immediately trade him because he's now in line to make big money. I don't think of myself as a doom-and-gloom guy, but this is a very disturbing trend, and I don't see how much longer things can continue like this. It now seems inevitable that there will a long, bloody work stoppage when the current Basic Agreement expires, probably the worst one ever. Won't *that* be fun!

Speaking of doom-and-gloom guys, did you read Hal Bodley's article in yesterday's *USA Today* entitled, "Guaranteed salaries cause for 'grave concern'"? Old Hal wants us to know how big this problem really is, so when he talks about how much money the teams have guaranteed their players, he writes out the whole figure: $2,596,185,253. It took me a minute to determine that the dollar figure he was talking about amounts to roughly $2.6 billion. *That* I could get a handle on, but apparently Hal figured we needed to picture each dollar bill individually in order to grasp the seriousness of the problem. He uses this technique through the whole article; I was surprised he didn't make it $2,596,185,253.27, a figure which is even more impressive and *much* more accurate. I don't know about you, but I'm really worried about whether the Expos (it must be them) are going to be able to come up with that $253 in a couple of years.

Enough of this. Let's talk about the baseball awards. Right before the playoffs started, Bill James asked some friends of his, along with the people in our STATS e-mail network, to submit ballots for the MVP, Cy Young and Rookie of the Year Awards. A total of 28 people wound up voting, roughly the name number that annually take part in the actual balloting. We voted the same way the writers do, picking our top 10 players for the MVP Award and a top three for the other awards. All in all, this seemed to be a pretty good straw poll. Let's look at the results.

We'll start with the two awards which have already been announced, the NL and AL Rookie of the Year (the number of first-place votes are in parentheses):

National League Rookie of The Year—1999

1. Scott Williamson (16)	101
2. Warren Morris (5)	61
3. Preston Wilson (4)	42
4. Ronnie Belliard (1)	18
5. Kris Benson (1)	8

The voters were right on the money, picking the actual winner, Scott Williamson of the Reds. Since the choice of Williamson was considered a bit of an upset, I think our poll's predictive ability is enhanced a little. We weren't perfect; Morris and Wilson were flip-flopped in the actual voting, and the Brewers' Ron Belliard, who finished fourth in our poll, didn't receive any votes from the writers. But we did pretty well.

American League Rookie of The Year—1999

1. Carlos Beltran (16)	98
2. Jeff Zimmerman (6)	44
3. Freddy Garcia (2)	42
4. Tim Hudson (3)	26
5. Brian Daubach	12
6. Chris Singleton	9

Carlos Beltran's selection as AL Rookie of the Year was less of an upset than the choice of Williamson, but at least a couple of publications predicted that he wouldn't win the award. The top six in our poll were Beltran, Zimmerman, Garcia, Hudson, Daubach, Singleton; in real life it was Beltran, Garcia, Zimmerman, Daubach, Hudson, Singleton. So the poll's predictive ability is again enhanced.

Now that we've established our credibility, how did our voters do in the awards that have yet to be announced? We'll start with Cy.

National League Cy Young—1999

1. Randy Johnson (21)	123
2. Mike Hampton (5)	57
3. Kevin Millwood (1)	47.5
4. Billy Wagner	10.5
5. Jose Lima (1)	8
6. Kevin Brown	4
7. Greg Maddux	1
8. Scott Williamson	1

And the winner is. The Big Unit. Bill James was surprised that Johnson won the award; I wasn't as shocked, but I *was* surprised by the ease in which Johnson won our voting. Bill thinks that Mike Hampton, whose won-loss record was five full games better than Johnson's (22-4 vs. 17-9), will give The Big Unit a run for his money and might end up actually winning the award. I think it will be close, but based on this, I'm going with Randy.

American League Cy Young—1999

1. Pedro Martinez (28)	140
2. Mike Mussina	64
3. Mariano Rivera	21
4. Bartolo Colon	14.33
5. David Cone	7.33
6. Aaron Sele	2.33
7t. Tim Hudson	1
7t. Troy Percival	1
7t. Jeff Zimmerman	1

No controversy here: Pedro Martinez was a unanimous selection, as he undoubtedly will be in real life. Mussina and Rivera for second and third look pretty solid to me, also. But I wonder which guy split his third-place vote between Colon, Cone and Sele?

National League MVP—1999

1.	Chipper Jones (22)	55
2.	Jeff Bagwell (4)	259
3.	Mark McGwire	160
4.	Mike Piazza	102
5.	Matt Williams	89
6.	Edgardo Alfonzo	83
7.	Sammy Sosa	80
8.	Robin Ventura	69
9.	Randy Johnson (1)	63
10.	Craig Biggio	58
11.	Larry Walker (1)	57
12.	Jay Bell	43.5

Another easy choice: Chipper Jones won easily in our poll, and will probably do the same in real life. Bagwell for runnerup looks right on to me, but I'm betting that Mark McGwire won't get anywhere near third place in real life. Also curious to me were the first-place votes for Johnson and Walker, both of whom finished well down in the balloting.

American League MVP—1999

1.	Derek Jeter (7)	247
2.	Manny Ramirez (4)	223
3.	Pedro Martinez (7)	211
4.	Ivan Rodriguez (4)	205
5.	Nomar Garciaparra (3)	193
6.	Roberto Alomar (2)	174
7.	Rafael Palmeiro (1)	130
8.	Shawn Green	70
9.	Bernie Williams	64
10.	Jason Giambi	41
11.	Alex Rodriguez	33
12.	Ken Griffey Jr.	30

This is the one that will be hardest to predict. Thinking about the AL MVP Award prior to casting my ballot, I felt that there was no clear-cut favorite, and that there were seven players who could legitimately be given first-place votes: Ramirez, Jeter, Martinez, Rodriguez, Garciaparra, Alomar and Palmeiro. That was how I ranked them on my own ballot, but I could see a decent argument being made for any of the seven. As it turned out, each of the seven guys received at least one first-place vote in our balloting, and no one got more than one-fourth of the first-place votes. The winner was Derek Jeter in a close vote over Ramirez and Martinez.

Will Jeter win in real life as well? That's really hard to say. I don't think Pedro Martinez has much chance: a starting pitcher hasn't won the award since 1986, and a lot of voters simply won't put a starting pitcher on their ballot. I don't think Garciaparra or Alomar have much chance, either; Nomar will split the Boston vote with Pedro, and I think Alomar will rank behind his teammate Ramirez in most people's eyes.

That leaves Jeter, Ramirez, Rodriguez and Palmeiro. Pudge and Raffy have the same problem that the Boston and Cleveland guys have: two worthy candidates on the same team. I was shocked when Palmeiro won the AL MVP Award in the *Baseball Weekly* poll a few weeks ago; the sportswriters I read have been talking up Rodriguez much more than his Texas teammate. So I don't think Palmeiro, a DH for almost the entire season, has much of a chance (his Gold Glove at first base this year was a good argument for why managers, players and coaches shouldn't be selecting award winners). Pudge, though, has a great chance: impressive offensive numbers and a still-growing reputation as a baserunner-intimidator behind the plate.

I, for one, would be very disappointed if Ivan Rodriguez won the AL MVP Award. While it's true that his throwing arm makes teams reluctant to steal bases, teams of the late 1990s are *already* reluctant to steal bases: why risk it, when it's so easy to score runs whether you steal or not? Nailed to first base though they were, Ranger opponents still averaged 5.3 runs per game last year, slightly more than the league average. Rodriguez undoubtedly kept that figure down a little, but the impact of his arm has been greatly exaggerated.

So has the impact of his offensive production. He hit homers and drove in runs, but so did a lot of other guys. He stole 25 bases in 37 attempts, basically a wash. He drew only 24 walks, and he hit into 31 double plays, more than anyone else in the majors. Overall, his offensive production was about 25 percent better than the average AL catcher using on-base plus slugging, a stat that doesn't penalize players for grounding into DPs. That's good, but Manny Ramirez' OPS was 31 percent higher than the average AL right fielder, Derek Jeter outperformed the average AL shortstop by 32 percent and Nomar Garciaparra was 36 percent ahead of the average SS.

This brings Nomar back into the picture. . . briefly. Unfortunately, he missed 27 games last year, too many to keep him in consideration, in my opinion. So in my head it came down to Ramirez and Jeter, and I think it may be that way with the writers as well. Ramirez missed 15 games himself, but he also drove in 165 runs—the most by any player in 61 years—in his 147 games. He batted .386 with runners in scoring position, and he hit .360 with 30 RBI in September, when the Indians were finally playing for something (home-field advantage throughout the playoffs). On the other hand, he's a sloppy fielder, an erratic baserunner and a guy who doesn't always have a head in the game. His weaknesses are Jeter's strengths, and Jeter's offense was outstanding, also, especially when seen in the context of the position he plays.

So it's close. Ultimately I voted for Ramirez because of the 165 RBI, but it wasn't a firm conviction. If Jeter wins, I'll be delighted. But then, neither one of them may win. We'll find out next week.

November 25—AL MVP Voting

Last week's column was written prior to the announcement of the American League Most Valuable Player voting, so I didn't get a chance to write about it. Let's do a Q&A:

HOW UNIQUE WAS THE VOTING?

There's never been anything quite like it. So many candidates were deemed worthy by the voters that a total of six players—Pudge Rodriguez, Pedro Martinez, Roberto Alomar, Manny Ramirez, Rafael Palmeiro and Derek Jeter—received at least one first-place vote. All except Jeter received at least four first-place votes.

Since the BBWAA took over the awards in 1931, there have been a number of years in which six or more players received first-place votes. In two elections—the 1947 NL (Bob Elliott was the winner) and 1977 AL (Rod Carew)—a total of 10 players received at least one first-place vote, which is pretty amazing. However, it's extremely rare for as many as five players to receive significant support. The number of writers voting has varied over the years, mostly as a result of expansion, but the only voting I could find which offered any kind of parallel to the 1999 AL vote was the American League MVP race in 1957. That year, a total of 24 ballots were cast (three in each city), and five players received at least four first-place votes: Mickey Mantle (6), Ted Williams (5), Nellie Fox (5), Roy Sievers (4) and Gil McDougald (4). That's the only year which roughly parallels 1999. In retrospect, the '57 voting seems absurd; all our methods for evaluating players tell us that Mantle and Williams had two of the greatest offensive seasons in history, and both played for contending teams. You could argue Williams over Mantle, who won the award, but Gil McDougald, a decent-fielding shortstop who batted .289 with 13 homers and 62 RBI? That's a joke. Will the 1999 AL vote seem as absurd in future years? Among intelligent fans, I think that's pretty likely.

DID PUDGE RODRIGUEZ DESERVE THE AWARD?

I covered this in an earlier column, and I'll be blunt: he shouldn't have come close to winning. Rodriguez is a wonderful defensive catcher, but his main talent—inhibiting the running game—is nowhere near so important in late-1990s baseball that it should be the difference in winning an MVP Award. His offensive numbers, while good for a catcher, aren't in the same league with the other candidates—even those playing equally important defensive positions like shortstop or second base.

HOW DID THE ZEE-MAN VOTE?

I'm a BBWAA member, but I don't have awards voting privileges yet. However, I did cast a ballot in the Bill James straw poll. If memory serves, my 10 players in order from 1 through

10 were Ramirez, Jeter, Martinez, Alomar, Nomar Garciaparra, Rodriguez, Palmeiro, Shawn Green, Jason Giambi and Bernie Williams.

SHOULD STARTING PITCHERS BE ELIGIBLE FOR THE MVP AWARD?

Of course they should. While starting pitchers work only every five games or so, their impact on those games is so important that it essentially makes up for the games they miss.

However, you have to be careful with this. In modern-day baseball, top starting pitchers don't work nearly as many games or innings as they did even a decade ago. Thus their contribution to their teams' success isn't what it used to be, and to me that makes them less "valuable." When Sandy Koufax won the NL MVP Award in 1963, he started 40 games and worked 311 innings, facing 1210 batters. When Roger Clemens won the AL MVP Award in 1986, he started 33 games and threw 254 innings, facing 997 batters. This year, Pedro Martinez started 29 games and pitched 213.1 innings, facing 835 batters. Koufax as MVP seems clear-cut to me. Clemens in '86 was a tougher sell, and Martinez in '99 tougher still.

WAS IT AN OUTRAGE THAT PEDRO MARTINEZ DIDN'T WIN THE MVP?

I've already answered this; it wasn't an outrage that he didn't win, but it *was* an outrage that two guys left him off the ballot. Martinez' pitching was so extraordinary that he was a very viable MVP candidate; that's why I had him third. To claim he wasn't as valuable as Shawn Green or Jason Giambi is patently ridiculous.

WILL A STARTING PITCHER EVER WIN AN MVP AWARD?

I think the flap over Martinez was strong enough that a starting pitcher posting extraordinary numbers will have a good chance to win an MVP Award in future years. That's as it should be. I think the guys who left Martinez off their ballots should forfeit their voting rights forever.

I could go on about this, but the holiday beckons. Happy Thanksgiving to all.

December 2—Pete Rose

OK, let's talk about Pete Rose:

HOW GOOD A BALLPLAYER WAS HE?

It's weird. . . I kind of think he's simultaneously both overrated (by the casual fan who puts too much importance on things like career hit totals) and underrated (by the stat crowd, which can't really calculate the impact of Rose's amazing will to win). From a numbers point of view, Pete's main problem is that he was a singles-and-doubles hitter playing home-run hitters' positions for most of his career. As a leadoff man he was very good but no Rickey Henderson: he didn't steal bases and his lifetime on-base percentage was a good but not sensational .375. But the guy could play, and he'd do anything to win a ballgame. Would I want him on my team? Until the last few years of his career, you betcha.

HOW STRONG IS THE EVIDENCE THAT HE BET ON BASEBALL?

The general consensus among people who have studied the subject is that it's pretty strong. Consider me part of that crowd. I encourage anyone interested in the subject to read the books *Collision at Home Plate: the Lives of Pete Rose and Bart Giamatti,* by James Reston Jr., and *Hustle: The Myth, Life and Lies of Pete Rose* by Michael Y. Sokolove. Both cover the evidence in considerable detail. There is also an excellent online overview of the subject which can be found on The Baseball Archive website (www.baseball1.com). Check it out.

In reviewing this material, it is important to note this: the legendary "betting slips" purported to be Pete's handwriting are hardly the only convincing evidence that he bet on baseball, or even the most compelling. There is the detailed testimony of Paul Janszen, Ron Peters and others, which has gone unchallenged for a decade (Yes, Peters and Janszen are convicted felons, but then so is Pete Rose). There is Rose's rambling and unconvincing testimony to investigator John Dowd, much of it flying in the face of the facts. There is the pattern of Rose's betting, confirmed by telephone records, which continued heavily during the months when baseball was the only thing he realistically could have been betting on. There is Rose's continuing refusal to deal with the specifics of the evidence apart from the betting slips, even after 10 years.

IS THERE A CHANCE THAT THIS EVIDENCE IS WRONG, AND THAT ROSE IS TELLING THE TRUTH?

It's possible. One of the frustrating things about this case is that until now, Pete and his lawyers have carefully avoided confronting the evidence and responding to it item by item. They could have had a hearing before Bart Giamatti in 1989, but Rose went to court to block it, arguing that Giamatti had prejudged him. This lawsuit was eventually moved to federal court, but Rose signed the agreement accepting permanent ineligibility before a full hearing on the matter could take place. It was a compromise agreement, in theory: baseball got Rose banned from the game, and Rose accepted his punishment without a formal ruling that he had bet on baseball.

WHY DID BASEBALL SIGN AN AGREEMENT THAT DID NOT ADDRESS THE ISSUE OF PETE'S BETTING ON GAMES?

That's a good question. Had the issue played out in the courts, the odds are very strong that the commissioner's absolute power to rule on matters affecting the interests of the game would have been reaffirmed yet again. On the other hand, this would have taken months to play out, and Giamatti would have been forced to defend his actions in open court in front of hostile attorneys. While nobody knew then how close he was to death, it was obvious that Giamatti's health was shaky. Frankly, the guy looked like hell, and it was beginning to affect his public behavior. In particular, Giamatti had performed poorly when grilled by Rose's attorneys during the Dowd hearings, chain-smoking and refusing to look people in the eye; to quote James Reston, "Giamatti was loose on facts, loose on words, and seemed confused and uncertain about the very legal concepts that were supposed to govern his judicial-like proceedings." So he might have won the case if forced to testify in federal court, but in the process he very well could have looked like a buffoon. The powers that be wanted to avoid that, so they settled after getting the thing most important to Giamatti, which was Rose's banishment.

HAS BASEBALL ACTED HONORABLY IN THIS CASE?

Anything but, and this is one area in which I've been in complete agreement with Bill James, who has been one of Pete's staunchest defenders. In essense, Major League Baseball:

1. Signed an agreement clearly saying they were making no formal ruling that Rose bet on baseball, and

2. Within minutes, began acting as if they *had* ruled that Rose had bet on baseball. And they've acted that way ever since then.

This is simply unfair to Rose, whatever you think about the merits of the case. It's more than that: it's unethical. As Bill put it, it's like having an employee you think is stealing from your company. You confront him with the evidence; he still denies the charge vehemently. Rather than fire him for stealing and risk the consequences of lawsuits, dragged-out court fights, etc., you negotiate a settlement in which he agrees to leave, and you specifically acknowledge that his exit was not based on the charge that he was stealing. The guy leaves, thinking, "I lost my job, but at least they didn't say I was a thief." Then as soon as the guy is out the door, you start telling everybody, "He was stealing. That's why we fired him."

There's something rotten about that. There's also something rotten about Bud Selig sitting on Rose's reinstatement petition for two years without doing a damned thing. As Pete put it, "Even Charlie Manson gets a hearing once a year."

WILL ROSE FINALLY GET HIS DAY IN COURT?

I hope so. The ideal thing would be to have Pete and his attorneys confront the evidence in at least a semi-open forum. Let them challenge the evidence and try to shake the case that baseball feels is so strong. Maybe they'll change people's minds about his guilt. . . or maybe the evidence and Pete's vague denials, presented again after 10 years, will convince even more people that he really *did* bet on baseball. Whatever, I hope all the evidence is presented pro and con, out in the open. I only wish this had happened in 1989.

Of course it may not happen like that at all. There's a good chance the hearing will be closed, and swift. Rose's attorneys will present their challenge, MLB will say, "Thanks. There's nothing new here," and that'll be it. I hope things don't unfold this way, but it's quite possible.

WILL ROSE BE REINSTATED AFTER HIS HEARING?

I'd say it's a long shot. Chances are, baseball will present the same evidence that it has always felt was convincing. Chances are, Pete will continue to deny that he bet on baseball. And there's the rub: we can all get behind forgiveness, but it's hard to forgive somebody who insists he didn't do what you're trying to forgive him for.

Of course, Bud could always say that he's changed his mind, and that betting on baseball isn't such a bad thing after all. . .

December 9—Offseason Newsmakers

In the news:

MARINERS SIGN OLERUD. Free agency has helped baseball in some ways, hurt it in others, but to me this is one of the good things: it allows a player to join the team he was always meant to play for. John Olerud was born in Seattle, went to high school in Bellvue, WA, and then became a big hitting and pitching star at Washington State University; one year he batted .464 and went 15-0 on the mound. If there was ever a "local hero," this is it. Now he can finally play for his hometown team. It's a nice story all-around, except maybe if you're a Mets fan.

The Olerud signing makes it a little more probable that the M's will trade Ken Griffey to the Reds, since they'll no longer be insisting that Cincinnati include Sean Casey in the deal. Supposedly the Mariners' offer is Griffey for Pokey Reese, Scott Williamson and somebody like Mike Cameron. This would be a pretty good deal for the M's, who are a long shot at this point to re-sign Griffey, but it's risky for the Reds since Griffey could walk after the 2000 season. Even so, there's a good chance that Cincy will take the plunge and even entice Griffey to stay by making his father, currently a Reds coach, the club's manager sometime between now and the start of the 2001 season.

Is this smart or crazy on Cincinnati's part? Part of it depends on how much the Reds give up; at this point they're reluctant to include Reese and Williamson in the deal, but if they want Griffey, they're going to have to part with at least one of their key players, probably more than one. I can see the temptation on the Reds' part, since Griffey would be a huge gate attraction right now, and an even bigger attraction when the Reds move into their new park in 2002 or 2003. His family history makes him a link to the great Reds teams of the 1970s, especially if Ken Sr. becomes the Reds manager. Conceivably this could energize the franchise even more than 1999's surprise contender did.

But I still wouldn't make the deal. The new park is still several years away, and who knows what kind of team the Reds will have at that point? If they give Junior the $20 million a year or so that will be required to keep him around, how much will the Reds have left for players to build around him? And who knows how well Ken Griffey Sr. can manage a major league team? In essense, this is putting all your eggs in the Griffey family's basket, and that's too risky for my taste.

METS SAY NO TO ROGERS AND HERSHISER. Along with losing Olerud, the Mets decided not to offer salary arbitration to Kenny Rogers and Orel Hershiser. The Rogers thing was kind of forced on them by Rogers' complicated contract; rather than get into a hassle with Rogers' agent, Scott "The Grinch" Boras, they decided to let him walk just like Rogers let Andruw Jones walk, ho ho ho. No great loss, in my book. But I was a little surprised that they let go of Hershiser, who pitched reasonably well during the regular season and very

286

well—unlike a few Mets pitchers I can think of—during the postseason. And besides, Hershiser is my wife's favorite player. But look on the bright side, Mets fans: Shawon Dunston will be back!

The interesting question concerning the Mets is what they'll do to replace Olerud. David Segui is supposedly one option, but that's a real step down from Olerud. Dave Nilsson is another possibly, and not a bad one; along with playing first base, he could relieve Mike Piazza behind the plate now and then and help keep Piazza fresher late in the year. Or the Mets could go all out and try to make a deal for Carlos Delgado. Then again, maybe Bobby Bonilla could dig out his first baseman's glove and make us all proud of him again. (And maybe pigs can fly after all.) I have my own good, and probably inexpensive, option for the Mets: Roberto Petagine, last seen tearing up Japan worse than Godzilla did. But I have that same dream every Christmas Eve. Whatever the Mets do, it's hard to see this team being as good as it was in 1999. Do you think Rickey Henderson can possibly play as well next year as he did in '99? Can Robin Ventura or Roger Cedeno have another year like '99? And how long will it be before things start getting ugly again for Bobby Valentine? No, I think the Mets had their big chance in '99, and couldn't quite get over the hump.

FROM ABBA DABBA TO ZORRO: THE WORLD OF BASEBALL NICKNAMES. And now a word from our sponsor. Did you know Christmas is coming? And did you know that the Zee-Man has a really good book out available now for the amazing low price of only $9.95? Incredible but true! I get a little embarrassed shamelessly hawking my own works, but this is really a fun book, full of good stories as well as a lot of illuminating information. Find out why Ross Grimsley was known as Scuzzy. Let Gary Carter tell you how Elias Sosa got the nickname Lights. Discover the members of the All Body-Parts Team. It's all here, and a whole lot more. Check it out on our website (www.stats.com), which has some sample pages. I think you'll like it.

December 16—Wheelin' And Dealin'

Let's talk about last week's deals and signings and how they affected the various teams:

ASTROS (traded Carl Everett for Adam Everett and Greg Miller) What gives here? The Astros are a playoff team about to move into a new park, yet they're dumping salary. And Mike Hampton could be next. Someone explain this to me. There is *some* logic at work here: the Stros had too many outfielders to begin with, and Adam Everett, the infielder they picked up, is a terrific defensive shortstop who started hitting with power late last year. This deal would make more sense if Adam E. were ready to plug Houston's shortstop hole next year, but he only has 119 games of minor league experience, and his highest level is the 98 games he played at Double-A Trenton last year. Overall this is not a terrible deal for Houston by any means—Miller, the other player, throws hard and has looked very good in the low minors—but they're probably going to be weaker next season. And when you're a contender moving into a new park, I would think you'd want as strong a team as possible the first year.

BREWERS (traded Jeff Cirillo and Scott Karl and got back Jamey Wright, Henry Blanco and Jimmy Haynes, signed Jose Hernandez) The word is that trading Cirillo and Karl was dictated by economics; with the Brewers forced to play another year in County Stadium, they're really hurting financially. OK, but why not trade them for prospects who can help you when the new park opens? You don't trade for guys like Jimmy Haynes and Henry Blanco; you wait until they get released, then pick them up for nothing. Blanco's not very good, either, though he did have some good throwing stats last year. Let me say this: I love Jeff Cirillo and am astounded that the Brewers got so little for him *and* Karl. And if they're hurting for money so much, why sign Jose Hernandez? None of these moves make the least bit of sense to me.

CUBS (signed Joe Girardi, traded Manny Alexander for Damon Buford, traded Terry Adams and Chad Ricketts for Ismael Valdes and Eric Young) People in Chicago are talking like the Cubs have made themselves instant contenders with these moves, but as Jim Callis points out, look at their lineup: nearly half their projected batting order for 2000 will consist of Damon Buford, Shane Andrews, Jose Nieves and either Joe Girardi or Jeff Reed. Does that look like a contender to you? The Dodger deal should make the Cubs a stronger team, but they don't look much better than .500 to me.

DEVIL RAYS (signed Greg Vaughn, drafted Chad Ogea, dealt Rolando Arrojo and Aaron Ledesma and got back Vinny Castilla) The Devil Rays are really excited about their new Murderers Row of Fred McGriff, Jose Canseco, Vaughn and Castilla, and saying they'll be contenders next year. I doubt it. Who's going to pitch, for one thing, and for another, Tropicana Field is *not* the home-run paradise Greg Vaughn seems to think it is, at least judging from 1999. The Devil Rays deepened their power alleys after a homer-crazy 1998 season, though the effect wasn't obvious because the outfield signs in 1998 had listed the wrong dimensions. The net result was that Tropicana went from a good home-run park for righty hitters to a very tough home-run park (it remains a good park for lefty power hitters). Canseco, Tampa Bay's leading righthanded slugger last year, hit only 12 of his 34 homers at home last year. Unless they change the configuration again, Vaughn and Castilla are going to hit a lot of warning-track flyballs. Yes, the Rays will be better, but contend? Get real.

DODGERS (traded Eric Young and Ismael Valdes for Terry Adams and Chad Ricketts) The always-mysterious Fox Dodgers have suddenly decided their payroll is too high, which is why they dumped Young and Valdes without getting a whole lot in return. It's hard to see how this deal is going to help make them a contender.

INDIANS (signed Chuck Finley for three years) This will help the Tribe, but it's not like getting Randy Johnson or Kevin Brown. Finley is basically a good No. 2 starter, not as good as Bartolo Colon but a little better than Charles Nagy or Dave Burba. (Mrs. Chuck Finley: now *there's* a "No. 1 starter"!) Nagy has won 32 games over the last two years despite ERAs of 5.22 and 4.95, so you have to figure Finley can win 18 games or more. But is this the pitcher who will get the Tribe over the hump at last? I doubt it.

MARLINS (traded Bruce Aven for Brant Brown, traded Todd Dunwoody for Sean McNally) I guess this is the Marlins' way of trying to compete with the Devil Rays for attention. I've always kind of liked Brant Brown, but neither of these deals is very exciting, unless Sean McNally—who hit 36 homers in a great hitters' park in his third season at Double-A Wichita—is a lot better than I think.

PIRATES (traded Brant Brown for Bruce Aven, traded Brad Clotz for Roberto Manzueta, signed Wil Cordero) I guess if you're the Pirates, Will Cordero qualifies as a big-name free-agent signing. He hit pretty well for the Indians last year, but I doubt he'll be that good for the Pirates this year. Put another way, his lifetime slugging average is .433, and that's not what you want from a guy who's playing a power hitter's position.

RANGERS (traded Sam Marsonek and Brandon Knight for Chad Curtis) To the Rangers, everyone in a Yankee uniform probably looks like a superstar. Curtis is a good fourth outfielder, but nothing more than that.

RED SOX (traded Damon Buford for Manny Alexander, traded Adam Everett and Greg Miller for Carl Everett) As I mentioned earlier, this is a salary-driven deal, with the Red Sox taking on Carl Everett, who is going to be making big money after his outstanding 1999 season. The two prospects the Red Sox gave up were affordable losses, and Everett should be a big offensive upgrade over the Damon Buford/Darren Lewis combo the Sox had out there in 1999. Everett's pretty good defensively, also, but the Sox probably won't be able to challenge the Yankees unless they find someone able to replace Tom Gordon.

ROCKIES (signed Tom Goodwin and Brent Mayne, traded Vinny Castilla, Jamey Wright and got back Jeff Cirillo, Rolando Arrojo, Scott Karl and Aaron Ledesma) Interesting moves. Castilla's better than some people think, but I'd rather have Cirillo, a terrific fielder who should hit 20-plus homers and be a batting title contender in Coors Field. Tom Goodwin doesn't excite me much, but he can catch the ball, which is important in Coors' big outfield. As for Arrojo and Karl, it's hard to predict how they'll be able to handle Coors. Still, this club is improved, and a possible contender in the NL West.

December 23—Happy Holidays

News items:

EXPOS ADD SALARIES. What's going on here? In the space of three days, the Montreal Expos—baseball's ultimate poor boys—have signed their first free agent in eons (Graeme Lloyd, three years for $9 million) and made a deal for Hideki Irabu, who's scheduled to make $2 million-plus this year and more than that in 2001. Can the Expos really be spending money at last? Yes, they are, thanks to new owner Jeffrey Loria, who says he wants to build a competitive team and keep the Expos in Montreal, with a new stadium to boot.

Admirable sentiments, but if you're going to spend money, spend it on someone useful, not a hood ornament like Lloyd whose narrow range of skills aren't going to help make a bad team like the Expos a contender. (Lloyd *would* be very useful to a good team looking for a setup man/lefty specialist.) As for Irabu, his career thus far could best be described as "interesting," which is a long way from "good." Would you give up one of your very best prospects (Jake Westbrook), plus two other players to be named later, to get him? I sure wouldn't, but it's nice to see the Expos at least *trying* to get better.

VINA FOR ACEVEDO. This is a one-sided deal at this point, but the Cardinals are supposed to sweeten the pot with a couple of minor leaguers. I like Fernando Vina, a very good defensive second baseman who's probably the best around these days at turning the double play. The Cardinals are also saying he "solves our leadoff problem," which would be true if Vina plays like he did in 1998, when he had a .386 OBP. The problem with that thinking is that Vina was probably playing over his head in '98; his lofty OBP was a product of his .311 batting average and 25 hit-by-pitches, both of which are out of context with the rest of his career. He's not an effective basestealer, either. I'd expect something more like our projection in the '99 *Major League Handbook*, which was a .288 average with a .337 OBP. In other words, Vina is *not* going to solve the Cards' leadoff problem. Offensively he's barely adequate for a second baseman.

I also wonder what the Cards are going to do with Adam Kennedy, who was projected to be their second baseman before they traded for Vina. Kennedy, who will be 24 next year, has less patience at the plate than Vina, but his power and superior basestealing ability give him greater overall offensive potential. He's also considered an excellent defensive player. The Cards are making an all-out effort to make the playoffs next year, so I can understand the desire to go with an established veteran. But I hate it when teams make deals which block the paths of their *good* young players. You need more faith in your farm system than this.

CUBS SIGN GUTIERREZ. Like the Cardinals, the Cubs think they can make the playoffs next year, so they're rounding up one veteran after another. I just can't get excited about the mediocre and eternally injured Ricky Gutierrez, who's never had a 500-AB season in his career and only two with more than 400.

MARINERS' MOVES. In one week, the M's have signed Arthur Rhodes, Mark McLemore, Stan Javier and Kazuhiro Sasaki, Japan's career saves leader. Sasaki, who had elbow surgery last year, is an unknown quantity, but the other guys are good, useful players, not very exciting but helpful to a team trying to contend. Every one of them excites me more than Ricky Gutierrez. Seattle still needs pitching help, but its roster is much deeper than it was in '99, and the lineup for 2000, at least right now, begins with Junior Griffey, Alex Rodriguez, Edgar Martinez and John Olerud. A lot can happen between now and the start of the season, but this looks like the team to beat in the AL West.

BELTRE STAYS PUT. I thought the decision here—Adrian Beltre remains a Dodger, the club gets fined and sanctioned—was proper under the circumstances. The worst thing would have been to make Beltre a free agent, because that would only encourage any 15-year-old signee to do what Beltre and Scott Boras tried to do: wait until the guy establishes himself as a major leaguer, then try to cash in.

If Beltre really is only 20 years old—he will apparently turn 21 on April 7—he's an even better prospect than most of us thought. He should be the best third baseman in baseball in two or three years, and he'll be all of 25 years old when he first becomes eligible for free agency. Pardon me if I don't shed any tears for him.

PADRES-BRAVES DEAL. If you're the Braves, this makes sense: you strengthen yourself in two places where you needed help (left field and leadoff), plus you get a little bit of a first-base insurance policy in Wally Joyner in case Andres Galarraga can't make it back next year. If you're the Padres, it makes sense, too, because you're unloading some big salaries, namely Joyner's. Assuming Reggie Sanders can stay healthy enough to get 450 at-bats—not exactly a given, since he's never had a 500-AB season in his career—the trade makes the Braves a little bit better, and they didn't really need to get a *lot* better.

This is typical Braves, never doing anything too outrageous, which making an all-out effort to get Griffey would have been. I wonder if it's enough. I also wonder about them giving up on Bret Boone so quickly. When they traded for Boone last year, we kept hearing about how fiery and competitive Boone was, and how this was just what those Atlanta sleepwalkers needed. Well, Boone didn't have a great year, but I watched the World Serious last year, and one of the few guys who *wasn't* sleepwalking was Bret Boone. I'm not saying, keep Boone, he has "intangibles," necessarily. But this team still *needs* a little fire, and a few more guys with Boone's personality wouldn't hurt. But maybe the Braves are thinking, we don't need more guys with fire. We already got John Rocker.

I was going to comment on the Rocker affair, but I think I'll let it go. The man apologized quickly and contritely, and that's good enough for me. Anyway, I've got my own work to do in trying to ensure peace on earth and goodwill toward men. Don't we all?

January 6, 2000—Hall of Fame Voting

Happy New Year, just in time for the Hall of Fame voting. Let's look at the players on this year's ballot:

PLAYERS I WOULD VOTE FOR:

CARLTON FISK. Not a truly dominant player, as he never led the American League in any important category (he won one triples title) and won only one Gold Glove. On the other hand, he caught more games and hit more homers than any catcher in history, and he performed at a high level for so long that I don't think you can keep him out. He'd get my vote, if I had one.

GARY CARTER. He didn't play as long as Fisk, but the two are fairly comparable. At his peak he probably was a better player than Fisk, with nine 20-homer seasons vs. Fisk's eight, and four 100-RBI seasons compared to two for Fisk. He also won three Gold Gloves to Fisk's one. Like Fisk, he clearly is one of the best catchers in history and I don't see how you could vote for one without the other. My hunch, though, is that Fisk will make it this year while Carter will fall well short.

BRUCE SUTTER and **GOOSE GOSSAGE.** Both Sutter and Gossage helped pioneer the role of closer—especially Sutter, who won five National League save titles in a six-year period from 1979-84. He also helped revolutionize baseball by popularizing the split-finger fastball. Gossage was nearly as dominant at his peak, and he lasted longer, working in more than 1,000 games. I say yes to both of them.

JIM RICE. Rice didn't have a long career, but at his peak he was as good as it gets, winning an MVP award and finishing in the top five in the MVP voting six times between 1975 and 1986. While it's true that Fenway helped him, he led the AL in road homers twice while winning three home-run crowns, two RBI titles and two slugging titles. He also led the AL in total bases four times. I like him a lot, and he'd get my vote.

LUIS TIANT. I wrote a column last year favorably comparing Tiant to Catfish Hunter, and some guy wrote me a long letter explaining why Catfish Hunter was no good. I remain unconvinced, and both Hunter and Tiant could anchor my staff anytime. Tiant's 229 wins are low for a Hall of Famer, but he won two ERA titles, had four 20-win seasons and compiled a splendid lifetime ERA of 3.16, despite spending his peak years pitching in Fenway. He also was an excellent postseason pitcher, going 3-0 in 1975 and almost pitching the Sox to a title over the mighty Big Red Machine.

BERT BLYLEVEN. My Tiant comments last year provoked another letter from a Bert Blyleven fan who insisted that Blyleven was just as worthy a Hall of Fame candidate, if not more so. That prompted me to take another look at Blyleven, and I'd vote for him this time around. While he never won an ERA title and won 20 games only once, Blyleven was a top-level pitcher for many years, winning 15 or more games 10 times in his career. In his best season, 1973, Blyleven worked 325 innings, threw 25 complete games and tossed nine shutouts while working at Metropolitan Stadium, a notorious hitters' park. His durability alone—nine seasons with more than 250 innings, eight years with 15-plus complete games—gives him a lot of value, and I'm now inclined to vote for him.

JACK MORRIS. First time on the ballot, and he's going to get some support, with 254 wins, a .577 lifetime winning percentage and a flair for dominant postseason pitching, especially in 1991, when he basically pitched the Twins to the World Title. The end of Morris' career was pretty bad, and that helped bring his lifetime ERA up to 3.90, which is awfully high for a Hall of Famer. But Morris won 15-plus games a total of 12 times in his career, he had three 20-win seasons, and before the postseason debacle with the 1992 Blue Jays that signaled his decline, he'd gone 7-1 with a 2.60 ERA in nine postseason starts. He gets my vote.

A LITTLE SHORT:

TONY PEREZ. I think Perez is going to get in, and it won't break my heart, as he was a quality run producer for a long time. On the other hand, he played for 23 years and never led his league in *any* positive category, including RBI. Are we supposed to put him in just because people say he was "the heart and soul of The Big Red Machine"? As I say, I like Tony and won't cry if he gets in, but to me it was a joke last year when all the old lady sportswriters were crying about Perez but didn't say a word about the fact that Dwight Evans—a better player than Perez by any reasonable standard—dropped off the ballot due to lack of support.

TOMMY JOHN and **JIM KAAT.** If Blyleven is worthy, why not John and Kaat? The three have very similar career numbers:

Pitcher	W-L	Pct	ERA	20+ Wins	15+ Wins	Awards or Led League
Blyleven	287-250	.534	3.31	1 time	10 times	1 SO, 3 ShO
John	288-231	.555	3.34	3 times	5 times	3 ShO
Kaat	283-237	.544	3.54	3 times	8 times	1 Wins, 1 ShO

Yes, similar numbers, but of the three, only Blyleven could have been considered a dominant pitcher at his peak, and that puts him ahead of the other two in my book. It's not a strong conviction—I could go either way on this.

DALE MURPHY. Murphy was a lot like Rice, with two MVP Awards and some very dominant seasons at the peak of his career. But his peak was much shorter than Rice's—his two MVP years were the only times he finished in the top five—and his fadeout a lot more dramatic. Rice's career numbers are simply superior:

Player	AB	R	H	HR	RBI	BB	SB	Avg	OBP	Slg
Rice	8225	1249	2452	382	1451	670	58	.298	.352	.502
Murphy	7960	1197	2111	398	1266	986	161	.265	.346	.469

Even after giving Murphy credit for his speed, his patience and his five Gold Gloves, Rice still comes out ahead in my estimation.

DAVE PARKER. Very dominant at his peak, with two batting titles, an RBI crown, three Gold Gloves and an MVP Award. Then he got into drugs and went into a serious decline before coming back to have some more productive years. Parker finished in the top five in the MVP race five times, and he was in the top three in four of them. I think he's a little short of Hall of Fame caliber, but he's not far away.

KEITH HERNANDEZ and **STEVE GARVEY.** Two former MVP first basemen and better candidates than a lot of people think, given Hernandez' brilliant defense (11 Gold Gloves) and .384 lifetime OBP and Garvey's outstanding postseason record (.338 with 11 homers in 55 games). I think they're a little short, but not by that much.

JEFF REARDON. Reardon was one of the first relievers to get 40 saves in a season—he did it three times—and his 367 saves still rank fourth all-time. I think he's worth consideration, but he won only one save crown, and I think any manager would rather have Goose Gossage or Bruce Sutter as his closer.

There were some other people I wanted to write about, including Ron Guidry and Dave Concepcion, but I'm about out of time. Here's what I think will happen in the voting: Perez and Fisk will get in, Gossage will come close while finishing third, and Morris will make a strong showing but not get in either. No one else will be within shouting distance.

January 13—Busy Week

Events of the week:

HALL OF FAME VOTING. Quick comments:

1. I was very happy for Carlton Fisk.

2. I would not have voted for Tony Perez, but he was an arguable choice and a good guy to boot. I'm happy for him, too.

3. Jim Rice, Gary Carter and Bruce Sutter all picked up a lot of votes over 1998, finishing third, fourth and fifth. As I wrote last week, I would have voted for all three of them, but I'm not sure any of them are going to make it for awhile. The next couple of years will see guys like Dave Winfield, Kirby Puckett and Ozzie Smith enter the balloting, and that will make it more difficult for Rice, Carter and Sutter. I'd give Carter the best chance, since more and more people will realize how well he compares to Fisk. But if the writers don't vote in any of these guys, however, I'm 90 percent sure that the Veterans Committee will put all of them in.

4. I was very surprised that Goose Gossage did so poorly (166 votes, 33 percent of the ballots) the first time around. I have to think that Gossage will get in sometime over the next few years, as he is eminently qualified.

5. Speaking of relief pitchers, Jeff Reardon got only 24 votes and is off the ballot forever after one year. I would not have voted for him either, but that's a little harsh for a guy who ranks fourth all-time in saves. Don't these relievers get any respect?

6. I'd like to know who the writers are who cast Hall of Fame ballots for Lonnie Smith, Dave Henderson, Bruce Hurst, Bill Gullickson, etc. And four people voted for Charlie Hough! The real question is why these players were on the ballot at all. A few years ago, there were very strict standards for putting someone on the Hall of Fame ballot, so strict that they left off Milt Pappas, who had as many career wins as Don Drysdale. When Pappas complained, they went the other direction. There ought to be a screening committee with *some* standards that leave off joke candidates like this.

RANGERS SIGN DARREN OLIVER. After adding Justin Thompson and Kenny Rogers to their roster this winter, the Rangers now have three lefties in their rotation. The common theory is that the only way to beat the Yankees is with lefties, but do you think the Yanks are trembling and saying, "Oh, no, now we'll have to face Darren Oliver and Justin Thompson in the postseason!"? And if The Gambler is toeing the rubber against the Bombers in Yankee Stadium, who's gonna blink—him or the New York fans, who have such fond memories of him pitching in the postseason for the Yankees and Mets?

SOX TRADE JAIME NAVARRO. As a lifelong Sox fan, I can tell you there are a lot of smiles on the South Side today. We would have taken *anything* for Navarro—Bobby Bonilla, a bag of Doritos, you name it. Even if he wins 25 games and pitches the Brewers to the World Championship—don't hold your breath here—we'll still be happy.

JOHN ROCKER. Am I the only one who's sick of this? "Hank Aaron Mad at Rocker." "Rocker Says He's Really, Really Sorry." "Rocker to Undergo Psychological Testing." "Rocker Apologizes (Again)." "'I'm a Redneck, Not a Racist,' Says Rocker." "Rocker Sentenced to Three Years on New York Subway." "Rocker to Guest Star on 'The Sopranos.'" This is like an episode of "The Simpsons," except that episodes of "The Simpsons" are funny. These are great days for America's Thought Police, but I'm not sure who else is benefiting.

February 3—Winter Leagues

Let's look at how some key young players are performing in Winter League action this year. These stats tend to be somewhat spotty and there were some guys I was looking for who I couldn't find, but the numbers are still interesting:

TONY ARMAS, JR, EXPOS. Currently 0-1, 4.76 in five games in Venezuela, but has 14 Ks in 11 innings. I really like the guy. John Sickels thinks he needs a half-year in Triple-A, but I think he'll be a contributing member of the Expos staff this year.

ROOSEVELT BROWN, CUBS. After a big minor league season in 1999 that put him in the prospect category, Brown is hitting only .119 in 59 AB in the Puerto Rican League. I like his bat but think he played over his head in '99; anyway, where's he going to find playing time with the Cubs?

TRAVIS DAWKINS, REDS. The Reds' shortstop or second baseman of the future is hitting .246 in Puerto Rico, with two walks in 21 games. I like him but don't think he'll be ready for the majors in 2000.

OCTAVIO DOTEL, ASTROS. Currently 1-1, 3.27 in five starts in the Dominican League. Dotel has a lot of talent, and I think Larry Dierker will help make him an even better pitcher.

RAFAEL FURCAL, BRAVES. Atlanta's presumed shortstop of the near future is hitting .281 in the competitive Dominican League, with 36 walks in 42 games. Negatives are 15 errors and only six extra-base hits. He should be a very good player in a couple of years but I doubt he'll have major league impact in 2000.

RUBEN MATEO, RANGERS. Having a somewhat disappointing year in the Dominican League, .265 with one homer in 68 AB. He remains an outstanding prospect, but a little more seasoning in Triple-A is a possibility if he struggles in spring training. I would caution against expecting too much this year.

MITCH MELUSKEY, ASTROS. Not showing much in Venezuela after missing almost all of 1999 with a shoulder injury. Currently .250 for 48 AB, with no homers. Meluskey can hit, but I wonder how much Dierker will trust him with his pitching staff. I'd like his chances a lot more with another team.

MELVIN MORA, METS. After his surprise starring role in the 1999 postseason, Mora is hitting .333 for 147 AB in Venezuela, with .517 slugging and a .440 OBP. I keep telling myself, "He isn't this good," and I still believe that. I'd take him if I could get him for next to nothing, but that's about the extent of it.

DAVID ORTIZ, TWINS. Hey, Tom Kelly! Ortiz is hitting .320 in 125 AB in the Dominican League! Ortiz can hit in the majors right now, but then he could hit in '99, also, and the Twins didn't seem to notice. He'll hit 25 homers and slug .500 if anyone will give him a chance.

ANGEL PENA, DODGERS. After blowing it big-time with the Dodgers in '99, Pena in hitting .225 in 125 AB in the Dominican League. This is no way to show people you're not fat and lazy.

ARAMIS RAMIREZ, PIRATES. After a huge year in Triple-A, Ramirez is hitting .282 in the Dominican League, albeit with only two homers in 131 AB. Errors remain a problem, as he has 13 in 42 games this winter. I still think he'll be the Pirates' third baseman this year and put up some good numbers.

ALFONSO SORIANO, YANKEES. The broken neck suffered by D'Angelo Jimenez in an auto accident opens up more possibilities for Soriano, but he's only hitting .203 in the Dominican League. I think he needs a year in Triple-A, and the Yanks also need to decide where to play him.

February 10—Veterans Committee

As I write this the Griffey deal is being finalized, but the exact details of the trade haven't been announced yet. So I thought I'd write about the Hall of Fame Veterans Committee, which will meet very soon to make its picks for induction to Cooperstown this summer.

The Veterans Committee has had various incarnations over the years, including an absurd period during the 1960s in which it was dominated by former Cardinals and Giants players who seemed determined to vote all their old teammates in. The current 15-person committee consists mostly of players, writers, broadcasters and executives from the postwar era, including Ted Williams, Stan Musial, Yogi Berra, Juan Marichal, Bill White, Bob Broeg, Leonard Koppett and Jerome Holtzman. For the last few years, the committee has been specifically instructed to hold separate votes to elect no more than one 19th-century figure and one former Negro Leaguer each year. We'll get to those guys later, but first I want to talk about the Veterans Committee candidates who mean the most to many of us: players whose prime years came after 1940. All of these players have previously been rejected by the baseball writers in the BBWAA's own voting. One obvious question is, how did the recent Veterans Committee electees do in the writers' balloting?

Here's a list of the post-1940 players voted into the Hall of Fame by the Veterans Committee over the last 20 years. Along with the year they were voted in, I'll list the highest percentage of votes each player received in the writers' balloting. Remember, a player needs to receive votes from at least 75 percent of the writers to win induction:

Veterans Committee Hall of Fame Selections, Post-1940 Players—1980-99

Player	Year Elected by Veterans	Highest % in Writers Voting
Johnny Mize	1981	44%
George Kell	1983	37%
Pee Wee Reese	1984	48%
Enos Slaughter	1985	69%
Bobby Doerr	1986	25%
Red Schoendienst	1989	43%
Hal Newhouser	1992	43%
Phil Rizzuto	1994	38%
Richie Ashburn	1995	42%
Jim Bunning	1996	74%
Nellie Fox	1997	74%
Orlando Cepeda	1999	74%

I deliberately left out Larry Doby, who was technically elected as a Negro Leaguer. Doby never got any support from the writers—he was on the ballot for three years, and his best showing was 10 votes (three percent) in 1967. I have some sympathy for voting him in as a courageous pioneer who broke the color line in the American League. In all honesty, though, Doby's major league numbers don't merit Hall of Fame consideration.

Of the others, only four received strong support from the writers: Jim Bunning, Nellie Fox and Orlando Cepeda came within one percent of being voted in by the BBWAA, and Enos Slaughter made a very strong showing in his last year of eligibility, getting 69 percent of the votes. The players generally considered among the worst recent inductees into the Hall of Fame, George Kell and Phil Rizzuto, also got the lowest percentage of support from the writers. The others are a mixed bag. I think Johnny Mize was an excellent Hall of Fame choice and I considered Pee Wee Reese and Richie Ashburn solid candidates, but I'm iffy about Red Schoendienst and don't think Hal Newhouser belongs.

While I'm happy for guys like Mize and Fox, I have always been uneasy about the "double eligibility" in the Hall of Fame voting, with candidates who were rejected by the writers getting a second chance with the Veterans Committee. If you come very close like Fox, Bunning and Cepeda did, I can understand getting a second review. Though they generally do a decent job, the writers do make mistakes: Mize, in particular, was a really excellent hitter who never got his due in the BBWAA balloting.

Now here's a list of post-1940 players who received at least 40 percent of the votes in a writers' balloting, but who have not yet been elected by the Veterans Committee:

Player	Highest % in Writers Voting
Gil Hodges	63%
Tony Oliva	47%
Roger Maris	43%
Ron Santo	43%
Bill Mazeroski	42%
Maury Wills	41%
Marty Marion	40%

Gil Hodges seems to have been forgotten as a Hall of Fame candidate, but he received more support from the writers than any player not eventually elected by the Veterans Committee. Hodges received more than 200 votes in nine different elections, peaking at 63 percent in 1983, his last year of eligibility. Somehow it doesn't seem right to be putting in guys like Kell and Rizzuto, who never received anywhere near the support Hodges did, and yet continuing to ignore Hodges year after year.

Of the other players on this second list, I think Ron Santo and Bill Mazeroski have serious Hall of Fame credentials, and they also have a group of rabid supporters who will keep their names in front of the Veterans Committee voters. I admired the careers of both players, especially Santo, but I remain uncomfortable with this whole process. Supposedly the candidates being considered by the Veterans Committee this year include Mel Harder, who never got more than 25 percent in a writers' balloting, and Dom DiMaggio, who peaked at a heady 11 percent. Both were fine players and quality human beings, but as far as I can tell, the main reason they're being considered is that Ted Williams, perhaps the most strong-minded member of the current committee, has been pushing for them. Apparently, Teddy Ballgame wants them in the Hall of Fame because he had trouble hitting Harder's slider, and good old Dom tracked down a lot of flyballs that Williams couldn't get to. I love Ted Williams, but isn't this how we ended up with Hall of Famers like Jesse Haines and Long George Kelly?

I would propose the following changes in how the Veterans Committee is allowed to operate:

1. The committee should continue to remain free to elect former executives, umpires and other non-players, as they do now.

2. Negro League and 19th-century should continue to be considered for a limited period of time—say, 10 more years—and then the books should be closed on them forever. Let a group of people who really *know* these candidates—like former Negro Leaguers themselves, or a group of SABR experts who know the 19th century—submit the list of nominees and make its case before the Veterans Committee, who will then review them over the next decade. After the 10 years are up, that's it.

3. Twentieth-century players whose careers took place primarily in the years before World War II should be handled like the Negro Leaguers and 19th-century players. Let a qualified group of experts submit a list of the *best* candidates—not just the best teammates and favorite opponents of the guys on the committee. Have the group present the candidates' credentials, and then let the Veterans Committee vote on the best of these candidates over the next decade.

4. The worthiest of the more recent players who failed to pass muster with the writers, like Santo and Mazeroski, should get another chance to make the Hall. Let the Veterans Committee itself submit one name a year, as the Pro Football Hall of Fame Veterans Committee does. This candidate would then go on the writers' ballot with the more recent players. If he gets 75 percent of the votes, he's in. If not, they can submit him again next year, with a limit of three chances.

One could tinker with this system in various ways. You could change No. 4, for instance, so that the Veterans Committee candidate gets voted on only by the more senior BBWAA voters, guys who were more familiar with the player's career. Maybe that would be 100 voters or so, with the same three-fourths requirement to get in. But let's bring some thought to the system. While I admire the individual members of the Veterans Committee and know they take their job seriously, it's simply a bad idea to have a small group of people, like the 15 people on the committee, deciding who's a Hall of Famer and who isn't. It just paves the way for cronyism. The Baseball Hall of Fame remains the best one there is. We ought to be doing things to keep it that way.

February 17—The Griffey Deal

Thoughts about the Griffey trade:

1. I'm still amazed that the Mariners got so little for him. Granted the Reds had most of the leverage here, but earlier offers from Cincinnati included guys like Scott Williamson, Dmitri Young, Steve Parris, Danny Graves, Dennys Reyes and Denny Neagle—not all of them in the same offer, of course, but usually several of them as part of the package. Mike Cameron is a decent player, but I would rather have almost any of the pitchers listed here than Brett Tomko.

2. Had the Mariners handled the situation quietly and diplomatically, they might have been able to get Griffey to consent to a trade last fall to another club. The Mets, in particular, offered much, much more than the M's ultimately received from Cincinnati. But rather than finesse and coddle him, Seattle tried to pressure Griffey into accepting a trade to a team other than Cincinnati, and that backfired on them big-time.

3. The Pirates were supposedly one of the late suitors for Griffey. I find that hard to believe. Griffey buying the Pirates, I can believe.

4. According to a *USA Today* article, the Cardinals offered J.D. Drew *and* Rick Ankiel for Griffey. I'm not sure I buy this one, either, but the idea is intriguing, offering two of the most heralded prospects in recent years for a 30-year-old superstar. Whether you like this deal

depends in part on your opinion of Drew, and in part on your estimate of how likely it is that Ankiel will hurt his arm. But if I were the Cardinals, I just couldn't do something like this.

5. Going into the offseason, I considered Jim Bowden and Pat Gillick to be two of the best general managers in baseball. But in this chess game, almost everything Gillick did went wrong, and almost everything Bowden did turned out brilliantly. At the last minute, Bowden told Gillick that he'd walk away from the trade rather than include both Cameron and Reyes in the deal, and Gillick blinked. Can you imagine Bowden holding a press conference and saying, "Well, we didn't get Griffey, but we still have Dennys Reyes!"? Amazing.

6. I love all the players and agents who are criticizing Griffey—mostly anonymously—for taking "only" $13 million a year to sign with the Reds. Is it really necessary for every player to squeeze every last nickel out of the game every time? According to some people, the answer is yes.

7. Every reasonable study I've ever seen indicates that a superstar like Griffey can improve a team by 10 wins, tops. Five or six is a lot more realistic. The Reds have other problems, like whether their overworked 1999 bullpen will be OK this year. I think they'll be fortunate to win 96 games again.

8. Despite losing Griffey, Seattle can still contend in the wide-open AL West this year. It's very possible that the M's will make the playoffs this year while the Reds stay home. . . but Cincinnati still made a great trade.

9. Right now Griffey and Cincinnati are a match made in heaven, and I think that's a great thing for baseball. But it's easy to see how this could all go bad in a couple of years. Say Ken Sr. gets named manager, doesn't win, and gets bounced after a year and a half. Will Junior sulk and demand to get traded again? Jim Bowden wins that one also: at "only" $13 million a year, Griffey would be very tradable.

10. If the Mariners lose Alex Rodriguez after dumping Griffey, I fear for the future of the franchise.

About STATS, Inc.

STATS, Inc. is the nation's leading sports information and statistical analysis company, providing detailed sports services for a wide array of commercial clients. In January 2000, STATS was purchased by News Digital Media, the digital division of News Corporation. News Digital Media engages in three primary activities: operating FOXNews.com, FOXSports.com, FOXMarketwire.com and FOX.com; developing related interactive services; and directing investment activities and strategy for News Corporation, as they relate to digital media.

As one of the fastest growing companies in sports, STATS provides the most up-to-the-minute sports information to professional teams, print and broadcast media, software developers and interactive service providers around the country. STATS was recently recognized as "One of Chicago's 100 most influential technology players" by *Crain's Chicago Business* and has been one of 16 finalists for KPMG/Peat Marwick's Illinois High Tech Award for three consecutive years. Some of our major clients are Fox Sports, the Associated Press, America Online, *The Sporting News*, ESPN, Electronic Arts, MSNBC, SONY and Topps. Much of the information we provide is available to the public via STATS On-Line. With a computer and a modem, you can follow action in the four major professional sports, as well as NCAA football and basketball and other professional and college sports. . . as it happens!

STATS Publishing, a division of STATS, Inc., produces 12 annual books, including the *Major League Handbook*, *The Scouting Notebook*, the *Pro Football Handbook*, the *Pro Basketball Handbook* and the *Hockey Handbook*. In 1998, we introduced two baseball encyclopedias, the *All-Time Major League Handbook* and the *All-Time Baseball Sourcebook*. Together they combine for more than 5,000 pages of baseball history. Also available is *From Abba Dabba to Zorro: The World of Baseball Nicknames*, a wacky look at monikers and their origins. A new football title was launched in 1999, the *Pro Football Scoreboard*. These publications deliver STATS' expertise to fans, scouts, general managers and media around the country.

In addition, STATS offers the most innovative—and fun—fantasy sports games around, from Bill James Fantasy Baseball and Bill James Classic Baseball to STATS Fantasy Football and our newest game, Diamond Legends Internet Baseball. Check out our immensely popular Fantasy Portfolios and our great new web-based product, STATS Fantasy Advantage.

Information technology has grown by leaps and bounds in the last decade, and STATS will continue to be at the forefront as both a vendor and supplier of the most up-to-date, in-depth sports information available. For those of you on the information superhighway, you always can catch STATS in our area on America Online or at our Internet site.

For more information on our products or on joining our reporter network, contact us on:

America Online — Keyword: STATS

Internet — www.stats.com

Toll-Free in the USA at 1-800-63-STATS (1-800-637-8287)

Outside the USA at 1-847-470-8798

Or write to:

STATS, Inc.
8130 Lehigh Ave.
Morton Grove, IL 60053

STATS Power Hitters

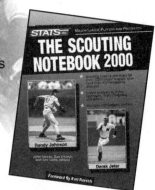

Rounding Out STATS'
Starting Lineup

STATS Player Profiles 2000

Extensive season and five-year breakdowns including:
- Lefty-righty splits for hitters and pitchers
- Breakdowns for clutch situations
- Home vs. road, day vs. night, grass vs. turf
- Batting in different lineup spots for hitters
- Pitching after various days of rest

"*Player Profiles* is my companion on all road trips."
Rod Beaton, *USA Today*

Item #PP00, $19.95, Available Now!
Comb-bound, $24.95, Available Now!

Bill James Presents:
STATS Batter Versus Pitcher Match-Ups! 2000

- Career stats for pitchers vs. batters
- Leader boards with best and worst match-ups
- Batter and pitcher performances for each major league ballpark
- Stats for all 1999 major league players

"No other book delivers as much info that's so easy to use."
Peter Gammons, *Boston Globe/ESPN*

Item #BVSP, $24.95, Available Now!

Order From ☰STATS☰ Today!

1-800-63-STATS   847-470-8798   www.stats.com

Free First-Class Shipping for Books Over $10
Order form in back of this book

Hard-Hitting Action!

STATS Pro Football Handbook 2000

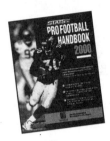

- A complete season-by-season register for every active NFL player
- Numerous statistical breakdowns for hundreds of NFL players
- Leader boards in both innovative and traditional categories
- Exclusive evaluations of offensive linemen
- Kicking, punting and defensive breakdowns

"*STATS Pro Football Handbook* is informative and easy to use."
-Will McDonough, *Boston Globe*

Item #FH00, $19.95, Available April!
Comb-bound #FC00, $24.95, Available April!

STATS Pro Football Scoreboard 2000

- STATS answers football's hottest questions
- Creative essays on every team, the league and the game in general
- Coach and team profiles, draft coverage

This unique book is a must-have for all football fans!
Item #SF00, $19.95, Available July!

Hot Coverage of the Winter Sports

STATS Hockey Handbook 2000-2001

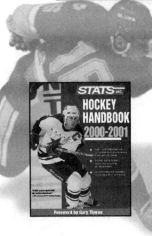

- Career stats for every NHL player who made an appearance in 1999-2000
- In-depth player profiles identifying strengths and weaknesses
- Leader boards for forwards, defensemen and goaltenders
- Team game logs

"STATS scores again with the **Hockey Handbook.**"
Bill Clement, *ESPN* Hockey Analyst

Item #HH01, $19.95, Available August

STATS Pro Basketball Handbook 2000-2001

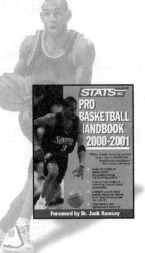

- Career stats for every player who logged minutes during the 1999-2000 season
- Team game logs with points, rebounds, assists and much more
- Leader boards from points per game to triple-doubles
- 1999-2000 and five-year player splits

"A great guide for the dedicated NBA fan."
Rick Telander, *ESPN Magazine*

Item #BH01, $19.95, Available Sept.

Order From STATS Today!

1-800-63-STATS   847-470-8798   www.stats.com

Free First-Class Shipping for Books Over $10
Order form in back of this book

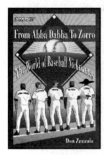

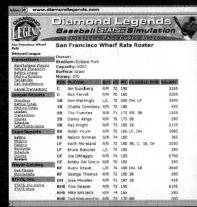

Books (Free first-class shipping for books over $10)

Qty	Product Name	Item Number	Price	Total
	STATS Major League Handbook 2000	HB00	$ 19.95	
	STATS Major League Handbook 2000 (Comb-bound)	HC00	**Sold Out**	
	The Scouting Notebook 2000	SN00	$ 19.95	
	The Scouting Notebook 2000 (Comb-bound)	SC00	**Sold Out**	
	STATS Minor League Handbook 2000	MH00	$ 19.95	
	STATS Minor League Handbook 2000 (Comb-bound)	MC00	**Sold Out**	
	STATS Player Profiles 2000	PP00	$ 19.95	
	STATS Player Profiles 2000 (Comb-bound)	PC00	**Sold Out**	
	STATS Minor League Scouting Notebook 2000	MN00	$ 19.95	
	STATS Batter Vs. Pitcher Match-Ups! 2000	BP00	$ 24.95	
	STATS Ballpark Sourcebook: Diamond Diagrams	BSDD	$ 24.95	
	STATS Baseball Scoreboard 2000	SB00	$ 19.95	
	STATS Diamond Chronicles 2000	CH00	$ 19.95	
	STATS Pro Football Handbook 2000	FH00	$ 19.95	
	STATS Pro Football Handbook 2000 (Comb-bound)	FC00	$ 24.95	
	STATS Pro Football Scoreboard 2000	SF00	$ 19.95	
	STATS Pro Football Sourcebook 2000	PF00	$ 19.95	
	STATS Hockey Handbook 1999-2000	HH00	$ 19.95	
	STATS Pro Basketball Handbook 1999-2000	BH00	$ 19.95	
	STATS All-Time Major League Handbook, 2nd Edition	ATHB	$ 79.95	
			Total	

Books Under $10 (Please include $2.00 S&H for each book/magazine)

Qty	Product Name	Item Number	Price	Total
	From Abba Dabba to Zorro: The World of Baseball Nicknames	ABBA	$ 9.95	
	STATS Baseball's Terrific 20	KID1	$ 9.95	
	STATS Player Projections Update 2000	PJUP	$ 9.95	
			Total	

Previous Editions (Please Circle appropriate years and include $2.00 S&H for each book)

Qty	Product Name		Price	Total
	STATS Major League Handbook	'91 '92 '93 '94 '95 '96 '97 '98 '99	$ 9.95	
	The Scouting Notebook/Report	'94 '95 '96 '97 '98 '99	$ 9.95	
	STATS Player Profiles	'93 '94 '95 '96 '97 '98 '99	$ 9.95	
	STATS Minor League Handbook	'92 '93 '94 '95 '96 '97 '98 '99	$ 9.95	
	STATS Minor League Scouting Notebook	'95 '96 '97 '98 '99	$ 9.95	
	STATS Batter Vs. Pitcher Match-Ups!	'94 '95 '96 '97 '98 '99	$ 9.95	
	STATS Diamond Chronicles	'97 '98 '99	$ 9.95	
	STATS Baseball Scoreboard	'92 '93 '94 '95 '96 '97 '98 '99	$ 9.95	
	Pro Football Revealed: The 100-Yard War	'94 '95 '96 '97 '98	$ 9.95	
	STATS Pro Football Handbook	'95 '96 '97 '98 '99	$ 9.95	
	STATS Pro Football Scoreboard	'99	$ 9.95	
	STATS Hockey Handbook	'96-97 '97-98 '98-99	$ 9.95	
	STATS Pro Basketball Handbook	'93-94 '94-95 '95-96 '96-97 '97-98 '98-99	$ 9.95	
	All-Time Major League Handbook (Slightly dinged)	First Edition	$ 45.00	
	All-Time Major League Sourcebook (Slightly dinged)	First Edition	$ 45.00	
			Total	

Qty	Product Name	Item Number	Price	Total
	Bill James Classic Baseball	BJCB	$ 129.95	
	Bill James Fantasy Baseball	BJFB	$ 89.95	
	STATS Fantasy Football	SFF	$ 49.95	
			Total	

TOTAL [   ]

1st Fantasy Team Name (ex. Colt 45's): _____
Which Fantasy Game is the team for? _____

2nd Fantasy Team Name (ex. Colt 45's): _____
Which Fantasy Game is the team for? _____

Note: $1.00/player is charged for all roster moves and transactions.

SPORTS TEAM ANALYSIS & TRACKING SYSTEMS

Mail:
STATS, Inc.
8130 Lehigh Avenue
Morton Grove, IL 60053

Phone:
1-800-63-STATS
(847) 677-3322

Fax:
(847) 470-9140

Bill To:
Company_____
Name_____
Address_____
City_____State_____Zip_____
Phone (   )_____Ext.____Fax (   )_____
E-mail Address_____

Ship To: *(Fill in this section if shipping address differs from billing address)*
Company_____
Name_____
Address_____
City_____State_____Zip_____
Phone (   )_____Ext.____Fax (   )_____
E-mail Address_____

Method of payment:
All prices stated
in U.S. Dollars

❏ Charge to my *(circle one)*
   Visa
   MasterCard
   American Express
   Discover

❏ Check or Money Order
   (U.S. funds only)

Please include credit card number
and expiration date with charge orders!

Exp. Date
Month Year

X_____
  Signature *(as shown on credit card)*

Totals for STATS Products:

Books	
Books Under $10 *	
Prior Book Editions *	
order 2 or more books/subtract: $1.00/book *(Does not include prior editions)*	
Illinois residents add 8.5% sales tax	
Sub Total	

Shipping Costs

Canada	Add $3.50/book	
* All books under $10	Add $2.00/book	
Fantasy Games		
Grand Total		

(No other discounts apply)

(Orders subject to availability)

Free First-Class Shipping for Books Over $10